Prentice Hall

# LITERATURE

PENGUIN  EDITION

# Reading Kit

## *Reading and Literacy Intervention*

*Grade Eight*

Upper Saddle River, New Jersey
Boston, Massachusetts
Chandler, Arizona
Glenview, Illinois

13-digit ISBN: 978-0-13-366702-8
10-digit ISBN: 0-13-366702-2

10 11 12 13 14 V001 15 14 13

# Contents

## BENCHMARK 8 SKILLS: UNIT 4, PART 2



## BENCHMARK 9 SKILLS: UNIT 5, PART 1



## BENCHMARK 10 SKILLS: UNIT 5, PART 2

## BENCHMARK 11 SKILLS: UNIT 6, PART 1 — Practice / Assess



## BENCHMARK 12 SKILLS: UNIT 6, PART 2



---

## PART 2: LITERATURE-BASED STRATEGIES

## PART 3: CLASSROOM MANAGEMENT STRATEGIES

### ■ Teacher-Mediated Classroom Reading Strategies



### ▼ Vocabulary and Concept Development



### ● Structuring Academic Discussion and Writing



## PART 4: PROFESSIONAL DEVELOPMENT ARTICLES



## ALPHABETICAL BY SKILL

## READING AND LITERARY ANALYSIS

# How to Use the Reading Kit

The *Reading Kit* has four parts, each designed to help you address the needs of students with varying ability levels.

- Use Part 1 to reteach and reassess unmastered skills
- Use Part 2 to develop independent application of active reading strategies
- Use Part 3 to ensure that students of all ability levels actively participate in learning activities and class discussions.
- Use Part 4 to devise strategies for addressing the special needs of diverse learners.

## Part 1 Practice and Assess

Part 1 is organized around the skills taught in the student edition and is organized in the order in which the skills are taught and assessed. These *Practice* pages are designed to reteach skills targeted by the benchmark, but you can use them at any time that you feel reteaching is needed. All *Practice* and *Assess* pages are also available electronically on Success Tracker.

- After administering a benchmark test, use the Interpretation Chart that accompanies the tests to determine which *Practice* pages should be assigned to students.
- After students complete the *Practice* assignments, use the *Assess* pages to check mastery of the specific skills that have been retaught.

## Part 2 Everyday Reading Strategies

Part 2 provides teacher and student pages for teaching reading strategies that develop active, thoughtful reading practices in *all* students. In addition, by giving direct instruction in these strategies, you will provide struggling readers with the tools they need to improve their comprehension and interpretation. These strategies can be used with any literature selection.

- Introduce the strategy, using the strategy plan and the graphic organizer.
- Once students are familiar with the strategy, encourage them to use the strategy independently with other selections.

## Part 3 Classroom Management for Differentiated Instruction

Part 3 describes practical, effective strategies for engaging students of all ability levels in learning activities and class discussions. These research-based, classroom-tested techniques allow you to support your struggling students and challenge your advanced students in the same discussion or activity. These frameworks can be used with any literature selection or discussion topic.

## Part 4 Language Arts Instruction—Professional Articles

Part 4 gives an overview of the diverse classroom. It also provides an analysis of the reading process, identifying the four aspects that need to be addressed to fully support diverse learners. Sections dedicated to specific characteristics of and challenges posed by three groups follow, along with discussion of strategies and resources for each: English language learners, less proficient learners, and special needs students.

## Part 2 Everyday Reading Strategies

## Part 3 Classroom Management for Differentiated Instruction

# Practice and Assess

Name ______________________________ Date ____________

# Reading: Make Predictions

## Practice

When you **make predictions** as you read, you make logical guesses about what will happen next in a story. You can make predictions based on *prior knowledge*, things you already know. You can *revise* predictions based on new information that is presented in the story. You can *support* predictions with details from the story.

Answer the questions about making predictions.

**1.** The title of a story is "Surf Dog." What do you predict this story will be about?

______________________________________________

**2.** On what did you base your prediction in question 1?

**A.** story details
**B.** new information
**C.** prior knowledge
**D.** song lyrics

**3.** Read the beginning of the story, and then answer the question that follows.

Milo is a little white mutt weighing only nine pounds. He lives in Hawaii and he loves to surf. It all began accidentally, when Milo fell off a fishing boat and went splashing into the sea.

With this new information, will you revise your prediction? Explain. ________

______________________________________________

______________________________________________

**4.** Read the next passage from the story, and then underline some of the story details that support your prediction.

He paddled until a chunk of driftwood floated past. He climbed onto it, panting. He stood on it as it drifted closer to shore, where surfers were waiting for the waves to come in. Milo's driftwood caught a wave! He held on and rode it in to shore. All the surfers cheered. They adopted the little surfing dog as their mascot.

Name ______________________________________________ Date ____________

# Reading: Make Predictions

## Assess

**A** Read the passage, and then answer the questions that follow.

### A Science Fair Blooper

Lila and Jim entered the district-wide science fair with hopes of winning a medal. Their project idea was so good, they thought, that no one could top it. They had trained a hamster named Bucky to drive a miniature car through a maze.

**1.** Based on the title of the story, and using your prior knowledge, what would you predict the story will be about?

**A.** a funny video

**B.** something funny that happens at a science fair

**2.** Based on the story details in this paragraph, what do you predict will happen next in the story?

______________________________________________

**3.** What story details did you use to make your prediction? ______________

______________________________________________

**B** Read the next paragraph in the story "A Science Fair Blooper." Then, respond to each item.

When the judges, Mrs. Peron and Mr. Adams, arrived at their station, Lila and Jim set the demonstration in motion. Bucky steered the car around the first corner, then the next. The judges looked impressed. Suddenly the car's engine accelerated. "Oops," whispered Jim. "How did that happen?"

**1.** Using the new information you now know, what do you predict might happen next? ______________________________________________

______________________________________________

**2.** Read the rest of the story below, and then underline story details that support your prediction.

The car hit a wall of the maze, and Bucky flew out of the car, into the air, and onto Mrs. Peron's head. "Oh! There's a hamster in my hair!" she screamed.

"I guess we won't be winning a medal," said Lila.

"Probably not," said Mr. Adams as he rescued Bucky from Mrs. Peron's hairdo, "but at least the hamster is all right."

Name ______________________ Date __________

# Reading: Use Information to Solve a Problem

## Practice

When you read schedules and maps, you use information to solve a problem: how to get from one place to another. Using text features can help you find the information you need. The chart below shows some text features of schedules and maps.

| Text Features of a Schedule | |
|---|---|
| **Headings** | Show where to find departure and arrival times |
| **Rows and columns** | Allow for easy scanning across and down the page |
| **Special type (boldface or italics) and special symbols (such as asterisks)** | Indicate exceptions or special information |

| Text Features of a Map | |
|---|---|
| **Labels** | Identify places shown on map |
| **Compass rose** | Shows directions (north, south, east, west) |

Use the schedule below to answer the questions that follow.

| Westmorland Birding Center | | | | |
|---|---|---|---|---|
| Open Thursday through Sunday, 8 a.m. to sunset, year-round. | | | | |
| Admission $5 per person. | | | | |
| Tour Schedule: | | | | |
| 8:30 a.m. | 11 a.m. | 2 p.m. | 5 p.m. | 7 p.m.* |
| *June-August only | | | | |
| No pets allowed. No children under age 7 admitted. Do not feed the birds. | | | | |

**1.** What days does the birding center offer tours? ______________________

**2.** Can you take the 7 p.m. tour in April? ______ In August? ______

**3.** Are pets allowed on the tours? ______________________

Name ______________________ Date __________

# Reading: Use Information to Solve a Problem

## Assess

Use the map and legend below to answer the questions that follow.

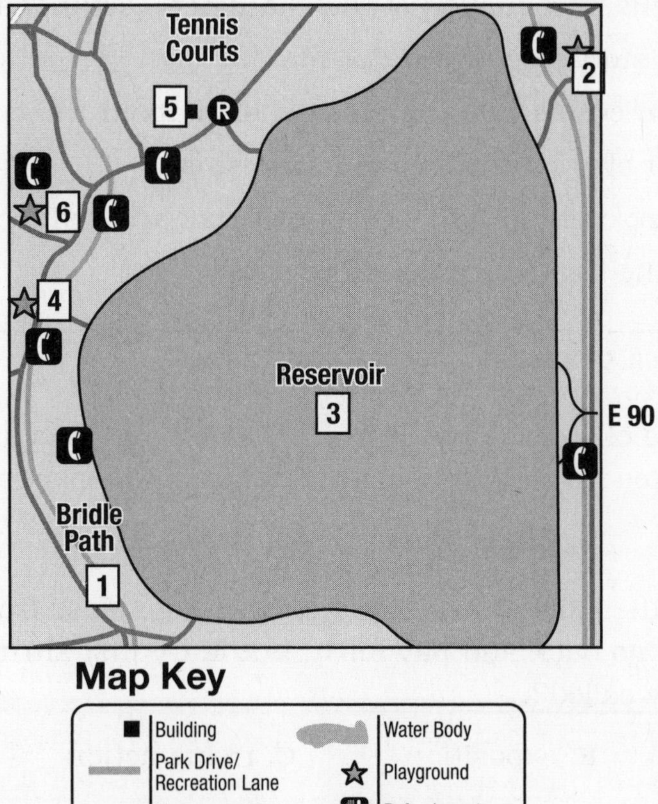


**1.** How many emergency call boxes are there near the Reservoir? _____

**2.** Are there any playgrounds? _____ If so, how many? _____

**3.** If you walk east from the Bridle Path, what will happen? _______________

**4.** Are the tennis courts closer to the Bridle Path or a Rest Station? ________

**5.** Are there any refreshment stands on this map? ______________________

Name ______________________________ Date ____________

# Literary Analysis: Plot

## Practice

**Plot** is the arrangement of events in a story. A story's plot includes these parts:

- **exposition:** the introduction of the characters, setting, and basic situation
- **conflict:** the story's central problem
- **rising action:** events that increase tension about the conflict
- **climax:** point of greatest tension in the story
- **falling action:** events that follow the climax and reduce tension
- **resolution:** the final outcome of the story

For each question, choose the letter of the best answer.

1. At the beginning of a story, you learn that Mary and Lisa are friends who always walk home from school together. What is this part of the story called?

   **A.** climax **B.** exposition **C.** rising action **D.** falling action

2. A little later in the story, Mary steals a tube of lip gloss from a drug store. Lisa tells her to go back and pay for it, but Mary just shrugs. What is this part of the story called?

   **A.** climax **B.** exposition **C.** rising action **D.** falling action

3. One day Mary dares Lisa to take something from the store. Lisa is torn between doing the right thing and proving herself to her friend. Finally, she takes a bottle of nail polish, but she is caught by the store manager. While the manager threatens to call the police, Mary sneaks away. What is this part of the story called?

   **A.** climax **B.** rising action **C.** falling action **D.** resolution

4. The next day, Mary apologizes to Lisa for getting her into trouble. What is this part of the story called?

   **A.** climax **B.** rising action **C.** falling action **D.** resolution

5. Mary and Lisa decide they have learned their lesson and will walk straight home without any stops from that day on. What is this story part called?

   **A.** climax **B.** rising action **C.** falling action **D.** resolution

Name ______________________________ Date ____________

# Literary Analysis: Plot

## Assess

Read each item. Choose the letter of the answer that tells which part of a story's plot is being described.

**1.** At the beginning of a story, you learn that Jack is an adventurous young man who loves mountain biking.

**A.** rising action
**B.** falling action
**C.** exposition
**D.** climax

**2.** A little later in the story, Jack decides to go biking alone. When a bad storm comes up, the pathways become slippery and treacherous. Jack searches for shelter.

**A.** rising action
**B.** falling action
**C.** exposition
**D.** climax

**3.** Before he can take cover, he gets caught in a mud slide. His bike slides down the hillside on a tide of mud and rocks, mangled. He has twisted a leg and cannot walk.

**A.** rising action
**B.** falling action
**C.** exposition
**D.** climax

**4.** A forest ranger sees the ruined bicycle wrapped around a tree, so he comes out in search of the rider. Luckily, he finds Jack.

**A.** rising action
**B.** falling action
**C.** climax
**D.** resolution

**5.** At the end of the story, Jack recovers in the hospital and decides never to go mountain biking alone again.

**A.** rising action
**B.** falling action
**C.** climax
**D.** resolution

Name ______________________________ Date ____________

# Literary Analysis: Conflict and Resolution

## Practice

The **conflict** in a literary work is a struggle between two forces. Conflict drives the action of the plot. There are different kinds of conflict:

- In an **external conflict,** a character is struggling against an outside force, such as another character, nature, or society.
- In an **internal conflict,** a character is struggling within himself or herself. The struggle is based on desires, beliefs, feelings, or needs.

The **resolution,** or outcome, of the conflict takes place when the problems have been worked out or when one force in the conflict wins over the other.

**A** Indicate whether each example of conflict is internal or external by writing *I* or *E.* Then, briefly explain your answer.

**1.** ______ Two Iditarod racers are sledding through the Alaskan wilderness. Both racers hope to win this year's trophy.

______________________________

**2.** ______ A hurricane hits a coastal area of the United States. Major floods spread throughout the area. A woman tries to drive her car to higher ground.

______________________________

**3.** ______ Angela tells a secret to her friend Adam about another friend, Steven. Adam thinks he should tell Steven what Angela said, but he doesn't want to lose Angela's friendship. Adam thinks about the problem for several hours.

______________________________

**B** Describe a brief resolution for each conflict listed above.

**1.** Possible resolution: ______________________________

______________________________

**2.** Possible resolution: ______________________________

______________________________

**3.** Possible resolution: ______________________________

______________________________

Name ______________________ Date ____________

# Literary Analysis: Conflict and Resolution

## Assess

**A** Indicate whether each example of conflict is internal or external by circling *I* or *E*. Then, briefly explain your answer.

1. Patrick and Ellen spent the day on the beach, but they forgot to bring sunscreen. Although the day was more hazy than sunny, both of them are bright pink when they return home. Their mother looks at them in dismay.

   I/E ______________________

2. A scientist in a small laboratory is studying the effects of global warming on Earth's climate. He is concerned about the development of too much carbon dioxide in the atmosphere.

   I/E ______________________

3. Paula has been assigned to design a poster for the eighth-grade musical. She'd like to ask Gina to help her with the poster, but they had a disagreement a few days ago. Will Paula swallow her pride to ask for Gina's help?

   I/E ______________________

**B** Briefly explain whether each item below describes a resolution for each conflict above.

1. The children tell their mother to calm down. They take showers and go out for a walk. Hours later, they feel uncomfortable and are sorry they forgot to protect their skin.

   ______________________

2. The scientist proposes an unusual idea that just might work. He suggests the construction of giant machines that can absorb carbon dioxide from the atmosphere and pump it deep underground.

   ______________________

3. Paula decides to overcome her fears. She asks Gina for help, and the two girls agree that their argument was silly to begin with.

   ______________________

Name ______________________ Date ____________

# Literary Analysis: Comparing Narrative Structure

## Practice

**Narrative structure** is the pattern a writer follows to tell a story. Part of the pattern of a story involves the writer's approach to time.

**Chronological order:** story events told in the order in which they happen

*The sky blackened. Then, the wind grew stronger, and the ship began to roll. Within minutes, the captain alerted the first mate to prepare for the storm.*

**Flashbacks:** scenes that show events happening in the past

*The sky blackened and the wind grew strong. Captain Tom Dell remembered his first big storm at sea. "Wake up, young Tom, and get yourself on deck. There's a whopper of a storm comin', and we have to secure the ship!"*

**Foreshadowing:** clues that hint at events that will happen later in the story

*The wind was gentle, and the sky was mostly clear. We saw a few wisps of dark clouds far off, but the captain assured us we had nothing to worry about.*

Identify each item as an example of chronological order, foreshadowing, or flashback. Explain your answers.

1. Today is my fortieth birthday. As I stare at the candles blazing on the cake, images of my childhood fill my head. *I am sitting on the stoop of the cabin we call home. Seven of us live here, including Gramps.*

______________________________________________

______________________________________________

2. Alison and Mike had been hiking for a couple of hours. Suddenly, Alison said, "Isn't that a bear track?" "Are you kidding?" Mike laughed. "There aren't any bears in these woods!"

______________________________________________

______________________________________________

3. "The fish are biting," said Sal. He and Joe headed for the stream with their poles and bait. An hour later, each had caught two fine trout for dinner.

______________________________________________

______________________________________________

Name ______________________ Date __________

# Literary Analysis: Comparing Narrative Structure

## Assess

**A** Idenfity each item below as an example of chronological order, foreshadowing, or flashback. Explain your answers.

**1.** Last winter, Dan and Eva made plans for what they would plant in their garden when spring came. In May, they planted several kinds of beans and asparagus. During late July, the vegetables started to sprout.

______________________

______________________

**2.** Now I am an old man, but I can remember—as though it were yesterday—when I first saw my wife . . . It's the second day of college, and I see this lovely young woman standing in the registration line behind me. She's a beauty, all right. "May I borrow your pen?" I ask, with a silly grin on my face.

______________________

______________________

**3.** Orson opens the front door, which creaks on its rusty spring. *Squeak, squeak.* The house is dark and empty. Why has no one come by to light the candles? Don't they know the master of the house is home? *Crash!* Oh, no—What is that noise?

______________________

______________________

**B** Read the following passage. Then, draw parentheses around the example of flashback, and underline the example of foreshadowing.

Tension is high at the ice-skating tournament. Janelle has reached the finals for the third time. She wonders, "Will this win be as exciting as the first? To think, I was only 15 . . ." The scores go up. The fans roar. The announcer's voice echoes over the ice, "Miss Janelle Ames, the youngest winner of the Ice Castle Tournament." Janelle suddenly hears her trainer's voice. "It's your turn, Janelle. Good luck." From the corner of her eye, she sees 15-year-old Mei Lee, the challenger, watching her and smiling calmly.

Name ______________________ Date __________

# Vocabulary: Word Roots *-trib-*, *-scop-*, *-limin-*, and *-jud-*

## Practice

A **root** is the basic unit of meaning of a word. Knowing the meanings of word roots can help you figure out the meanings of many new words. Study these examples.

Examples:

| Root | Meaning | Words with the Root |
|---|---|---|
| *-trib-* | to give in return, repay | retribution, tribute, contribution, tributary |
| *-scop-* | an instrument for seeing or observing | periscope, telescope, scope, microscope |
| *-limin-* | threshold, the entrance or beginning point of something | preliminary, eliminate, sublime |
| *-jud-* | judge | judicious, prejudice, judge, judiciary, judgment |

**A** Replace each underlined word or phrase with the most appropriate word from the chart above.

1. ________________ Jeremy composed a tune as a <u>mark of respect</u> to his music teacher.
2. ________________ Because of her allergy, Monica had to <u>remove</u> peanuts from her diet.
3. ________________ I often find it hard to <u>evaluate</u> whether clothes look good on me.
4. ________________ I brought some canned goods as a <u>donation</u> to the school food drive.

**B** Complete each sentence with a word from the chart above.

1. The astronomer used a ________________ to view other planets.
2. The Ohio River is a ________________ of the Mississippi.
3. Use your best ________________ about what to include in your report.
4. Learning the alphabet is a ________________ step in learning to read.

Name ______________________ Date __________

# Vocabulary: Word Roots *-trib-*, *-scop-*, *-limin-*, and *-jud-*

## Assess

**A** Circle *T* if the statement is true or *F* if the statement is false. Then, write a sentence to explain your answer.

**1.** T/F A microscope is a tool that submarines use for seeing above the water.

______________________

**2.** T/F A person who is judicious would think carefully before making a decision.

______________________

**3.** T/F Prejudice helps people get along with each other.

______________________

**4.** T/F If you forgive someone who has harmed you, you will seek retribution.

______________________

______________________

**B** Circle the root in each word, and think about its meaning. Then, write the word's meaning on the first line. Use a dictionary to check the meaning. Finally, use each word in a new sentence.

**1.** judgment ______________________

______________________

**2.** distribute ______________________

______________________

**3.** stethoscope ______________________

______________________

**4.** judiciary ______________________

______________________

Name ______________________________ Date ____________

# Grammar: Common and Proper Nouns

## Practice

A **common noun** names any one of a group of people, places, things, or ideas. Common nouns are capitalized only when they begin a sentence. A **proper noun** names a specific person, place, thing, or idea. Proper nouns are always capitalized.

| Common Nouns | Proper Nouns |
|---|---|
| athlete | Brett Favre |
| arena | Madison Square Garden |
| book | *To the Lighthouse* |
| city | Toronto |

In the sentence below, the proper nouns are in bold, and the common nouns are in italics.

My *brother* **Brad** and I went to **Denver** to watch the **Broncos** play in an important *game* against an undefeated *team*.

**A** Underline each common noun once and each proper noun twice.

1. Ernest Hemingway was born in Oak Park, which is in Illinois.
2. During World War I, Hemingway was a volunteer for the Red Cross in Italy.
3. For six weeks, he drove an ambulance and worked at a canteen.
4. This important writer won a Pulitzer Prize in 1952.
5. His heroes often face violence and destruction with great courage.
6. Hemingway lived in Paris for several years and then returned to the United States.
7. He also lived and worked in Spain for a time.
8. The Spanish Civil War is the setting of the novel *For Whom the Bell Tolls.*
9. One of his best stories is "A Clean, Well-Lighted Place."
10. In his later years, Hemingway suffered from physical and mental illnesses.

Name ______________________________ Date __________

# Grammar: Common and Proper Nouns

## Assess

**A** Complete each sentence by writing a proper noun that fits the description in parentheses.

1. The library on ______________________ will be closed tomorrow. (a specific street)

2. My sister was nervous about her first day at ______________________. (a specific school)

3. Have you studied the poetry of ______________________ in class? (a specific poet)

4. ______________________ has starred in at least fifteen films. (a famous movie actor)

5. Seeing the ______________________ was the highlight of the trip. (a famous monument)

**B** Circle the letter of the sentence that has correct capitalization.

1. **A.** The touring Cast of the musical *Cats* arrived early.
   **B.** The touring cast of the musical *Cats* arrived early.
   **C.** The touring cast of the Musical *Cats* arrived early.
   **D.** The touring cast of the musical *cats* arrived early.

2. **A.** The Family saw a Show at Radio City Music Hall in New York City.
   **B.** The family saw a show at Radio City music Hall in New York city.
   **C.** The family saw a show at radio city music hall in New York City.
   **D.** The family saw a show at Radio City Music Hall in New York City.

3. **A.** Which holiday is more popular, Thanksgiving or Labor Day?
   **B.** Which holiday is more popular, thanksgiving or labor day?
   **C.** Which Holiday is more popular, Thanksgiving or Labor Day?
   **D.** Which Holiday is more popular, Thanksgiving or labor day?

4. **A.** One state that borders the Pacific ocean is Oregon.
   **B.** One state that borders the Pacific Ocean is Oregon.
   **C.** One State that borders the Pacific Ocean is Oregon.
   **D.** One State that borders the pacific ocean is Oregon.

Name ______________________ Date __________

# Grammar: Plural Nouns

## Practice

A **plural noun** refers to more than one person, place, thing, or idea. The plural of most nouns is formed by adding *-s* or *-es.* Some nouns, however, form their plurals in different ways. Study the rules and examples below to learn how to form plurals.

| Rule | Examples |
|---|---|
| For nouns that end in *-s, -x, -ch,* or *-sh,* add *-es.* | tax—taxes; dish—dishes; match—matches; pass—passes |
| For nouns that end in a consonant plus *y,* change the *y* to an *i* and add *-es.* | county—counties; berry—berries |
| For some nouns that end in *-f* or *-fe,* use *-ves.* (Some just add *-s.* Consult a dictionary.) | wolf—wolves; loaf—loaves; chief—chiefs; gulf—gulfs |
| Some nouns change their spelling to form the plural. | mouse—mice; child—children; foot—feet; basis—bases |

**Underline each misspelled plural noun. Then, write the correct spelling of the plural.**

1. ______________ Professional chefs learn to use sharp knifes carefully.

2. ______________ Pottery and stenciling are popular hobbys among creative people.

3. ______________ The rolling hilles and valleys of Pennsylvania make beautiful scenery.

4. ______________ Big cities are no place to try to raise gooses.

5. ______________ In Europe, professional guides show tourists through old churchs.

6. ______________ Before the highwais were built, many supplies were transported on the railroads.

7. ______________ The ladies and gentlemans of the jury have reached a verdict.

8. ______________ The children enjoyed stories about elfs and other fantasy creatures.

Name ______________________________ Date ____________

# Grammar: Plural Nouns

## Assess

**A** Write the plural form of each noun.

1. shelf ______________
2. brush ______________
3. submarine ______________
4. gallery ______________
5. belief ______________
6. turkey ______________
7. country ______________
8. branch ______________
9. fox ______________
10. painting ______________

**B** Rewrite these sentences, changing each noun in parentheses to its plural.

1. Both (man) and (woman) can become (astronaut).

______________________________________________

2. (Exhibit) at (zoo) often include (giraffe), (wolf), and (monkey).

______________________________________________

3. (Child) like to make (wish) on their (birthday).

______________________________________________

4. Older (house) often have many narrow (hallway).

______________________________________________

5. Grand (display) of artwork decorated all the (lobby) in the county courthouse.

______________________________________________

6. (Sheriff) and (deputy) usually carry (handcuff) with them.

______________________________________________

7. In some (city), food (bank) collect (box) of food for (citizen) who are struggling.

______________________________________________

8. Most (plant) have broad (leaf), but narrow (leaf) are found on (grass).

______________________________________________

Name ____________________ Date __________

# Grammar: Concrete, Abstract, and Possessive Nouns

## Practice

**Nouns** are words that name people, places, things, or ideas.

**Concrete nouns** name people, places, or things that can be perceived by the five senses (sight, hearing, taste, touch, smell). **Abstract nouns** name ideas, beliefs, qualities, or concepts—things that cannot be perceived by the senses.

| | |
|---|---|
| Concrete Nouns | bicycle, house, sun, Kenneth, teacher, mountain, glass |
| Abstract Nouns | freedom, confidence, joy, wealth, beauty, mood, existence |

**Possessive nouns** are used to show ownership or belonging. To form the possessive of most singular nouns, add an apostrophe and an *s*. To form the possessive of a plural noun that ends in *s*, add an apostrophe. For plural nouns that do not end in *s*, form the possessive by adding an apostrophe and an *s*.

| Singular Possessive Nouns | | | |
|---|---|---|---|
| uncle | **uncle's** address | James | **James's** notebook |
| parrot | **parrot's** food | story | **story's** plot |

| Plural Possessive Nouns | | | |
|---|---|---|---|
| teenagers | **teenagers'** concerns | Gomezes | the **Gomezes'** driveway |
| people | **people's** homes | countries | **countries'** leaders |

Identify the underlined noun as concrete, abstract, or possessive.

**1.** ____________ Tragic heroes in literature often suffer because of their <u>pride</u>.

**2.** ____________ <u>Mark's</u> favorite playwright is Neil Simon.

**3.** ____________ Rain, snow, hail, and <u>sleet</u> are all made up of fresh water.

**4.** ____________ Martin Luther King, Jr., tried to end <u>racism</u>.

**5.** ____________ <u>Mrs. Peterson</u> has been elected to the city council.

Name ______________________________ Date __________

# Grammar: Concrete, Abstract, and Possessive Nouns

## Assess

**A** Underline each concrete noun once and each abstract noun twice.

1. Italy is known for its rich cultural heritage.
2. Visitors are drawn by the beauty of its beaches, vineyards, and mountains.
3. Cities such as Florence, Rome, and Venice also attract tourists.
4. People find inspiration in the great artworks displayed at the museums.
5. They seek relaxation in the Italian countryside.

**B** Identify each noun as either concrete or abstract.

1. ____________ loyalty
2. ____________ Pacific Ocean
3. ____________ whale
4. ____________ generosity
5. ____________ basket
6. ____________ love
7. ____________ humanity
8. ____________ snowflakes
9. ____________ justice
10. ____________ Mrs. Perry

**C** Write the possessive form of each noun in parentheses.

1. ____________ (Teresa) friend
2. ____________ the (Joneses) front yard
3. ____________ the (bloodhound) search
4. ____________ the (children) toys
5. ____________ the (artist) style
6. ____________ her (parents) careers
7. ____________ the (men) tennis team
8. ____________ the (teachers) lounge

Name ______________________ Date __________

# Writing: New Ending

## Practice

The ending of a short story is important. Sometimes, endings are happy. Sometimes, endings surprise you. Sometimes, it is interesting to imagine a different ending to the story.

When you **write a new ending** to a story, remember to match the style of the original story. If characters have a distinctive way of speaking in the story, keep that way of speaking in your new ending. The story might have been written from the third-person point of view, with a narrator telling events from "outside" and using the pronouns *he, she,* and *they* when referring to the characters in the story. When writing a new ending for a story such as this, keep the third-person point of view. The story might have been written using the first-person point of view, with the narrator being part of the action and using the pronouns *I, me, my,* and *we* when referring to himself or herself. When writing a new ending for a story such as this, use the first-person point of view.

Read the story. Then, answer the questions.

Well, I tell ya, I farmed this land my whole life. It's rough, hard soil, and oftentimes I've had an aching back. But I've always brought in the harvest, and we've always had enough to live on. My son Mike doesn't understand me. "Dad!" he says, "We could sell this patch of dirt and be rich! People would buy up the lots and build big houses. You're sitting on a gold mine! Let's sell!"

I almost agreed to, but then I just could not do it. "Don't matter, son," I said. "I'd rather live right here in our old farmhouse than anywhere else on Earth." Mike's a touch angry now. He'll come around.

1. Sum up the ending of this story. ______________________

______________________

2. From what point of view is this story told? ______________________

3. Write one sentence to describe a different ending to this story.

______________________

4. On a separate sheet of paper, write a new ending for this story. Remember to use the same point of view. Use the pronouns *I* and *me* when referring to yourself.

Name ______________________________ Date __________

# Writing: New Ending

## Assess

**Read this story. Then, respond to the items that follow.**

Dr. Marina Hall is a scientist who works at a top-secret laboratory high in the mountains of Peru. No one has heard of the lab; it is called only "Zone 1." The people who are chosen to work there are sworn to secrecy. Their mission is to raise the remarkable alien children who have been left in their care. No one knows when their warrior parents will be returning for them.

The children are gifted. They learn subjects as difficult as microbiology by the age of three, they speak every language of this world as well as some interplanetary tongues, and they are stronger than Earth's strongest man.

Their parents entrusted these incredible children to the most advanced citizens of planet Earth. There was only one rule: never let it be known. Dr. Marina Hall has often worried what would happen if the media ever found out about Zone 1. She is glad that such a thing is impossible. The laboratory is well hidden and well protected. She spends her days creating new and wonderful lessons for her charges.

**1.** Summarize the ending of this story. ______________________________

______________________________

**2.** From what point of view is this story told? ______________________________

**3.** In one sentence, describe a different ending for this story.

______________________________

**4.** Write the new ending for the story. Remember to keep the same point of view as in the original story.

______________________________

______________________________

______________________________

______________________________

______________________________

______________________________

______________________________

______________________________

Name ______________________________ Date __________

# Writing: Letter

## Practice

A **letter** is a written form of communication from one person or group to another. It is written in a standard format that includes a heading, greeting, body, closing, and signature. There are two main types of letters:

- A *friendly letter* is written to someone with whom the writer wants to communicate in a personal, friendly way.
- A *business letter* is written for a formal purpose. A letter to a company requesting product information is an example of a business letter.

You can write a friendly letter to someone you do not know or do not know well. However, the less well you know the person, the more respectful and formal your style needs to be.

**A** Read the example. Then, respond to the items that follow.

HEADING [ 327 Winding Way
Louisville, KY
October 14, 2007

Hi Jess, ←——GREETING

I just got your package, and I'm so excited! I can't believe you made all of those cookies for me! They're all so good, I can't decide which one I like best.

Mom says we can come out to visit you again in the spring. I can't wait! I'm saving my money so we can go to the mall and the movies like last time. ] BODY

Love, ←——CLOSING
Asha ←——SIGNATURE

**1.** Is this a friendly letter or a business letter? ______________________

**2.** Circle the letter of the item that is *not* an example of a friendly letter.

**A.** a letter to a pen pal in another country
**B.** a letter to a company asking for a replacement part for a camera
**C.** a letter to former neighbor asking about her life in a new town

**3.** List the names of three people to whom you might send a friendly letter.

______________________________________________

**4.** List two topics you might discuss in a letter to one of the people on your list.

______________________________________________

______________________________________________

Name ______________________ Date __________

# Writing: Letter

## Assess

Complete these activities about writing a letter.

1. Name a person to whom you might send a letter. ______________________

2. List two or three topics you might discuss in a letter to that person.

______________________

______________________

3. Fill in the lines below to draft your letter. If you are writing a business letter, use a polite, formal style. If you are writing a friendly letter, you can use a more relaxed style.

HEADING

GREETING

BODY

CLOSING

SIGNATURE

Name ______________________ Date ________

# Writing: Descriptive Essay

## Practice

A **descriptive essay** creates a picture in words to share a vivid experience. Many writers create a description of a person who has had an important impact on their lives. This type of descriptive essay includes the following:

- a main impression of the person
- concrete examples or anecdotes (stories) that show his or her personality
- sensory details that show how the person appears, behaves, or speaks
- information about how the person affected the writer's life

**A** Read each example from a descriptive essay. Then, answer each question.

1. He had once been a strong man, but the years of working outside had taken their toll on him. Grandpa used to be able to pick me up and twirl me around for hours. Now, he walked slowly, leaning on his old hand-carved walking stick.

   What is the main impression you get about the writer's grandfather? ______

   ______________________

2. When Lila walked into a room, everyone turned around. It wasn't that she was beautiful, or even especially brilliant. But when she smiled at you, you felt as though there were no one else around. She made you feel special.

   How would you describe Lila, based on this example? ______

   ______________________

**B** Write information about a person in your family who has had an impact on you. Then, on a separate sheet of paper, write a short paragraph that describes him or her.

1. Main impression of the person: ______________________
2. Concrete example/anecdote about the person: ______________________

   ______________________

3. Two details about his or her appearance/behavior/speech: ______

   ______________________

4. How he or she affected you: ______________________

   ______________________

Name ______________________ Date __________

# Writing: Descriptive Essay

## Assess

**A** Circle one of the following people to describe, or select a person of your own choosing. Then, respond to each item.

| | | | |
|---|---|---|---|
| a teacher | a movie star | a president | a neighbor |
| a friend | a club advisor | a friend's parent | a scientist |

**1.** Write four sensory details that could describe the person you chose.

______________________

______________________

**2.** What single, overall impression sums up this person?

______________________

______________________

**3.** List at least two details about the appearance, behavior, or speech of this person. ______________________

______________________

______________________

**4.** What impact has this person had on you? How do you think his or her impact on you will affect your future?

______________________

______________________

______________________

**B** Write a paragraph describing the person you chose, using your answers above.

______________________

______________________

______________________

______________________

______________________

Name ______________________________ Date ____________

# Reading: Author's Purpose

## Practice

An **author's purpose** is his or her main reason for writing. The most common purposes for writing are to inform, to persuade, and to entertain. To determine an author's purpose, notice the types of details included in the work. Writers may use facts and statistics to inform or persuade. They may use stories about personal experiences to inform or entertain. Often, authors will have more than one purpose—to inform while entertaining, for example.

**Read each paragraph. Then, respond to each item.**

When you buy a bicycle helmet, make sure it fits you well. The foam pads should touch your head all around, and the helmet should sit level. Tighten the straps so that they are snug but comfortable. You must not be able to pull off the helmet, no matter how hard you try.

**1.** Is the author's main purpose to entertain, to inform, or to persuade?

____________________

**2.** List two details from the paragraph to support your answer to question 1.

______________________________________________________________________

It was a beautiful day. Ramona put on her helmet, hopped on her bike, and headed to a desert bike path near her house. She was peddling merrily along when suddenly she heard a loud, hissing sound. "Oh, no," she thought, "not a snake!" She peddled faster but noticed that her bike was bouncing badly. When she looked back, she saw that her rear tire was flat. "So that was the hissing!" No snake, after all—just a flat tire and a ruined bike ride.

**3.** Is the author's main purpose to entertain, to inform, or to persuade?

____________________

**4.** List two details from the paragraph to support your answer to question 3.

______________________________________________________________________

Name ______________________ Date __________

# Reading: Author's Purpose

## Assess

**A** Read the paragraph. Then, answer the questions that follow.

Wherever and whenever you ride your bicycle, you should wear a helmet. You may not know it, but statistics show that a bike rider can expect to crash at least once for every 4,500 miles of riding. Every year, more than 600 people die in bicycle crashes, mostly from head injuries. Your bicycle helmet can protect you. Don't go biking without it!

**1.** Is the author's main purpose to entertain, to inform, or to persuade?

______________

**2.** List two details from the paragraph to support your answer to question 1.

______________________________

______________________________

**B** Circle the letter of the best answer to each question. Then, explain your choice.

**1.** In an article about a new movie, a writer briefly describes the story, names the main actors and the director, and tells the movie's rating. What is the writer's purpose?

**A.** to persuade **B.** to inform **C.** to entertain **D.** all three

______________________________

**2.** In an article about the same movie, another writer tells the story in detail. He describes a confusing, slow-moving plot, actors who are not right for their roles, and dull background music. He ends with the line, "If you need to catch up on your sleep, this is the movie for you." What is the writer's purpose?

**A.** to persuade **B.** to inform **C.** to entertain **D.** all three

______________________________

**3.** Another writer describes the movie in glowing terms—exciting story, great acting, terrific special effects. He ends his article with the line, "Don't miss it!" What is this writer's main purpose?

**A.** to persuade **B.** to inform **C.** to entertain **D.** all three

______________________________

Name ______________________________ Date ____________

# Reading: Identify Main Idea and Details

## Practice

The main idea is the central point or message conveyed in a passage or text. Details are the facts and examples that support the main idea. Before you begin to read an article or other informational text, preview the text features and a few sample paragraphs. Doing so will help you identify the main idea. Then, as you read, you will be able to identify details that support the main idea.

**Questions to Help You Preview an Article**

- What do headings and subheadings tell me about the topic?
- What information do photographs, diagrams, illustrations, and captions provide?
- What subjects are mentioned in the first sentences of paragraphs?
- What kinds of statistics, quotations from experts, or facts appear in the text?

**Read the passage below, looking for the main idea and supporting details. Then, answer the questions that follow.**

### Heavy Lifting

Strength training is becoming more popular among younger teens. This form of exercise can have benefits for teens, as long as it is done properly and under adult supervision.

BENEFITS There are many benefits to strength training. The first, of course, is greater strength. It may also increase endurance and focus in athletics and other pursuits. It helps protect tendons, bones, and joints, so may decrease athletic injuries. Strength training also may help prevent some health problems when you get older.

CAUTIONS It is important to gear up to strength training gradually. You should do it no more than three days a week, and never two days in a row. Forty minutes is a good workout for a young person. It is best to do many repetitions at a lower weight. Do not do maximum lifts. Always work out with a person to help you and under trained adult supervision.

1. What is the main idea of this passage? ______________________________

______________________________________________________________

2. Write two things to be careful about during strength training. ____________

______________________________________________________________

Name ______________________ Date __________

# Reading: Identify Main Idea and Details

## Assess

**Read the passage below, looking for the main idea and supporting details. Then, answer the questions that follow.**

It is important to understand what goes into medical reports so that you can evaluate them. Medical reports on television can give you information but can also be scary. Complicated information is difficult to present in a short period of time. The job of a medical reporter is to achieve a combination of accuracy and dramatic presentation. To get people to pay attention to the story, a reporter may use stories of real people to dramatize a problem or benefit. These are called anecdotes.

ANALYZE Sometimes a report about a new health danger can cause unnecessary fears. People hear certain words and focus on them. For example, something may be shown to double your chance of contracting a disease. That sounds bad! But the real question is, what is your chance of getting the disease in the first place? If the chance is very, very small, then doubling it means that it is still very small. If the disease is more common, then doubling the chance may be something to worry about.

INVESTIGATE If a medical news report seems to apply to you, use a variety of sources, including longer and more detailed reports and your doctor, to investigate further.

1. What is the main idea of the passage? ______________________

______________________

2. Is the main idea implied or stated? Explain. ______________________

______________________

3. Give two details that support the main idea. ______________________

______________________

4. The subheads give clues to two things you should do when you hear a medical report. What are they? ______________________

5. Summarize the recommendations under the two subheads. ______________________

______________________

______________________

Name ______________________ Date ____________

# Literary Analysis: Mood

## Practice

**Mood** is the overall feeling a literary work creates in a reader. The mood of a work can often be described in a single word. For example, a mood can be *gloomy, hopeful,* or *tense.* A variety of elements contribute to mood:

- Word choice and images. Words such as *serene* and images such as *the starry sky* would contribute to a peaceful mood, for example.
- Setting, or where the action takes place. For example, a setting of a deep, echoing cavern will contribute to a mood of danger or mystery.
- Events, or things that happen. Having a circus come to town, for example, could contribute to a happy mood.

**A** Read the passage. Then, respond to each item.

Nan had been out running after dark before, but never this late at night. She had her reflective vest on and carried a flashlight, but still she did not feel comfortable. "Oh, I'm just not used to it," she thought. "People do it all the time." She kept a steady pace and focused on her breathing. Except for the occasional car driving by, the roadway was deserted. Trees swaying in the breeze looked as if they were doing an eerie dance. She wished she had remembered to bring her cell phone. A crashing sound made her stop in her tracks. Something was running out of the woods.

**1.** Which word best describes the mood of the passage? Circle its letter.

**A.** unexcited **B.** relaxed **C.** fearful **D.** melancholy

**2.** Which event does *not* help create that mood? Circle its letter.

**A.** The trees danced eerily.
**B.** Nan wore a vest.
**C.** Nan went running in the dark.
**D.** Something ran out of the woods.

**3.** Does the setting contribute to the mood in this passage? Explain.

______________________________________________

**B** Read the selection. Then, tell what its mood is, and underline two words or images that convey this mood.

Bright kites fly in the wind / And the world seems full of joy.
A field of daisies smiles at the sun / And children, laughing, run.

The mood is ________________.

Name ______________________________ Date ____________

# Literary Analysis: Mood

## Assess

**A** Read the following passage. Then, respond to each item.

Our whole family went kayaking on the lake one early September day. It was cool and sunny, perfect for paddling on the water. The hillsides were beginning to show some autumn color, and the sky was vivid blue. As we kayaked along, ducks followed us, hoping for a treat. A regal-looking heron stood at the water's edge, watching. The dragonflies swooped by like brightly colored darts. A fish leaped out of the water right in front of me, a silver arc. Everything seemed to be full of color and life. "I'll always remember this," I thought.

**1.** Which word best describes the mood of this passage? Circle its letter.

**A.** delighted
**B.** serious
**C.** unhappy
**D.** hopeful

**2.** Write down two events that contribute to the mood.

______________________________

______________________________

**3.** Does the setting contribute to the mood in this passage? Explain.

______________________________

**4.** Which of these best defines *mood* in a literary work?

**A.** the reader's opinion about the work
**B.** language that describes the physical senses
**C.** the overall feeling the work creates in the reader
**D.** the writer's purpose in writing

**B** Read the poem. Then, tell what its mood is, and underline three words or images that convey this mood.

It is empty / Our old house. / Every wall blank now, every room packed in crates.

A dusty toy soldier is stuck in the radiator's coils still, / A forgotten captive from our living room wars. / Our new house holds no memories for me yet.

The mood is ________________.

Name ______________________________ Date ____________

# Literary Analysis: Author's Style

## Practice

An author's **style** is his or her particular way of writing. It is made up of these elements:

- **Word Choice:** Some writers use everyday language: *Ben plays on lots of sports teams.* Other writers use formal, more difficult words: *Ben participates in several competitive sports.*
- **Length and Rhythm of Sentences:** Some writers use simple, straightforward sentences: *The game was almost over. I was tired. I tried as hard as I could.* Others write longer, more complicated sentences: *Toward the end of the fourth quarter of the game, I felt exhausted. However, I was determined to do my best.*
- **Tone:** Writers have certain attitudes toward their subjects and readers. For example, a writer might write an article to help young soccer players. That positive attitude toward the readers would lead the writer to use a helpful, gentle tone.

Read the passage. Then, circle the letter of the best answer to each question.

Please sit down. Do not talk. Just listen to me. You must stop being mean to your little sister. It's against the rules. She can be a pest, I know. But you must be patient. She's just a little girl. Please try to be kind to her.

**1.** Which answer best describes the writer's word choice?

**A.** many formal, difficult words
**B.** many simple, everyday words
**C.** many descriptive, lively words
**D.** many humorous expressions

**2.** Which answer best describes the writer's sentences?

**A.** short and straightforward
**B.** declarative and exclamatory
**C.** compound and complex
**D.** long and complicated

**3.** How would you describe the tone that is created by the writer's word choice and sentence structure in this passage?

**A.** natural, conversational
**B.** formal, sophisticated
**C.** technical, instructive
**D.** mysterious, suspenseful

**4.** Which answer best describes the writer's attitude toward his or her audience?

**A.** humorous and light
**B.** harsh and angry
**C.** stern but gentle
**D.** proud but happy

Name ______________________________ Date __________

# Literary Analysis: Author's Style

## Assess

**A** For each question, circle the letter of the best answer.

1. What is the best definition of an author's **style**?
   - A. his or her particular way of writing
   - B. a story the author tells
   - C. the type of nouns the author uses
   - D. a formal way of using language

2. What is the best definition of an author's **tone**?
   - A. the length and rhythm of the sentences the author uses
   - B. the figurative language the author uses
   - C. the subject or topic of the author's passage
   - D. the author's attitude toward the subject and readers

**B** Read the following two paragraphs. Then, respond to each item.

1 Believe it or not, we had to wake up at 4 A.M. to catch the bus to catch the train to catch the ferry! But the Statue of Liberty was totally worth it. It was awesome. We saw people sailing around it in fancy yachts. I kept thinking of the people who had looked at this same statue from overcrowded ships.

2 I found our trip to the Statue of Liberty really fascinating and also surprisingly emotional. It was a long and draining trip. Any amount of travel was worth seeing this awe-inspiring sight, though. I was reminded of the waves of immigrants who had sailed past her on their way to Ellis Island.

1. ______________ Which paragraph is written in an informal or casual style?

2. ______________ Write a word or phrase that is an example of this informal style.

3. ______________ Write a more formal word or phrase from the other paragraph.

4. ______________ What word would you use to describe the writer's attitude toward the subject in the first paragraph?

5. ______________ Which paragraph uses longer sentences?

Name ____________________ Date __________

Literary Analysis: Comparing Characters of Different Eras

## Practice

Just as in real life, characters in stories are affected by their living conditions. Characters living in different historical eras often have different problems to face. For example, characters in a story set long ago might suffer because they are on a dangerous whaling voyage. By contrast, modern characters might suffer because they are on a dangerous mission in space. When you read stories set in different historical eras, think about how the characters' situations are alike and different.

The characters in these two passages live in different historical eras. As you read, think about how their situations are alike and different. When you have finished reading, answer the questions.

A It was freezing cold out on the prairie, but Daniel trudged on. He had to find firewood. His mother was ill. She needed the warmth of a fire. So many people on the wagon train had died. Daniel was scared. He wondered if they would ever reach Oregon by the end of 1861.

B "Hello, Chicago Power Company?" Bob said into the phone. "I need you to come fix our furnace. The heat won't come on, and it's very cold. My mother's sick. It's a fairly new furnace, too. Mom said it was installed in 2005. Can you come right away?" He hung up and got blankets out of the closet to cover his mother until help came.

**1.** What is the time and place of Passage A? What problem does Daniel face?

______________________________

______________________________

**2.** How does the historical era affect Daniel's problem? ______________

**3.** What is the time and place of Passage B? What problem does Bob face?

______________________________

______________________________

**4.** How does the historical era affect Bob's problem? ______________

**5.** How are Daniel and Bob's problems alike and different? ______________

______________________________

______________________________

Name ______________________________ Date __________

## Literary Analysis: Comparing Characters of Different Eras

### Assess

**Read the two passages. Then, answer the questions that follow.**

A Fire Chief Adams held onto the reins with one hand and clanged the firetruck bell with the other. As the horses galloped into the lane leading to Will Fischer's farm, he could see flames leaping from the barn. 1902 had been a dry year in Acton, and this was the fourth major fire he'd faced. "Whoa," he yelled to the horses. He was thankful to see that men from surrounding farms had come to help. Someone had even started the bucket brigade—a line of people from the barn door to the duck pond, passing bucket after bucket along to fight the blaze. Together they'd try to save Fischer's barn.

B When the alarm clanged, the firefighters leaped into their protective suits and climbed aboard the firetrucks. The engines roared as the trucks hurtled out of the station. Lightning had hit a building in the heart of Detroit, and the top floors were ablaze. Luckily, the building had just been completed in 2006, so there were no workers in the offices yet. However, the firefighters would have to climb the 25 flights of stairs to fight the blaze. Luckily, they could also rely on firefighting helicopters to drop water and other chemicals to help douse the flames.

1. What is the time and place of Passage A? What problem does Chief Adams face? ______________________________

______________________________

2. How does the historical era affect his problem? ______________________________

______________________________

3. What is the time and place of Passage B? What problem do the firefighters face? ______________________________

______________________________

4. How does the historical era affect their problem? ______________________________

______________________________

5. How are the problems in these passages alike and different? ______________________________

______________________________

______________________________

Name ______________________________ Date ______________

# Vocabulary: Word Roots *-duc-*, *-lum-*, *-sol-*, and *-equi-*

## Practice

A **root** is the basic unit of meaning of a word. Knowing the meanings of word roots can help you figure out the meanings of many new words. Study these examples.

Examples:

| Root | Meaning | Words with the Root |
|---|---|---|
| *-duc-* | to lead, to bring | reduce, introduction |
| *-lum-* | light | luminous, illuminate |
| *-sol-* | alone | solo, solitude, desolate |
| *-equi-* | equal | equivalent, equitable |

**A** Circle the letter of the word that completes each sentence correctly.

**1.** The other instruments were silent during the violin ________________.

**A.** illumination **B.** introduction **C.** solitary **D.** solo

**2.** I was able to ________________ the meaning based on what I knew about word roots.

**A.** deduce **B.** equate **C.** equivocate **D.** reduce

**3.** I traded my dollars for the ________________ amount in euros.

**A.** desolate **B.** equivalent **C.** luminous **D.** solitary

**4.** The cave walls shone with a faint ________________.

**A.** equality **B.** induction **C.** luminescence **D.** solitude

**B** Replace each underlined word or phrase with the most appropriate word from the chart above.

**1.** ________________ Her skin was so healthy it appeared <u>radiant</u>.

**2.** ________________ The desert landscape looked absolutely <u>barren</u>.

**3.** ________________ I thought his plan to share the computer was <u>fair</u>.

**4.** ________________ I left some books at school to <u>lessen</u> the weight of my backpack.

Name ______________________________ Date ____________

# Vocabulary: Word Roots *-duc-*, *-lum-*, *-sol-*, and *-equi-*

## Assess

**A** Revise each sentence so that the underlined vocabulary word is used logically. Be sure not to change the vocabulary word.

**1.** I switched off the lights to illuminate the room.

______________________________

**2.** I spent a solitary evening visiting with my friends.

______________________________

**3.** Electricity travels easily through water because it is a poor conductor.

______________________________

**4.** The two sides of an equation should have different values.

______________________________

**5.** The introduction to a book comes at the end.

______________________________

**6.** I fell down the stairs because I maintained my equilibrium.

______________________________

**B** Answer each question. Then write a sentence explaining your answer.

**1.** If your house and your friend's house are equidistant from your school, which of you has a longer trip to school? ______________

______________________________

**2.** Would an actor deliver a soliloquy to several other characters in the play? ___

______________________________

**3.** Would most people be happy about being abducted? ______________

______________________________

**4.** When would a room be most likely to need illumination? ______________

______________________________

Name ______________________________ Date __________

# Grammar: Personal Pronouns

## Practice

A **personal pronoun** is used in place of a noun in a sentence. Personal pronouns change their form, or **case,** depending on how they function in a sentence. The three case forms are *nominative, objective,* and *possessive.*

| | |
|---|---|
| Nominative Case Pronouns | I, you, he, she, it, we, they |
| Objective Case Pronouns | me, you, him, her, it, us, them |
| Possessive Case Pronouns | my, mine, your, yours, his, her, hers, its, our, ours, their, theirs |

Use the nominative case when the pronoun is the subject of a verb.

> **They** make memory chips for computers. [*They* is the subject of the verb *make.*]

Use the objective case when the pronoun is used as a direct object or an indirect object.

> Keith took the computer apart and studied **it.** [*It* is the direct object.]
> Miss Hobbs showed **him** the hard drive. [*Him* is the indirect object.]

Use the possessive case to show ownership.

> Jasmine enjoys adding components to **her** personal computer.
> The keyboard mouse with the blue logo is **mine.**

**Underline the personal pronoun in each sentence. Then, identify the case of the pronoun by writing *nominative, objective,* or *possessive.***

**1.** ____________ Raymond showed me a photograph of an iris.

**2.** ____________ Irises are his favorite flowers.

**3.** ____________ The iris is easy to recognize because it has an unusual shape.

**4.** ____________ Irises grow in temperate regions; they may be planted in spring or fall.

**5.** ____________ Many people cultivate them in backyards and gardens.

Name ________________________________ Date ____________

# Grammar: Personal Pronouns

## Assess

**A** Complete each sentence by writing an appropriate personal pronoun. The hints in parentheses tell you which case the pronoun should be in.

1. The team members have chosen ____________ as their captain. (objective)

2. The blue raincoat with the torn pocket is ____________. (possessive)

3. At the beginning of practice, ____________ stretched and ran drills. (nominative)

4. Please share ____________ ideas with the rest of the group, Alise. (possessive)

5. Then, ____________ went over the details of the case with the police chief. (nominative)

6. Wes played ____________ a song on the guitar. (objective)

7. Rose sent ____________ two tickets to *The Sound of Music.* (objective)

8. ____________ wants to become a landscape architect. (nominative)

**B** Write the case of the underlined personal pronoun in each sentence.

1. ____________ Albert Einstein is well known for his theory of relativity.

2. ____________ Australia is a country, and it is also a continent.

3. ____________ After baby birds hatch, their parents must bring them food.

4. ____________ Pueblo craftswomen make pottery and decorate it with painted designs.

5. ____________ Giant anteaters use their claws to rip open ants' nests.

Name ______________________________ Date __________

# Grammar: Reflexive Pronouns

## Practice

A **reflexive pronoun** reflects the action of the verb back to the subject. A reflexive pronoun always ends with *-self* or *-selves* (*myself, yourself, himself, herself, itself, ourselves, yourselves, themselves*).

> Most domestic cats will groom **themselves**. [The reflexive pronoun *themselves* reflects the action of the verb *groom* back to the subject *cats*.]

A reflexive pronoun always refers back to another word in the sentence (its **antecedent**). The reflexive pronoun should agree in number with the antecedent. Sometimes the antecedent is a compound construction.

> Mindy prides **herself** on being a good skater. [*Mindy* is the antecedent of the reflexive pronoun *herself*. Both *Mindy* and *herself* are singular.]
> Karen and I found two seats and made **ourselves** comfortable. [The antecedent of *ourselves* is the compound subject *Karen and I*. Both *Karen and I* and *ourselves* are plural.]

Do not use a reflexive pronoun to take the place of a noun or pronoun.

> INCORRECT Dan, Lily, or myself will run the video camera.
> CORRECT Dan, Lily, or I will run the video camera.

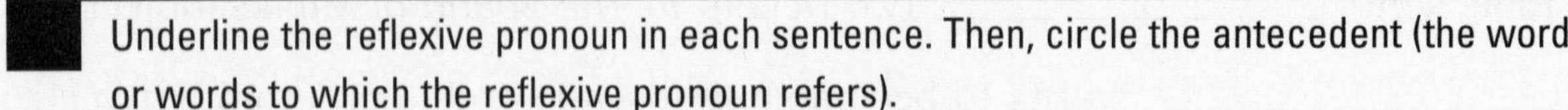

Underline the reflexive pronoun in each sentence. Then, circle the antecedent (the word or words to which the reflexive pronoun refers).

1. Viewers of television owe it to themselves to choose shows wisely.
2. Usually a producer of a TV show will not willingly censor himself.
3. My sisters and I make ourselves viewing schedules, and our parents review them.
4. Because the TV does not turn itself off, we limit our viewing to one hour per night.
5. You can make yourself smarter by choosing interesting, informative shows to watch.

Name ______________________________ Date ____________

# Grammar: Reflexive Pronouns

## Assess

**A** Complete each sentence by writing the correct reflexive pronoun. Then, underline the antecedent of the reflexive pronoun. (Remember, an antecedent can be compound.)

**1.** A mother chimp occupies ________________ with taking care of her baby until it is about five years old.

**2.** My teammates and I drove ________________ hard to prepare for the big game.

**3.** Aren't you being a bit too hard on ________________?

**4.** The jenny wren makes ________________ at home in cities, where people often build birdhouses for it.

**5.** Although Mr. Hannigan is a skilled architect, he does not think of ________________ as an artist.

**6.** Dr. Jane Goodall and Dr. Louis S. B. Leakey prided ________________ on their findings about primates.

**7.** Heather announced, "I like to think of ________________ as a courageous person."

**B** Circle the letter of the sentence that uses pronouns correctly.

**1. A.** Everyone except myself seemed to understand the math problem.
**B.** Everyone except me seemed to understand the math problem.

**2. A.** All of you dancers should do yourself a favor and stretch more.
**B.** All of you dancers should do yourselves a favor and stretch more.

**3. A.** She and Kelly took themselves out of the tennis tournament.
**B.** She and Kelly took herself out of the tennis tournament.

**4. A.** Reggie and myself will both attend the sports banquet.
**B.** Reggie and I will both attend the sports banquet.

**5. A.** The group consisted of two guides, a family of six, and us.
**B.** The group consisted of two guides, a family of six, and ourselves.

Name ______________________ Date __________

## Grammar: Revising for Pronoun-Antecedent Agreement

### Practice

A **pronoun** usually stands for a noun or another pronoun, which is called the **antecedent.**

Antecedent Pronoun
**Mr. Jacobs** asked **his** students to write reports on marine animals.

Pronouns should agree with their antecedents in *person* and *number.* **Person** tells whether the pronoun refers to the one speaking (*first person*), the one spoken to (*second person*), or the one spoken about (*third person*). **Number** tells whether a pronoun is singular or plural.

I would like to write **my** report on penguins. [The first-person singular pronoun *my* agrees with its antecedent, *I.*]
**Penguins** walk with a waddle because **they** have short legs and tall bodies. [The third-person plural pronoun *they* agrees with its antecedent, *Penguins.*]

Sometimes the antecedent of a pronoun is an indefinite pronoun. The indefinite pronouns *anybody, anyone, anything, each, either, everybody, everyone, everything, neither, nobody, no one, nothing, one, somebody, someone,* and *something* are singular. The indefinite pronouns *both, few, many,* and *several* are plural. Make sure the pronoun agrees with the indefinite pronoun in number.

**One** of the penguins was feeding **its** baby. [singular pronoun and antecedent]
**Many** of the penguins were sliding on **their** stomachs on the ice. [plural pronoun and antecedent]

**On the line provided in each sentence, write a pronoun that agrees with its antecedent. Then, underline the antecedent.**

**1.** As the moon rose, ______________ cast a soft glow on the mountains.

**2.** I bought a used bike, but it broke down and left ______________ stranded.

**3.** Neither of the kittens is ready to leave ______________ mother yet.

**4.** The children took their baths, and then ______________ went to bed.

**5.** Everyone in the room seemed to be holding ______________ breath.

Name ______________________________ Date __________

## Grammar: Revising for Pronoun-Antecedent Agreement

### Assess

**A** Underline the indefinite pronoun that is the antecedent of the pronoun in parentheses. Then, circle the pronoun in parentheses that agrees with the antecedent.

1. Several of the science teachers took (his or her, their) classes on field trips.
2. Anyone in our class can go on the field trip if (he or she, they) has permission.
3. Fill out one of these permission slips and give (it, them) to your teacher.
4. Everyone was eager to describe (his or her, their) experience at the Field Museum in Chicago
5. Each of the museum's resource centers provides books and museum samples to educate (their, its) visitors.

**B** Rewrite each sentence, correcting any errors in pronoun-antecedent agreement. If a sentence is correct as written, write *Correct.*

Each of the men took their uniform to the dry cleaners.
Each of the men took his uniform to the dry cleaners.

1. The ladies in the card club have postponed its next meeting.

______________________________

2. Ask someone on the girls' swim team to show you their technique.

______________________________

3. Nobody on the boys' soccer team ever forgets their cleats.

______________________________

4. The drawer had two pencils and a notepad inside them.

______________________________

5. Several of the homes had their roofs torn off during the storm.

______________________________

Name ______________________ Date __________

# Spelling: Commonly Misspelled Words

## Practice

Look at the Word List on this page. If you have ever had trouble spelling one or more of these words, you are not alone. These words are just some of the **commonly misspelled words.** The words on this list are often misspelled because a letter is added or left out.

Many words are misspelled because a consonant is doubled when it should not be or not doubled when it should be. Others simply have unusual letter combinations. Analyze each word on the list, focusing on the single and double consonants.

| always | aggravate | business | career | occasion |
|---|---|---|---|---|
| parallel | possession | really | recommend | until |

**A** For each misspelled word below, find the correct spelling in the box above. Then, write the correct spelling on the line.

**1.** reccommend ______________

**2.** ocassion ______________

**3.** realy ______________

**4.** agravate ______________

**5.** paralell ______________

**B** Underline the five misspelled words in the following paragraph. Then, write the correct spelling for each one on the lines below.

I once thought about pursuing a carreer in bussiness. My parents always reccommend this as a sure path to financial security. But I am not sure that this is what I realy want to do. I guess I won't know for sure untill I graduate from college.

**1.** ______________ **4.** ______________

**2.** ______________ **5.** ______________

**3.** ______________

Name ______________________ Date __________

# Spelling: Commonly Misspelled Words

## Assess

**A** Write the correct spelling of each word in the space provided. If the word is spelled correctly, write *Correct* in the space.

**1.** recommend ____________

**2.** possession ____________

**3.** occassion ____________

**4.** realy ____________

**5.** untill ____________

**6.** busines ____________

**7.** agravate ____________

**8.** allways ____________

**9.** career ____________

**10.** parrallel ____________

**B** Underline the seven misspelled words in the following paragraph. Then, write the correct spelling for each one on the lines below.

My math teacher told me that there is a special kind of geometry in which paralell lines meet at some point. I said to her, "This idea realy sounds crazy to me! In fact, I clearly remember the occassion when you told the class that such lines never meet." She then offered to reccommend a book that might explain this idea. I answered, "Untill I read this book, I won't believe that it is possible." I have now read this book and have begun to understand this other kind of geometry. I have even begun to consider a carreer in advanced mathematics, even though my parents want me to get a degree in bussiness administration.

**1.** ____________

**2.** ____________

**3.** ____________

**4.** ____________

**5.** ____________

**6.** ____________

**7.** ____________

Name ______________________________ Date __________

# Writing: Personal Narrative

## Practice

When you write a **personal narrative,** you tell the story of one of your own experiences. That experience might have led to an insight, a solution to a problem, or a change in thinking. For example, you might write about going skiing for the first time. In your narrative, you would do the following:

- **Tell events in order.** You might begin by telling about putting on the ski equipment. Then, you might tell about going up a bunny hill on a rope tow.
- **Give descriptive details.** You might tell how steep the hill was, how cold the day was, how sunny it was, how windy it was, and so on.
- **Give your reactions and thoughts.** You might have felt a little nervous. You might have wondered if you would fall and hurt yourself. You might have realized just how difficult skiing is, and how hard it is to try something new. These details are important to your personal narrative.

**A** Read the passage, and then complete the activities that follow.

My family and I drove to the Grand Canyon this summer. At first I didn't want to go. Slowly, though, I changed my mind. We drove through the incredible scenery of the desert. The sunsets were astonishing, coloring the faraway mountains with shades of gold and orange. Even before we got to the Grand Canyon, I realized that I would not have wanted to miss this for the world.

1. Underline three words or phrases in this passage that indicate time order.
2. Draw a double-underline under one descriptive detail in the paragraph.
3. Circle the narrator's initial feeling about the trip, as well as the narrator's final feeling about the trip.

**B** Complete these activities for a personal narrative of your own.

1. List a personal experience that made you realize something new. You might choose a trip, a sporting event, or a play.

   ______________________________

2. Give a descriptive detail from this experience.

   ______________________________

3. Describe one of your reactions to the experience.

   ______________________________

Name ______________________ Date __________

# Writing: Personal Narrative

## Assess

**A** Complete the following activities to prepare to write a personal narrative.

**1.** List two personal experiences you might write about. Think about trips you have taken, events you have seen or participated in, or adventures you have had that led to an insight or a change in thinking.

**A.** ______________________

**B.** ______________________

**2.** Choose one of the experiences you listed. List three or four events that were part of it, in time order.

______________________

______________________

______________________

**3.** Give three descriptive details about the experience.

**A.** ______________________

**B.** ______________________

**C.** ______________________

**4.** Give two thoughts or feelings you had about the experience, especially something you realized.

**A.** ______________________

**B.** ______________________

**B** On a separate sheet of paper, write your personal narrative. Tell events in order. Include the descriptive details, thoughts, and feelings that you listed in activity A.

Name ______________________ Date __________

# Writing: Observations Journal

## Practice

An **observations journal** is a written record of your thinking about a specific topic. Outlining your ideas in an observations journal is a good way to prepare for writing a problem-and-solutions essay. Use these steps:

- Begin by describing the problem. Include details, true stories, or examples to show why the situation needs to change. Use complete sentences.
- Then, suggest possible solutions. Describe how they might improve the problem situation. Use complete sentences.

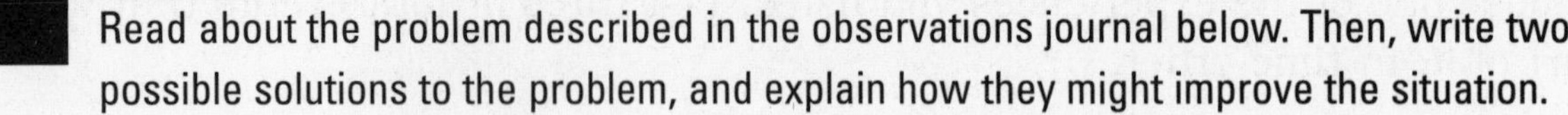

Read about the problem described in the observations journal below. Then, write two possible solutions to the problem, and explain how they might improve the situation.

**Problem:** The school cafeteria is too crowded at lunch time.
**Details:** Often, there is no place to sit. Sometimes arguments break out when people stay too long even though others are waiting for a table. Students standing between tables are a safety hazard.
**Examples:** At least three times a week, I cannot find a place to sit when I arrive at 12:30. Last Friday, I waited with my tray for ten minutes before there was a free seat.
**True Stories:** One day, someone fainted at lunchtime. Cafeteria monitors had to push through the crowds in the aisles to help the victim lying on the floor.

**Possible Solutions:**

**1.** ______________________

**Why it would help:** ______________________

______________________

______________________

**2.** ______________________

**Why it would help:** ______________________

______________________

______________________

Name ______________________ Date __________

# Writing: Observations Journal

## Assess

**1.** Choose one of the following problems that you would like to solve.

☐ lack of school spirit
☐ poor attendance at a specific event
☐ lack of money for field trips
☐ traffic problems around your school
☐ other: ______________________

**2.** Below, write an observations journal about the problem you chose in Step 1.

**Problem:** ______________________

______________________

**Details:** ______________________

______________________

**Examples:** ______________________

______________________

**True Stories:** ______________________

______________________

**Possible Solutions:**

**1.** ______________________

**Why it would help:** ______________________

______________________

______________________

**2.** ______________________

**Why it would help:** ______________________

______________________

______________________

Name ____________________ Date ____________

# Writing: Autobiographical Essay

## Practice

An **autobiographical essay** tells the story of a memorable event, time, or situation in the writer's life. A well-written autobiographical essay includes a clear sequence of true events from the writer's life, descriptive details about the setting and the characters, and remembered feelings about the experience. Autobiographical essays may include a conflict or problem the writer faces. They can include characters besides the writer.

**A** Read the paragraph. Then, answer the questions and follow the directions.

One summer, when I was nine years old, we rented a cottage near the ocean. The first morning there, I woke when everyone else was still asleep. It was warm and foggy, and the tide was way out, so I decided to explore. The sand squished between my toes as I splashed from tide pool to tide pool, farther and farther out. The tidal basin seemed to stretch out forever! After a while, my stomach began to grumble and I turned to go home, hoping breakfast might be ready. It was then that I realized I was lost. The fog was so thick that I couldn't see if I was walking toward shore or farther into the ocean. The more I walked, the more frightened I became. I worried the tide would come in before I found my way home. Then, through the fog, I heard voices calling. I moved toward the sound, yelling and calling for help. Soon I saw my dad and my brother Josh. I was safe at last!

1. What time period does the essay cover? Give details to support your answer.

______________________________

______________________________

2. Circle three details that tell about the setting.

3. Underline three details that tell about the main character.

4. Explain the problem or conflict the writer faces in this essay. ____________

______________________________

______________________________

**B** Imagine that you wrote the above essay. On a separate sheet of paper, write a few sentences that tell what happens next. Include a description of at least one other character.

Name ______________________ Date ____________

# Writing: Autobiographical Essay

## Assess

Respond to each item to help you prepare your autobiographical essay.

1. What memorable situation or event will your autobiographical essay cover?

___

2. What is the setting?

___

3. What characters will you include?

___

___

4. List the events and a problem or conflict that you will describe.

___

___

___

5. Arrange the events in order. How is the problem solved?

___

___

___

6. List some descriptive details about the setting.

___

___

___

7. List some descriptive details about the characters you have chosen.

___

___

___

Name ______________________ Date __________

# Reading: Compare and Contrast

## Practice

When you **compare** two people or things, you explain how they are alike. When you **contrast** two people or things, you tell about how they are different. A good tool for comparing and contrasting literature is to ask questions, so you can notice similarities and differences in characters, settings, moods, and ideas. Here are some questions you might ask:

- How is one character different from another?
- How is this story like another that I have read?
- How is this character's experience different from my own experience?

As you read literature, pay attention to dialogue and descriptions of how the characters speak and act. Pay attention to words that compare and contrast characters or events. Examples of words that compare are *both, alike,* and *like.* Examples of words that contrast are *although, but, while, both,* and *however.*

**Sample Comparison:** Juliet in *Romeo and Juliet* and Maria in *West Side Story* are both young women in love.

**Sample Contrast:** Juliet is a girl of noble birth, while Maria is an immigrant.

Read each item. Then, answer the questions.

1. Both Olympic athletes had the patience to work hard to achieve their dreams. They had trained on the race track for years, in all kinds of weather.

   **A.** What or whom is being compared or contrasted? ______________________

   **B.** Is comparison or contrast being used? ______________________

   **C.** What clues helped you decide whether it was a comparison or a contrast?

   ______________________

2. San Francisco was enjoying weather in the 50s in late January. However, New York City was in the midst of a frosty chill. Mark was glad to be on a plane headed toward a milder climate.

   **A.** What or whom is being compared or contrasted? ______________________

   **B.** Is comparison or contrast being used? ______________________

   **C.** What clues helped you decide whether it was a comparison or a contrast?

   ______________________

Name ______________________________ Date __________

# Reading: Compare and Contrast

## Assess

**A** Read each item. Then, answer the questions.

1. Jacques called up his friend Susanne, who had moved to Pennsylvania. She described how much she loved climbing the hills and swimming in the mountain lakes. He laughed and said it sounded great—but he was going to stay right where he was, in Kansas. He liked the broad flat land, with its glowing wheat fields. He felt as though he could see for miles and miles.

   **A.** What or whom is being compared or contrasted? ______________

   **B.** Is comparison or contrast being used? ______________

   **C.** What clues helped you decide whether comparison or contrast was being used?

   ______________________________

   ______________________________

2. The old copper mine was like a deep, dark, abandoned cave. It seemed to go on forever with no end in sight. Wilhelm wanted to explore it and make a map of it.

   **A.** What or whom is being compared or contrasted? ______________

   **B.** Is comparison or contrast being used? ______________

   **C.** What clues helped you decide whether comparison or contrast was being used?

   ______________________________

   ______________________________

**B** Read the passage. Then, underline the examples of contrast, and circle the examples of comparison.

Jeanine was the talker. However, her twin sister Janet was quiet and shy. They were both outstanding musicians. Jeanine called herself "the noisemaker of the orchestra." She played percussion instruments, while Janet played the flute with a lovely, gentle touch. They had different musical styles, but they were alike in that they appreciated each other's talents.

Name ______________________________ Date ____________

## Reading: Comparing an Original Text With Its Summary

### Practice

When you **compare an original text with its summary,** you will notice that only certain details have been included in the summary. A summary should capture the main ideas and meaning of the original text; include important characters and plot details; and present accurate information in chronological order. However, a summary is shorter than the original work because it does not include every original detail, as in this example:

Original work:

It was quiet and still early enough so that Marie was alone on the street as she walked to her job at the bakery. She could not believe she was actually living and working here, in tiny Capriglia, Italy. Marie had been frightened about leaving her home town after graduating college. However, she wanted to strike out on her own. *I will make desserts that will be known all over the world*, she thought.

Summary:

The story describes a young woman named Marie who has just started living and working in Italy on her own. She is planning to become a pastry chef, and she is nervous but determined.

**Read the story. Then, answer the questions.**

"I found a peanut!" cried out Jaclyn.

"Here's one—and another, and another!" shouted Martino.

The children were excited. If they gathered enough peanuts, they could win a prize. They rushed around the bushes and trees, looking for more.

All of the carnival games were going beautifully. Mr. Cesar had arranged Carnival Day to help raise money for the playground project.

Just then, Rusty, Mr. Cesar's dog, hopped out of the back of a pickup truck. He was running straight for the table that held the hot dogs and hamburgers that were waiting to be cooked.

"Look out!" yelled Martino, "Dog on the loose!"

**1.** What information about the main characters would a summary include?

______________________________

______________________________

**2.** Which events should be included in a summary of the story? ____________

______________________________

______________________________

Name ______________________________ Date ____________

## Reading: Comparing an Original Text With Its Summary

### Assess

**Read the story below. Then, answer the questions.**

"We'll be there in a few hours," said Tom Anders. "Just try to hold on."

"But Tom, the children are so hungry," cried Maybelle Anders. "They haven't had anything to eat for days."

"I know, honey, but just tell them to hang on. My sister Nancy's place is just a few miles up the road. Can't be too far away now."

The family was dirty and exhausted, their faces streaked with the dust of the road. Their old wagon was barely holding together. Any minute, one of the wheels was likely to fall off. Their aging horse Steel wasn't doing much better. He was limping along, weakly putting one hoof in front of the other.

"Hmph! 'Steel' ain't exactly the right name for this nag," thought Tom to himself. "He should'a been named Scrawny. I paid too much for him, that's for sure."

The children sat huddled in the wagon, trying to calm their stomach pains with thoughts of a warm house that would soon welcome them. Surely Aunt Nancy and Uncle Fred would have some soup or potatoes for them. They had come such a long way west from Oklahoma, believing things might be better for them out here.

Just as he was about to give up hope, Tom Anders saw a light. A porch light. Yes, they were waiting—he could almost smell the cooking fire from here. It smelled like hope.

**1.** What information about the main characters would a summary include?

______________________________________________

______________________________________________

**2.** Which events should be included in a summary of the story? ____________

______________________________________________

______________________________________________

**3.** What detail from the original story does not need to be included in a summary? ______________________________

______________________________________________

**4.** What main idea of the story should be included in a summary? ____________

______________________________________________

______________________________________________

Name ______________________________ Date ____________

# Literary Analysis: Setting

## Practice

The **setting** of a story is the time and place of a story's action. The time may be the past, present, or future. The place can be a person's home, the ocean, a circus tent—anywhere. The setting helps create the mood of the story. Certain details help contribute to the setting:

- the characters' customs, values, and beliefs
- what the land looks like
- what the weather is like or what the season is
- the historical time period of the action

Read the following passage.

**Example:** It was a dark, dull day in late November. As was the custom, I had to gather the coal to fuel the morning fire. My father would be awake soon, and he would take care of the early morning feeding for the horses. But first I had to start the fire for our breakfast, even though I was half-awake and hungry.

**What we learn from understanding the setting:** The setting is a farm in late fall, and the mood is grim because the weather is grey and cold, and chores await the child.

**Read the selection, looking for clues that will help you figure out the time and place of the events. Then, answer the questions.**

The day dawned sunny and bright. I awakened to the noise of fishermen offering their wares, as I always did.

"Fish for sale! Fresh fish for sale!"

Today was different, though. Today was going to be a great day. We would carry out our plan to teach the British a lesson. It was December 16, 1773.

I had heard the men talking about it for weeks. They had had enough of the British, and quite enough of their taxes. As a son of one of the "Sons of Liberty," I planned to be there for the main event.

That evening, my father and many others were going to dress themselves as Mohawk Indians and dump tons and tons of tea into the Boston Harbor. It promised to be a wonderful, if unusual, sort of tea party!

1. What is the setting, or time and place, of the passage?

______________________________

2. What is the mood of the passage?

______________________________

Name ______________________ Date ________

# Literary Analysis: Setting

## Assess

**Read the following selection, looking for clues about the time and place. Then, answer the questions.**

We landed our Jetstar on the first pod we could locate. Traffic was heavy on Andaron at this time of the morning—8027 onstar time—and we needed to hurry. It was another gloomy morning. The sky was filled with huge blue and white drops that threatened to splatter all over the windshield.

Laura and I were the first people to arrive at work. Commander Voss took one look at us and said, "What happened to you two? You look like you were caught in a meteor avalanche!"

"No, boss," said Laura calmly. "Just a blue-and-white shower; a little heavier than usual, I guess. We forgot to wear our auto-protective devices."

Voss wasn't impressed. "Well, what do I train you for? Never mind, let's get to work. We have a lot to talk about today. Our planet is in grave jeopardy of disintegrating from this disturbing weather pattern."

That was Voss—always exaggerating. The fact is that Andaron has not had any bad weather in hundreds of years, so people tend to overreact if the sun doesn't shine.

**1.** When are the events in the story probably taking place?

______________________________

**2.** Underline the clues you used to figure out your answer to question 1.

**3.** Where does the selection take place?

______________________________

**4.** Circle the clues you used to figure out your answer to question 3.

**5.** What is the mood of the story? Explain.

______________________________

______________________________

______________________________

______________________________

______________________________

______________________________

______________________________

Name ______________________________ Date __________

# Literary Analysis: Character Traits

## Practice

**Character traits** are the personal qualities, attitudes, and values that make a character unique. For example, one character may be lazy and untrustworthy, while another is hardworking and dependable.

- **Round characters** are complex, showing many different character traits. For example, a character's actions and dialogue might reveal that, although she is tough and demanding, she can also be sensitive, considerate, and humble.
- **Flat characters** are one-sided, showing just a single trait. For example, the villains in many TV and movie comedies are flat characters. They are portrayed only as "bad guys."

Read the selection. Then, respond to each item.

Simon and Leonard were always playing elaborate practical jokes. If people got upset, the boys laughed and told them to get a sense of humor. Ginger lived next door to Simon and Leonard. Like them, she enjoyed a good joke, but she didn't like to upset people. She thought the brothers' jokes sometimes went too far. She decided it was time they learned a lesson. A few nights before Halloween, Ginger went from door to door, telling her neighbors about her plan to beat the boys at their own game. Most of the neighbors were happy to play along. The only holdout was Mr. Cruthers. He was a grumpy man who never said hello to anyone and always kept his lights off on Halloween. He didn't even answer the door when Ginger knocked, although she knew he was home.

**1.** Which character trait does Simon display in the selection?

**A.** thoughtfulness **B.** insensitivity **C.** unfriendliness **D.** cruelty

**2.** List the character traits that the other characters display.

Leonard: ______________________________

Ginger: ______________________________

Mr. Cruthers: ______________________________

**3.** Which character(s) would you describe as flat? Explain. ______________________________

______________________________

**4.** Which character(s) would you describe as round? Explain. ______________________________

______________________________

Name ______________________ Date __________

# Literary Analysis: Character Traits

## Assess

**A** Read the passage, and then respond to each item.

Matt was a daredevil on the slopes, doing flips in the air and other stunts. He could snowboard with the best of them, and he knew it. When it came to asking out girls, however, he was a coward. He'd liked Anna for years but could never get up the courage to call her.

**1.** Circle the character traits displayed by Matt.

confidence shyness honesty adventurousness

**2.** What is the difference between a flat character and a round character?

______________________

**3.** Is Matt a flat or round character? Explain. ______________________

______________________

**B** Read these two passages, and then tell whether each character is flat or round. Use details to support your answer.

Liah was one of the most popular girls at school. She was the star of the debate club and a co-captain of the track team. She also managed to get straight A's. Teachers admired her work ethic and found her charming. It was a different story once she got home, however. There, Liah was quiet and moody, often locking herself in her room and ignoring her little sister's pleas for attention.

Liah: ______________________

______________________

Frankie dropped his backpack to the floor. He tossed his jacket over the chair and kicked his sneakers off across the room. He yanked open the refrigerator door and pulled out three dishes of leftovers before he found what he was looking for—the lasagna. He ripped off the foil covering, crumpled it into a ball, and then grabbed a fork from the sink. After polishing off the pasta, he pushed the dish aside, where it cluttered the countertop along with the other three dishes he never put back. He grabbed a bag of chips and went to watch TV in the next room.

Frankie: ______________________

______________________

Name ______________________ Date __________

# Literary Analysis: Comparing Types of Narratives

## Practice

A **narrative** is a story about characters and the events that happen to them. Every narrative has a plot, a series of related events told in chronological order. There are two main types of narratives:

- A **fictional narrative** tells about imaginary characters and events. Short stories and novels are fictional narratives. Read this passage from a fictional narrative:

  Teddy shouted to the house, ". . . Our mongoose is killing a snake"; and Rikki-tikki heard a scream from Teddy's mother. His father ran out with a stick, but by the time he came up, Karait [the snake] had lunged out once too far, and Rikki-tikki had sprung, jumped on the snake's back, dropped his head far between his forelegs, bitten as high up the back as he could get hold, and rolled away.

- A **nonfictional narrative** is a true story about real characters and events. Biographies and autobiographies are nonfictional narratives. Read this passage from a nonfictional narrative:

  One day when I was eight years old, I came upon an injured raccoon lying in our backyard. I ran to help the poor suffering creature. Suddenly, my mother, a few feet behind me, rushed forward and let out a heart-stopping scream.

  "James! No! Stop immediately! Do not take another step. That animal might have rabies."

Circle the choice that best completes the statement or answers the question.

**1.** Both passages are narratives because they both include

**A.** fictional characters.
**B.** real people.
**C.** a plot involving characters and events.
**D.** facts and opinions about animals.

**2.** The fictional narrative above might be part of a(n)

**A.** short story. **B.** biography. **C.** autobiography. **D.** poem.

**3.** The nonfictional narrative above might be part of a(n)

**A.** short story. **B.** novel. **C.** autobiography. **D.** poem.

**4.** In what way does the nonfictional narrative borrow the elements of a fictional narrative?

**A.** It describes an imaginary setting.
**B.** It creates a feeling of suspense.
**C.** It includes imaginary characters.
**D.** It uses chronological order.

Name ________________________________ Date ____________

## Literary Analysis: Comparing Types of Narratives

### Assess

**Read this example of a nonfictional narrative. Then, answer the questions.**

Suddenly a queer quivering ran under me, apparently the whole length of the ship. Startled by the very strangeness of the shivering motion, I sprang to the floor. With too perfect a trust in that mighty vessel I again lay down. Someone knocked at my door, and the voice of a friend said, "Come quickly to my cabin; an iceberg has just passed our window; I know we have just struck one."

. . . Then, and not until then, did I realize the horror of an accident at sea. Now it was too late to dress . . . the stewardess put on our life-preservers. . . . Our lifeboat, with thirty-six in it, began lowering into the sea. . . . As only one side of the ropes worked, the lifeboat at one time was in such a position that it seemed we must capsize in mid-air. At last the ropes worked together, and we drew nearer and nearer the black, oily water. The first touch of our lifeboat on that black sea came to me as a last good-bye to life, and so we put off—a tiny boat on a great sea. . . .

—from the memories of Elizabeth Shutes, a survivor of the sinking of the *Titanic*

**1.** What makes this passage a narrative?

**A.** It describes real people and places.
**B.** It tells a story and has characters and events.
**C.** It gives facts about the sinking of the *Titanic.*
**D.** It includes fictional characters.

**2.** How can you tell that this narrative is nonfiction?

**A.** It tells a true story about real people.
**B.** It is taken from a short story.
**C.** It is written by a famous person.
**D.** It describes real places.

**3.** How would a fictional narrative about a shipwreck be different from this one?

**A.** It would include more facts.
**B.** It would include more opinions.
**C.** It would include imaginary characters and events.
**D.** It would take place in an imaginary setting.

**4.** In what way does this nonfictional narrative borrow the elements of fiction?

**A.** It describes an imaginary setting.
**B.** It includes imaginary characters.
**C.** It creates a mood of danger and suspense.
**D.** It uses chronological order.

Name ______________________ Date __________

# Vocabulary: Prefix *de-* and suffixes *-ee* and *-ity*

## Practice

A **prefix** is added to the beginning of a word or word root to change its meaning. The prefix *de-* can change word meanings in two ways. In some words, *de-* means "away" or "from." In other cases, it means "down."

de + tour = detour: "a route that leads away from the normal route"
de + scend = descend: "to go down"

A **suffix** is added to the end of a word to change its meaning or part of speech. The suffix *-ee* refers to someone who receives an action or has been put in a certain position. It is often used to change verbs to nouns. The suffix *-ity* changes adjectives to nouns.

train + ee = trainee: "someone who is being trained for a job"
rare + ity = rarity: "something that is rare, or hard to find"

**A** Circle the letter of the correct answer to each question.

**1.** What is happening if the price of something declines?
**A.** the price goes down **B.** the price goes up

**2.** What do you do when you decode a message?
**A.** hide its meaning **B.** figure out its hidden meaning

**3.** What do you do when you defer a decision?
**A.** you put off making the decision **B.** you make the decision right away

**B** Add *-ee* or *-ity* to each underlined word to form a new word that fits the meaning of the sentence.

**1.** ______________ He was the newest appoint to the state's highest court.

**2.** ______________ She hurt many people's feelings because of her insensitive.

**3.** ______________ His timid made it hard for him to ask girls out on dates.

Name ______________________________ Date __________

# Vocabulary: Prefix *de-* and suffixes *-ee* and *-ity*

## Assess

**A** Circle the meaning of the prefix *de-* that is used in each word. Then use the word in a sentence.

1. deficiency: a lack of something that is needed — down/away

______________________________

2. descendants: children, grandchildren, great-grandchildren, and so on — down/away

______________________________

3. deny: to claim something is untrue — down/away

______________________________

4. depart: to leave — down/away

______________________________

5. depressed: pushed down, or sad and low-spirited — down/away

______________________________

6. deduct: to subtract from the total — down/away

______________________________

**B** Add the suffix indicated to each underlined word to form a new word. Write this word on the line. Then rewrite the original sentence to use the new word.

1. ______________ We will honor him at the banquet tonight. (add *-ee*)

______________________________

2. ______________ The problem is hard to solve because it is complex. (add *-ity*)

______________________________

3. ______________ The best thing about this brand of soap is that it is pure. (add *-ity*)

______________________________

4. ______________ Her party nominated her to run for the Senate seat. (add *-ee*)

______________________________

5. ______________ After three futile attempts to solve the problem, he called in an expert. (add *-ity*)

______________________________

Name ______________________________ Date ____________

# Grammar: Action and Linking Verbs

## Practice

An **action verb** indicates an action. The action may be visible (*run, write, return, practice, give, contain*) or mental (*think, like, dream, believe, understand*).

A **linking verb** connects the subject with a word that describes it or identifies the subject. Common linking verbs include *seem, appear, feel, sound, taste, smell, look*, and forms of *be* (*am, is, are, was, were, have been, had been*). Depending on how they are used, some verbs may be action or linking.

| **Action Verbs** | **Linking Verbs** |
|---|---|
| Sheila likes cooking. | Sheila is a great *baker* (*Baker* identifies *Sheila.*) |
| Sheila tastes the apple pie. | The pie tastes *good.* (*Good* describes *pie.*) |
| She appeared on television. | She appeared *happy.* (*Happy* describes *she.*) |

**A** Underline the verb in each sentence. Then, write ***A*** if it is an action verb or ***L*** if it is a linking verb.

1. ______ At the queen's order, her servant tasted the food.
2. ______ The house seemed very lonely last night.
3. ______ The girls became lifeguards last summer.
4. ______ A dinner bell sounded in the banquet hall.
5. ______ The bald eagle is our national symbol.
6. ______ Amy looked through the telescope.

**B** Each sentence contains a linking verb. Underline the subject with one line and the verb with two lines. Circle the word that either describes or identifies the subject.

**Example:** Her new sweater looks (beautiful).

1. Her rug is too small for her room.
2. Television is an important tool of education.
3. Dana may be the most likely choice for the office.
4. The girls were hoarse from cheering.
5. The aroma of freshly baked bread smells wonderful to me.

Name ______________________________ Date ____________

# Grammar: Action and Linking Verbs

## Assess

**A** Underline the verb in each sentence. Then, write ***A*** if it is an action verb or ***L*** if it is a linking verb.

**1.** ______ Our neighbor remained a close friend for years.

**2.** ______ My mother felt my head often during my illness.

**3.** ______ Your perfume smells too strong today.

**4.** ______ Grandmother tasted our fresh bread.

**5.** ______ This red sweater is the one I made.

**6.** ______ My grandmother is my favorite relative.

**7.** ______ The new snow shovel looks sturdy.

**8.** ______ We grew two varieties of tomatoes last summer.

**9.** ______ Harrison Ford is a famous actor.

**10.** ______ The next bus was an express to the train station.

**B** Each sentence below contains a linking verb. Underline the subject with one line and the verb with two lines. Circle the word that either describes or identifies the subject.

**1.** *Frankenstein* is a famous novel.

**2.** The dinosaur is a prehistoric animal.

**3.** The afternoon speaker appears very confident.

**4.** After their swim, the boys felt very refreshed.

**5.** Jerry has been president of his class for three years.

**6.** A good dictionary is a valuable tool for writing assignments.

**7.** The plant grew sturdy in the hothouse.

**8.** The new chorus sounds even better than the old.

**9.** Rhode Island is the smallest state in the Union.

**10.** The visitor became more and more demanding.

Name ______________________________ Date __________

# Grammar: Principal Parts of Regular Verbs

## Practice

Every verb has four **principal parts** that are used to form tenses which show action occurring at different times. These principal parts are the *present* (*base form*), the *present participle*, the *past*, and the *past participle*. A regular verb forms its past and past participle by adding *-ed or -d* to the basic form. Sometimes you will have to double a final consonant, add a *-d* if the verb ends in *e*, or change *y* to *i* before adding *-ed* or *-ing*.

| Principal Part | Description | Examples |
|---|---|---|
| Present | Basic form | call, try |
| Present Participle | Add *-ing*. Use after a *to be* verb. | (is) calling, (are) trying |
| Past | Add *-ed* or *-d*. | called, tried |
| Past Participle | Add *-ed* or *-d*. Use after *has, have, had.* | (had) called, (had) tried |

Underline the verb or verb phrase in each sentence. Then, identify the principal part used to form the verb.

**Example:** ____past____ We watched the tennis match.

1. ______________ My uncle lives on an island.
2. ______________ Gary waited half an hour for the bus.
3. ______________ Karen is visiting her relatives in Iowa.
4. ______________ Are you listening to the explanation?
5. ______________ The speaker had paused for the moment.
6. ______________ She has drawn many cartoons.
7. ______________ Mr. Kelly coached the football team last season.
8. ______________ Amy had remembered to pack a flashlight.
9. ______________ We are planning a number of surprises.
10. ______________ These musicians usually play some contemporary music.

Name ______________________ Date __________

# Grammar: Principal Parts of Regular Verbs

## Assess

**A** Underline the verb or verb phrase in each sentence. Then, identify the principal part used to form the verb.

1. ______________ Barbara filled the fish tank with fresh water.
2. ______________ The president is holding a press conference tomorrow.
3. ______________ My brother is enrolling in college in the fall.
4. ______________ Have the judges announced the winner?
5. ______________ The sweater always shrinks in the wash.
6. ______________ The head chef personally prepares each dish.
7. ______________ The first guests had already arrived.
8. ______________ We are planning a trip to Yellowstone Park next summer.
9. ______________ Steve drives me home every day.
10. ______________ I am calling Dr. Johnson tomorrow.

**B** Write the form of the verb in parentheses that correctly completes the sentence.

1. ______________ Kevin has (live) in Kentucky all his life.
2. ______________ The players were (discuss) their strategies.
3. ______________ I still (exercise) every day.
4. ______________ We have (agree) to meet at 7 P.M.
5. ______________ Before he spoke, the entertainer (smile) at the audience.
6. ______________ Frank had already (perform) his act before I arrived.
7. ______________ He is (attempt) to run a four-minute mile.
8. ______________ Yesterday Jennifer (promise) she would join our group.
9. ______________ Kenneth is (practice) a new song on his clarinet.
10. ______________ I am (suggest) that you make several changes.

Name ____________________ Date ________

# Grammar: Revising Irregular Verbs

## Practice

**Irregular verbs** are verbs whose past and past participle forms do not follow a predictable pattern. For regular verbs, the past tense is formed by adding *-ed* or *-d* to the tense form, as in *follow, followed.* With an irregular verb, the past and past participle are *not* formed according to this rule.

**Present Tense:** School begins at 8:00.
**Past Tense:** School began at 8:00.
**Past Participle:** School has begun at 8:00.

**Some Irregular Verbs**

| Present | Present Participle | Past | Past Participle |
|---|---|---|---|
| bring | (is) bringing | brought | (have) brought |
| rise | (is) rising | rose | (have) risen |
| go | (is) going | went | (have) gone |
| choose | (is) choosing | chose | (have) chosen |
| do | (is) doing | did | (have) done |
| see | (is) seeing | saw | (have) seen |

Underline the correct form of the verb.

1. The dough should (raise, rise) for about twenty more minutes.
2. You mean I (did, done) the wrong page of math homework?
3. Now I wish that I had (went, gone) with you.
4. Marco Polo (saw, seen) many strange sights in his travels.
5. Amelia Earhart (did, done) what few other people dared to do.
6. The patriot said, "I (done, did) my best for my country."
7. They (went, gone) away without saying goodbye.
8. Kerry, have you (brung, brought) your tennis racket?
9. Our little kitten has (drank, drunk) all its milk.
10. Have you (chose, chosen) your partner yet?

Name ______________________________ Date __________

# Grammar: Revising Irregular Verbs

## Assess

**A** Underline the correct form of the verb.

1. The referee had (blew, blown) the whistle.
2. The quarterback dropped back and (threw, thrown) a pass.
3. The receiver had (sprang, sprung) high in the air but missed the ball.
4. The audience (began, begun) to shout and boo the players.
5. Clearly the crowd had (became, become) upset.
6. The receiver (run, ran) to catch the ball.
7. The running back had not (saw, seen) a tackler behind him.
8. Both players had (went, gone) down.
9. The ball had (flew, flown) out of the running back's hands.
10. Everyone had (knew, known) it would be a close game.

**B** Rewrite each sentence to make the verb correct.

1. I had grow to love my car.

______________________________

2. I had swore never to get rid of it.

______________________________

3. Now its engine has wore out somewhat.

______________________________

4. The seat belt buzzer has rang its last warning.

______________________________

5. Among my friends I have sang its praises.

______________________________

Name ______________________________ Date ____________

# Writing: Description of an Imagined Setting

## Practice

When writing a **description of an imagined setting,** writers use their knowledge of the real world to create a fictional environment. To be effective, a description of an imagined scene should include the following elements:

- **concrete language** identifying the objects in the scene (for example, "a wooden rocking chair")
- **sensory details** that describe how the place looks, smells, sounds, or feels (for example, "the hot, muggy air")
- **vivid descriptions** that bring the scene to life (for example, "A parade of determined black ants marched across the patio.")

**A** Read the following example. Then, follow the directions below.

Deena pressed her sturdy hands against the heavy oak window frame and pushed upward. In rushed the jarring sounds of honking horns and screeching tires and the pungent smells of exhaust and uncollected trash, all piggybacking on a welcome current of cool September air. Deena had been in the one-room apartment nearly two months now and had managed to acquire no more than a small cot in the corner opposite the door, a folding table and two chairs beside the window, and an assortment of colorful milk crates in which to store her meager belongings.

1. Give three examples of concrete language in the scene. ______________

______________________________

2. List at least three adjectives used to describe these objects. ______________

______________________________

3. Find a sensory detail in the scene for each of the senses listed below.

Sound: ______________________________

Smell: ______________________________

Sight: ______________________________

Touch: ______________________________

**B** Imagine that you are standing by the window in the apartment described above. On the back of this page or on a separate sheet of paper, write a brief description of the scene outside your window.

Name _______________________________________________ Date ____________

# Writing: Description of an Imagined Setting

## Assess

Respond to each item below.

**1.** Choose a setting to imagine yourself in.

a two-room apartment above a bakery

a densely wooded forest in early autumn

the home office of a famous author

a campground by a lake in mid July

**2.** What objects will your setting include? ____________________

____________________________________________

**3.** What adjectives will you use to help readers visualize these objects? ________

____________________________________________

**4.** Give three sensory details that you will use to describe the scene.

____________________________________________

____________________________________________

____________________________________________

**5.** Write your description of the setting on the following lines.

____________________________________________

____________________________________________

____________________________________________

____________________________________________

____________________________________________

____________________________________________

____________________________________________

____________________________________________

____________________________________________

____________________________________________

Name ______________________ Date __________

# Writing: Character Profile

## Practice

When you write a **character profile,** you describe that character's personality traits. A character profile can help show how a character's personality affects his or her actions and the part he or she plays in the story's plot. For example, if you describe a character as being good-hearted and easily swayed by others, it is easy to understand how that character might be tricked into doing extra work for someone else. If you describe a character as being clever, observant, and hardworking, it makes sense that that character will be good at solving problems.

**A** Read the character profile. Then, circle the letter of the best answer to each question.

Anne, the main character of the book *Anne of Green Gables,* is a determined and spunky girl. Adversity does not stop her from trying to get what she wants. She is very intelligent and works hard to succeed at home and at school. However, she is high-spirited and daring and tends to get into mischief. She sees the world as an adventure, while those around her, especially Marilla, her guardian, are far more practical. Anne is a dynamic and imaginative character and often influences those around her.

1. Based on this character profile, why would it make sense that Anne is often in some sort of trouble?

   **A.** She is determined and intelligent.
   **B.** She is spunky, high-spirited, and daring.
   **C.** She works hard.
   **D.** She is not very practical.

2. Based on this character profile, how would you predict Anne would deal with conflicts?

   **A.** She would probably be bold and creative in resolving conflicts.
   **B.** She would probably shy away from resolving conflicts.
   **C.** She would probably not bother to resolve conflicts.
   **D.** She would probably not have the strength to resolve conflicts.

**B** Choose one of the following: a character from a story or novel, a character from a movie or TV show, or someone you know. List at least four character traits of that person.

______________________________________________

______________________________________________

______________________________________________

______________________________________________

Name ______________________ Date __________

# Writing: Character Profile

## Assess

Use the following prompts to help create a character profile.

1. Choose a character from fiction, movies, television shows, or drama. Write the character's name on the line.

2. List at least four personality traits of that character, or more if you wish.

3. Think about a conflict that your character has been involved in. Write one sentence about how your character deals with conflict.

4. Think about a problem your character has faced. Write one sentence about how your character has solved a problem.

5. On the lines provided, write a character profile for the character you have chosen, using the information in items 1–4.

Name ______________________ Date __________

# Writing: Critical Review

## Practice

In a **critical review,** a writer responds to one or more pieces of literature. If the review covers more than one piece of literature, both pieces should be similar in some way. For example, a writer might write a critical review of two poems with the same topic or theme. Or, the writer might write a critical review of two stories by the same author.

In the introduction to the review, the writer identifies the piece or pieces of literature and describes the ways in which they are similar. Then, the writer states his or her opinions about the works. The writer is free to express both positive and negative opinions, and to include ideas and arguments that demonstrate independent thinking. However, each opinion must be supported effectively with facts, details, or examples.

**A** Read this excerpt from a critical review. Then, answer the questions.

The poems "Storm," by Nick Scott, and "Snowy Wonderland," by Sally Pierre, both describe a winter setting. However, the two poems are very different in content and tone. Scott's poem uses powerful imagery, as in the line *Driving pellets like icy needles,* to allow the reader to "feel" the cold, hard sleet. By contrast, Pierre's poem is softer and more songlike. For example, the lines *Snowman, snowman, look at that! Here's your pipe and here's your hat* seem simple and childish.

1. According to the reviewer, how are the poems alike and different? ______

______

2. What is the reviewer's overall opinion of "Storm"? ______

______

3. What fact, detail, or example does the reviewer use to support that opinion?

______

4. What is the reviewer's overall opinion of "Snowy Wonderland"? ______

______

5. What fact, detail, or example does the reviewer use to support that opinion?

______

**B** On a separate sheet of paper, write a brief critical review of two poems, songs, or stories that are similar in some way. Include your opinions, backed by facts, details, or examples.

Name ________________________________ Date ____________

# Writing: Critical Review

## Assess

**A** Read this excerpt from a critical review. Then, answer the questions.

The short stories "Westward Ho!," by Matthew Williams, and "Follow the Trail," by Rebecca Hall, are both about pioneers traveling to the American West. *Westward Ho!* was a very exciting book. In it, the Wells family must deal with diseases, lack of food and water, and an attack by a pack of wolves. Because the narrator was Jen, a 15-year-old girl, I identified with her and felt a lot of suspense as she and her family faced each incredible challenge. I was thrilled when they finally made it to Oregon. By contrast, I found *Follow the Trail* to be dull. The main characters, two families named the Fultons and the Goods, face far fewer outside challenges than the Wells family. Instead, they face inner problems. They argue about which trail to follow, and what they will do once they make it to the West. They were so disagreeable that I couldn't identify with any of them, and I lost interest halfway through the book.

**1.** According to the reviewer, how are the stories alike? ____________________

______________________________________________

**2.** What is the reviewer's overall opinion of "Westward Ho!"? ____________________

______________________________________________

**3.** What facts, details, or examples does the reviewer use to support that opinion? ____________________

______________________________________________

______________________________________________

**4.** What is the reviewer's overall opinion of "Follow the Trail"? ____________________

______________________________________________

**5.** What facts, details, or examples does the reviewer use to support that opinion? ____________________

______________________________________________

______________________________________________

**B** Think of two plays, short stories, or movies that are similar in some way. On a separate sheet of paper, write a brief critical review of them. Be sure to include your opinions, supported by facts, details, or examples.

Name ______________________ Date __________

# Reading: Make Inferences

## Practice

Readers often have to **make inferences,** or logical guesses, about characters, setting, and events by recognizing and using details in the story. For example, the detail that a girl is smiling added to the detail that she is looking at a photograph helps you infer that looking at the photograph makes her happy.

**A** Read the paragraph. Then, respond to each item.

Lana paced back and forth across the living room carpet. She stopped and picked up a magazine from a table. After flipping through the pages impatiently, she let it drop. She tugged at a strand of hair and continued her pacing, back and forth, back and forth. She sighed, then stopped and slumped down on the sofa.

1. How do you think Lana feels?

______________________

2. Underline two details that helped you infer Lana's feelings.

**B** Read each passage. Then, respond to each item.

You ask your brother how his first day at his new job went. He frowns and says, "I don't even want to talk about it."

1. What would you guess happened?

______________________

Your friend promises you that you can borrow her roller skates, but when she comes over, she forgets to bring them. When you remind her, she says, "Oh, right. Maybe some other day." The next time you get together, she never mentions the skates. You ask her one last time. She looks away from you as she says, "I think they are probably the wrong size for you."

2. What can you infer about your friend and her skates?

______________________

3. Underline two details that support your inference.

Name ______________________ Date __________

# Reading: Make Inferences

## Assess

**A** Read the passage. Then, answer the questions that follow.

Tom rushed through the doorway, out of breath. The teacher was about to begin the history lesson. Tom had gotten lost in the wrong wing of the school and was late. Some of the kids stared at him, and somebody whispered a joke and laughed. Tom bit his thumbnail and looked at the floor. He made his way to the back of the room, where there was an empty desk. He sat down and glued his eyes to the desk.

**1.** Who is Tom? Circle the letter of the likely answer.

**A.** a new student in the class  **B.** a substitute teacher

**2.** Underline two details in the paragraph that support your answer.

**3.** How does Tom feel? Circle the letter of the likely answer.

**A.** nervous  **B.** bored

**4.** Underline two details in the paragraph that support your answer.

**B** Read the passage. Then, respond to each item.

Above all, Paula loved writing her own music. She could hear a symphony in her head, and someday she planned to write every note of it. She hummed as she walked from class to class. She jotted down melodies and chords as she thought of them, sometimes in the middle of chemistry class or Spanish.

"What's this, Miss Smith?" asked Dr. Tern, her chemistry teacher. "Are you writing a formula? Or just fooling with your musical doodles again?"

**1.** What is Paula's plan? Circle the letter of the likely answer.

**A.** to write a symphony  **B.** to go to a concert

**2.** Underline two details in the passage that support your answer.

**3.** How does Dr. Tern feel about Paula's music? Circle the letter of the likely answer.

**A.** He does not appreciate it.  **B.** He wants to know more about it.

**4.** Underline a detail from the passage that supports your answer.

Name ______________________________ Date ____________

# Reading: Recognize Appeals to Emotion

## Practice

When you **recognize appeals to emotion,** you notice arguments that are based on feelings rather than on logic and reason. Appeals to emotion are used in advertisements, as well as in political speeches and other forms of persuasive writing. Read the example below, and notice the appeals to emotion the writer uses.

**Sample Advertisement:** If you want to be part of the "in" crowd, you've got to buy Sneeks, the hottest new sneaker for teens. "I wear them everywhere!" says Kira J, the singer. You will simply love these shoes—they've got that magic ingredient that everyone wants—style.

**Appeals to Emotion Used in Advertisement:**
The **bandwagon appeal** is designed to appeal to everyone's desire to belong: "be part of the 'in' crowd."
**Loaded language** uses words that cannot be proved but sound important: "the hottest new sneaker."
**Testimonials** suggest that just because a celebrity or an expert says the product is good, it must be true: "'I wear them everywhere!' says Kira J, the singer."
**Generalizations** include broad or vague claims: "You will simply love these shoes."
**Factual evidence for claims:** None.

**Read the passage. Then, answer the questions.**

I urge you to join your neighbors in voting for me for senator. I offer an alternative to the dangerous, wild policies of my opponent. In fact, Mr. Yuri Jackson of the Clarksville lumber mill is supporting my candidacy. Surely you agree that he's smart enough to know a good candidate when he sees one! Come on, folks. If you vote for me, life will be better here in Clarksville—you'll see.

**1.** Which part of the speech includes a bandwagon appeal? Explain.

______________________________________________

**2.** Which part of the speech includes loaded language? Explain.

______________________________________________

**3.** Which part of the speech includes a testimonial? Explain.

______________________________________________

**4.** Which part of the speech includes a generalization? Explain.

______________________________________________

Name ______________________ Date __________

# Reading: Recognize Appeals to Emotion

## Assess

**Read the advertisement. Then, answer the questions.**

Hurry, folks, before time runs out! We're running a special sale on the Triple Flex action vitamins—three bottles for the price of only two. But we have a limited supply, so you must act now!

Do you want to be the guy on your block who's huffing and puffing while your friends and family are bouncing through life with energy and vigor? Do you want to be sitting on the couch while your wife is getting ready to set a new record in the statewide marathon race?

No, of course you don't. And you're smart. According to Dr. Ulrich Patterson of the Life Fitness Center, after just one week on Triple Flex, you'll feel ten years younger. You'll sleep better, too.

You deserve a better life. Now you can have one. Feel the Triple Flex difference. You'll be glad you did.

**1.** Which part of the advertisement includes a bandwagon appeal? Explain.

______________________________

______________________________

**2.** Which part of the advertisement includes loaded language? Explain.

______________________________

______________________________

**3.** Which part of the advertisement includes a testimonial? Explain.

______________________________

______________________________

**4.** Which part of the advertisement includes a generalization? Explain.

______________________________

______________________________

**5.** Are there any facts included in the advertisement? Do they contribute to making it more persuasive? Explain.

______________________________

______________________________

______________________________

Name ______________________________ Date __________

# Literary Analysis: Point of View

## Practice

**Point of view** is the perspective from which a story is told.

In **first-person point of view,** the story is told by a character who is in the story and is part of the action. The first-person narrator uses the pronouns *I, me,* and *we* when speaking about himself or herself. The reader sees and knows only what the narrator sees and knows.

In **third-person point of view,** the storyteller is not a character in the story but tells events from the "outside." This narrator can describe the thoughts and actions of any or all of the characters in the story and uses pronouns such as *he, she,* and *they* to describe the characters.

Read the story excerpts. Write F-P if the excerpt is told from the first-person point of view. Write T-P if the excerpt is told from third-person point of view.

**1.** ______ Ted says that being a good magician isn't easy. He and Gina practice their tricks for hours a day. Sometimes they watch themselves in the mirror as they do the tricks. Sometimes they might invite an audience to watch. "The hand is quicker than the eye!" Ted always says.

**2.** ______ Laura and I were completely silent. We crouched down behind the bushes, afraid to even breathe. Was that really a bear in our woods? What should we do?

**3.** ______ I watched Mario as he took his time putting on the skates. Why had he told Lola that he could play hockey? I noticed that she hadn't been that impressed. Why did he always have to make up stories? I could tell that Mario was feeling nervous. He was stalling for time, trying to stay off the ice as long as possible.

**4.** ______ Identical twins Max and Bart used to dress the same way, speak the same way, and go everywhere together. However, ever since they started high school, the boys look quite different. Max dresses in khakis and button-down shirts. Bart wears all black, all the time.

**5.** ______ "A storm is coming," said Marla. "We'd better get off the beach." Dark clouds were forming, and the wind was getting stronger. Marla, Kara and Grace quickly folded the towels while D. J. called her dad on her cell phone. When Mr. Martin got the call, he was already about to leave to pick up the kids at the lake.

Name ______________________________ Date ____________

# Literary Analysis: Point of View

## Assess

**A** Circle the letter of the choice that best answers each question.

1. In first-person point of view, who is the narrator, or person telling the story?

   **A.** a character in the story **B.** a person outside the story

2. In third-person point of view, who is the narrator?

   **A.** a character in the story **B.** a person outside the story

3. When a story is told from the third-person point of view, what do readers know?

   **A.** only what the narrator experiences **B.** what many of the characters do and say

4. When a story is told from the first-person point of view, what do readers know?

   **A.** only what the narrator experiences **B.** what most characters think

**B** Read each passage. Then, answer the questions.

I would love to be an archaeologist when I grow up. The study of ancient civilizations fascinates me. Central America, the home of the Aztecs and Mayas, is the place I would like to explore. I dream of discovering ruins and artifacts deep in a jungle.

1. What is the point of view? Explain. ______________________________

______________________________

______________________________

Mike and Julio volunteer at the North Street Animal Shelter after school twice a week. They do the hardest part first: cleaning all the dogs' cages. Then, they do the fun part: exercising the dogs. Dog walking takes some skill when you are walking four or five dogs at a time! Mike and Julio are even teaching some of the dogs tricks.

2. What is the point of view? Explain. ______________________________

______________________________

______________________________

Name ______________________________ Date ____________

# Literary Analysis: Theme

## Practice

The **theme** of a literary work is its central idea, insight, or message. It is usually a generalization about life or people. A **stated theme** is expressed directly. For example, in most fables, the story teaches one or more animal characters a lesson. This lesson is directly stated at the end of the fable as a moral, such as "Always tell the truth." An **unstated, or implied, theme** is not directly stated. Instead, the writer presents it through the actions and experiences of the characters. For example, picture a story about a tiny man who must defeat a wicked dragon. He is no match for a huge dragon physically, so he uses cleverness to win. The story events and outcome suggest the theme of "Brains are mightier than brawn." Readers can often find more than one theme in a story. Each interpretation of a theme is valid as long as it can be supported with details from the text.

Read the passages. Then, respond to each item.

A A dog named Harry found a meaty bone and wanted to save it for later. But he was too lazy to bury the bone. He decided to trick another dog into doing it for him. "Hey, Fuzzy! If you bury this bone for me, I'll share it with you," he said. Fuzzy agreed and trotted off to bury the bone. Later that day, Harry was hungry. He dug up an entire field, but he couldn't find his bone. He learned that laziness does not lead to success. Meanwhile, Fuzzy enjoyed his tasty, meaty bone.

B Two birds, Marge and Helen, saw a birdhouse in an apple tree. Both thought it was a perfect place for a nest, but it was only big enough for one of them. "Let's rest a bit, Helen," Marge said. When Helen fell asleep, Marge started building a nest. By the time Helen woke up, Marge was almost finished. Helen flew over to the birdhouse.

"I'll bet your nest is lovely," she said. "May I go inside and see it?"

"Well, all right," agreed Marge.

Once inside, Helen pushed straw up against the opening. "Thanks, Marge," she said. "It's really cozy in here."

1. Does Passage A or B have a stated theme? ______ Underline its theme.

2. In your own words, state the implied theme of the other passage.

______________________________________________

3. A story can have more than one theme. In Passage A, what theme might Fuzzy's actions and the story outcome suggest? ______________________

______________________________________________

Name ______________________________ Date __________

# Literary Analysis: Theme

## Assess

**A** Answer the questions. Circle the letter of the best answer.

1. Which statement about the theme of a work is true?

   A. There is usually just one correct interpretation of a work's theme.
   B. The theme of a work is usually directly stated at the end.
   C. The theme of a work is never directly stated but is always implied.
   D. The theme of a work is often a generalization about life or people.

2. Which statement about an unstated theme is true?

   A. It must always be supported by details in the text.
   B. It is always an important lesson that an animal character learns.
   C. It appears as a written moral at the end of the story.
   D. It is not implied.

**B** Read this passage. Then, answer the questions that follow.

A cat cornered a mouse in a barn and was about to eat it. "Save me!" the mouse cried. "And someday I may save you!" The cat was haughty. "How can a tiny mouse ever save a cat?" she asked. "I may be tiny," the mouse answered, "but I have thirty-four brothers and sisters. Together, we will help you someday when you are in grave danger."

The cat was amused. She decided to let the mouse go. One day, weeks later, a snarling, growling dog cornered the cat in the same barn.

"Help!" cried the cat. "I'm in grave danger!" Suddenly, thirty-five mice leaped out of a hole in the wall. They began nipping at the dog with all their might. The dog yelped as he raced away.

"Thank you," the cat said to the mice. "You really did save me!"

1. Is the theme of this passage stated or unstated? ______________________

2. What is the theme of this passage? Circle the letter of the best answer.

   A. Don't underestimate others.
   B. Cats are haughty.
   C. Barns can be dangerous.
   D. Animals sometimes talk.

3. Which is an additional theme of the passage? Circle the letter of the best answer.

   A. Mice often have large families.
   B. Dogs are never as smart as cats.
   C. Cats live in barns.
   D. Teamwork pays off.

Name ______________________________ Date __________

# Literary Analysis: Comparing Symbols

## Practice

A **symbol** is a person, place, or thing that represents something beyond its literal meaning. For example, a heart might be a symbol for love; a handshake might be a symbol for peace or cooperation. When you **compare symbols,** think about what meaning each symbol has, and what significance each symbol has in the story.

**A** Each sentence contains an underlined symbol. Identify what each one might stand for.

1. ________________ A traveler comes to a fork in the road. He can go in either direction.

2. ________________ A wild horse kicks against the fence of the corral, trying to break free.

**B** Read the following passages. Then, complete the chart to compare the symbols.

A Tomorrow, Mary will have to take her turn singing a solo in front of the music class. She is upset because she thinks that her singing voice is bad. As she sits in her room worrying, she notices a big black crow outside on the lawn. "Caw! Caw!" it cries harshly. Suddenly, a large flock of crows swoops in to join the first crow. They all caw together happily as they peck at the grass.

B "No! I don't want to move!" Jim yelled. He ran out in the yard. Everything was perfect here—his friends lived nearby, and the soccer fields were across the street. Why did everything have to change? As he sat brooding, he noticed that milkweed pods in the garden were shaking and wiggling. Then he noticed that each one held a cocoon. Suddenly, one cocoon burst open, and a beautiful orange butterfly emerged. It unfolded its brand new wings, wobbled a little bit, and then fluttered away, to begin a new part of its life. Maybe moving would be okay, Jim thought.

| | Mary | Jim |
|---|---|---|
| Symbol | 1. | 4. |
| What does the symbol mean to the character? | 2. | 5. |
| What does the symbol suggest about the theme of the story? | 3. | 6. |

Name ______________________________ Date ____________

# Literary Analysis: Comparing Symbols

## Assess

**A** Each sentence contains one or more underlined symbols. Identify what each one might stand for.

**1.** ________________ Their disagreements had turned into an impossible knot.

**2.** ________________ Grandma says that a rainbow can appear even after the worst storm.

**3.** ________________ The first man to land on the moon said, "One small step for man, one giant step for mankind."

**B** Read the following passages. Then, complete the chart to compare the symbols.

A Larry's assignment was to write a piece of short fiction based on a true experience. "There's nothing exciting about my life," he grumbled. That weekend, he was at his grandmother's house. As they watched TV together, Grandma sewed. "What are you making?" Larry asked.

"This is just an old, plain shirt," Grandma answered. "So I've decided to get out my embroidery thread and make it fancy. Look what I've done with just a few stitches and some bright thread!" That gave Larry an idea about how to write his story.

B Dana struggled to learn how to dance. She practiced and practiced, but she still felt clumsy. She was really discouraged and sad. Then, one morning at breakfast with Dad, she glanced out the window. A squirrel was trying to get food from a birdfeeder Dad had hung on a tree. Over and over again, the squirrel would leap from a nearby branch onto the feeder. Each time, he would fall to the ground. Then, he'd shake himself off, climb the tree, and try again. He kept at it and at it until finally, he succeeded. Then, he gobbled up all of Dad's birdseed. "That squirrel!" Dad said with a laugh. "He never quits!" Dana had the same idea. Maybe she could be a squirrel, too.

| | Larry | Dana |
|---|---|---|
| Symbol | 1. | 4. |
| What does the symbol mean to the character? | 2. | 5. |
| What does the symbol suggest about the theme of the story? | 3. | 6. |

Name ______________________________ Date ____________

# Vocabulary: Word Roots *-spec-* and *-nounc-/-nunc-* and Prefixes *mis-* and *per-*

## Practice

A **root** is the basic unit of meaning of a word. A **prefix** is one or more syllables added to the beginning of a word or word root to form a new word with a different meaning. Study these examples.

Examples:

| Root or Prefix | Meaning | Words with the Root |
|---|---|---|
| *-spec-* [root] | to look | spectator, inspect |
| *-nounc-* or *-nunc-* [root] | messenger | announce, pronounce, enunciate |
| *mis-* | opposite; badly or wrongly | misplace, mistake |
| *per-* | thoroughly; throughout | persistent, persuade |

**A** Replace the underlined word in each sentence with a word from the chart above containing the root *-spec-* or *-nunc-*.

**1.** ____________ The <u>audience</u> at the baseball game cheered wildly.

**2.** ____________ He <u>declared</u> that he intended to run for mayor.

**3.** ____________ I <u>examined</u> the clothes carefully for signs of damage.

**4.** ____________ When speaking in public, you need to <u>articulate</u> your words clearly.

**B** Circle the letter of the correct answer to each question.

**1.** What does it mean if I <u>misunderstand</u> your meaning?

**A.** I know what you are saying **B.** I do not know you are saying

**2.** What kind of odor could be described as <u>pervasive</u>?

**A.** one that seems to be everywhere **B.** one that is centered in one place

**3.** How would you describe something that is in <u>perpetual</u> motion?

**A.** it never moves **B.** it never stops moving

Name ______________________________ Date ____________

# Vocabulary: Word Roots *-spec-* and *-nounc-*/*-nunc-* and Prefixes *mis-* and *per-*

## Assess

**A** Circle the letter of the word that is closest in meaning to the underlined word or phrase.

**1.** Sometimes you can solve a problem by looking at it from a new <u>viewpoint</u>.

**A.** announcement **B.** miscalculation **C.** perspective

**2.** He <u>criticized</u> his rival for using her family connections unfairly.

**A.** denounced **B.** misused **C.** respected

**3.** After months of temporary jobs, she finally found a <u>long-term</u> position.

**A.** circumspect **B.** misstated **C.** permanent

**4.** I <u>lost</u> my favorite umbrella.

**A.** inspected **B.** misplaced **C.** renounced

**5.** The bad weather <u>lasted</u> for an uncomfortably long time.

**A.** mistrusted **B.** persisted **C.** pronounced

**6.** As an experiment, I decided to <u>give up</u> television for a month.

**A.** mistake **B.** persuade **C.** renounce

**B** Revise each sentence so that the underlined vocabulary word is used logically. Be sure not to change the vocabulary word.

**1.** I wear <u>spectacles</u> because my vision is perfect.

______________________________________________

**2.** The mayor was pleased about being <u>misquoted</u> in the local paper.

______________________________________________

**3.** She was so <u>persuasive</u> that no one ever did as she suggested.

______________________________________________

**4.** I could always understand him because his <u>pronunciation</u> was terrible.

______________________________________________

Name ______________________________ Date __________

# Grammar: Verbs—Simple Tenses

## Practice

The **tense** of a verb shows the time of an action or a condition. The three simple tenses are *present, past,* and *future.* A regular verb forms its past tense by adding *-ed* or *-d* to the base form. Sometimes you will have to double a final consonant, add a *-d* if the verb ends in *e*, or change *y* to *i* before adding *-ed.*

| Present Tense | Past Tense | Future Tense |
|---|---|---|
| Base Form | Add *-d* or *-ed* to base form. | Use *will* before the base form. |
| I play<br>you play<br>he, she, it plays | I played<br>you played<br>he, she, it played | I will play<br>you will play<br>he, she, it will play |

**A** Underline each verb, and tell what tense it is.

1. ________________ In 1969, American astronauts landed on the moon.
2. ________________ The idea of space travel started long ago.
3. ________________ Maybe we will travel to the moon again.
4. ________________ Today scientists explain the value of space travel.
5. ________________ In 1957, the Soviet Union launched *Sputnik I* into orbit.
6. ________________ The shuttle crews continue the launching of satellites and space telescopes today.
7. ________________ The space shuttle measures about 184 feet in length.

**B** Rewrite each sentence, changing the underlined verb to the tense in parentheses.

1. Jon and Tina <u>study</u> their parts alone and together. (past)

________________________________________________

2. They still <u>needed</u> a few more hours of practice. (present)

________________________________________________

3. Jon <u>accompanies</u> Tina on the piano. (future)

________________________________________________

Name ______________________________ Date ____________

# Grammar: Verbs—Simple Tenses

## Assess

**A** Underline each verb, and tell what tense it is.

**1.** ________________ Tim and Phil are junior mountain climbers for our school.

**2.** ________________ They climb Mt. Somerset at least once every year.

**3.** ________________ Last summer they climbed it twice.

**4.** ________________ They and their group will scale it tomorrow.

**5.** ________________ Thomas, their guide, trained the whole group well.

**6.** ________________ Phil completes his last lesson with Thomas today.

**7.** ________________ All group members conditioned themselves for instructions.

**8.** ________________ Some of the group members departed at 4:00 A.M.

**9.** ________________ They will wait at the base camp until the others arrive.

**10.** ________________ They shopped for all the food last night.

**B** Rewrite each sentence with the verb form called for in parentheses.

Example: We ——— a sailboat on our vacation. (use, *past*)
We used a sailboat on our vacation.

**1.** The band _____ their rehearsal. (stop, *past*)

________________________________________

**2.** By next week, the workers _____ the job. (finish, *future*)

________________________________________

**3.** Only one train _____ at this station. (stop, *present*)

________________________________________

**4.** The audience _____ closely to the speaker. (listen, *past*)

________________________________________

Name ______________________________ Date ____________

# Grammar: Verbs—Perfect Tenses

## Practice

The **tense** of a verb shows the time of an action. The **perfect tense** describes an action that was or will be completed at a certain time. In perfect tenses, the helping verb changes tense. The chart lists the perfect tenses.

| Verb Tense | invite (invited) |
|---|---|
| Present Perfect: action begun in the past that continues up to the present<br>have + past participle | I *have invited* my friends to the party. |
| Past Perfect: action begun in the past that ended<br>had + past participle | I *had invited* my friends to the party, but some couldn't make it. |
| Future Perfect: action begun in the past or present, completed in the future<br>will have + past participle | By tonight, I *will have invited* everyone. |

**Underline the perfect tense verbs in the sentences, and write what tense forms they are.**

Example: ______________ Suzie had hoped to win last week's race.
past perfect Suzie had hoped to win last week's race.

1. ______________ Have you heard of the lost city of Atlantis?

2. ______________ I had not thought about it for years.

3. ______________ Soon I will have read almost everything on the subject.

4. ______________ They say that Atlantis had been a rival of Athens.

5. ______________ There have been many references to this strange place in myths.

6. ______________ Perhaps Atlantis had sunk during an earthquake.

7. ______________ Since then, many adventurers and scholars have looked for it.

8. ______________ By now, they will have searched both seas and oceans.

9. ______________ They will have discovered many lost cities in the process.

10. ______________ No one has ever found evidence of Atlantis's existence.

Name ______________________________ Date __________

# Grammar: Verbs—Perfect Tenses

## Assess

**A** Underline the perfect tense verbs in the sentences, and write what tense forms they are.

Example: ______________ I have enjoyed all kinds of sports.
present perfect I have enjoyed all kinds of sports.

1. ______________ I have taken swimming lessons since October.
2. ______________ By June 20, I will have attended thirty lessons.
3. ______________ My teacher has complimented me on my backstroke.
4. ______________ My diving has improved.
5. ______________ I have practiced even more lately.
6. ______________ By the end of August, I will have raced in several events.
7. ______________ Neither of them had swum before.
8. ______________ In a week, each of them will have taken three lessons.

**B** Rewrite the sentences, adding the suggested form of the verb.

Example: I _____ a great experiment. (*complete*, present perfect)
I have completed a great experiment.

1. I _____ about a life without friends (*wonder*, present perfect)

______________________________________________

2. Now I _____ it is no life at all. (*conclude*, present perfect)

______________________________________________

3. Until yesterday, I _____ to no one for thirty days. (*talk*, past perfect)

______________________________________________

4. I _____ no one. (*visit*, past perfect)

______________________________________________

5. I finally _____ what friendship means. (*learn*, present perfect)

______________________________________________

Name ______________________________ Date __________

# Grammar: Revising for Subject/Verb Agreement

## Practice

**A verb must agree with its subject in number.** In grammar, the number of a word can be either *singular* (indicating *one*) or *plural* (indicating *more than one*). Unlike nouns, which usually become plural when *-s* or *-es* is added, verbs with *-s* or *-es* added to them are singular.

| **Nouns and Pronouns** | |
|---|---|
| Singular | Plural |
| apple, child, I, you, it | apples, children, we, you, them |
| **Verbs** | |
| Singular | Plural |
| walks, plays, eats, runs | walk, play, eat, run |

Here are some examples of correct subject/verb agreement. In each case, subjects are underlined and verbs are set in italics.

Singular: The girl *walks* to school every day.
Plural: The girls *walk* to school every day.
Compound, Plural: Sarah and Vicky *drive* to the mountains on weekends.

**Underline the correct singular or plural form of the verb in parentheses.**

**1.** Two dogs and a cat (lives, live) in that house.

**2.** They (is, are) always playing together.

**3.** Mr. Mitchell and one dog (takes, take) long walks.

**4.** Jerry and his sisters (want, wants) to put on a pet show.

**5.** Both Megan and Sandy (has, have) agreed to help.

**6.** Jamie (has, have) entered a snake.

**7.** Ron (expects, expect) to win a prize.

Name ______________________________ Date __________

# Grammar: Revising for Subject/Verb Agreement

## Assess

**A** Underline the correct singular or plural form of the verb in parentheses.

1. A tall tree (stand, stands) in our front yard.
2. The ships (was, were) passing the island.
3. It seems that the baby (grows, grow) an inch every day.
4. Our blackboards (was, were) all scratched.
5. Candles (is, are) quite expensive.
6. Yesterday the newspaper (was, were) not delivered.
7. His pictures (belongs, belong) in the gallery.
8. Mr. Thompson (was, were) reading poems in a dramatic voice.
9. At sunrise the ships (sails, sail) from the harbor.
10. At the quarry the noises (is, are) deafening.

**B** Rewrite the sentences. Correct the agreement mistakes.

Example: My sisters never enjoys arguing anymore.
My sisters never enjoy arguing anymore.

1. The mail carrier deliver mail about noon.

______________________________

2. The cities closes the beaches in September.

______________________________

3. The toy soldier and the stuffed dog was thrown away in the trash.

______________________________

4. My brother and sister has been very cooperative lately.

______________________________

5. A box of cookies are in the cupboard.

______________________________

Name ______________________ Date __________

# Spelling: Tricky or Difficult Words

## Practice

Sometimes, when saying a word, people make the mistake of adding or subtracting syllables. If this mistake leads them to mispronounce the word, they are likely to misspell the word as well.

Let's take the example of adding an extra syllable that should not be there: If you say pen-tath-a-lon, you will probably misspell the word *pentathlon*, which has only three syllables, not four. It is just as big a problem if you subtract a syllable that should be there. For example, the word *beverage* has three syllables—BEV(1)-ER(2)-AGE(3)—but it is often pronounced as though the middle syllable—ER—were not there. So, people often pronounce only two of the syllables—BEV(1)-RAGE(2)—and they often misspell it that way too: *bevrage.*

The best solution to this problem is to consult a dictionary. Carefully note how many syllables the word contains. As you count the number of syllables, say each syllable aloud—even the unstressed ones. This method is your best protection against adding or omitting a syllable when you say and spell the word.

| | | | | |
|---|---|---|---|---|
| opera | mischievous | chocolate | beverage | wintry |
| basically | aspirin | gardener | blustery | electoral |

**A** In the blank space next to each word below, write the number of syllables it contains. (You may consult a dictionary if you wish.)

**1.** mischievous ______________

**2.** chocolate ______________

**3.** wintry ______________

**4.** aspirin ______________

**5.** gardener ______________

**B** Underline the five misspelled words in the paragraph. Give the correct spelling for each on the lines that follow.

In a mischievious move, my parents told us we were going someplace special. We ended up going to see an opra! So we traveled twenty miles in blustry, wintery weather to see four hours of loud, old-fashioned singing. Luckily, the theater sold choclate candy between acts, so all was not lost.

**1.** ______________

**2.** ______________

**3.** ______________

**4.** ______________

**5.** ______________

Name ______________________________ Date ____________

# Spelling: Tricky or Difficult Words

## Assess

**A** Circle the letter of the sentence in which the underlined word is spelled correctly.

1. **A.** In the winter, everyone enjoys a hot bevrage.
   **B.** When I had the flu, the doctor told me to take asprin.
   **C.** Most soda pop is basically sugar water.
   **D.** Carla is a superb all-around athalete.

2. **A.** It can be dangerous to drive in wintery conditions.
   **B.** Saying that my younger brother is mischevous is putting it mildly.
   **C.** Some nutritionists say that small amounts of choclate are good for you.
   **D.** My sister is a talented amateur gardener.

3. **A.** My dad and I have basickly different tastes in music.
   **B.** When we discuss this topic, the atmosphere can grow pretty blustery.
   **C.** My dad says that after listening to hours of my hip-hop CDs, he needs to take an asprin.
   **D.** I tell him that I feel the same way after listening to hours of his opra CDs.

4. **A.** A special feature of U.S. presidential elections is the Electorial College.
   **B.** Some doctors recommend so-called sports bevridges for runners.
   **C.** The gardner says he has an emotional relationship with the trees and flowers.
   **D.** Our cat is mischievous, but in an endearing way.

**B** Circle the letter of the correctly spelled word.

1. Golf is ______ a sport of relaxation and patience.

   **A.** basicly **B.** basickly **C.** basically **D.** basickcally

2. ______ is used as a pain reliever and as a blood thinner.

   **A.** Aspirin **B.** Asipirin **C.** Aserprin **D.** Asprin

3. It is important to dress warmly in ______ weather.

   **A.** blustry **B.** blusetry **C.** blusatry **D.** blustery

4. We agreed on an ______ procedure for voting for a new student council.

   **A.** electral **B.** electoral **C.** electorial **D.** elecktoral

Name ______________________ Date ____________

# Writing: Dialogue

## Practice

**Dialogue** is conversation that is written as part of a script for a play or a film. It is spoken aloud. As you prepare to write dialogue, follow these steps:

- Think of someone real or imagined. Draw a picture, list a few details, or ask questions to yourself about how the character might behave.
- Imagine your character in a particular time and place.
- Think of a conversation that could take place between two or more characters.
- Write each character's name, followed by a colon (:). Then, write the words the character says, as shown in the example below.
- Use words that seem natural for each character.

Ursula: John, I think we will have to have a talk with Adam.
John: Why? What's wrong?
Ursula: I had to take out the garbage again last night. He's neglecting his chores and his schoolwork.

You learn information from this dialogue. You can guess that Ursula and John are Adam's parents. You can infer that Ursula is upset and that John will become concerned. You can predict that both parents will be talking to Adam soon.

**A** Read the dialogue below, and then answer the questions.

Hector: Ah, me. I have loved Julia from afar since we were children. But there is no hope for us. She lives inside those walls, and I am a nobody.
Ian: Do not fear, my friend. When the king learns who killed the great dragon, I am sure he will let you marry his daughter.

1. What setting have the characters been placed in? ______________________

______________________________________________

2. How would you describe the character of Ian, based on his words? __________

______________________________________________

**B** On a separate sheet of paper, write at least four lines of dialogue, using a story or situation concerning events that took place a time long ago. Make sure that you use words that seem natural for each character.

Name ______________________ Date ____________

# Writing: Dialogue

## Assess

**A** Read the dialogue, and then answer the questions.

**Molly:** Donna, come inside! The wind is blowing like crazy—I think we'll have to head down to the storm cellar tonight. I'd better bring the horses into the barn.
**Donna:** I'm coming, Auntie. I just have to run next door and pick up Trixie. Ollie was taking care of her today while I was at the county fair.
**Molly:** All right, but hurry. Lands' sakes, child! You fuss too much about that silly old dog, and I don't like the looks of the sky.
**Donna:** Yes, ma'am. I'll be right back—don't worry!

1. What setting have the characters been placed in? ______________________

______________________________________________

2. How would you describe the character of Aunt Molly, based on her words?

______________________________________________

3. What prediction can you make about what will probably happen to the characters?

______________________________________________

4. Do the characters' words seem natural to you? Explain why or why not.

______________________________________________

______________________________________________

**B** Using a story or situation that you know about, write at least six lines of dialogue having to do with an event that involves older people. Make sure that you use words that seem natural for each character.

______________________________________________

______________________________________________

______________________________________________

______________________________________________

______________________________________________

______________________________________________

Name ______________________ Date __________

# Writing: Personal Essay

## Practice

A **personal essay** shares the writer's thoughts about a personal experience, an event, or an idea. A strong personal essay includes these elements:

- The writer is the main character and writes in the first person.
- It includes the writer's personal feelings and ideas.
- It shows a connection between events and ideas.
- It shares the writer's insights, such as those based on a new understanding or lessons that have been learned.

You might write a personal essay based on something you have read. In this case, you would connect your reading to a personal experience that reflects similar themes or ideas, as in this example:

When I read the story "Quiet Boy," I felt an instant connection to the main character. Like him, I struggled for many years with shyness. Luckily, I was able to discover a hidden ability—I can juggle! Finding my talent opened up the rest of my personality, and I am now much more comfortable with people.

**A** Read the example. Then, answer the questions that follow.

When my teacher announced that our class would be on a televised quiz show on the topic of U.S. history, I felt overwhelmed. As the captain of our team, I felt pressure to make sure that we all did well. So I did something about it. For an entire month before the show, we met every day after school to hold drills and practice sessions. Knowing that we were making the best possible effort made everyone feel better. We might not win, but we knew we had tried our hardest.

**1.** What event does the writer describe? ______________________

**2.** How does the writer feel about the event? ______________________

**3.** What insight does the writer gain? ______________________

**B** Think of a team or group in which you have had to accomplish a specific task. What might be the theme of a personal essay about your experience with this team or group?

______________________________________________

______________________________________________

Name ______________________ Date __________

# Writing: Personal Essay

## Assess

Respond to each item below.

1. Think of an event or experience from your life, or a book, story, or poem you have read that connects to something in your life, that you would want to describe in a personal essay. What is the main theme or idea you would want to convey to your readers?

2. List three details about the event or experience.

3. Describe your thoughts and feelings about the event.

4. What new understanding did you gain as a result of the event, or what lesson did you learn?

5. Write the first paragraph of your personal essay on the lines below.

Name ______________________________ Date ____________

# Writing: Narration—Short Story

## Practice

A **short story** is a brief piece of fiction. Short stories include the following elements:

- one or more characters
- a clear setting, or time and place in which the action occurs
- a conflict or problem that is faced by the main character
- a plot that develops the conflict, leads to a climax (or turning point), and a resolution of the conflict
- a theme that reflects an idea about life or human nature
- dialogue that reveals the characters' thoughts and feelings

**A** Read the following passage. Then, answer the questions.

All day, the snow kept falling. The weatherman reported on television that the Northeast could expect at least ten inches by the end of the day. Newscasters were telling people not to drive unless it was an emergency. The Sampsons weren't worried, though. They had plenty of food. They invited their next-door neighbors, the Thomas family, to come over and play some board games with them. Everything was fine until a few hours later, when Mrs. Sampson started to feel cold. Something was wrong with the heat.

**1.** Who are the main characters in this passage?

______________________________

**2.** What conflict faces the main characters?

______________________________

**B** Reread the passage above and prepare to add to it. Using the lines provided or a separate sheet of paper if needed, add one or more characters, and create a brief dialogue between the characters. Make sure the dialogue is related to the story and helps build the action.

______________________________

______________________________

______________________________

______________________________

______________________________

Name ______________________ Date __________

# Writing: Narration—Short Story

## Assess

**A** Circle one of these topics to create a short story. Then, complete the activities.

when Mrs. Yardley's cat disappeared
how Oliver learned his lesson
where Tasha found courage
the weirdest weather we ever had

1. Briefly summarize your idea for a story. ______________________

2. List the characters you will include in your story, as well as their names, ages, and a detail about each of their personalities. ______________________

3. Write at least two details of the setting, including the time and place. ______________________

4. What problem or conflict is faced by one or more characters? ______________________

5. Create a brief dialogue that fits each character's personality and moves the story forward. ______________________

6. What is the theme of the story? ______________________

**B** On a separate sheet of paper, write the first few paragraphs of your short story. It should include one or more characters; a clear setting; a conflict; a plot that develops the conflict, leads to a climax, and resolves the conflict; a theme; and dialogue.

Name ______________________________ Date __________

# Reading: Main Idea

## Practice

The **main idea** is the most important point in a work of literature. Writers usually convey their main ideas in an introduction. Then, the main idea is supported by the paragraphs that follow.

- Sometimes the main idea is **stated.** The writer directly tells the reader the main idea.
- Sometimes the main idea is **implied.** The writer suggests, rather than directly tells, the main idea.
- Whether it is stated or implied, the main idea is supported by **details.**

In the following example, the main idea is that the writer was having a bad morning. The writer does not directly state this idea. Instead, the writer describes the events that made the morning bad.

> The train was late this morning, and I forgot to pack a sandwich to take to work. When I got off the train, it was raining—but I had forgotten to take my umbrella! By the time I got to work, I was ready to turn around and head back home. What a morning!
>
> Main Idea: The writer had a bad morning.

In the example, several details support the main idea, such as the late train, the missing lunch, and the rain. These details all show that the writer was having a bad morning.

**Read the passage, looking for the main idea. Then, answer the questions that follow.**

Alaska offers excellent opportunities for people who like to fish. You can enjoy fly-fishing, saltwater fishing, freshwater fishing, and even ice fishing. You'll find over 600 kinds of fish in Alaska. Alaska is home to over 3 million lakes, 3,000 rivers, and numerous streams, so you can't help but bring home something great to cook.

**1.** What is the main idea of the passage?

______________________________

**2.** Is the main idea implied or stated? Explain. ______________________________

______________________________

**3.** What are two details that support the main idea? ______________________________

______________________________

Name ______________________________ Date ____________

# Reading: Main Idea

## Assess

**A** Look for the main idea in the following passage. Notice whether it is implied or stated. Find details that support the main idea.

Researchers are finding that eating dark chocolate rather than milk chocolate or white chocolate can help lower blood pressure. Dark chocolate is an *antioxidant*, which means that it helps attack molecules in the body that can lead to heart disease. Of course, eating dark chocolate is a great idea—but watch out for the extra calories! Balance them by exercising more.

**1.** What is the main idea of the passage? ______________________________

______________________________________________________________

**2.** Is the main idea implied or stated? Explain. ______________________________

______________________________________________________________

**3.** What are two details that support the main idea? ______________________________

______________________________________________________________

**B** Read the list of details below. Then, write a main idea that these details can support. Explain your choice for a main idea.

| | | |
|---|---|---|
| sunshine | flowers in bloom | blanket on the ground |
| pond with ducks | sitting and reading | smile on my face |

Sample main idea: ______________________________

______________________________________________________________

Explanation of my choice for a main idea: ______________________________

______________________________________________________________

______________________________________________________________

Name ______________________________ Date ____________

# Reading: Analyze Treatment, Scope and Organization of Ideas

## Practice

The study of history involves two types of sources. A primary source, such as a diary or letter, is created at the time an event is occurring, often by a participant or onlooker. A secondary source, such as a textbook or encyclopedia entry, interprets or describes a past event.

When you read any historical resource, analyze the treatment, scope, and organization of ideas. Treatment refers to the way the writer regards and presents a topic. Scope is the range of information that the writer discusses. Ask these questions to help you identify and analyze the treatment, scope, and organization of texts:

Read the email that follows. Then, answer the questions.

Hi Jenny,

I'm having a wonderful time in New Orleans for Mardi Gras. The weeks before Mardi Gras Day are full of dozens of elaborate parades. I've already been to eight over the last four days! The parades are full of bands, dancers, and huge floats with masked and costumed riders throwing beads to the crowds. The floats are all colorfully painted and covered with lights, and they travel slowly down the streets.

Mardi Gras means Fat Tuesday. Fat Tuesday is the very last day of Mardi Gras. It brings both kids and adults out to stand along the parade routes. Tourists from all over the world visit New Orleans just to see Mardi Gras. Maybe we can come together sometime. I'm so lucky my aunt and uncle live here and my parents let me come.

See you soon,

Audrey

**1.** Is this a primary or secondary source? ______________________________

**2.** What is the purpose of this email? ______________________________

Name ____________________ Date __________

# Reading: Analyze Treatment, Scope and Organization of Ideas

## Assess

**Read the following two passages on the same topic. The first was written to a pen pal by Raymond Jones in 1969. The second was published in a magazine in 1999. Then, answer the questions that follow.**

August 1, 1969

Dear Erik:

The big excitement here has been the moon landing and moon walk last week. I have told you before that I am very interested in space. It is hard to believe that it really happened, and I was around to see it. Even though we could not see too clearly on television, it was still amazing to see Neil Armstrong walk on the moon.

It is almost as incredible to think that they flew there. I thought Neil Armstrong's words were cool, too.

Did you get to see it? Was there a lot of publicity in Denmark? Were people excited?

I know that this is something I will remember my whole life.

Write soon.

Your friend, Ray

### Twentieth-Century Miracle

One of the most dramatic moments of the twentieth century was the day a man first walked on the moon. On July 20, 1969, American astronaut Neil Armstrong took those historic steps.

Around the world, millions watched this take place on their televisions. While today we would find the grainy image unacceptable, at the time it seemed incredible. We are used to seeing fantastic images beamed back from satellites heading to distant planets. But to people almost 40 years ago, it seemed like a miracle.

**1.** Which passage is a primary source? Why? ____________________

____________________

**2.** Which passage is a secondary source? Why? ____________________

____________________

**3.** Describe the tone of each passage. ____________________

____________________

Name ______________________________ Date __________

# Literary Analysis: Narrative Essay

## Practice

A **narrative essay** is a short piece of nonfiction that tells the story of real events, people, and places. Narrative essays share these features with fictional stories:

- People's traits and personalities are developed through their words, actions, and thoughts.
- They include significant details that help move the story forward.
- The setting of the action may be an important element.

For each item, circle the letter of the best answer.

**1.** In a short work, a writer describes a neighbor, Jeff Summers, who became a champion figure skater. If the work is a narrative essay, then which of the following must be true?

**A.** Jeff Summers has skated in the Olympics.
**B.** The characters in the essay are fictional.
**C.** The writer is a best-selling author of nonfiction books.
**D.** Jeff Summers is a real person.

**2.** The essay about Jeff includes this significant detail: Jeff often invites the writer to join him and his friends for dinner. What might the writer want to reveal about Jeff's personality through this detail?

**A.** Jeff is friendly.
**B.** Jeff is famous.
**C.** Jeff is ambitious.
**D.** Jeff is humorous.

**3.** Which of these details is likeliest to help move Jeff's story forward?

**A.** Jeff has blonde hair.
**B.** Jeff was born in August.
**C.** A professional coach comes to watch Jeff at a skating competition.
**D.** Jeff's father is from Kentucky.

**4.** Why might the writer include details about Jeff's childhood in a poor rural town?

**A.** to tell the complete story of his life
**B.** to compare his upbringing with that of other skaters
**C.** to show how his childhood setting influenced his desire to excel
**D.** to show that people everywhere enjoy skating

Name ______________________________ Date __________

# Literary Analysis: Narrative Essay

## Assess

**For each item, circle the letter of the best answer.**

**1.** Which work is a narrative essay?

**A.** a fictional story that uses a character who is like the writer's sister
**B.** a book giving the life story of a famous politician
**C.** a true story showing how the writer's mentor inspired the writer
**D.** an explanation of the difference between football and soccer

**2.** In a narrative essay, Vanessa explains how her uncle changed careers in mid-life and became a professional storyteller. The essay includes this significant detail: Vanessa's uncle often told funny stories at dinner. Why might Vanessa include this detail?

**A.** to show what her aunt had to put up with
**B.** to show that her uncle's stories inspired her to tell stories herself
**C.** to show that she knew her uncle well
**D.** to show that her uncle is a man who enjoys entertaining people

**3.** Which detail is likeliest to move the story of Vanessa's uncle forward?

**A.** Vanessa and her uncle enjoy reading the same books.
**B.** Vanessa's uncle was born in 1960.
**C.** Vanessa's uncle enjoys horseback riding.
**D.** Vanessa's uncle would tell stories to Vanessa and her cousins.

**4.** Which quote might Vanessa include to show that her uncle is caring?

**A.** "I don't own a television; I prefer to read for entertainment."
**B.** "When you bring laughter into a child's life, you give him a true gift."
**C.** "Every story is a new experience, no matter how often I've told it before."
**D.** "I've lived in the same house for twenty-five years."

**5.** Which detail about the setting would Vanessa use to show how her uncle's interest in storytelling grew?

**A.** Her uncle's house was large and inviting.
**B.** Laughing children passed by her uncle's house every day on their way to school.
**C.** A large vegetable garden grows in her uncle's backyard.
**D.** The afternoons are often warm and sunny in her uncle's coastal town.

Name ______________________ Date __________

## Literary Analysis: Biographical and Autobiographical Essay

### Practice

**Biographical and autobiographical essays** describe important facts and events from a person's life. However, there are important differences between the two kinds of essays.

- In a **biographical essay,** the writer tells about the life of another person. A biographical essay uses the pronoun *he* or *she,* relies on research, and is usually more objective than an autobiographical essay.

  Example: Jackson Pollock was a modern abstract artist who used form and color to express himself. He lived from 1912 to 1956.

- In an **autobiographical essay,** the writer tells about his or her own experience. An autobiographical essay uses the pronoun *I,* relies on the author's own thoughts and feelings, and tells a more personal story.

  Example: I realized at a very early age that my talents did not lie in the world of art.

**A** Write *B* if the statement describes a biographical essay or *A* if it describes an autobiographical essay. Write *B* and *A* if the statement describes both forms.

**1.** ______ The writer uses the pronoun *I* to express the writer's feelings.

**2.** ______ The writer may need to do research about someone's life.

**3.** ______ The writer presents a true account of a person's experience.

**4.** ______ The writer uses the pronoun *he* or *she* to tell a person's story.

**B** Write either *biographical* or *autobiographical* to describe each passage. Then, explain your answer.

**1.** I was young—only about four years old—when I first experienced the joy of sledding down the snow-covered hill in the park down the block from our house. ______________________

______________________

**2.** Mr. Barns was a handsome man, and he had always been athletic. His skill with a golf club was well known in Ridgeville. ______________________

______________________

Name ______________________________ Date ____________

## Literary Analysis: Biographical and Autobiographical Essay

### Assess

**A** Write *T* if the statement is *true* or *F* if it is *false*.

**1.** ______ Both biographical and autobiographical essays are nonfiction.

**2.** ______ Both biographical and autobiographical essays describe events from someone's life.

**3.** ______ Both biographical and autobiographical essays are based on research done on the Internet or in the library.

**4.** ______ The author of an autobiographical essay uses the pronoun *I*.

**5.** ______ An autobiographical essay is less personal than a biographical essay.

**6.** ______ A biographical essay uses the pronoun *he* or *she*.

**7.** ______ A biographical essay reveals the writer's thoughts and feelings.

**8.** ______ Both biographical and autobiographical essays might describe a person's achievements.

**B** Write either *biographical* or *autobiographical* to describe each passage. Then, explain your answer.

**1.** "Cookies are my business!" was my Uncle Jimmy's motto. Jimmy was determined to find the recipe for the richest chocolate chip cookie in the world. ______________________________

______________________________

**2.** It was a great relief to me when I heard that my aunt and uncle had finally returned home after last week's snowstorm. I had been listening to the weather reports for hours. ______________________________

______________________________

**3.** John Coltrane was a great saxophonist who influenced the style of modern jazz. He played with both Dizzy Gillespie and Miles Davis. ______________________________

______________________________

Name ______________________________ Date ____________

# Literary Analysis: Comparing Types of Organization

## Practice

**Organization** describes methods that writers use to present information clearly. There are several **types of organization** from which writers can choose. Here are three of the most common methods:

- **Comparison-and-contrast** organization shows similarities and differences and uses clue words such as *like, unlike, both,* or *however.*
- **Cause-and-effect** order shows the relationship between events and their results and uses clue words such as *because, as a result,* and *caused.*
- **Chronological** order shows events in the order in which they occurred and uses clue words such as *first, next, then,* and *finally.*

Read the passages. Notice the three different ways in which the same topic has been organized. The italicized words are clues that show each type of organization.

Comparison-and-contrast organization: Yesterday, my friends and I explored an old cave. We saw stalactites and stalagmites. *Both* of these cave features are made from limestone that has been dissolved by acidic water. *However,* stalactites grow down from the ceiling, *while* stalagmites build up on the cave floor.

Cause-and-effect order: Yesterday, my friends and I explored an old cave. We learned how stalactites and stalagmites are created. *Because* acidic water flows into cracks in the cave's limestone walls and ceiling, the limestone dissolves. *As a result,* the dissolved limestone flows down from the ceiling to create stalactites and builds up on the cave floor to produce stalagmites.

Chronological order: Yesterday, my friends and I explored an old cave. *First,* we used our flashlights to check out the stalactites that grew on the ceiling. *Then,* we noticed the stalagmites that were building up on the floor. The acidic water that flows into the cave dissolves the limestone rock and creates these interesting features.

Respond to each item about types of organization.

1. Write two clue words that indicate comparison-and-contrast organization.

______________________________

2. Write two clue words that indicate cause-and-effect order.

______________________________

3. Write two clue words that indicate chronological order.

______________________________

Name ______________________________ Date ____________

# Literary Analysis: Comparing Types of Organization

## Assess

**A** Read each passage. Then, answer the questions.

Avalanches are caused by a variety of conditions. When the temperature is cold and snow falls, the snow sticks to the ground. However, when the air temperature changes, the snow may slide away in pieces or slabs. Basically, an avalanche happens when the gravity of snow heading downhill is greater than the gravity that holds snow together on the ground. Steep slopes on mountains, a recent heavy snowfall, a weak layer in the snow cover, changes in the weather, and changes in pressure on the surface (such as a skier's sudden weight) can all contribute to the creation of an avalanche.

Avalanches happen in a series of stages. First, while the temperature is cold and there is a heavy snowfall, the snow will stick to the ground. Suppose that what happens next is that the air temperature changes after the snow has fallen. Then, a layer of the snow may weaken. Next, suppose that a skier lands on the weakened snow. The snow may then slide away from the ground in pieces or slabs. As the slabs head downhill, their gravity is greater than the snow underneath. They may slide down a steep slope, creating a major avalanche.

1. In the first paragraph, did the writer use comparison-and-contrast organization, cause-and-effect order, or chronological order to organize information? Explain. ______________________________

______________________________

______________________________

______________________________

2. In the second paragraph, did the writer use comparison-and-contrast organization, cause-and-effect order, or chronological order to organize information? Explain. ______________________________

______________________________

______________________________

______________________________

**B** Look again at the above paragraphs. On a separate sheet of paper, compare the two methods used to organize information by explaining how the two paragraphs are alike and how they are different.

Name ______________________ Date __________

# Vocabulary: Suffixes *-ly* and *-ance* and Word Roots *-val-* and *-nym-*

## Practice

A **suffix** is added to the end of a word to change its meaning or part of speech. The suffix *-ance* changes a verb or adjective into a noun. The suffix *-ly* is generally used to turn adjectives into adverbs.

> ignore + ance = ignorance: "the state of being ignorant, or unaware of something"
>
> calm + ly = calmly: "in a calm or peaceful manner"

A **root** is the basic unit of meaning of a word. The Greek root *-nym-* means "name." The Latin root *-val-* means "to be strong."

> homo (same) + nym (name) = homonym: "a word that sounds like another word"
>
> val (strong) + ue = value: "worth"

**A** Add *-ance* or *-ly* to each underlined word to form a new word that fits the meaning of the sentence.

**1.** ______________ It's a mistake to judge people based only on appear.

**2.** ______________ She answered the question thoughtful.

**3.** ______________ The room was comfortable furnished.

**4.** ______________ The developer asked for a vary in the building codes.

**B** Match each word with the sentence in which it fits best.

| | |
|---|---|
| **1.** I don't think your assumption is ______________. | anonymously |
| **2.** "Soft" is a ______________ for "quiet." | synonym |
| **3.** The writer published the article ______________. | valid |
| **4.** The soldier received a medal for ______________. | valor |

Name ______________________________ Date __________

# Vocabulary: Suffixes *-ly* and *-ance* and Word Roots *-val-* and *-nym-*

## Assess

**A** Choose the correct word to complete each sentence. Write the word on the line.

**1. horrible** **horribly**

The car made a ____________ squealing sound.

The car squealed ____________.

**2. alliance** **allied**

The two nations ____________ with each other to fight the war.

The two nations formed an ____________ to fight the war.

**3. immediate** **immediately**

He decided it was best to leave ____________.

He decided it was best to make an ____________ exit.

**B** Circle the root in each word, and think about its meaning. Then, write the word's meaning on the first line. Use a dictionary to check the meaning. Finally, use each word in a new sentence.

**1.** valuable ______________________________

______________________________

**2.** pseudonym ______________________________

______________________________

**3.** anonymous ______________________________

______________________________

**4.** evaluate ______________________________

______________________________

Name ______________________ Date __________

# Grammar: Adjectives and Articles

## Practice

An **adjective** is a word that describes a noun or pronoun. Adjectives are also called *modifiers* because they modify, or change, the noun. An adjective adds detail to a noun by answering one of these questions: *What kind? Which one? How many? How much? Whose?*

Three common adjectives that answer the question *Which one?* are also called **articles:** *a, an,* and *the.*

**A** Underline the adjectives in each sentence, including the articles *a, an,* or *the.*

1. The older man stopped us on the street.
2. Did you speak to the newspaper reporter?
3. He flew in a supersonic jet to the airport.
4. The weary citizens sought out the shadiest spots.
5. The long, hot day drew to a close in a fiery sunset.

**B** Underline the two adjectives in each sentence. Circle the words they modify. Do not underline *a, an,* or *the.*

Example: The vast, flat (desert) stretched before him.

1. The sleek gray horse galloped across the pasture.
2. This fine novel was written by a friend of mine.
3. The long, narrow column of soldiers marched through the pass.
4. Every qualified person can enter the contest.
5. Bob loaded the plate with four large sandwiches.
6. Make one special wish and blow out the candles.
7. The car was a powerful and efficient vehicle.
8. During the winter, we had little snow and no temperatures below zero.
9. Our history teacher gave us a special assignment.
10. Great flocks of large birds migrate here in the spring.

Name ______________________________ Date __________

# Grammar: Adjectives and Articles

## Assess

**A** Underline the adjectives in each sentence, including the articles *a, an,* or *the*. Then, circle the noun or pronoun each one modifies.

Example: A hungry (lion) stalked the frightened (animals.)

**1.** Laura bought a blue blouse with white trim.

**2.** Each one in the class will develop an original project.

**3.** I made three attempts to reach the local representative.

**4.** A gracious hostess greeted us at the flower show.

**5.** We packed the fragile glassware in a reinforced container.

**6.** The investigator hopes to get some answers from the lone witness.

**7.** The decorator suggested using three large paintings to cover the bare wall.

**8.** My foreign car is equipped with radial tires.

**9.** The many rings of Saturn glowed in the blurry photograph.

**10.** Several athletes complained about the old stadium.

**B** Write *A* if the adjective answers the question *what kind?* Write *B* if the adjective answers the question *which one?* Write *C* if the adjective answers the question *how many?*

**1.** ______ **few** passengers

**2.** ______ **easy** answer

**3.** ______ **powerful** crew

**4.** ______ **black** flag

**5.** ______ **highest** cloud

**6.** ______ **third** line

**7.** ______ **many** friends

**8.** ______ **these** boats

**9.** ______ **large** apartment

**10.** ______ **thirty-two** helicopters

Name ______________________________ Date __________

# Grammar: Adverbs

## Practice

An **adverb** is a word that modifies, or adds to the meaning of, a verb, an adjective, or another adverb. Adverbs often end in the suffix *-ly* and answer the questions *When? Where? In what manner?* and *To what extent?*

| When? | Where? | In What manner? | To What extent? |
|---|---|---|---|
| Yesterday I decided on a special project. | Many students live close to the school. | A firefighter ran swiftly past her. | *Treasure Island* is an extremely exciting story. |

**A** Underline each adverb, and then write which word it modifies on the line.

Example: applauded The crowd applauded wildly.

1. ______________ Today we watched an exciting sailboat race on the lake.
2. ______________ Many crews enthusiastically competed for first prize.
3. ______________ The clear blue water glistened brightly in the sun.
4. ______________ Colorful pennants flapped loudly in the strong wind.
5. ______________ The crews scurried around to their captains' sharp commands.

**B** Underline the adverb that modifies a verb in each sentence. On each line, write the question the adverb answers—*Where? When? In what manner?*

Example: When? I have seldom seen a better performance.

1. ______________ The ice storm completely destroyed several buildings.
2. ______________ The emergency crew arrived promptly.
3. ______________ Our neighbors will be moving away.
4. ______________ Dad seemed genuinely surprised by the party.
5. ______________ Did you return the call immediately?

Name ______________________________ Date ____________

# Grammar: Adverbs

## Assess

**A** Underline each adverb, and then write the word it modifies on the line.

Example: ____walks____ The lion walks slowly into the clearing.

1. ____________ Lauren studied for a very difficult history test.
2. ____________ She began early in the evening.
3. ____________ First she listed the important events.
4. ____________ She reviewed her notes carefully.
5. ____________ She studied quite hard until eleven o'clock.
6. ____________ That night she slept soundly.

**B** For each sentence, underline the adverb once and the word it modifies twice. Then, write the question the adverb answers—*Where? When? In what manner? To what extent?*

Example: ____________ Greg wrote the newspaper article yesterday.

____When?____ Greg wrote the newspaper article yesterday.

1. ____________ The crash happened suddenly.
2. ____________ Lights flashed outside.
3. ____________ The police came instantly.
4. ____________ It was very important that an ambulance arrived.
5. ____________ A man promptly received aid.
6. ____________ His arm was badly hurt.
7. ____________ The traffic moved slowly.
8. ____________ An officer soon fixed that.
9. ____________ Trucks pulled the cars away.
10. ____________ It was particularly frightening to watch.

Name ______________________ Date __________

# Grammar: Comparative and Superlative Forms

## Practice

When you use adjectives and adverbs to compare items, use the comparative and superlative forms. The **comparative form** is used to compare two items. The **superlative form** is used to compare three or more items.

- The most common way to form these degrees is by adding *-er or -est* to words with one or two syllables.
- *More* and *most* (and *less* and *least*) are used with most adverbs ending in *-ly* and with modifiers of three or more syllables.
- Irregular adjectives and adverbs have unpredictable patterns that must be memorized.

| Positive | Comparative | Superlative |
|---|---|---|
| happy | happier | happiest |
| interesting | more interesting | most interesting |
| bad, badly | worse | worst |
| good, well | better | best |
| many, much | more | most |
| far (distance) | farther | farthest |
| far (extent) | further | furthest |

Comparative: One road is narrower than the other.
Superlative: This road is the narrowest of the three we've traveled.

Underline the correct form of the modifier in parentheses.

1. The meeting was the (longer, longest) one we ever had.
2. Of all my friends, Gregory is the (more, most) patient.
3. Carol is the (better, best) violist in our school.
4. This antique is (older, oldest) than any other in my collection.
5. Samantha has been waiting (longer, longest) of all.
6. When I began dancing, I was much (clumsier, clumsiest) than Rebecca.
7. Scranton is the (closer, closest) of the two locations.

Name ______________________________ Date ____________

# Grammar: Comparative and Superlative Forms

## Assess

**A** Fill in each blank with the correct form of the modifier in parentheses.

Example: ___best___ This is the (good) story I have ever written.

1. ____________ I feel (bad) today than I did yesterday.
2. ____________ Of all my friends, Joseph lives the (far) from school.
3. ____________ Air travel is (safe) than travel by car.
4. ____________ This is the (good) news I have heard all day.
5. ____________ John is the (wealthy) of their four nephews.
6. ____________ It is (sunny) this week than it was last week.
7. ____________ That crew sailed (early) of all.
8. ____________ Jack swam out (far) than he should have.
9. ____________ We should have ordered (many) pizzas for the party.
10. ____________ Snow is (heavy) than usual after a rainfall.

**B** Rewrite each sentence by correcting the modifier.

1. The Jacksons are the friendlier people on the block.

   ______________________________

2. Teddy seems to be the brightest of the twins.

   ______________________________

3. She is the most popular of the two candidates.

   ______________________________

4. Venus is the more brilliant of all the planets.

   ______________________________

5. The larger of all snakes is the anaconda.

   ______________________________

Name ______________________________ Date ____________

# Writing: Biographical Sketch

## Practice

A **biographical sketch** is a brief narrative work that presents high points in the life of a notable person. A well-written biographical sketch should include

- a first sentence that clearly states the main idea you want readers to know about the person: *Rosa Parks was a courageous woman and a role model for many Americans.*
- facts and details that support the main idea, arranged according to their sequence in time: *Parks refused to accept unfair treatment; she allowed herself to be arrested for her beliefs; and she fought the law despite risks to her own safety.*
- a strong concluding sentence that restates your main idea in different words: *Parks' courage in the face of adversity is an inspiration to all.*

**A** Read the following example. Then, complete the activities that follow.

My Uncle Royce is not wealthy, but he is one of the richest men in the world. Uncle Royce is rich in goodness, kindness, and compassion. He runs errands for sick or elderly neighbors. He volunteers for the fire department, the Red Cross, and other local organizations. During the holidays, he visits hospitals and homeless shelters, spreading cheer and optimism. Uncle Royce is my role model for the only kind of wealth that matters: spiritual wealth. His pockets may be empty, but his heart is full.

**1.** Write the main idea expressed in this passage. ______________________

______________________________________________

**2.** List two details that support the main idea.

______________________________________________

______________________________________________

**3.** Underline the writer's conclusion.

**B** On the back of this page, write a brief paragraph about a teacher, a neighbor, or a relative whom you admire. Explain why you admire that person, and include at least two supporting details. Conclude by using different words to restate your main idea.

Name ______________________________ Date __________

# Writing: Biographical Sketch

## Assess

Respond to each item to help you write a biographical sketch about someone whose accomplishments you find inspiring.

**1.** Choose one of the following subjects for your biographical sketch:

| | | |
|---|---|---|
| a historical figure | an athlete or entertainer | a politician |
| a respected scientist | a humanitarian | other: __________ |

**2.** Write a statement that clearly expresses why you find this person inspiring.

______________________________

______________________________

**3.** List a few of your subject's personal qualities. ______________________________

______________________________

**4.** List two of your subject's accomplishments.

______________________________

______________________________

**5.** Provide another detail or an anecdote that shows why you admire him or her.

______________________________

______________________________

**6.** Now, write your biographical sketch. ______________________________

______________________________

______________________________

______________________________

______________________________

______________________________

______________________________

______________________________

______________________________

Name ________________________________ Date ____________

# Writing: Reflective Composition

## Practice

A **reflective composition** is a brief prose work that presents a writer's thoughts and feelings, or reflections, about an experience or idea. A writer may write a reflective composition when these thoughts and feelings are especially strong or important.

**A** Read the following example. Then, respond to the items that follow.

Last summer, I spent a lot of time feeling angry. I also spent a lot of time chopping wood. Whenever my temper got the best of me, my dad would quietly say my name and point to the back door. The message was clear. Usually, I stormed out in a huff. To me, chopping that wood was nothing more than a punishment. I never seemed to realize that after an hour or so of slamming my ax into thick logs, I felt lighter—if not quite "happy," then at least less stressed. By the end of the summer, the woodpile was almost as tall as I was, but only recently have I realized its importance. This winter, a snowstorm knocked out our power for three days straight. It was the wood from my pile that fed the wood stove and heated our home. It felt good knowing that my hard work was keeping my family warm. My dad showed me how to turn my anger into something constructive, and that's a lesson I can take with me throughout my life.

1. What experience does the writer describe? ________________________________

________________________________

2. Cite two passages that express the writer's thoughts or feelings about the experience. ________________________________

________________________________

________________________________

________________________________

3. What insight does the writer offer about the importance of this experience?

________________________________

________________________________

________________________________

**B** On the back of this page, write a paragraph about a song, poem, painting, or other work of art that made a strong impression on you. Be sure to explain why it is important to you.

Name ______________________________ Date ____________

# Writing: Reflective Composition

## Assess

Respond to each item to help you write your reflective composition.

1. Choose one of the following topics for your reflective composition:

   a time when you succeeded or failed at something new
   a meaningful childhood experience
   a camping trip, hike, or other outdoor experience
   a positive encounter with a teacher or another authority figure

2. What were you thinking or feeling during this experience?

   ______________________________

   ______________________________

3. What do you think or feel about this experience now?

   ______________________________

4. Why was this experience important to you?

   ______________________________

   ______________________________

5. Now, write your reflective composition.

   ______________________________

   ______________________________

   ______________________________

   ______________________________

   ______________________________

   ______________________________

   ______________________________

   ______________________________

   ______________________________

   ______________________________

Name ______________________ Date __________

# Writing: How-to Essay

## Practice

A **how-to essay** is a short piece of expository writing. Its purpose is to explain how to do something. An effective how-to essay includes these elements:

- a focused topic that can be fully explained in an essay
- definitions of terms or materials that may be unfamiliar to the reader
- a clear sequence of steps the reader must follow, presented in chronological order
- transitional words and phrases, such as *first, next,* and *last,* to make the order clear

**A** Read this how-to essay. Then, respond to each item.

To make homemade applesauce, you will need 6 red apples, 3/4 cup sugar, and a teaspoon or two of cinnamon. You will also need a large covered pot, a colander or strainer, a food mill (a kitchen utensil that mashes and grinds food), and a large bowl. First, cut the apples into quarters and remove the cores and seeds. (Leaving the skins on will give your applesauce a warm, pink color.) Then, place the cut apples into the large pot. Add water to cover them. Next, cover the pot, place it on a stove burner, and bring the water to a boil. After that, turn the heat down to low and let the apples simmer until they are soft, about twenty minutes. Place the colander in a sink and carefully drain the apples into it. Next, place the drained apples into the food mill and grind the contents into a large bowl. Discard the skins that collect in the mill. Finally, stir the sugar and cinnamon into your applesauce.

1. What does this essay instruct readers to do? ______________________

2. What ingredients and equipment are needed? ______________________

______________________________________________

3. Which piece of equipment did the writer define? Why? ______________________

______________________________________________

4. List three transitional words that help readers follow the steps.

______________________________________________

**B** On a separate sheet of paper, write a how-to essay to explain how to do something that you enjoy. For example, explain how to make a craft project, do a science experiment, or play a board game. Explain any terms that may be unfamiliar to the readers, and make sure you give the steps in the correct order.

Name ______________________________ Date ____________

# Writing: How-to Essay

## Assess

**A** Read this how-to essay. Then, respond to each item.

It's easy and fun to make old-fashioned cornbread, and once you taste it, you will never use a packaged mix again. First, gather the ingredients: 1 cup cornmeal, 1 cup sifted flour, 1 teaspoon baking soda, 1 teaspoon salt, 3/4 cup sugar, 1 egg, and 1 cup milk. You will need the following equipment: a 10- to 12-inch cast-iron skillet (a heavy, ovenproof frying pan) or a shallow, 9 x 13-inch baking pan; a mixing bowl; a wire whisk or wooden mixing spoon; and a wire cooling rack. Now, you can begin to cook.

Begin by preheating the oven to 400 degrees. Then, grease the skillet or baking pan with butter or cooking spray. After that, combine the cornmeal, flour, baking soda, salt, and sugar in the mixing bowl. Next, lightly whisk in the egg and milk. (Stir only until blended; overbeating will make your cornbread tough.) Pour the mixture into the greased pan, and bake until golden on top, about 25 minutes. Cool slightly on wire rack. Then, slice into wedges and serve immediately.

1. What does this essay instruct readers to do? ____________

2. What ingredients and equipment are needed? ____________

____________

____________

____________

3. Which piece of equipment did the writer define? Why? ____________

____________

4. List three transitional words that help readers follow the steps.

____________

**B** On a separate sheet of paper, write a how-to essay to explain how to do something that you enjoy. For example, explain how to put a friend's phone number into a cell phone's memory, how to put a zipper into a sewing project, or how to use a computer to make a greeting card. Explain any terms that may be unfamiliar to the readers, and make sure you give the steps in the correct order.

Name ______________________________ Date ____________

# Reading: Fact and Opinion

## Practice

A **fact** is something that actually happened or that can be proved. An **opinion** is a person's judgment or belief and cannot be proved. To determine if something is a fact, sometimes you may have to do some research by checking encyclopedias, almanacs, or reliable Web sites. To determine if something is an opinion, look for statements that have clue words that suggest judgments that cannot be proved.

Fact: There are thirteen stripes in the American flag. (The stripes can be counted, so the statement can be proved.)
Opinion: The colors orange and green go together well. (The writer is expressing his or her judgment. Someone else might think the two colors do not go together well. The word *well* is a clue word because it expresses a judgment.)

**A** Read the following paragraph. Then, answer the questions.

Marianna Smith was leading her opponent 40–30. Then, the referee called the tennis match to a halt for a few minutes, while he silenced the cheering crowd. It was the wrong thing to do. Marianna ended up losing the game.

**1.** Is the first sentence a fact or an opinion? Explain. ______________________

______________________________________________

**2.** How could you prove that the second sentence is a fact? ______________________

______________________________________________

**3.** Why is the third sentence an opinion? ______________________

______________________________________________

**4.** Is the fourth sentence a fact or an opinion? Explain. ______________________

______________________________________________

**B** Write *F* if the statement is a fact. Write *O* if the statement is an opinion.

**1.** ______ George Washington was America's first president.

**2.** ______ Lincoln was one of America's best presidents.

**3.** ______ The birthday of Martin Luther King, Jr., is honored as a national holiday in the U.S., and all government buildings are closed on that day.

Name ______________________________ Date ____________

# Reading: Fact and Opinion

## Assess

**A** Read the following paragraph. Then, answer the questions.

The photographer seated the family and told them to sit quietly and smile. As he clicked the first picture, the baby started to scream. It was an awful, embarrassing moment for the baby's parents. The father picked the baby up and walked around the room for a few minutes. He was trying to get the baby to calm down.

**1.** Is the first sentence a fact or an opinion? Explain. ______________________

______________________________________________

**2.** How could you prove that the second sentence is a fact? ______________________

______________________________________________

**3.** Why is the third sentence an opinion? ______________________

______________________________________________

**4.** Is the fourth sentence a fact or an opinion? Explain. ______________________

______________________________________________

**B** Write *F* if the statement is a fact. Write *O* if the statement is an opinion.

**1.** ______ A chorus combines the singing voices of many people.

**2.** ______ The people in my school choir are very talented.

**3.** ______ I prefer playing piano to playing guitar.

**4.** ______ A piano is an instrument that has both strings and a keyboard.

**5.** ______ The Martin company is known for making handcrafted guitars.

**6.** ______ Musicians are very smart people.

Name ______________________ Date __________

# Reading: Analyze Proposition and Support Patterns

## Practice

In editorials and speeches, a writer or speaker often presents a proposition, a statement of a position on an issue, and then gives details as support for that proposition. Support may include facts, expert opinions, or personal observations. As you read a text with a proposition, analyze the support to see if the proposition is logical.

Here are some examples of statements that show errors in logic:

**Read the following editorial. Then answer the questions that follow.**

### Every Vote Counts

Americans live in a democracy. That means we have the right to vote for our leaders. When Americans turn eighteen, they are legally able to vote. There are elections for mayor, city council, congress, senator, and many more positions.

The right to vote is something that not all citizens take seriously. Some believe that their vote doesn't make a difference. Others think that everyone else votes, so why should they? Some people believe politicians are ineffective and that their actions won't make a difference in their lives. However, others take voting very seriously. Groups who only gained the right to vote more recently, like women, African Americans, and new citizens, often vote in higher percentages than other groups. They don't take their right to vote for granted since they were unable to vote for hundreds of years in America. Of course, everyone should vote. There have been many elections, including the presidential election in 2000, where the winner was determined by just a few votes. One of the most patriotic things you can do is to take advantage of your right to vote.

1. Does this editorial present a strong point of view? Explain. ______________

______________________________________________

2. Give a fact the writer uses to support the point of view. ______________

______________________________________________

3. Give one opinion from the editorial that is not supported by evidence. ______

______________________________________________

Name ______________________ Date __________

# Reading: Analyze Proposition and Support Patterns

## Assess

**Read the following editorial about a widespread issue. Then answer the questions that follow.**

### Cat Suffering Must Be Ended

Millions of cats live in the United States. Many are purchased or adopted and brought into wonderful homes. Unfortunately, some people who own cats later decide they don't want their pets and abandon them. Other times cats get outside accidentally and become lost. Without their owners to feed and protect them, they wander the streets looking for food and shelter. They can contract serious diseases. Cars hit some and larger animals kill others. It's a very sad situation.

Even worse, if these homeless cats have not been spayed or neutered, the females will become pregnant. The Feral Cat Coalition reports that the number of homeless cats that can result from one male and one female pair is stunning. If each pair of cats averages 2.8 surviving kittens, one pair and their offspring will produce 66,088 kittens in only six years. After 11 years, that number grows to 11,506,077! There are not nearly enough homes for all of these cats.

Veterinarians and animal support groups agree. The best solution is for owners to spay and neuter all cats when they are young so they cannot reproduce. Then perhaps there will only be enough cats for people who can and will care for them properly.

1. What is the main problem stated in this editorial? ______________________

2. Does the title state the author's position clearly? ______________________

3. What is the solution that the author proposes? ______________________

______________________________________________

4. Does the author give sources for the statistics and opinions quoted? ________

If so, what are the sources? ______________________

5. Do you agree with the proposition and its supporting evidence? Why or why not?

______________________________________________

______________________________________________

Name ______________________ Date __________

# Literary Analysis: Persuasive Techniques

## Practice

**Persuasive techniques** are the methods that a writer uses to make readers think or act in a certain way. Such techniques include:

- **Repetition:** Using the same word, phrase, or idea over and over to make a point. *Example:* Who works the hardest in this country? We taxpayers! Who pays for government waste? We taxpayers!
- **Rhetorical questions:** Asking questions with obvious answers to lead readers to agree with an argument. *Example:* Why should people vote? Because we deserve our freedom.
- **Appeals to emotions:** Using words that lead readers to have strong feelings, such as pride, patriotism, or anger. *Example:* If you love your country, you'll vote for Senator Adams.

Read this passage. Then, respond to each item.

There is little, if any, "storm" in the new movie *Storm Fever.* Aren't actors supposed to act, and aren't directors supposed to direct? Actor Robert Pierre seems to wander aimlessly around the set. And director Sue Smith can't seem to figure out how to present a good story. This movie was advertised as "full of adventure." It isn't. This movie was advertised as "full of stunning action." It isn't. This movie is like a sleeping pill. So if you have any sense at all, avoid *Storm Fever.*

1. Which is the best summary of the author's persuasive message?

   A. *Storm Fever* is a great movie.
   B. *Storm Fever* is a poor movie.
   C. Buy lots of popcorn.
   D. Movies should be full of adventure.

2. To what emotion or desire does the clause *if you have any sense at all* appeal?

   A. affection
   B. anger
   C. pride
   D. curiosity

3. Underline the rhetorical question in this passage.

4. What point does the author make by using this rhetorical question?

   A. The movie is like a sleeping pill.
   B. The story is not adventurous.
   C. The movie was poorly advertised.
   D. The cast and director did poorly.

5. What point does the writer attempt to drive home through use of repetition?

   A. Smith is a poor director.
   B. This movie was widely advertised.
   C. The movie doesn't live up to its ads.
   D. *Storm Fever* is about a bad storm.

Name ______________________________ Date ____________

# Literary Analysis: Persuasive Techniques

## Assess

**Read this passage. Then, respond to each item.**

What should a mayor do for his city—lead the people or play a lot of golf with his pals? Mayor Flaherty promised to fix the transportation system. Still not done. He promised to build a new sports arena. Still not done. Perhaps it's asking too much that he accomplish much as mayor. After all, he does seem to spend most of his time at the City Golf Club, entertaining business leaders. Enough is enough! Charles Digby is a far better candidate for this important office. He's got plenty of experience: look at his tenure as Chester County Commissioner. He's got plenty of energy, too: look at his successful drive to improve our schools. If you want to keep a dull mayor, stick with Flaherty. However, if you want to bring prosperity and honesty back into city government, vote for Digby.

1. Which is the best summary of the author's persuasive message?

   **A.** Flaherty doesn't have experience.
   **B.** We need to improve our schools.
   **C.** Digby has lots of energy and drive.
   **D.** Digby should be elected mayor.

2. To what emotion does the clause *if you want to bring prosperity and honesty back into city government* appeal?

   **A.** a desire to improve the schools
   **B.** a desire to improve local government
   **C.** a desire to help one's friends
   **D.** a desire to be honest and fair

3. Underline the rhetorical question in this passage.

4. Which is the best summary of how the author answers the rhetorical question?

   **A.** The mayor's office is the most important post in local government.
   **B.** Mayor Flaherty entertains business leaders at the City Golf Club.
   **C.** Mayor Flaherty has not led the people well.
   **D.** Charles Digby has both the experience and the energy he needs.

5. What point does the writer attempt to make through use of the repeated phrase *Still not done*?

   **A.** Mayor Flaherty doesn't spend his time wisely.
   **B.** Mayor Flaherty has not accomplished what he promised to do as mayor.
   **C.** Charles Digby will bring prosperity and honesty to city government.
   **D.** Charles Digby will promise to fix the transportation system and build an arena.

Name ______________________________ Date __________

# Literary Analysis: Word Choice

## Practice

An author's **word choice** refers to his or her selection of particular words to convey meaning and to express specific ideas and attitudes.

- **Connotations:** Writers often choose words that convey their feelings and attitudes about their topics. For example, the words *slender* and *skinny* both mean "slim." However, *slender* has positive connotations, and *skinny* has negative connotations.
- **Specific words:** Writers choose vivid adjectives and verbs to help readers visualize descriptions and actions exactly. For example, the sentence *A big dog went by* is vague and dull. By contrast, *An enormous dog with curly black hair trotted down the gravel driveway* is much more specific and vivid.

Read this passage. Then, respond to each item.

Sharon glanced around the table and saw that most of her classmates had already begun to eat their lunch. Betty was delicately nibbling on a crisp green salad with juicy tomatoes. Across from her, Ralph was gulping down some soggy chicken, loaded with fat. Next to Ralph sat Angel, sipping spoonfuls of a hearty beef stew. Just across from Sharon, Roberto was eating a sandwich.

**1.** Which phrase best conveys a positive feeling?

**A.** already begun to eat
**B.** juicy tomatoes
**C.** soggy chicken
**D.** loaded with fat

**2.** Which verb or verb phrase conveys a negative connotation?

**A.** glanced
**B.** delicately nibbling
**C.** sipping
**D.** gulping down

**3.** The clause *Roberto was eating a sandwich* seems dull and vague. Rewrite it, using vivid adjectives and verbs.

______________________________________________

**4.** The phrase *hearty beef stew* has positive connotations. Write a phrase with positive connotations that describes another food.

______________________________________________

Name ______________________________ Date ____________

# Literary Analysis: Word Choice

## Assess

**A** Write *P* if a phrase's connotation is positive or *N* if its connotation is negative.

1. ______ a cozy cottage
2. ______ a cramped house
3. ______ a scrawny puppy
4. ______ a petite kitten
5. ______ differing points of view
6. ______ a loud argument
7. ______ a worthy rival
8. ______ a bitter enemy
9. ______ a nasty lie
10. ______ a heroic legend

**B** Read this passage. Then, respond to each item.

Exhausted from round-the-clock labor, the rescue workers knew they had to reach out and keep going. Victims of the devastating flood formed a long line that stretched around the battered building. Courageously, the workers had rescued helpless children and pets as the violent storm raged on and on. Now family members huddled together, waiting patiently for warm food and the kind generosity of a helping hand.

1. Which phrase best conveys a positive feeling?

   **A.** round-the-clock labor
   **B.** reach out and keep going
   **C.** a long line
   **D.** battered building

2. Which verb or verb phrase conveys a negative connotation?

   **A.** raged on
   **B.** formed
   **C.** stretched around
   **D.** huddled together

3. What does the writer's choice of words convey about his or her attitudes toward the relief workers? Give two examples that support your answer.

   ______________________________________________________________

   ______________________________________________________________

4. What does the writer's choice of words convey about his or her attitudes about the flood? Give two examples that support your answer.

   ______________________________________________________________

   ______________________________________________________________

Name ______________________ Date __________

# Literary Analysis: Comparing Tone

## Practice

The **tone** of a literary work is the writer's attitude toward his or her subject and characters. The tone can often be described by a single adjective, such as *formal, playful,* or *respectful.* Factors that contribute to the tone include word choice, details, sentence structure, and sentence length. When **comparing tone,** consider both authors' reasons for writing. For example, the tone of a work meant to inform readers about a certain event will differ from the tone of a piece meant to entertain readers with an account of the same event.

| Tone | Example |
|---|---|
| Matter-of-fact: | Leon wore a black tuxedo with a maroon cummerbund. |
| Complimentary: | Leon looked so handsome in his black tuxedo! |

Read the following passages. Then, respond to each item.

A: To make Aunt Serena's cranberry-pumpkin pancakes, you mix one cup of whole-grain pancake mix with a quarter cup of mashed pumpkin, a cup of water, a tablespoon of oil, and a handful of fresh or frozen cranberries. They cook best on a preheated griddle. Use a quarter cup of batter per pancake, and brown gently on both sides.

B: Aunt Serena makes the best pancakes in the world! It's like Thanksgiving on a plate. She mixes just the right amount of cranberries and mashed pumpkin into her batter. My mouth waters in anticipation as I watch her flip those thick, autumn-colored pancakes into the air and catch them again in the pan. She serves them up with a big pitcher of maple syrup—warmed, of course.

**1.** Circle the author's reason for writing each passage.

| | | | |
|---|---|---|---|
| A: | to entertain | to narrate an event | to explain a process |
| B: | to entertain | to narrate an event | to explain a process |

**2.** Which answer best describes the tone of each passage?

**A.** A is lighthearted, while B is serious.
**B.** A is informative, while B is appreciative.
**C.** A is serious, while B is dreamy.
**D.** A and B are both playful.

**3.** Circle the words and details in each passage that suggest the author's tone.

Name ____________________ Date ____________

# Literary Analysis: Comparing Tone

## Assess

**Read each passage. Then, respond to the items that follow.**

A: Tessa had never picked so many peaches in her life. Her hands hurt from pulling, her shoulders hurt from reaching, and her legs hurt from climbing up and down the ladder. In all, she lugged fourteen baskets of peaches up the dirt trail to her back porch. The orchard was all she had left these days, besides her old dog Roy. But Roy wasn't much company anymore; he spent most days under the porch. Tessa stood at the kitchen sink and splashed cool water on her face. She gazed out at the orchard and remembered a time when it had echoed with the laughter of rough-and-tumble boys, falling over one another to get the first peach of the season.

B: "Childhood obesity on the rise!" "A couch potato generation!" These are the headlines we see over and over again. And we see proof of these headlines right in our own schools! Yet what is anyone doing to help solve this critical problem? When we propose renovating the playground, the voters say no. When we propose building a town pool, the voters say no. If we don't create safe places for our children to play, who will? It's time to take action! It's time to say YES, we care! Next Tuesday, vote YES for the proposed bicycle trail. Let's help our children help themselves!

**1.** Circle the letter of the best description of the authors' reasons for writing.

**A.** A is written to narrate an story; B is written to persuade readers.
**B.** A is written to explain a process; B is written to entertain readers.
**C.** A is written to persuade readers; B is written to inform readers.
**D.** A is written to entertain readers; B is written to explain a process.

**2.** What is the overall tone of Passage A?

**A.** lonely **B.** frightened **C.** cheerful **D.** depressed

**3.** List the details from the passage that suggest this tone. ____________________

____________________________________________

____________________________________________

**4.** What is the overall tone of Passage B?

**A.** optimistic **B.** passionate **C.** anxious **D.** furious

**5.** List the details from the passage that suggest this tone. ____________________

____________________________________________

____________________________________________

Name ________________________ Date ____________

# Vocabulary: Word Roots *-bell-*, *-vad-*, *-pass-*, and *-tract-*

## Practice

A **root** is the basic unit of meaning of a word. Knowing the meanings of word roots can help you figure out the meanings of many new words. Study these examples.

Examples:

| Root | Meaning | Words with the Root |
|---|---|---|
| *-bell-* | war | bellicose, belligerent, antebellum |
| *-vad-* | to go | pervading, evade, invade |
| *-pass-* | to suffer, to endure | compassionate, passion, passive |
| *-tract-* | to pull, to drag | distract, attract, tractor |

**A** In the paragraph, underline each word that contains one of the roots listed above.

When soldiers from Eastland invaded Westland, most of the Westlanders accepted it passively. However, some Westlanders were more passionate about their freedom. They planned a rebellion against the Eastlanders. They worked hard to attract more people to their cause. Then they set up several small attacks to distract the Westlander forces. This helped them evade enemy troops while they marched toward the capital.

**B** Now, write each underlined word from part A in the correct column to show which word root it contains.

| -bell- | -vad- | -pass- | -tract- |
|---|---|---|---|
| | | | |
| | | | |

Name ______________________________ Date ____________

# Vocabulary: Word Roots *-bell-*, *-vad-*, *-pass-*, and *-tract-*

## Assess

**A** Circle the letter of the word that best completes each sentence.

1. The bully ________________ threatened his classmates.
   **A.** belligerently **B.** evasively **C.** passively
2. The barn was filled with the ________________ smell of cow manure.
   **A.** attractive **B.** impassive **C.** pervasive
3. The aid worker always showed ________________ to the poor and unfortunate.
   **A.** compassion **B.** evasion **C.** rebellion
4. The factory ________________ the metal from the raw ore.
   **A.** extracted **B.** invaded **C.** pervaded
5. She tried to be calm and take a ________________ view of the problem.
   **A.** belligerent **B.** dispassionate **C.** distracted

**B** Circle T if the statement is true or F if the statement is false. Then, write a sentence to explain your answer.

1. T/F A <u>rebellious</u> teen would always obey her parents and teachers.

________________________________________

________________________________________

2. T/F If a person is <u>impassive,</u> it is hard to tell what he is thinking.

________________________________________

________________________________________

3. T/F An unflattering haircut might <u>detract</u> from a person's appearance.

________________________________________

________________________________________

4. T/F If you <u>evade</u> the person who is "it" in a game of tag, you will get caught.

________________________________________

________________________________________

Name ______________________________ Date __________

# Grammar: Conjunctions

## Practice

Words that connect sentence parts and help you add information to sentences are called **conjunctions.** The chart shows some common conjunctions.

| Type | Function | Example |
|---|---|---|
| coordinating | connects parts of similar importance | *and, but, for, nor, or, so, yet* |
| correlative | connects pairs of equal importance | *both/and, either/or, neither/nor* |
| subordinating | connects two ideas, one dependent on the other | *although, because, even though, if, since, while, until* |

Examples:
One leader was very powerful, *and* the other was very weak. (coordinating)
We will play *either* soccer *or* volleyball. (correlative)
He built a fire *because* the cabin was cold. (subordinating)

Underline the conjunctions in these sentences.

1. I sent an invitation and a map to the guests.
2. I go to either movies or early evening shows to avoid crowds.
3. When I received the package, I jumped for joy.
4. Both Sandy and I will participate.
5. Our team can win the championship if it continues to train hard.
6. My brother is in the crowd, but I can't see him.
7. They all went fishing while their father slept.
8. Neither Michael nor she could explain the strange noises.
9. I don't care much about money, nor am I careless with it.
10. Although I understand his reason, I cannot go with him.

Name ______________________________ Date ______________

# Grammar: Conjunctions

## Assess

**A** Underline the conjunctions in these sentences.

1. Tommy entered the store while everyone else waited in the store.
2. Two of my brothers and three of my sisters have jobs.
3. My mother wants a new car so she can drive herself to work.
4. Neither Frank nor I could come to an agreement.
5. I have to take my medicine before breakfast or before dinner.
6. Uncle Gary always phones whenever he is in town.
7. We expect them either in the evening or in the morning hours.
8. Whether we win or lose depends on you.
9. She liked the painting, yet she didn't buy it.
10. Both my parents and the rest of my family have given in to me.

**B** Underline each conjunction. Label it *coordinating*, *correlative*, or *subordinating*.

1. ____________________ We bought a small yet comfortable car.
2. ____________________ I can't go to the concert because I have to study for my finals.
3. ____________________ Grandfather was either reading or napping.
4. ____________________ The actor was handsome but untalented.
5. ____________________ I will wash the car since Father needs it tomorrow.
6. ____________________ She trains for the marathon both in the morning and in the afternoon.
7. ____________________ Darryl's art was the best, so he won first prize.
8. ____________________ He lost his way because he forgot to take a map.
9. ____________________ The eagle soared, swooped, and landed on its nest.
10. ____________________ I will either buy or make her a birthday card.

Name ______________________________ Date ____________

# Grammar: Prepositions and Prepositional Phrases

## Practice

A **preposition** relates the noun or pronoun following it to another word in the sentence.

Examples: above, before, between, during, in, of, over, through, under, with

The group of words beginning with a preposition and ending with a noun or a pronoun is called a **prepositional phrase.**

Example: We were sitting on the front porch.

**A** Underline each preposition in the sentences below. The numbers in parentheses tell how many prepositions are in each sentence.

1. I placed the lawn mower in a corner of the garage. (2)
2. During the spring, I often visit a flower show. (1)
3. The invading army marched into the valley without warning. (2)
4. The book is underneath the pillow near the headboard. (2)
5. She almost never leaves her clothes on the floor. (1)

**B** Underline the prepositional phrases in each sentence. The numbers in parentheses tell how many prepositional phrases are in the sentence.

1. The actress with red hair held a book in her hand. (2)
2. She stood in the very center of the huge stage. (2)
3. She was auditioning for the director and the producer. (1)
4. The stage manager sat inside the wings to the right. (2)
5. Behind him stood various members of the cast. (2)

Name ______________________________ Date __________

# Grammar: Prepositions and Prepositional Phrases

## Assess

**A** Underline the prepositional phrases below. Some sentences contain more than one.

1. From the meeting we strolled into the restaurant.
2. We listened intently throughout the manager's presentation.
3. A group of students demonstrated in front of the building.
4. The sound of falling rain can be very soothing.
5. At dawn we attempted to cross the river.
6. The investigators from the police station found evidence under the bridge.
7. We raced through the enemy town at great speed.
8. Instead of hamburgers, we had salads for lunch.
9. The road marker is some distance in front of the chalet.
10. According to the travel agent, we should arrive about noon.

**B** Underline the preposition in each sentence. Then, rewrite the sentence using a different preposition.

**Example:** My brother walked near the park. *My brother walked into the park.*

1. The ticket holders waited patiently outside the theater.

______________________________

2. The telephone book is under the table.

______________________________

3. A housing development has been built across the river.

______________________________

4. Let's pick the strawberries near the fence.

______________________________

5. We were sitting on the front porch.

______________________________

Name ______________________ Date ________

# Grammar: Combining Sentences With Conjunctions

## Practice

**Conjunctions** connect words or groups of words. They can be used to create a compound or complex sentence. There are two categories of conjunctions that serve different functions.

**Coordinating conjunctions** join words of the same kind and equal rank, such as two nouns or two verbs. When they join two independent clauses, these conjunctions make a compound sentence.

> **Example:** Jerry enjoys playing tennis. Tommy enjoys playing tennis.
> **Compound Subject:** Jerry and Tommy enjoy playing tennis.
>
> **Example:** Crocodiles look slow. They can move swiftly.
> **Compound Sentence:** Crocodiles look slow, but they can move swiftly.

**Subordinating conjunctions** create complex sentences by connecting two complete ideas and showing that one is dependent on the other.

> **Example:** Carol had searched for several days. She found the perfect gift.
> **With Subordinating Conjunction:** After Carol had searched for several days, she found the perfect gift.

| Common Conjunctions | |
|---|---|
| **Coordinating** | and, but, for, nor, or, so, yet |
| **Subordinating** | after, although, as, because, before, if, since, unless, until, when, while, whenever |

Underline the coordinating or subordinating conjunction in each sentence.

1. When my relatives discuss music, different opinions emerge.
2. Terry will clean the garage, or his parents will be disappointed.
3. We read stories before we go to bed.
4. If it does not rain tomorrow, we will go to the lake.
5. The radio announcer warned of a storm, but no one paid any attention.

Name ______________________________ Date ______________

# Grammar: Combining Sentences With Conjunctions

## Assess

**A** Combine each pair of sentences, using the coordinating or subordinating conjunction in parentheses.

**Example:** I need money. I've started walking dogs. (because)
**Answer:** Because I need money, I've started walking dogs.

1. We were late for school. We missed the bus. (because)

______________________________

2. According to legend, Betsy Ross made our first flag. There is little evidence. (but)

______________________________

3. Skin divers must follow safety precautions. They may be injured. (or)

______________________________

4. We stood by the Washington Monument. We felt very small. (when)

______________________________

5. My schedule varies. I try to exercise every day. (although)

______________________________

**B** Write an appropriate coordinating or subordinating conjunction on the line to complete each sentence.

1. Aunt Jennifer came with us, ______________ Uncle Steve stayed home.
2. ______________ she has the time, Mom volunteers at the hospital.
3. ______________ you need help, please call me.
4. Napoleon was a brilliant general, ______________ he made several costly mistakes.
5. ______________ I sent the letter off, I remembered the stamp.
6. Carla has not called, ______________ has she written.
7. ______________ the rain stops, the firewood will be too wet to burn.

Name ______________________________ Date __________

# Spelling: Homonyms and Homophones

## Practice

**Homophones** are words that sound alike but have different meanings and spellings. Homophones are sometimes called **homonyms.** The words *cite, sight,* and *site* are homophones. Two of the words are nouns: *site,* meaning "place," and *sight,* meaning "the act of seeing." One of the words is a verb: *cite,* meaning "to quote." Notice the different ways in which the words are used in the following sentences.

> What sources did he *cite* in his report?
> The *site* of the new library is on Main Street.
> The *sight* of the shark's teeth made me shiver.

The spell-check feature on your computer cannot always tell whether you have used the wrong homophone. You might have used the wrong word but spelled it correctly—for example, "I love the cite of a mountain range." So even after you have used spell-check, proofread your work carefully for any mistakes the computer might have overlooked.

| except | accept | bored | board | waste | our |
|---|---|---|---|---|---|
| waist | foul | fowl | through | threw | hour |

**A** Next to each word below, write the homophone from the box that matches it.

1. ____________ board
2. ____________ through
3. ____________ except
4. ____________ hour
5. ____________ foul
6. ____________ waste

**B** Underline the six misspelled words, and then write the correct spellings on the lines below.

I was hoping to get a new surf bored for my birthday. But my parents thought that would be a waist of money. Instead, they through out the idea of a chess set with hand-carved game pieces. I was so board at the thought of sitting indoors playing chess! My father asked me to give chess just one our of my time. I was hooked! I gladly decided to except their offer.

1. ____________
2. ____________
3. ____________
4. ____________
5. ____________
6. ____________

Name ______________________________ Date ____________

# Spelling: Homonyms and Homophones

## Assess

**A** Underline the correct homophone in each sentence.

1. The two-hour speech on the new waste-disposal site left me (bored/board).
2. (Our/Hour) new sedan had that unmistakable new-car smell.
3. After the flood in our basement, the water came up to my (waste/waist).
4. The umpires could not agree on whether the ball was fair or (fowl/foul).
5. We decided to take a shortcut (through/threw) the neighbor's backyard.
6. Everyone liked the film (accept/except) Chan.

**B** Choose the word that best completes each sentence.

1. Our coach said that he would like to ____________ the trophy on behalf of the whole team.

   **A.** except  **B.** accept

2. The president ____________ out the first ball on the opening day of the new baseball season.

   **A.** through  **B.** threw

3. Juana had to wait more than an ____________ to renew her driver's license.

   **A.** our  **B.** hour

4. The school ____________ ruled that make-up exams would be held on the following Wednesday.

   **A.** bored  **B.** board

5. The student council debated the merits of the city's ____________ recycling program.

   **A.** waist  **B.** waste

6. A main dish of ____________ is traditional for many Americans over the holidays.

   **A.** fowl  **B.** foul

Name ________________________________ Date ____________

# Writing: Evaluation

## Practice

An **evaluation** is a brief work that analyzes the overall effectiveness of a persuasive essay, speech, or advertisement. A well-written evaluation should

- **clearly identify** the author's position and supporting points: *The author expresses the belief that everyone should eat organically. She cites proven health benefits of an organic diet to support her position.*
- **discuss the kinds of persuasive techniques** the author uses: *She uses attention-grabbing words, such as "tainted food," and emotional words, such as "energetic" and "pure," and she repeats key phrases, such as "Eat well, live well." She also appeals to authority by citing statistics.*
- **assess** how well the author deals with **counterarguments:** *The author effectively addresses the argument that organic foods cost too much by offering money-saving tips. She also points out that, while organic foods cost more, an organic diet results in lower medical bills.*

**Read the following persuasive speech. Then, answer the questions.**

Next week I turn sixteen and can apply for my license. However, I've decided not to. We've all seen the headlines: "Teen driver killed in crash" or "Teen driver causes pile-up." Sixteen-year-olds are just too young to handle the responsibility of a car. The statistics don't lie. Sixteen-year-olds have a higher crash rate than drivers of any other age. They're three times more likely to die in a car crash. Some say it's necessary for sixteen-year-olds to drive. They need to get to work. They need to free their parents from the chore of driving them everywhere. Those things may be true, but there are alternatives, such as carpools and public transportation. Too inconvenient, you say? I for one would rather be inconveniently alive than conveniently dead.

1. What position does the speaker express in this speech?

   ______________________________________________

2. Underline two supporting points. Are they convincing? Why or why not?

   ______________________________________________

3. Identify a persuasive technique used in the speech. Is it effective? Explain.

   ______________________________________________

4. Underline one sentence that deals with counterarguments.

5. Overall, how effective is this speech? Explain. ______________________

   ______________________________________________

Name ______________________ Date __________

# Writing: Evaluation

## Assess

Respond to each item to help you write an evaluation of an advertisement.

1. Think of the many ads that you see on television or in magazines. Choose an ad for one of the following items to evaluate.

| | | | |
|---|---|---|---|
| food | electronic device | phone service | makeup |
| book | sports equipment | clothing | other: ________ |

Write a brief description of the ad you will evaluate.

______________________________________________

2. What position does the ad express? ______________________

______________________________________________

3. How does the ad support this position? ______________________

______________________________________________

______________________________________________

4. What persuasive techniques does the ad use? ______________________

______________________________________________

5. Does the ad address any counterarguments? Explain. ______________________

______________________________________________

6. Did the ad make you want to buy the product? Why or why not? __________

______________________________________________

7. Now, write your evaluation of the ad's overall effectiveness. __________

______________________________________________

______________________________________________

______________________________________________

______________________________________________

______________________________________________

Name ______________________ Date __________

# Writing: Response

## Practice

A **response** is a brief work that expresses the writer's thoughts and feelings about an idea. A response should contain the following elements:

- a statement of agreement or disagreement with the idea: *I agree that all students should spend time volunteering in their community.*
- an explanation of how the idea applies—or does not apply—to your own experience: *Working at the local nursing home has helped me appreciate the wisdom of our elderly citizens.*
- examples that support your explanation: *Mrs. Garcia told me some stories about her past that showed me the value of strong family ties.*

**A** Read the following passage. Then, answer the questions.

Students entering the ninth grade should automatically begin block scheduling, which divides the school year into two terms with four classes per term—as opposed to traditional scheduling, which stretches seven or eight classes over the course of a full year. With block scheduling, classes meet for approximately 80 minutes each day, and students take a final exam at the end of the term. The following term, students take a different set of classes. This gives students a manageable workload and allows them to fit in up to eight full classes per year. It also prepares them for college life, where this type of schedule is the norm.

1. What idea does the writer of this passage express? ______________________

______________________________________________

2. Do you agree or disagree with this idea? ______________________

3. How does this idea apply—or not apply—to your own expectations for your high-school education? Include at least one example that supports your explanation.

______________________________________________

______________________________________________

______________________________________________

______________________________________________

**B** On a separate sheet of paper, write a response to the following statement: Every middle- and high-school student should be required to participate in at least one sport per year.

Name ______________________ Date __________

# Writing: Response

## Assess

**Respond to each item to help you write a response to an idea about a current issue.**

Cell phone companies are no better than tobacco companies. Both companies sell a product that is highly profitable, highly addictive—and highly dangerous. Studies suggest that radiation from mobile phones can cause heavy users to

- suffer from headaches.
- damage DNA and other cells in their body.
- develop tumors.
- increase their chances of dying from brain cancer.

Despite studies documenting these and other potential effects of cell phone use, manufacturers continue to deny the dangers, and millions of Americans continue to use them. Yes, we depend on our cell phones, but there are ways to reduce their risk. Here are just a few: Carry your cell phone on something other than your body. Buy cell phones that have the lowest amount of radiation. Use your cell phone on speakerphone. The brain you save may be your own.

**1.** What opinion does the author of this work express? ______________________

______________________

______________________

**2.** Do you agree or disagree with this idea? ______________________

**3.** How does this idea apply—or not apply—to your own experience? Explain.

______________________

______________________

**4.** Jot down two examples that support your explanation.

______________________

______________________

**5.** Now, write your response. Continue on the back of this page if you need more space.

______________________

______________________

Name ______________________ Date __________

# Writing: Editorial

## Practice

When you use written words to change people's thinking or influence their actions, you are using persuasive writing. One type of persuasive writing is an **editorial,** a brief essay published in a newspaper, magazine, or Web site. An editorial states and defends an opinion on a current issue. An effective editorial includes these elements:

- a strong statement that clearly states the writer's opinion on an issue
- strong evidence to support that opinion, including facts and statistics
- a response to possible opposing arguments
- persuasive language to sway readers, including emotional appeals and words with positive or negative connotations

**A** Circle the letter of the best answer to each question about an editorial favoring the building of a teen center.

1. Which is the strongest statement of opinion regarding a teen center?

   A. It would probably be nice to have a teen center somewhere in town.
   B. The nearby city of Oakdale has a very attractive and busy teen center.
   C. Studies show that teens often benefit from organized activities.
   D. Our town needs a teen center—now!

2. Which statement supports the writer's opinion with a fact or statistic?

   A. People just don't seem to understand the needs of young people.
   B. The Oakdale teen center's computer workshops have helped teens develop job skills.
   C. Some students may not want a teen center at first, but they'll catch on.
   D. If you don't think that a teen center is needed, you're wrong.

3. Which statement best responds to an opposing view about a teen center?

   A. My research shows that building a teen center will *not* cost a lot.
   B. People who are against the teen center are stupid.
   C. A teen center could provide athletic programs and useful homework help.
   D. It doesn't take a rocket scientist to see that a teen center would be good.

**B** On a separate sheet of paper, write a brief editorial expressing and supporting an opinion about a current issue at school or in your community. Be sure to include the elements listed at the top of this page.

Name ______________________ Date __________

# Writing: Editorial

## Assess

**A** Circle the letter of the best answer to each question about an editorial favoring the building of a public swimming pool.

1. Which is the strongest statement of opinion promoting the pool?

   **A.** Learning to swim is an important life skill.
   **B.** Many wealthy families can swim at home, but most of us can't.
   **C.** A public swimming pool would greatly improve citizens' recreational opportunities.
   **D.** Swimming is good exercise and a wonderful way to beat the heat.

2. Which statement supports the writer's opinion with a fact or statistic?

   **A.** Many cities with public pools have successful competitive swim teams.
   **B.** Working as a lifeguard sounds like a great summer job.
   **C.** Don't oppose the pool just because you feel it would raise taxes.
   **D.** Young children would probably enjoy free swim classes.

3. Which statement best responds to an opposing view about the pool?

   **A.** If you're an adult who doesn't swim, you're likely in bad physical shape.
   **B.** To insure safety, the pool would be staffed with trained lifeguards.
   **C.** It's high time that our city provide more recreational facilities for the public.
   **D.** Some people are opposed to the building of a swimming pool.

4. Which statement makes the most effective use of persuasive language?

   **A.** As the long, hot summer drags on, let's find relief and lots of fun at our new pool.
   **B.** What could possibly be a better way to spend our tax money?
   **C.** If you don't want a pool, perhaps you'd prefer to build a soccer field.
   **D.** We need a public swimming pool.

**B** On a separate sheet of paper, write a brief editorial on a current issue at school or in your community. Be sure to start with a clear statement expressing your opinion. Then, support it with strong evidence. Address an opposing viewpoint, and use persuasive language effectively. Sample topics include lowering the age at which a person can get a driver's license, putting soda and snack machines in the school cafeteria, establishing a local film festival, and hiring middle-school students to write about school activities in local newspapers.

Name ______________________________ Date __________

# Reading: Context Clues

## Practice

**Context** is the text around a particular word. When you come across an unfamiliar word, ask yourself: "How is this word used?" (For example: *to describe something.*) Then, look for clues in the context to help you determine a possible meaning for the word. Look for these types of clues:

- **synonyms** or **definitions:** words that mean the same as the unfamiliar word
- **antonyms:** words that are opposite in meaning
- **explanations:** words that give more information

Example: Paula feels apprehensive about her new school. She is worried that no one will sit with her at lunch.
Unfamiliar word: apprehensive
How is this word used? to describe how someone feels
Context clues: *worried* (synonym) and *no one will sit with her* (explanation)
Possible meaning: anxious

**A** Circle the context clue that helps you determine the meaning of each underlined word. Write the meaning in the space provided.

1. ______________ Jed thought the documentary was intriguing. He is fascinated by unsolved mysteries.

2. ______________ Amy has an aptitude for math. Her friends envy her natural ability.

**B** Read the passage. Then, complete the activities that follow.

Because of my diminutive size, opposing soccer players always tease me. They call me "shorty" and "small fry" almost every day. It doesn't matter that I'm the best player on the soccer team; the teasing is nonstop. Their incessant teasing bothers me so much that I've decided to retaliate. Won't they be surprised when they can't find their uniforms!

1. How is the word diminutive used? What context clues point to this meaning?

______________________________________________

2. What type of context clue for incessant is the word *nonstop*? ______________

3. Underline the phrase that helps you figure out the meaning of retaliate.

Name ______________________________ Date __________

# Reading: Context Clues

## Assess

**A** Use context clues to determine the meaning of the underlined words. Then, circle the letter of the correct answer.

1. It's too risky to drive anywhere in these hazardous conditions.

   A. predictable
   B. sticky
   C. windy
   D. dangerous

2. Jim is an amazing orator. No other speaker moves me like he does.

   A. speaker
   B. actor
   C. politician
   D. referee

3. The rescue workers were glad to see that food was abundant. There was enough for everyone.

   A. plentiful
   B. scarce
   C. restricted
   D. excessive

4. Our dispute was so long-standing that we had no hope of reaching an agreement.

   A. relationship
   B. quarrel
   C. resentment
   D. unhappiness

**B** Read the passage. Then, answer the questions.

When Aunt Theresa decided to build a house, she insisted on hiring a seasoned builder, someone with many years of experience. She was adamant in her refusal to consider anyone but the best. As inflexible as she was on this point, she was open to our ideas about the style and design of the house.

1. How is the word seasoned used in the above passage?

   A. to describe the way someone looks
   B. to describe someone's personality
   C. to describe someone's job experience
   D. to describe what someone is cooking

2. What is the meaning of the word seasoned? ______________________________

3. What type of context clue helped you determine the meaning of adamant?

   A. a synonym B. an antonym C. an explanation D. all of these

Name ______________________________ Date __________

# Reading: Compare and Contrast Features of Consumer Materials

## Practice

Different types of documents offer different types of information. For example, a cookie recipe tells you how to make cookies, but it might not tell you the cookies' nutritional content. When you read consumer materials, take note of the features and elements and the types of information offered within them. As you read the following text, note types of information that are particular to it.

**EXERCISE CHART**

Your body weight, how hard you workout, your conditioning level, and your metabolism affect the number of calories you burn during exercise. Some examples of average calories burned per hour are listed below. These numbers are for sample body weights of 130, 155 and 190 pounds, for recreational versions of the sports.

| Activity (1 hour) | 130lbs. | 155lbs. | 190 lbs. |
|---|---|---|---|
| Aerobics | 354 | 422 | 518 |
| Basketball | 354 | 422 | 518 |
| Bicycling | 236 | 281 | 345 |
| Bowling | 177 | 211 | 259 |
| Frisbee | 177 | 211 | 259 |
| Golf | 236 | 281 | 345 |
| Skateboarding | 295 | 352 | 431 |
| Soccer | 413 | 493 | 604 |
| Swimming Laps | 472 | 563 | 690 |

1. Name two activities that burn the same amount of calories. ______________

2. If you are trying to get in the best condition, which two of these activities should you participate in? Why? ______________________________

______________________________________________

3. Does the chart explain why some activities burn more calories? ______ Why do you think frisbee and golf have the lowest number of calories burned per hour? ______________________________

______________________________________________

Name ______________________________ Date __________

# Reading: Compare and Contrast Features of Consumer Materials

## Assess

**Read the recipe and nutritional information below. Then, answer the questions that follow.**

Banana Breakfast Smoothies (serves 4)

Equipment: knife, blender, glasses for serving

Ingredients:
1 cup orange juice
2 cups plain low-fat yogurt
4 small bananas
1 teaspoon honey or artificial sweetener

Instructions:
Cut up bananas into small pieces. Place all ingredients in blender. Process until desired consistency. Enjoy!

Nutritional Content Per Serving
Number of Servings: 4
Serving Size: approximately 1 cup

| | | | |
|---|---|---|---|
| Calories | 212 | Carbohydrate | 40 g |
| Fat | 5 g | Fiber | 3 g |
| Protein | 6 g | Saturated Fat | 3 g |
| Sodium | 59 mg | | |

**1.** Name the four categories of information in this recipe. ______________

**2.** Compare the carbohydrate versus protein content of this recipe.

**3.** Would the nutritional content be useful to someone who is on a diet that restricts carbohydrates? Why or why not? ______________

______________________________

**4.** What is the value of having the nutritional information accompany all recipes? ______________________________

______________________________

Name ______________________ Date __________

# Literary Analysis: Sound Devices

## Practice

**Sound devices** help poets draw on the musical quality of words in order to express ideas. Here are some of the most common of these sound devices:

- **Onomatopoeia:** words that imitate sounds—*buzz, crash, pop*
- **Alliteration:** repetition of sounds at the beginning of words—*a red rose*
- **Repetition:** repeated use of a sound, word, or phrase—*Yes, yes, you can!*
- **Rhyme:** repetition of sounds at the ends of words—*brown / gown*

**A** Decide what type of sound device is used in each item. Circle the letter of the correct answer.

**1.** The more I try, the more I learn.

**A.** onomatopoeia **B.** alliteration **C.** repetition **D.** rhyme

**2.** The great debate: What is our fate?

**A.** onomatopoeia **B.** alliteration **C.** repetition **D.** rhyme

**3.** Feathers floating freely on the breeze.

**A.** onomatopoeia **B.** alliteration **C.** repetition **D.** rhyme

**4.** Never, never tell a lie.

**A.** onomatopoeia **B.** alliteration **C.** repetition **D.** rhyme

**5.** We were awakened by the eerie honking of wild geese in flight.

**A.** onomatopoeia **B.** alliteration **C.** repetition **D.** rhyme

**B** Circle the letter of the best answer for each question.

**1.** Which is the best example of the use of alliteration?

**A.** a fearful sneer **C.** a barking dog
**B.** a sudden shower **D.** the tone of my phone

**2.** Which is the best example of the use of onomatopoeia?

**A.** a twinkling star **C.** the clang of a gong
**B.** a wiggly worm **D.** frost on the window

Name ______________________ Date __________

# Literary Analysis: Sound Devices

## Assess

**A** Decide what type of sound device is used in each item. Circle the letter of the correct answer.

**1.** At break of day, few words to say.

**A.** onomatopoeia **B.** alliteration **C.** repetition **D.** rhyme

**2.** a bouncing blue balloon

**A.** onomatopoeia **B.** alliteration **C.** repetition **D.** rhyme

**3.** The horses responded to the crack of the whip.

**A.** onomatopoeia **B.** alliteration **C.** repetition **D.** rhyme

**4.** A lifelong friend is joy without end.

**A.** onomatopoeia **B.** alliteration **C.** repetition **D.** rhyme

**5.** March on, march on, through storms and darkness.

**A.** onomatopoeia **B.** alliteration **C.** repetition **D.** rhyme

**6.** the chirping of the birds

**A.** onomatopoeia **B.** alliteration **C.** repetition **D.** rhyme

**B** Circle the letter of the best answer for each question.

**1.** Which is the best example of the use of onomatopoeia?

**A.** a flash of lightning
**B.** a crash of thunder
**C.** a ray of sunlight
**D.** the smooth, shiny stone

**2.** Which is the best example of the use of rhyme?

**A.** the beat of the drum
**B.** fresh green grass
**C.** a wild little child
**D.** the kindness of strangers

**3.** Which is the best example of the use of alliteration?

**A.** a pineapple pie
**B.** a purring kitten
**C.** an open window
**D.** a mellow fellow

Name ______________________________ Date __________

# Literary Analysis: Figurative Language

## Practice

**Figurative language** is language that is not meant to be taken literally. Writers use figures of speech to express ideas in vivid and imaginative ways. Common figures of speech include the following:

- A **simile** compares two unlike things using a word such as *like* or *as*.
  Example: His smile was as warm as springtime.
- A **metaphor** compares two unlike things by stating that one thing is another thing.
  Example: My brother is a pillar of strength in hard times.
- **Personification** gives human characteristics to a nonhuman subject.
  Example: The ocean waves beckoned to the surfers.

**A** Determine which figure of speech has been used in each item. Then, write the figure of speech on the line.

**1.** ____________________ The boats bobbed back and forth like rocking horses.

**2.** ____________________ My new dog is a gem.

**3.** ____________________ The crow chuckled at us, then winked and flew away.

**B** Circle the letter of the example for each type of figurative language.

**1.** simile

**A.** Marty's shout rattled the windows.
**B.** Her voice was as clear as a bell.
**C.** He is a bear in the morning.
**D.** The blossoms in the garden nodded their heads.

**2.** metaphor

**A.** The storm was a furious beast coming our way.
**B.** The baby smelled as fresh as daisies.
**C.** The airport was as busy as an ant colony.
**D.** The blank sheet of paper mocked me.

**3.** personification

**A.** The breeze ruffled the baby's hair and kissed her cheek.
**B.** The dog snarled and backed away.
**C.** Eliza jumped over hurdles like a deer.
**D.** The crowd roared like a pride of lions.

Name ______________________________ Date ____________

# Literary Analysis: Figurative Language

## Assess

**A** Give an example of each type of figurative language listed below. Your example may be one you have made up or one you remember from your reading.

**1.** personification ______________________________
______________________________

**2.** simile ______________________________
______________________________

**3.** metaphor ______________________________
______________________________

**B** Decide what type of figurative language is contained in each item. Write your answer on the line.

**1.** ____________ He was as big as a mountain but as gentle as a lamb.

**2.** ____________ The chilly breeze nipped at her nose.

**3.** ____________ Marco was as carefree as a bird in the air.

**4.** ____________ The raindrops tapped at the windowpane.

**5.** ____________ The wind was a beast.

**6.** ____________ My mother is a shining star.

**7.** ____________ The luna moths flew by, pieces of dreams in the night sky.

**8.** ____________ The ocean played its old, lonely song.

Name ______________________________ Date ____________

# Literary Analysis: Comparing Poetry and Prose

## Practice

Two major types of literature are **poetry** and **prose.**

| Prose | Poetry |
|---|---|
| Common form of written language | Language with a strong musical quality not heard in daily life |
| Includes both fiction and nonfiction | Makes use of the following: precise words; deliberate line lengths; sound devices such as rhythm, rhyme, and alliteration |
| Includes stories, essays, articles, and novels | Often hints at meaning rather than stating it directly, relying heavily on figurative language |

When **comparing poetry and prose,** you should notice the differences in the authors' styles to convey the **mood** (overall feeling) and describe the **setting** (where and when the action takes place).

"The Charge of the Light Brigade" by Alfred, Lord Tennyson is a poem written to memorialize a suicidal charge by British forces in the Battle of Balaclava (Ukraine) in the Crimean War (1854-56). Read the excerpt from the poem. Then, answer the questions.

Cannon to right of them,
Cannon to left of them,
Cannon in front of them
  Volley'd and thunder'd;
Storm'd at with shot and shell,
Boldly they rode and well,
Into the jaws of Death,
Into the mouth of Hell
  Rode the six hundred.

**1.** What are three qualities that make this poetry?

______________________________

**2.** What details about the setting help you picture the scene?

______________________________

**3.** What is the mood of the passage? ______________________________

Name ______________________________ Date ____________

# Literary Analysis: Comparing Poetry and Prose

## Assess

**A** Write *Poetry* for each characteristic of poetry. Write *Prose* for each characteristic of prose.

**1.** ________________ Makes use of deliberate line lengths.

**2.** ________________ Language heard in everyday life.

**3.** ________________ Includes both fiction and nonfiction.

**4.** ________________ Uses sound devices such as rhythm and rhyme.

**5.** ________________ Relies on figurative language to hint at meaning rather than stating it directly.

**B** "O Captain! My Captain!" by Walt Whitman was inspired by the tragic death of President Abraham Lincoln. Read the excerpt from the poem. Then, answer the questions.

O Captain! my Captain! our fearful trip is done,
The ship has weathered every rack, the prize we sought is won,
The port is near, the bells I hear, the people all exulting,
While follow eyes the steady keel, the vessel grim and daring;
  But O heart! heart! heart!
    O the bleeding drops of red,
      Where on the deck my Captain lies,
        Fallen cold and dead.

**1.** What are three qualities that make this excerpt poetry?

______________________________________________________________

______________________________________________________________

**2.** What details about the setting help you picture the scene?

______________________________________________________________

______________________________________________________________

**3.** What is the mood of the passage? ______________________________

Name ______________________________ Date __________

# Vocabulary: Prefix *im-* and Suffixes *-ous* and *-ive*

## Practice

A **prefix** is added to the beginning of a word or word root to change its meaning. The prefix *im-* can change word meanings in two ways. In some words, *im-* means "in" or "into." In other cases, it means "not."

im + press = impress: "to press inward, to make a dent or groove"
im + possible = impossible: "not possible"

A **suffix** is added to the end of a word to change its meaning or part of speech. The suffix *-ous,* meaning "full of" or "characterized by" often changes nouns to adjectives. The suffix *-ive* often changes verbs to adjectives.

joy + ous = joyous: "full of joy, happy"
act + ive = active: "likely to act"

**A** Match each word with the sentence in which it fits best.

immature

immediate

improvement

improvise

1. He demanded that I make an ____________________ decision.
2. I didn't have an answer prepared, so I had to ____________________.
3. The new sidewalks are a big ____________________ in our neighborhood.
4. I think he acts very ____________________ for his age.

**B** Add *-ous* or *-ive* to each underlined word to form a new word that fits the meaning of the sentence.

1. ____________________ The view from the mountain was <u>glory</u>.
2. ____________________ The screaming toddler was very <u>disrupt</u> during the airplane flight.
3. ____________________ She often does <u>outrage</u> things to get attention.
4. ____________________ I hope the town will take a <u>progress</u> approach to its traffic problems.

Name ______________________________ Date ____________

# Vocabulary: Prefix *im-* and Suffixes *-ous* and *-ive*

## Assess

**A** Circle the meaning of the prefix *im-* that is used in each word. Then use the word in a sentence.

**1.** immigrant: someone who moves into a country into/not

______________________________

**2.** immobile: unmoving into/not

______________________________

**3.** immerse: to submerge something in water into/not

______________________________

**4.** imports: goods shipped into a country into/not

______________________________

**B** Add the suffix indicated to each underlined word to form a new word. Write this word on the line. Then rewrite the original sentence to use the new word.

**1.** ____________ He is known for his virtue. (add *-ous*)

______________________________

**2.** ____________ She always gives a quick response to my suggestions. (add *-ive*)

______________________________

**3.** ____________ The TV show was full of humor. (add *-ous*)

______________________________

**4.** ____________ My quick lesson helped instruct me on how to skate. (add *-ive*)

______________________________

**5.** ____________ Their house was full of luxuries. (add *-ous*)

______________________________

Name ______________________________ Date __________

# Grammar: Subject Complements

## Practice

A **subject complement** is a noun, a pronoun, or an adjective that appears with a linking verb and tells something about the subject. Three types of subject complements are *predicate nouns, predicate pronouns,* and *predicate adjectives.*

A **predicate noun** is a noun that *identifies* or *renames* the subject of the sentence.

The banjo is a stringed **instrument** used in bluegrass music. [The noun *instrument* renames the subject *banjo*. The linking verb is *is*.]

A **predicate pronoun** is a pronoun that *identifies* or *renames* the subject of the sentence.

The featured performer at the bluegrass festival might be **he**. [The pronoun *he* identifies the subject *performer.* The linking verb is *might be*.]

A **predicate adjective** is an adjective that *describes* the subject of the sentence.

Does bluegrass music sound **good** to you? [The adjective *good* describes the subject *music*. The linking verb is *Does sound*.]

Underline the subject complement in each sentence. Then, identify it by writing *PN* for *predicate noun, PP* for *predicate pronoun,* or *PA* for *predicate adjective.*

**1.** ______ Buzz Aldrin became an astronaut in 1963.

**2.** ______ The second person to set foot on the moon was he.

**3.** ______ The American people were proud of the moon landing.

**4.** ______ Space exploration would be an exciting career.

**5.** ______ The special food for astronauts might taste strange.

**6.** ______ To many people, NASA astronauts are American heroes.

Name ______________________________ Date ____________

# Grammar: Subject Complements

## Assess

**A** Identify the underlined subject complement by writing *PN* for *predicate noun, PP* for *predicate pronoun,* or *PA* for *predicate adjective.*

**1.** ______ Fish, tofu, and rice are traditional Japanese foods.

**2.** ______ Does Japanese food taste delicious to you?

**3.** ______ Peking duck is a specialty of northern China.

**4.** ______ Egg rolls and dumplings are popular in China.

**5.** ______ Favorite lunchtime foods are they.

**6.** ______ Many people in India are vegetarians.

**7.** ______ Our dinner at the Indian restaurant was enjoyable.

**8.** ______ The owner of the restaurant is she.

**B** In each sentence, circle the linking verb and underline the subject complement.

**1.** Horses have been useful to humans for thousands of years.

**2.** The shire is the largest breed of horse.

**3.** Two thousand pounds would be a typical weight for a shire.

**4.** Running bands of wild horses must look beautiful.

**5.** Descendants of tame horses from long ago are they.

**C** Underline the subject complement in each sentence. Then, identify it by writing *PN* for *predicate noun, PP* for *predicate pronoun,* or *PA* for *predicate adjective.*

**1.** ______ Mrs. Diaz has become knowledgeable about Latin America.

**2.** ______ In fact, one of the best-known experts is she.

**3.** ______ Mexico is a large country in Latin America.

**4.** ______ Much of the land in Mexico is too dry for farming.

**5.** ______ Mexico City is the capital of Mexico.

Name ________________________________ Date __________

# Grammar: Direct and Indirect Objects

## Practice

A **direct object** is a noun, pronoun, or word group that receives the action of the verb and answers the question *Whom?* or *What?*

Bruce studies **geography** every night. [Bruce studies *what*? Geography.]
Carlos will help **him** with his geometry homework. [Carlos will help *whom*? Him.]

An **indirect object** is a noun, pronoun, or word group that follows an action verb and answers the question *To whom? To what? For whom?* or *For what?* Notice that every sentence that has an indirect object will also have a direct object.

Bruce's dad bought **him** a globe. [The indirect object *him* tells *for whom* Bruce's dad bought the globe. *Globe* is the direct object.]

Bruce gave the **globe** a special spot on his desk. [The indirect object *globe* tells *to what* Bruce gave a special spot. *Spot* is the direct object.]

Do not confuse an indirect object with the object of a preposition.

| | |
|---|---|
| INDIRECT OBJECT | Mr. Jacobs handed **Bruce** the geography test. [*Test* is the direct object, and *Bruce* is the indirect object.] |
| OBJECT OF A PREPOSITION | Mr. Jacobs handed the geography test to **Bruce**. [*Test* is still the direct object. *Bruce* is the object of the preposition *to*.] |

**Underline the direct object in each sentence. If a sentence has an indirect object, circle it.**

1. Julio has taken many courses in lifesaving.
2. As a lifeguard, he will help drowning victims.
3. Julio once gave me a swimming lesson.
4. He teaches his students safety techniques.
5. Only a trained lifeguard should attempt a rescue.

Name ______________________ Date __________

# Grammar: Direct and Indirect Objects

## Assess

**A** Identify the underlined word by writing *IO* for *indirect object* or *OP* for *object of a preposition.*

**1.** ______ Last night Tamesa wrote a letter to the editor of the paper.

**2.** ______ The librarian reads stories to the children each day.

**3.** ______ The dog trainer handed her a special training collar.

**4.** ______ Reggie made a birthday card for his grandmother.

**5.** ______ Ellie has taught the parrot a new trick.

**B** Underline the direct object in each sentence. If a sentence has an indirect object, circle it.

**1.** Aunt Mae sent us two bus tickets to Chicago.

**2.** She took us to the most popular museums.

**3.** The Great Chicago Fire destroyed a large part of the city in 1871.

**4.** Chicago has an excellent symphony orchestra.

**5.** The tour guide showed our group the beautiful lakefront.

**6.** Aunt Mae handed the man our tickets.

**7.** The Brookfield Zoo houses a variety of baby animals.

**C** Identify the underlined word by writing *DO* for *direct object, IO* for *indirect object,* or *N* for *neither.*

**1.** ______ The professor gave his students a chance for extra credit.

**2.** ______ The city council has approved the budget for next year.

**3.** ______ The volunteers delivered hot meals to people in need.

**4.** ______ Once my brother drew me a picture of a daisy.

**5.** ______ Melissa sent Judy the directions to her house.

Name ______________________ Date __________

# Grammar: Revising Active and Passive Voice

## Practice

A verb is in the **active voice** when its subject performs the action. A verb is in the **passive voice** when the action is done *to* the subject.

ACTIVE VOICE Tina **hit** two home runs. [The subject is *Tina.* Tina performs the action of hitting.]

PASSIVE VOICE Two home runs **were hit** by Tina. [The subject is *home runs.* The action of hitting is done *to* the home runs.]

Notice that the passive voice is formed by using a form of *be* plus the past participle.

Your writing will sound stronger and more direct if you use mostly active-voice verbs. However, the passive voice is appropriate when you want to emphasize the receiver of the action or when the performer of the action is unknown.

An umpire **was injured** in an unfortunate collision. [*Umpire,* the receiver of the action, is emphasized.]
The announcer's booth **was vandalized** in the middle of the night. [The writer does not know who did the vandalizing.]

Identify the voice of the underlined verb in each sentence by writing *active* or *passive.* Then, rewrite each passive-voice sentence in the active voice.

1. ______________ Photographs of the mountains were taken by Aunt Lila.

______________________________________________

2. ______________ Bill makes beautiful picture frames out of wood and handmade paper.

______________________________________________

3. ______________ Aunt Lila's photographs were put in the special frames by Bill.

______________________________________________

4. ______________ A group of these photos now hangs on the wall in the hallway.

______________________________________________

Name ______________________________ Date ______________

# Grammar: Revising Active and Passive Voice

## Assess

**A** Underline the verb in each sentence. Then, identify the voice of the verb as *A* for *active* or *P* for *passive.*

**1.** ______ The Greek festival was enjoyed by all the visitors.

**2.** ______ Hints of oregano, garlic, and cinnamon were detected in the air.

**3.** ______ Troupe Hellas performed traditional dances from Greece.

**4.** ______ The audience admired the costumes and the skill of the dancers.

**5.** ______ In the dining hall, volunteers served souvlaki, lamb, and more.

**6.** ______ Pastries such as baklava were offered for dessert or carryout.

**7.** ______ Vendors sold Greek sailor hats, jewelry, and handcrafted items.

**B** If the use of passive voice in a sentence is appropriate, write *okay.* If not, rewrite the sentence using the active voice.

**Example:** The rooftops were covered by a blanket of snow.

A blanket of snow covered the rooftops.

**1.** A powerful speech against the Stamp Act was delivered by Patrick Henry.

______________________________________________

**2.** Saint Augustine was founded in 1565 by a Spanish explorer.

______________________________________________

**3.** A bright smile was flashed by the orchestra conductor.

______________________________________________

**4.** Large pyramids with temples on top were built by the Toltec Indians.

______________________________________________

**5.** Some of the buildings in the historic district were restored years ago.

______________________________________________

Name ______________________________ Date ____________

# Writing: Introduction

## Practice

An **introduction** gives an overview of written or spoken material and grabs the attention of the audience. It might draw attention to the author's intentions in writing the piece and the methods the author uses to achieve those intentions. It also might mention the effect the piece will probably have on the audience.

**A** Read the introduction. Then, respond to the items that follow.

The poem "Annabel Lee" by Edgar Allan Poe is a haunting tribute to a beautiful maiden who has died. It describes the love shared by the narrator and the maiden, the illness that she suffered, and the sorrow he feels now that she is gone. As I read this poem aloud to you, notice the repetition of certain sounds, phrases, and rhythms. In addition, notice the rhyme pattern. Think about how all these elements contribute to the sorrowful mood of the poem.

1. Bracket the phrase that gives a brief overview of the poem.
2. Underline the sentence that gives details about the subject matter of the poem.
3. Name the methods used by the poet to achieve his intentions, according to the speaker of this introduction. ______________________________

______________________________

4. What effect does the speaker suggest the poem will have on the audience?

______________________________

**B** Think of one of your favorite recorded songs. Write an introduction you might use if you were getting ready to play that song for other students.

______________________________

______________________________

______________________________

______________________________

______________________________

______________________________

Name ______________________________ Date ____________

# Writing: Introduction

## Assess

**A** Read this passage from "The Highwayman" by Alfred Noyes. Then, respond to each item to help you prepare an introduction.

The wind was a torrent of darkness among the gusty trees,
The moon was a ghostly galleon tossed upon cloudy seas,
The road was a ribbon of moonlight over the purple moor,
And the highwayman came riding—
  Riding—riding—
The highwayman came riding, up to the old inn door.

1. Give three examples of vivid descriptions that the poet uses. ____________

2. Give an example of alliteration (repetition of initial sounds) from this poem.

3. Give an example of repetition. ____________

4. Which pairs of words rhyme at the ends of lines? ____________

5. What do you think a listener would most appreciate about this poem?

**B** Write an introduction, based on your answers above, that you might use before a poetry reading of "The Highwayman."

Name ______________________ Date __________

# Writing: Study for a Poem

## Practice

A **study for a poem** is a good way to prepare to write a poem. When you write a study for a poem, follow these steps:

- Choose a subject.
- Jot down objects associated with the subject.
- List sensory experiences (sights, sounds, smells, tastes, and touches) associated with some or all of the objects.
- Make comparisons (similes and metaphors) based on those sensory experiences.

To get ideas for similes and metaphors, you might want to complete sentences like this one: __?__ is like ____?____ because ____?____.

Read this study for a poem. Then, respond to the items that follow.

**Subject:** open-air market on Saturday morning
**Objects associated with subject:** fruits, vegetables, flowers, breads, cheeses, oils, vendors, stalls, shoppers, shopping bags, money, scales for weighing produce
**Sensory experiences:** sweet aromas of fruits and flowers; silky feel of oils; bright colors of oranges, apples, onions; sounds of coins changing hands
**Simile:** The peaches are like suede because of their downy covering.

**1.** What is the subject of this study for a poem? ______________________

______________________________________________

**2.** Name three objects associated with this subject. ______________________

______________________________________________

**3.** List three sensory experiences associated with the subject. ____________

______________________________________________

______________________________________________

**4.** Which sense is *not* represented in the sensory experiences listed in this study?

______________________________________________

**5.** Which of the five senses does the writer employ to show the similarity between peaches and suede? ______________________

Name ______________________________ Date ____________

# Writing: Study for a Poem

## Assess

Choose a setting that you enjoy. It might be a beach, the forest, a museum, a city street, a park, or any other place that you know well. With this setting in mind, answer these questions about it.

**1.** What setting did you choose? ____________________

**2.** What objects do you associate with this setting? Name at least eight.

______________________________

______________________________

______________________________

**3.** List sensory experiences associated with four of those objects.

______________________________

______________________________

______________________________

______________________________

______________________________

**4.** Based on the sensory experiences you listed, complete the following sentences:

______________ is/are like ______________ because

______________________________

______________ is/are like ______________ because

______________________________

______________ is/are like ______________ because

______________________________

______________ is/are like ______________ because

______________________________

Name ______________________________ Date ____________

# Writing: Problem-and-Solution Essay

## Practice

A **problem-and-solution essay** identifies a problem and presents one or more ways to solve it. A good problem-and-solution essay includes clear, easy-to-follow steps. It also gives evidence that explains why each step is important.

Read the problem and suggested solution below. Step 1 of the solution has been completed for you. Write three more steps for the solution. For each step, include evidence that explains why that step is important.

**Problem:** Middle school begins half an hour earlier than elementary school. New middle-school students are often late and are given detention if they are late too often.

**Solution:** New students need a plan to help them arrive at school on time.

**Step 1.** Before going to bed, make sure all your homework is packed up and you have everything you need for the next morning.

**Evidence:** Before I started doing this, I wasted precious time in the morning, running around looking for books, homework, and clean clothes, getting papers signed, and asking for lunch money.

**Step 2.** ______________________________

**Evidence:** ______________________________

______________________________

**Step 3.** ______________________________

**Evidence:** ______________________________

______________________________

**Step 4.** ______________________________

**Evidence:** ______________________________

______________________________

Name ______________________ Date ____________

# Writing: Problem-and-Solution Essay

## Assess

Read the following problem and the suggested solution. Fill in additional steps and evidence to complete the solution.

**Problem:** New immigrants to the United States might have trouble figuring out how to shop and find bargains in a huge American grocery store or shopping mall.

**Solution:** New immigrants need to make a plan before they go shopping in a grocery store or mall.

**Step 1.** Make a list of everything you need.

**Evidence:** ______________________

______________________

**Step 2.** ______________________

**Evidence:** ______________________

______________________

**Step 3.** ______________________

**Evidence:** ______________________

______________________

**Step 4.** ______________________

**Evidence:** ______________________

______________________

Name ______________________________ Date __________

# Reading: Paraphrase

## Practice

When you **paraphrase**, you restate an author's words in your own words. Paraphrasing is especially important in helping you understand poetry because poems often use words or phrases that are different from the way we speak.

Read this stanza from "The Courage That My Mother Had" by Edna St. Vincent Millay. Then, read the strategies for paraphrasing the poem.

1 The courage that my mother had
2 Went with her, and is with her still:
3 Rock from New England quarried;
4 Now granite in a granite hill.

- **Use the punctuation** in the poem to help you. Using punctuation helps you group words into complete, meaningful thoughts. For example, in the above poem, lines 1 and 2 represent one complete thought.
- **Stop and reread** difficult lines. When you stop and reread lines 1 and 2, you can get the meaning: "My mother will always have courage."
- **Look up** unfamiliar words, and replace them with words you know. For example, in line 3, the word *quarried* might be unfamiliar. You will understand the line better if you know that *quarried* means "dug out."
- **Restate** the lines in your own words. For example, you might paraphrase line 3: "Rock that has been dug out of the New England earth."
- **Reread** to see whether your paraphrase makes sense.

Read the last stanza of "The Courage That My Mother Had." Then, answer the questions.

Oh, if instead [of a piece of jewelry] she'd left me
The thing she took into the grave!—
That courage like a rock, which she
Has no more need of, and I have.

**1.** Why is the mother's courage compared to a rock? ______________________________

______________________________

**2.** Write a sentence or two to paraphrase this part of the poem. ______________

______________________________

______________________________

______________________________

Name ______________________ Date __________

# Reading: Paraphrase

## Assess

**A** Read the poem "Success is counted sweetest" by Emily Dickinson. Then, answer the questions. Use a dictionary if you need help.

Success is counted sweetest
By those who ne'er succeed.
To comprehend a nectar
Requires sorest need.

Not one of all the purple Host
Who took the Flag today
Can tell the definition
So clear of Victory

As he defeated—dying
On whose forbidden ear
The distant strains of triumph
Burst agonized and clear!

1. What is the meaning of the phrase "to comprehend a nectar," if you know that nectar is sweet and was thought to be the liquid of the gods in ancient times?

______________________

2. What is the most likely meaning of *sorest* in line 4? ______________________

3. What does the word *Host* in line 5 seem to refer to? Use lines 6–9 to help you understand its meaning. ______________________

4. Why does the writer choose to use the word *forbidden* to describe the ear of the person who is dying? Use lines 11–12 to help you understand its meaning.

______________________

______________________

______________________

**B** Use the lines below to write two or three sentences that paraphrase the poem above. Then, check them against the poem to make sure they effectively convey its meaning.

______________________

______________________

______________________

Name ______________________________ Date ____________

# Reading: Analyze Technical Directions

## Practice

Instruction booklets and manuals **are technical directions.** When you analyze technical directions you should notice each detail and complete the steps in order. Sometimes it is useful to paraphrase the information presented in a manual, or restate it in your own words, to help you understand directions.

**Read this excerpt from an instruction manual. Then, answer the questions.**

Installing Ink Cartridge into Printer

a. First, lift the top cover of the printer. The print-cartridge carriage will move to the center of the access area.
b. Raise the blue latch on the print carriage.
c. Insert the ink cartridge into the slot. Do not force the ink cartridge. Make sure the label is facing you.
d. Push the blue latch down and press to close.

**1.** Which is the best paraphrase of Step a?

**A.** The first thing you should do is open the printer and put the ink in.
**B.** The first thing you should do is take the cartridge out of the box.
**C.** Open the printer cover, and the print-cartridge carriage will move to the middle.
**D.** Lift the printer up, and put the print-cartridge carriage in the center.

**2.** Which of these is most important in analyzing the technical directions of the task described above?

**A.** memorizing the steps in order
**B.** skimming over the steps
**C.** understanding the order of the steps
**D.** knowing what a print-cartridge carriage is.

**3.** Which is the best paraphrase of Step c?

**A.** Push the ink cartridge into the slot, but do not push too hard. The label should be showing.
**B.** Make sure the ink cartridge goes into the right slot. Otherwise, the label will be wrong.
**C.** Do not push the ink cartridge too hard or it might break.
**D.** If the label is not facing you, you are putting the cartridge in wrong.

Name ______________________ Date ____________

# Reading: Analyze Technical Directions

## Assess

**Read the excerpt from an instruction manual. Then, answer the questions that follow.**

*Starting up*
Please note: You must fully charge your phone's battery prior to initial use!

*Installing the phone's battery*
Insert the bottom of the battery into the opening on the back of the phone. The battery is fully inserted when the latch clicks.

*Charging the phone's battery*
Please note: Use only the desktop charger provided with the phone. Using any other charger may damage your phone or your battery.

1. Plug the charger into a wall outlet.
2. Insert the phone with an installed battery into the charging slot. The red light indicates that the battery is charging. When the battery is fully charged, the green light will go on.

**1.** Which of these is most important in analyzing these technical directions?

**A.** paying attention to the details and completing the steps in order
**B.** memorizing the steps and doing well on the quiz
**C.** skimming the instructions for important words
**D.** getting the main idea

**2.** What is the best paraphrase of "Please note: You must fully charge your phone's battery prior to initial use!"?

**A.** Important: Put your initials on your phone.
**B.** Important: Charge your phone if you want to use it.
**C.** Important: You have to charge your phone's battery completely before you use it the first time.
**D.** Important: Use the batteries every time you use your phone.

**3.** What is the best paraphrase of Step 2 of "Charging the phone's battery"?

**A.** Put the phone into the slot, and watch the red light.
**B.** Put the phone without a battery into the charger, and wait for the green light.
**C.** Put the phone with the battery into the charging slot. The red light will go on. The green light will go on when the charging is done.
**D.** Put the phone battery in, and wait for the green light to come on.

Name ______________________________ Date ______________

# Literary Analysis: Lyric and Narrative Poetry

## Practice

There are a few main types of poetry, including the following:

- **lyric poetry** expresses the thoughts and feelings of the speaker, the person who "says" the poem. "Fog" by Carl Sandburg is an example of a lyric poem: *The fog comes / on little cat feet. / It sits looking / over harbor and city / on silent haunches / and then moves on.*
- **narrative poetry** tells a story. Like a short story, a narrative poem has a setting, characters, plot, and conflict. These lines from "Annabel Lee" by Edgar Allan Poe are an example of a narrative poem: *It was many and many a year ago, / In a kingdom by the sea / That a maiden there lived whom you / may know. / By the name of Annabel Lee.*

**Read each excerpt. Then, answer the questions.**

Listen, my children, and you shall hear
Of the midnight ride of Paul Revere
. . .
He said to his friend, "If the British
march
By land or sea from the town to-night
Hang a lantern aloft in the belfry arch
Of the North Church tower as a
signal light, —

—from "Paul Revere's Ride" by
Henry Wadsworth Longfellow

Between two hills
The old town stands.
The houses loom
And the roofs and trees
And the dusk and the dark,
The damp and the dew
Are there.

—from "Between Two Hills"
by Carl Sandburg

1. Which poem tells a story? ______________________________
2. What is the subject of the narrative poem? ______________________________
3. What is the subject of the lyrical poem? ______________________________
4. Summarize the thoughts and feelings of the speaker in the lyrical poem.

______________________________

______________________________

______________________________

Name ______________________________ Date __________

# Literary Analysis: Lyric and Narrative Poetry

## Assess

**A** Respond to each item.

**1.** What is the main purpose of a narrative poem? ____________

**2.** Give two examples of elements that are found in both a narrative poem and a short story. ____________

**3.** What is the main purpose of a lyric poem? ____________

**4.** In lyric poetry, what is the role of the "speaker"? ____________

**B** Read each excerpt. Then, answer the questions.

Excerpt #1
Loveliest of trees, the cherry now
Is hung with bloom along the bough,
And stands about the woodland ride
Wearing white for Eastertide.
—from "Loveliest of trees, the cherry now"
by A. E. Housman

Excerpt #2
Once upon a midnight dreary, while I pondered, weak and weary,
Over many a quaint and curious volume of forgotten lore,
While I nodded, nearly napping, suddenly there came a tapping,
As of some one gently rapping, rapping at my chamber door.
—from "The Raven"
by Edgar Allan Poe

**1.** Which excerpt is the beginning of a narrative poem? ____________

**2.** Based on this excerpt, what is the subject of the narrative poem? ____________

____________

____________

**3.** What is the subject of the lyrical poem? ____________

**4.** Summarize the thoughts and feelings of the speaker in the lyrical poem.

____________

____________

____________

Name ______________________________ Date ____________

# Literary Analysis: Imagery

## Practice

**Imagery** is language that uses **images**—words or phrases that appeal to the senses of sight, hearing, smell, taste, and touch. Writers use imagery for several reasons:

- to create moods
- to express emotions
- to help readers imagine sights, sounds, textures, tastes, and smells

An image can appeal to more than one sense. For example, "the icy snow crunched under Sally's boots" appeals to the senses of touch ("icy snow") and hearing ("crunched").

Read the poem below. Then, tell what kinds of imagery it uses by writing a sense word or phrase in the corresponding column in the chart. The first entry has been made for you. One column may remain empty.

The wind billowing out the seat of my britches
My feet crackling splinters of glass and dried putty,
The half-grown chrysanthemums staring up like accusers,
Up through the streaked glass, flashing with sunlight,
A few white clouds all rushing eastward,
A line of elms plunging and tossing like horses,
And everyone, everyone pointing up and shouting!
—"Child on Top of a Greenhouse" by Theodore Roethke

| Sight | Hearing | Smell | Taste | Touch |
|---|---|---|---|---|
| | | | | wind |

Name ______________________ Date __________

# Literary Analysis: Imagery

## Assess

**A** Read each example of imagery. Then, choose the sense to which it most clearly appeals.

**1.** The summer wind gently brushed against my face.

**A.** sight **B.** hearing **C.** smell **D.** touch **E.** taste

**2.** The sweet perfume of night-blooming jasmine filled the air.

**A.** sight **B.** hearing **C.** smell **D.** touch **E.** taste

**3.** The spectacular pinks, reds, and yellows in the rose garden took Anna by surprise.

**A.** sight **B.** hearing **C.** smell **D.** touch **E.** taste

**4.** With a deafening roar, the crowd cheered for their victorious team.

**A.** sight **B.** hearing **C.** smell **D.** touch **E.** taste

**5.** The ice cream was cold, sweet, and fruity.

**A.** sight **B.** hearing **C.** smell **D.** touch **E.** taste

**B** Read the following poem. Then, tell what kinds of imagery it uses by listing the sense words or phrases from the poem in the corresponding column in the chart. One column may remain empty.

I'm going out to clean the pasture spring; / I'll only stop to rake the leaves away / (And wait to watch the water clear, I may): / I shan't be gone long.—You come too.

I'm going out to fetch the little calf / That's standing by the mother. It's so young / It totters when she licks it with her tongue. / I shan't be gone long.—You come too.

—"The Pasture" by Robert Frost

| Sight | Hearing | Smell | Taste | Touch |
|---|---|---|---|---|
| | | | | |

Name ______________________________ Date ______________

# Literary Analysis: Comparing Types of Description

## Practice

Poets use words creatively to produce different levels of meaning.

- **Literal language:** the actual, everyday meanings of words
- **Figurative language:** figures of speech, images that appeal to the readers' senses, symbols, and analogies

An **analogy** compares two or more things that are similar in some ways but are otherwise not alike. For example, a poem might describe "a voyage of discovery." The literal meaning might be sailing to a distant place. However, the voyage could also be interpreted as an analogy—a spiritual or emotional "voyage" in which a person learns something important about life.

Read the poem "A Fence" by Carl Sandburg. Then, respond to each item.

Now the stone house on the lake front is finished and the
workmen are beginning the fence.
The palings are made of iron bars with steel points that
can stab the life out of any man who falls on them.
As a fence, it is a masterpiece, and will shut off the rabble
and all vagabonds and hungry men and all wandering
children looking for a place to play.
Passing through the bars and over the steel points will go
nothing except Death and the Rain and To-morrow.

**1.** What is the literal subject of the poem? ______________________

**2.** Describe that subject in your own words, based on the description in the poem.

______________________________________________________________

______________________________________________________________

**3.** What is the everyday purpose of the thing described in the poem? ________

______________________________________________________________

**4.** Now, think of the poem as an analogy. Which is the best expression of the deeper, symbolic meaning of the poem's subject? Circle the letter of your answer choice.

**A.** a barrier that prevents dogs from digging in the homeowner's garden
**B.** a protection against falling into the lake
**C.** a protective wall against wandering children
**D.** a barrier to isolate wealthy people from everything in the outside world

Name ______________________ Date ____________

# Literary Analysis: Comparing Types of Description

## Assess

**A** Circle the letter of the best answer.

**1.** Which reflects the actual, everyday meaning of words?

**A.** imagery
**B.** literal language
**C.** figurative language
**D.** analogy

**2.** Which reflects a deeper, symbolic meaning for words?

**A.** literal language
**B.** figurative language
**C.** expository writing
**D.** jargon

**3.** Which is the best example of the use of analogy in a poem?

**A.** a comparison of an old house and a new house
**B.** a comparison of a bright bluebird and a dark crow
**C.** a comparison of a deserted island and a sense of loneliness
**D.** a comparison of a young boy and a tired old man

**B** Read the poem "Choose" by Carl Sandburg. Then, answer the questions.

The single clenched fist lifted and ready,
Or the open asking hand held out and waiting.
Choose:
For we meet by one or the other.

**1.** The literal subject of this poem involves two people greeting each other.

What literal "choice" do they have? ______________________

**2.** What does "clenched fist lifted and ready" suggest about mood?

______________________

**3.** What does "open asking hand held out and waiting" suggest about mood?

______________________

**4.** Circle the letter of the best choice to complete this sentence: The deeper, symbolic meaning of the "choice" is a choice between being

**A.** enemies or friends.
**B.** manager or employee.
**C.** a teacher or a student.
**D.** a child or an adult.

Name ________________________________ Date ____________

# Vocabulary: Prefixes *in-* and *trans-* and Word Roots *-cede-/-ceed-* and *-vert-*

## Practice

A **root** is the basic unit of meaning of a word. A **prefix** is one or more syllables added to the beginning of a word or word root to form a new word with a different meaning. Study these examples.

Examples:

| Root or Prefix | Meaning | Words with the Root |
|---|---|---|
| *in-* (prefix) | not, lacking | insufficient, inconsiderate, incredible |
| *trans-* (prefix) | through, beyond, change | transfer, transmit, transition |
| *-cede-* or *-ceed-* (root) | go, yield | proceed, recede, exceed |
| *-vert-* | turn, top | invert, divert, vertical |

**A** Replace each underlined word or phrase with the most appropriate word from the chart above.

**1.** ________________ We had too little evidence to make an informed decision.

**2.** ________________ I try not to go over the speed limit on highways.

**3.** ________________ I might need to switch to another school if we change neighborhoods.

**4.** ________________ I tried to redirect my guests' attention from my messy kitchen.

**B** Circle the letter of the word that best completes each sentence.

**1.** I ________________ in my goal of making the basketball team.

**A.** inverted **B.** transmitted **C.** succeeded

**2.** Although he means well, he is often ________________ to other people's feelings.

**A.** excessive **B.** incredible **C.** insensitive

**3.** We decided to ________________ our basement to a family room.

**A.** concede **B.** convert **C.** transfer

Name ____________________ Date __________

# Vocabulary: Prefixes *in-* and *trans-* and Word Roots *-cede-/-ceed-* and *-vert-*

## Assess

**A** Add the prefix to each base word. Write the meaning of the new word on the line. Then use the new word in a sentence.

**1.** plant + trans- = ____________, meaning ____________

____________________

**2.** direct + in- = ____________, meaning ____________

____________________

**3.** adequate + in- = ____________, meaning ____________

____________________

**4.** action + trans- = ____________, meaning ____________

____________________

**B** Revise each sentence so that the underlined vocabulary word is used logically. Be sure not to change the vocabulary word.

**1.** I was pleased by his <u>ingratitude</u> for all the favors I had done him.

____________________

**2.** The <u>vertical</u> stripes ran all the way along the wall from side to side.

____________________

**3.** I had to flip ahead to the <u>preceding</u> chapter to remember what had just happened.

____________________

**4.** The politician was forced to <u>concede</u> that he had won the election.

____________________

**5.** I needed a <u>translator</u> because I was familiar with the local language.

____________________

Name ______________________________ Date __________

# Grammar: Prepositions and Prepositional Phrases

## Practice

A **preposition** shows the relationship between two words or two phrases. In *Sarah was working in her office, and Jane was working in hers*, the first preposition *in* relates the noun *office* to *Sarah*: It tells where Sarah is. The second *in* relates the pronoun *hers* to *Jane*. It tells where Jane is.

Common prepositions include *above, across, behind, below, during, for, from, near, of, on, over, under,* and *with*. Compound prepositions, which consist of more than one word, include *ahead of, because of, instead of.*

A **prepositional phrase** begins with a preposition and ends with the noun, noun phrase, or pronoun related to it. In this example, the prepositional phrase is underlined: *We were sitting* ***on** the front porch.*

**A** Underline each prepositional phrase. (Some sentences have more than one.)

1. Snacks before dinner may spoil your appetite.
2. We agreed to the plan without any hesitation.
3. The wagon in the barn once belonged to my grandfather.
4. Paul Revere rode through the countryside on his horse.
5. We walked along the riverbank until sundown.
6. Mom found my keys in the clothes hamper.
7. The wood stove in the kitchen heats the whole house.
8. Jerry hasn't changed much since last year.
9. Carrie brought her camera with her to the museum.
10. Steam sometimes rises from warm water.

**B** Fill in each blank with a suitable preposition.

1. The news reporter stood ______________ the candidate.
2. Lisa sat ______________ Kristin and Jackie.
3. The squirrels chased each other ______________ the park.
4. The cat raced ______________ the stairs.

Name ______________________ Date __________

# Grammar: Prepositions and Prepositional Phrases

## Assess

Underline the prepositional phrase in each sentence. Then, rewrite the sentence with a different prepositional phrase.

1. We planted marigolds around the vegetable garden.

_______________________________________________

2. The huge dog dragged his master along the path.

_______________________________________________

3. The person standing near the kitchen seems angry.

_______________________________________________

4. Every morning he passes by on roller blades.

_______________________________________________

5. Katherine walked out the door.

_______________________________________________

6. The child played outside the pool.

_______________________________________________

7. The runners raced up the hill.

_______________________________________________

8. No one can make that horse go over a bridge.

_______________________________________________

9. An old house near the glen caught fire last night.

_______________________________________________

10. He hid the money in a tin can.

_______________________________________________

Name ______________________________ Date __________

# Grammar: Infinitive Phrases

## Practice

An **infinitive** is a form of a verb that comes after the word *to* and acts as a noun, an adjective, or an adverb.

| | |
|---|---|
| NOUN | Grace wants **to become** a dolphin trainer. [direct object of *wants*] |
| ADJECTIVE | Sea World is one place **to see** dolphins. [modifies the noun *place*] |
| ADVERB | Are training methods easy **to learn**? [modifies the adjective *easy*] |

An **infinitive phrase** consists of an infinitive plus its modifiers and complements. The entire phrase acts as a single part of speech (a noun, an adjective, or an adverb).

| | |
|---|---|
| NOUN | **To travel in space** is an ambitious goal. [The infinitive phrase functions as the subject of the sentence. The infinitive *To travel* is modified by the prepositional phrase *in space*.] |
| ADJECTIVE | Neil Armstrong was the first person **to walk on the moon.** [The infinitive phrase modifies the noun *person*. The infinitive *to walk* is modified by the prepositional phrase *on the moon*.] |
| ADVERB | The astronauts prepared **to board the space shuttle.** [The infinitive phrase modifies the verb *prepared*. The infinitive *to board* has a complement, *the space shuttle*.] |

Underline the infinitive phrase in each sentence. Then, tell whether it is used as a *noun*, an *adjective*, or an *adverb*.

1. ____________ To become a professional dancer requires dedication and hard work.

2. ____________ Ms. Furr may have an opportunity to see the Grand Canyon.

3. ____________ The best person to speak to about zoning is Council Member Sanchez.

4. ____________ Her goal is to climb Mount McKinley.

5. ____________ Mr. Watson wants to visit Cambodia next year.

6. ____________ Commuters cross the Golden Gate Bridge to get to San Francisco.

7. ____________ Tomorrow would be a good day to take a long bike ride.

8. ____________ Are you ready to leave for the Earth Day Festival?

Name ______________________________ Date ____________

# Grammar: Infinitive Phrases

## Assess

**A** Underline the infinitive or infinitive phrase in each sentence.

1. To find information about Peru, check the Internet and other sources.
2. I would like to read more poems by Alice Walker.
3. Basic yoga poses are not very difficult to learn.
4. Kangaroos use their powerful hind legs to leap over obstacles.
5. The next student to propose a solution was Evan.
6. To master the martial art of judo takes practice and patience.
7. The person to ask would be Manuel.
8. Autumn is a great time to take a scenic tour of New Hampshire.

**B** Use each infinitive phrase below in an original sentence. Try to vary your sentences as much as possible.

**Example:** to succeed as an artist

To succeed as an artist takes commitment and talent.

1. to hike to the summit of Wheeler Peak

______________________________

2. to get into a good college

______________________________

3. to try new hobbies and activities

______________________________

4. to travel to Brazil

______________________________

5. to meet the new neighbors

______________________________

Name ______________________ Date __________

# Grammar: Revising to Vary Sentence Patterns

## Practice

When you review your writing, you might notice that many of your sentences begin with nouns. In most cases, these nouns are probably the subject and are followed by the verb. To avoid this dull subject-verb pattern, try varying your sentence beginnings. For example, you can start a sentence with an adjective, an adverb, or a prepositional phrase.

| | |
|---|---|
| *DULL* | Sam walked to the stage to accept his award. |
| ADJECTIVE | **Thrilled,** Sam walked to the stage to accept his award. |
| ADVERB | **Finally** Sam walked to the stage to accept his award. |
| PREPOSITIONAL PHRASE | **After a long pause,** Sam walked to the stage to accept his award. |

Another way to vary sentence patterns, and to pack more information into your sentences, is to include appositives and appositive phrases. An **appositive** is a noun or pronoun placed beside another noun or pronoun to define or explain it. An **appositive phrase** consists of an appositive and its modifiers.

| | |
|---|---|
| APPOSITIVE | My *cousin* **Belinda** makes origami swans for gifts. |
| APPOSITIVE PHRASE | They have a new *dog*, **a beagle mix from the shelter.** |

Revise each sentence according to the directions in parentheses.

1. The park was crowded on that early Saturday morning. [Move the prepositional phrase to the beginning.]

______________________________________________

2. Sara approached the soccer field. [Add an adjective at the beginning.]

______________________________________________

3. She asked the coach to let her try out for the team. [Add an adverb at the beginning.]

______________________________________________

4. She emptied her gym bag's contents onto the grass. [Add an appositive phrase.]

______________________________________________

Name ______________________________ Date ____________

# Grammar: Revising to Vary Sentence Patterns

## Assess

**A** Underline the appositive or appositive phrase in each sentence.

1. Daniel showed us photos of one of England's major tourist attractions, Stonehenge.
2. Stonehenge, an ancient monument, consists of huge stones arranged in circles.
3. The monument is located in Wiltshire, a county in southwestern England.
4. In the 1950s, British archaeologist R.J.C. Atkinson began excavating the site.
5. At Stonehenge, ancient tribes held religious ceremonies linked to the summer solstice, June 21.

**B** Revise each sentence according to the directions in parentheses.

1. Darren somberly lumbered out of the room. [Move the adverb *somberly* to the beginning.]

   ______________________________

2. The puppy flopped down on the rug and immediately fell asleep. [Add an adjective at the beginning.]

   ______________________________

3. We went to the back yard to watch the meteor shower. [Add a prepositional phrase at the beginning.]

   ______________________________

4. Next week our team will take on the Lakeland Tigers. [Add an appositive phrase.]

   ______________________________

5. A team of French and American scientists found the wreckage of the *Titanic* in 1985. [Move the prepositional phrase *in 1985* to the beginning.]

   ______________________________

   ______________________________

Name ______________________________ Date __________

# Spelling: Words With Prefixes and Suffixes

## Practice

A **prefix** is a syllable, group of syllables, or word added to the *beginning* of another word to change its meaning. Adding a prefix does not change the spelling of the base word: mis + understand = misunderstand.

A **suffix** is a syllable or syllables added to the *end* of a word to change its meaning. Unlike a prefix, a suffix sometimes does change the spelling of the base word:

- ✓ Drop the final *e* of the base word if the suffix begins with a vowel: collapse + -ible = collapsible.
- ✓ If, however, the suffix begins with a consonant, do *not* drop the final *e* of the base word: taste + -less = tasteless.
- ✓ If the base word ends with a consonant followed by a *y* (for example, *hazy*), change the *y* to *i* *except* when the suffix begins with *i*: hazy/haziness; hurry/hurried; hurry/hurrying.
- ✓ If the suffix begins with a vowel, double the final consonant of the base word *if*
  1. the base word has only one syllable: knit + -ing = knitting.
  2. the base word ends in a single vowel followed by a single consonant *and* the accent falls on the last syllable: occur + -ence = occurrence.

*Note:* Some suffixes, such as *-ance* and *-ence* or *-able* and *-ible*, sound the same but vary in spelling: collapsible/immovable.

Write the word from the word box that is related to each list word below. If the list word has a prefix, underline the prefix. If the list word has a suffix, underline the suffix.

| dizziness | immovable | reference | illegal | reenact |
|---|---|---|---|---|
| impractical | collapsible | occurrence | tasteless | traveled |

1. taste ____________ 4. move ____________

2. refer ____________ 5. legal ____________

3. travel ____________

Name ______________________ Date __________

# Spelling: Words With Prefixes and Suffixes

## Assess

**A** Add the indicated suffix to each word. Write the new word on the line.

1. taste + -less ______________
2. dizzy + -ness ______________
3. occur + -ence ______________
4. collapse + -ible ______________

**B** Add the prefix to each word. Write the new word on the line.

1. im- + practical ______________
2. re- + enact ______________
3. im- + movable ______________
4. il- + legal ______________

**C** Circle the letter of the sentence that contains no spelling mistakes.

1. **A.** The fallen tree was immoveable.
   **B.** Pure water is tastless.
   **C.** Littering in the park is illegal.
   **D.** His wild schemes were immpractical.

2. **A.** Every occurence in my dream seemed crazy.
   **B.** If you enjoy dizziness, then this roller coaster is for you.
   **C.** Last summer we travilled to Canada.
   **D.** The film tried to renact the crime just as it happened.

3. **A.** The comedy routine was hilarious, but some found it tasteless.
   **B.** I did most of my research in the referrence section of the library.
   **C.** Although his actions were not ileggal, they were still not moral.
   **D.** How do those figure skaters avoid dizzinness after those spins?

4. **A.** The bullet train travaled at 150 miles per hour.
   **B.** The collapsable umbrella fit right in my pocket.
   **C.** A stubborn person is like an imovable object.
   **D.** The architect's design was beautiful but impractical.

Name ______________________________ Date __________

# Writing: Lyric or Narrative Poem

## Practice

Two major forms of poetry are **lyric poetry** and **narrative poetry.**

- A **lyric poem** expresses the thoughts and feelings of a single speaker—the person "saying" the poem—to create a unified impression about a single incident or experience. It has a musical quality and uses vivid images.
- A **narrative poem** tells a story in verse and has all the elements of a short story—characters, setting, conflict, and plot.

**A** Read these lines from a lyric poem. Then, follow the directions.

Softly glowing embers warm the quiet, darkening room
When through my cabin door you crash and stomp,
Tugging off hat and gloves, trailing freezing air,
A current of cold in a warm lagoon

1. Describe the feelings expressed in this poem. ______________________________

______________________________

2. Underline two vivid images in the poem.
3. Add two more lines to the above poem. Include at least one vivid image.

______________________________

______________________________

**B** Read these lines from a narrative poem. Then, follow the directions.

"Oh, Donna-Lee, come play with me,"
My sister did request.
I quickly spun into a run
To flee the little pest.

1. What characters are introduced in the poem? ______________________________
2. Describe the conflict introduced in the poem. ______________________________

______________________________

3. On a separate sheet of paper or on the back of this page, write four more lines of the above poem. Introduce at least one new character and one detail that describes the setting.

Name ______________________ Date __________

# Writing: Lyric or Narrative Poem

## Assess

**A** Answer one of the following sets of questions to help you write a lyric or narrative poem about a rainy day.

**For a Lyric Poem:**

- Who will the speaker be in your poem? ______________________
- What thoughts and feelings does the rain evoke for this speaker? ______________________
- What images will you include to convey those thoughts and feelings? ______________________

**For a Narrative Poem:**

- What story will you tell in your poem? ______________________
- What characters will your poem include? ______________________
- In what setting will the events of your story occur? ______________________

**B** Use the information above to write your poem on the following lines.

Name ______________________________ Date ____________

# Writing: Review

## Practice

A **review** of a literary work is an assessment of its strengths and weaknesses. When you review a poem or collection of poems, you can evaluate the poetry based on sound, word choice, and imagery.

- To evaluate the sound of a poem, read it aloud and decide how its sounds and rhythms match its subject. For example, the line "A flea and a fly in a flue" uses a playful, bouncy rhythm. The repetition of the "fl" sound suits the silliness of the poem.
- To evaluate word choice and imagery, determine whether the poems use vivid and appropriate words and images. For example, in Eve Merriam's poem "Simile: Willow and Ginkgo," the line "The willow is sleek as a velvet-nosed calf" uses strong imagery that appeals to the senses of sight and touch. The artful word choices and natural imagery suit this lyric poem.

When you write a review of a poem or a collection of poems, support your opinions with references to specific lines from the poetry. Offer your overall opinion of each poem you are reviewing.

Read the review. Then, answer the questions.

Some poetry is art, and some poetry is pure nonsense. Let's look at two limericks by Edward Lear, "The Young Lady of Bute" and "The Old Person in Gray." At the heart of these limericks are the humorous word choice and outlandish imagery. The old person in gray, who "purchased two parrots / and fed them with carrots," or the young lady of Bute, who "played several jigs / to her uncle's white pigs," have made readers chuckle for generations.

1. What is the reviewer's opinion of the poetry? ______________________

2. Does the reviewer feel that word choices and imagery of these poems are appropriate? Explain your answer. ______________________

______________________________________________

3. The complete limerick "The Young Lady of Bute" follows. Read the poem, and then write the next paragraph of the review by evaluating the sounds and rhythms in it. Use a separate sheet of paper or the back of this page.

There was a Young Lady of Bute, / Who played on a silver-gilt flute; / She played several jigs, / To her uncle's white pigs, / That amusing Young Lady of Bute.

Name ______________________ Date __________

# Writing: Review

## Assess

Read the poems. Then, answer the questions and complete the activities that follow.

**Poem A**

After the moon sets
slow through the forest, shadows
drift and disappear.
—Buson

**Poem B**

Let the rain kiss you
Let the rain beat upon your head
with silver liquid drops.
Let the rain sing you a lullaby.
—from "Rain Song"
by Langston Hughes

1. What is the subject of Poem A? ______________________

2. Describe an image in the poem. ______________________

3. Is the image suitable to the subject of the poem? Explain. ______________________

4. What is the subject of Poem B? ______________________

5. Describe an element of the sound of poem B, such as the repeated words or letter-sounds, rhythm, or rhyme. ______________________

6. Is the sound element that you described appropriate to the subject of the poem? Explain. ______________________

7. On a separate sheet of paper or the back of this page, write a review of the two poems. Evaluate the sound and imagery in each poem, including whether the sound and imagery are suitable to the subjects of the poems. Offer your opinion of each poem.

Name ______________________ Date __________

# Writing: Comparison-and-Contrast Essay

## Practice

In a **comparison-and-contrast essay,** a writer tells about similarities and differences between two or more things. To show these similarities and differences, the writer gives facts and details about each thing. A well-written comparison-and-contrast essay includes these elements:

- a topic involving two or more subjects
- subjects that have some important similarities and some important differences
- facts and descriptions that show how the subjects are alike and different
- an organizational pattern that helps readers understand the comparison. In **block organization,** or subject-by-subject organization, the writer presents all the features of one subject and then all the features of the second subject. In **point-by-point organization,** the writer discusses one point about both subjects and then moves on to a second point.

Read the passage. Then, respond to each item below.

Cats do not mind being left alone during the day. They are so independent, they may not even come when you call them.

Dogs, on the other hand, need companionship. They like to play with their owners and can be trained to come, fetch, and beg.

1. Circle the type of organization used in this example.

   block point-by-point

2. What are the two points of comparison in the example?

   ______________________

   ______________________

3. What could be a third point of comparison between cats and dogs?

   ______________________

4. On a separate sheet of paper or the back of this page, write a paragraph in which you compare two animals. Use at least two points of comparison. You may use either block organization or point-by point organization.

Name ______________________________ Date ____________

# Writing: Comparison-and-Contrast Essay

## Assess

Circle one of the following topics. Then, complete the activities that follow.

two characters in a movie you have seen
two sports or activities
two places you have visited
two people you know
two seasons or times of day
two items of your choice

**1.** Write your specific topic on the line. ______________________________

**2.** List facts and details about each subject.

______________________ ______________________

______________________ ______________________

______________________ ______________________

______________________ ______________________

**3.** List three similarities and/or differences that you will write about.

______________________________________________

______________________________________________

______________________________________________

**4.** Choose an organization—either block or point-by-point—for your essay.

______________________________________________

**5.** Write the first paragraph of your comparison-and-contrast essay below.

______________________________________________

______________________________________________

______________________________________________

______________________________________________

______________________________________________

______________________________________________

______________________________________________

______________________________________________

Name ______________________ Date __________

# Reading: Draw Conclusions

## Practice

A **conclusion** is a reasonable opinion or decision you reach by analyzing several facts and details. To draw conclusions about a play, notice what characters say and do. Pay attention to how characters interact with each other. Then, use your own experience and knowledge about people to assess this information and make a decision about the characters.

Read the example. Then, answer the questions.

Sarah: Could you please get the cake pan from the upper shelf? I can't reach it.
Jean: Here it is. Is that everything we need?
Sarah: Let me check the recipe. I think we're ready to start mixing.
Jean: Shouldn't we turn the oven on now? Mom usually does that so the oven preheats while she's mixing the batter.
Sarah: You're right, she does. In fact, that's what the recipe says, too.

**1.** What do you think Sarah and Jean are doing? Circle the letter of the best answer.

**A.** performing an experiment
**B.** playing a trick on their mother
**C.** baking a cake
**D.** fixing dinner

**2.** Who do you think is taller, Sarah or Jean? ______________________

**3.** Why do you think so?

______________________________________________

______________________________________________

**4.** Which of the following conclusions does *not* seem correct, based on the interaction of the characters? Circle the letter of the best answer.

**A.** Sarah and Jean work well together.
**B.** Sarah and Jean are sisters.
**C.** The girls are skilled bakers.
**D.** The girls have learned from their mother.

Name ______________________________ Date ____________

# Reading: Draw Conclusions

## Assess

**Read the following passage. Then, answer the questions.**

**Kevin:** What is that roaring sound? I've been hearing it ever since I got here.
**Todd:** Roaring sound? [*Listens*] Oh, you mean *that*. That, farm boy, is the sound of the Pacific Ocean. And those crying sounds? Seagulls. And that blue thing over our heads? Out here we call it "sky."
**Kevin:** Very funny, cousin. I never realized you lived so close to the ocean. You'll have to teach me how to surf, right away.
**Todd:** Sure thing, Kev, but you got in late last night. We've got all summer, after all. Let's take it easy today. I want to hear about your thousand-mile journey in a twelve-year-old car. What was your junior year like? Does your little sister still wear braces?
**Kevin:** Can we at least wade in the surf while we talk?

**1.** Based on details in this passage, has Kevin visited Todd's home before?

______________________________

**2.** What are two details that helped you draw this conclusion?

______________________________

______________________________

**3.** Which conclusion does *not* seem correct, based on the passage? Circle the letter of the best answer.

**A.** Todd likes to tease his cousin.
**B.** The cousins live far apart.
**C.** Kevin is afraid of the ocean.
**D.** The cousins are good friends.

**4.** What details in the passage helped you answer question 3?

______________________________

______________________________

**5.** Which of these best describes a conclusion? Circle the letter of the best answer.

**A.** a prediction
**B.** an argument
**C.** a decision
**D.** a cause

Name ______________________________ Date ____________

# Reading: Compare and Contrast Features and Elements

## Practice

Different types of texts use different techniques to convey information. For example, a contract might contain numbered lists. Comparing and contrasting these features and elements will help you better understand the meanings of informational texts.

Review the document below, a portion of an athletic participation contract. Then, answer the questions that follow.

**Student Athletic Participation Contract**

Please Print – complete all items
Sport/Team______________________________
Name ______________________ ID # ____________
Birth date ______________ Grade ________

Stipulations

The student-athlete and his or her parent/guardian have received and read the *Student-Parent Athletic Participation Information.* Based on this information, the student and parent/guardian understand and agree to the following:

1. I understand the eligibility regulations required for participation.
2. I affirm that the student has satisfied all of the eligibility requirements, including age, residence, and academics.
3. I affirm that the student will exert effort to maintain a high level of academic achievement.
4. I understand there is potential for serious injury associated with participation in a sport.
5. I affirm that the student will not participate in hazing at any time, of any nature.

**1.** What have the parent/guardian and student agreed that they have read?

______________________________________________

**2.** What is the guideline about hazing? ______________________

Name ______________________________ Date ____________

# Reading: Compare and Contrast Features and Elements

## Assess

The document that follows provides guidelines for participation in recycling of household items. Read the document and then answer the questions that follow.

**Guidelines for Recycling**

*Residents must use the special bins provided. Place bins curbside before 7 a.m. on your designated recycling pickup day.*

The following items may be recycled:

✓ plastic containers with number 1–7 in triangles
✓ plastic bags
✓ aerosol cans (empty and with nozzle removed)
✓ aluminum cans and pie tins
✓ glass jars and bottles (rinsed, with lids removed)
✓ newspaper and regular office paper
✓ tin and steel containers
✓ magazines, catalogs, junk mail, and telephone books

The following items may NOT be recycled:

✗ auto parts and motor oil containers
✗ foil wrapping paper
✗ light bulbs
✗ coat hangers (plastic or wire)
✗ clothing and shoes
✗ plastic utensils

**1.** What technique is used to reinforce these recycling guidelines for what may and may not be recycled? ______________________________

**2.** What technique is used to make the rules for type of bins stand out? ______

**3.** Make a generalization about what types of items may be recycled. __________

**4.** What is the intended audience for these guidelines? ______________________

Name ______________________ Date __________

## Literary Analysis: Stage Directions (Setting and Character)

### Practice

**Stage directions** are notes in a script that tell how a play should be performed. They help a reader imagine how a play would look and sound when performed onstage. Stage directions

- tell how the characters feel, move, and speak.
- describe scenery, lighting, and sound.
- are usually printed in italics and put in brackets, as shown below.

[*A woman stands at a kitchen sink, humming as she washes dishes. Evening sunlight slants through the windows. Offstage, a steady, continuous hammering sound is heard. Suddenly, there is a cry of alarm, followed by a loud thud and a comically extended clash and tinkle of breaking glass. The woman rushes off stage left, dishcloth still in her hand.*]

The stage directions above offer the following information about the story:

The **characters** on stage: a woman at a kitchen sink

The **movements** of the characters: washing dishes, rushing off stage

The **lighting:** slanting evening sunlight

The **sounds:** hammering, a cry, a thud, glass tinkling

Read the selection below. Then, answer the questions.

[*Darkness, pierced by a baby's crying. A door creaks open, a light clicks on: instantly the crying stops. The light reveals a sleepy man in pajamas standing in a nursery. He shuffles over to the crib, peers at the silent baby, and then returns to the door. He switches off the light. The crying begins immediately. He switches on the light; the crying stops. This happens three more times. Finally, the man leaves the light on. Silence. The man tiptoes out, closing the door.*]

1. What can you tell about the time and setting of the play from this passage?

______________________________

2. What are the most important elements of these stage directions? Circle the letter of the best answer.

   A. characters' costumes and actions
   B. characters' words and emotions
   C. lighting and sound effects
   D. details of setting

Name ____________________ Date ____________

## Literary Analysis: Stage Directions (Setting and Character)

### Assess

**Read the following stage direction. Then, answer the questions.**

*[The set is a brightly lit, empty locker room. A door at center stage opens, letting in a muffled crowd noise and the sound of a band playing. Ten basketball players file in slowly. The door closes, cutting off all noise. The players are silent. They sag to their benches in postures of weariness. Some drape their heads in towels; others merely stare at the floor. No one moves to unlace or undress. The silence lengthens. Finally, someone begins to murmur, but a fist savagely bashes a locker door, producing a stunning metallic din that stops all words. It is still too soon to talk.]*

**1.** What information is included in these stage directions?

**A.** the characters' lines
**B.** the central theme
**C.** the characters' movements
**D.** the characters' costumes

**2.** What can you tell about the setting from this passage?

**A.** The setting is a fitness center, after a class workout.
**B.** The setting is a gymnasium, after a big victory.
**C.** The setting is a gymnasium, after a loss.
**D.** The setting is an auditorium, before a pep rally.

**3.** What do you learn about the characters from these stage directions?

**A.** how they feel about one another
**B.** how they feel about the outcome of the game
**C.** why they are in the locker room
**D.** how they will deal with reporters

**4.** To whom might these stage directions be most useful?

**A.** to a viewer of the play
**B.** to someone reading the play
**C.** to an actor in the play
**D.** to a reviewer of the play

Name ______________________ Date __________

# Literary Analysis: Setting

## Practice

The **setting** of a story is the time and place of the action.

**A** Choose the best answer for each question. Circle the letter.

1. What does the setting of a story include?

   **A.** the time and place **B.** only the time **C.** only the place

2. Which of these words tells where a story happens?

   **A.** time **B.** beginning **C.** place

3. Which of these words tells when a story happens?

   **A.** time **B.** beginning **C.** place

**B** Read the description of each problem. Match it with the most likely setting.

1. A colony of tourists has lost communication with Earth.

   **A.** the past in New York **B.** the future on the moon **C.** the present in San Diego

2. A group of men in America want to be free of England.

   **A.** the future in Boston **B.** the present in Detroit **C.** the past in Boston

3. A sixteen-year-old wants to work at a computer store, but his parents say no.

   **A.** ancient Egypt **B.** Florida now **C.** Illinois in 1900

4. A teenager loses her cell phone.

   **A.** New York in 1950 **B.** New York in 1850 **C.** New York today

Name ______________________ Date ________

# Literary Analysis: Setting

## Assess

**A** Read the description. Circle the two answers that fit the setting.

**1.** Two friends are at a street fair. The mood is happy.

**A.** heartbreaking sobs **B.** the smell of hot dogs **C.** sounds of music

**2.** An elevator has stopped between floors. It is late at night.

**A.** an alarm ringing **B.** the lights go out **C.** sunshine

**3.** Twelve people are on a river raft. They are laughing and paddling.

**A.** animated conversation **B.** sound of trucks on a road **C.** life jackets

**B** Circle the answer that best describes the tone of each setting.

**1.** The green meadow was covered with beautiful purple wildflowers. Just then, a graceful deer bounded across the meadow. Nearby, a robin was looking for worms.

**A.** appreciation of nature **B.** dislike of animals **C.** fear of animals

**2.** Rain pounded the ground. Thunder rumbled, and lightning streaked across the sky. It seemed that all the forces of cruel nature were at work today.

**A.** fondness for storms **B.** fear of storms **C.** admiration for nature

**C** Read the paragraph. Then write *true* or *false* for each of the following statements.

The black ocean was cold and ugly. All around were pieces of ice that had broken off icebergs. The temperature was twenty degrees below zero. Would the crew survive this Arctic expedition?

**1.** ______________ The setting points to a story of adventure.

**2.** ______________ The setting points to a story about the beauty of nature.

**3.** ______________ The setting points to a story about a father's love for his son.

**4.** ______________ The setting points to a story of survival.

Name ______________________________ Date ____________

## Literary Analysis: Comparing Adaptations to Originals

### Practice

A **literary adaptation** is a work that has been changed from one literary form to another. For example, a writer may adapt a novel or short story into a script for a play or movie. The script is a literary adaptation. Look at these examples:

Short Story: Melissa entered the room with a big smile, barely able to control her excitement. "Guess what!" she exclaimed to her friend Anna. "I won the contest!"

Anna jumped to her feet. "No way!" she said in disbelief.

*adapted to*

Drama Script: MELISSA. [*enters, smiling*] Guess what! I won the contest!
ANNA. [*jumping to her feet*] No way!

**Based on the definition and examples above, circle the letter of the best answer to each question.**

**1.** What is a literary adaptation?

**A.** a work that has been made shorter
**B.** a work that has been made longer
**C.** a work that has been changed from one form to another
**D.** any screenplay or script

**2.** What is one difference between the short-story form and the script form?

**A.** The short-story form does not use quotation marks.
**B.** The script form does not use quotation marks.
**C.** The short-story form has stage directions in parentheses.
**D.** The script form has a narrator who tells the story.

**3.** When you compare an adaptation to an original, which changes are most noticeable?

**A.** changes in characters
**B.** changes in setting
**C.** changes in mood
**D.** changes in form

**4.** Which of the following is a literary adaptation?

**A.** a sequel to a movie
**B.** a poem that is read aloud
**C.** a short story changed into a play
**D.** a movie that is shortened for TV

Name ______________________________ Date ____________

## Literary Analysis: Comparing Adaptations to Originals

### Assess

**A** Write *T* if the statement is *true* or *F* if it is *false*.

**1.** ______ A movie script based on a novel is a literary adaptation.

**2.** ______ A movie review is a literary adaptation.

**3.** ______ A play tells more about a character's thoughts than a novel does.

**4.** ______ A short story uses quotation marks to set off each character's words.

**5.** ______ A script uses a character's name, followed by the character's words, without quotation marks.

**B** Rewrite the following lines from a short story to adapt them into a script.

"Why do we always end up doing what *you* want to do?" Jesse complained, tugging his hat down over his eyes.

"Because I'm the one with all the good ideas," Luke said with a grin, pulling Jesse's hat back up. "Now, come on, let's go, we'll have a good time."

**JESSE.** ______________________________

______________________________

______________________________

______________________________

**LUKE.** ______________________________

______________________________

______________________________

______________________________

Name ______________________ Date __________

# Vocabulary: Suffixes *-ory* and *-ist*

## Practice

A **suffix** is added to the end of a word to change its meaning or part of speech. The suffix *-ory* means "of, related to, or characterized by."

obligatory: resulting from an obligation; required
transitory: in transition; passing; temporary

The suffix *-ist* means "one who does, makes, practices, is skilled in, or believes in."

art + *-ist* = artist: someone who produces a work of art
moral + *-ist* = moralist: someone concerned with morals

**A** For each definition listed, write a word that combines the underlined word with the suffix *-ory* or *-ist* to form a new word that matches the definition. Then use the new word in a sentence.

**1.** ____________ person who plays the violin

______________________________

**2.** ____________ good enough to give satisfaction

______________________________

**3.** ____________ promising to do or pay something

______________________________

**4.** ____________ person who rides a bicycle

______________________________

**5.** ____________ based on an illusion

______________________________

**6.** ____________ person who studies geology

______________________________

Name ______________________________ Date __________

# Vocabulary: Suffixes *-ory* and *-ist*

## Assess

**A** Write the word from the list that best fits the meaning of each sentence.

celebratory directory mandatory migratory transitory

1. ________________ birds travel south every winter.
2. I called ________________ assistance to get the phone number.
3. In some countries, military service is ________________ for everyone.
4. The mayor made a ________________ speech in honor of the town's centennial.
5. Some writers say that every pleasure in life is ________________.

**B** Choose the correct word to complete each sentence. Write the word on the line.

**1. pianist** **piano**

I am learning to play the ________________.

I hope to become a skilled ________________.

**2. loyal** **loyalists**

During the American Revolution, some people remained ________________ to England.

These people were known as ________________.

**3. humor** **humorist**

The well-known ________________ published many books.

All her books were full of ________________.

**4. psychiatrist** **psychiatry**

My brother is studying ________________.

He intends to become a ________________.

**5. science** **scientist**

The ________________ made a fascinating discovery.

This discovery would be a great advance to ________________.

Name ______________________________ Date ____________

## Grammar: Participles and Participial Phrases

### Practice

A **participle** is a verb form that is used as an adjective. Participles commonly end in *-ing* (present participle) or *-ed* (past participle). Some past participles are formed in irregular ways (for example, *broken, shaken, known, born*).

| | |
|---|---|
| PRESENT PARTICIPLE | **Laughing,** the girl chased the dog outside. [modifies *girl*] |
| PAST PARTICIPLES | The parents, **worried,** stayed at the hospital. [modifies *parents*]<br>Among other injuries, the child had a **broken** leg. [modifies *leg*] |

A participle together with its complements and modifiers forms a **participial phrase.**

One detective **studying the case** discovered a clue. [*Case* is the direct object of the participle *studying.* The participial phrase modifies the noun *detective.*]

Sometimes you can combine two related sentences by changing one sentence into a participial phrase and adding it to the other sentence.

| | |
|---|---|
| ORIGINAL | The suspect was arrested by the local police. The suspect cooperated with the authorities. |
| COMBINED | **Arrested by the local police,** the suspect cooperated with the authorities. [The participial phrase modifies the noun *suspect.*] |

**Underline the participle or participial phrase in each sentence.**

1. Losing control, the skier took a bad fall.

2. Megan, noticing the accident, grabbed her binoculars.

3. Several concerned spectators made their way over to the skier.

4. The shaken skier slowly got to her feet.

5. Discouraged by the fall, she made her way down the hill carefully.

Name ______________________ Date ____________

# Grammar: Participles and Participial Phrases

## Assess

**A** Underline the participle in each sentence, and circle the word it modifies. Then, write *PrP* if the participle is a present participle or *PaP* if it is a past participle.

1. ______ Mosaic artists set small pieces of colored glass or stone into mortar.
2. ______ Carved relief sculptures were used in ancient Egyptian temples.
3. ______ William Blake was one of the leading engravers of the 1800s.
4. ______ In one kind of fresco work, the artist paints on moistened plaster.
5. ______ Leonardo da Vinci had both artistic talent and an inquiring mind.

**B** Underline the participial phrase in each sentence. Then, circle the word it modifies. (Remember, some past participles are formed in irregular ways.)

1. Believing in many gods and goddesses, the ancient Romans developed a mythology.
2. The god of war, known as Mars, was important in their mythology.
3. Romulus and Remus were twins born to Mars and a mortal mother.
4. Raised to adulthood by a wolf, the twins decided to build a city.
5. Romulus, quarreling with his brother, killed Remus and then founded Rome.

**C** Combine each pair of sentences by changing one into a participial phrase.

1. The puppy was trembling with fear. The puppy slowly walked toward me.

_______________________________________________

2. A large woman walked into the courtroom. She was followed by a little boy.

_______________________________________________

3. He opened the door slowly. He peeked into the darkened shed.

_______________________________________________

4. A course of study can lead to a good career. The course of study must be chosen carefully.

_______________________________________________

Name ______________________________ Date __________

Grammar: Revising Sentences by Combining With Gerunds and Participles

## Practice

A **gerund** is a verb form ending in *-ing* that is used as a noun.

> **Playing** chess is Lisa's favorite pastime.    Lyle enjoys **cooking** for his family.

A **participle** is a verb form that is used as an adjective. Participles commonly end in *-ing* (present participle) or *-ed* (past participle). Some past participles are formed in irregular ways (for example, *beaten, hidden, written, spoken, torn*).

> The **scurrying** hamster was quickly lost. [modifies *hamster*]
> Jake's essay, **written** in a hurry, got him a poor grade. [modifies *essay*]

Sometimes you can combine two related sentences by using a gerund or a participle.

| | |
|---|---|
| ORIGINAL | Amber enjoys hiking. She also likes to jog. |
| COMBINED | Amber enjoys hiking and **jogging.** [gerund] |
| ORIGINAL | The kitten rubbed against my arm. It purred softly. |
| COMBINED | **Purring** softly, the kitten rubbed against my arm. [participle] |

**Combine each pair of sentences using either a gerund or a participle.**

**1.** The butterfly can be a graceful swim stroke. It has to be performed correctly.

______________________________

**2.** Jack enjoys learning new swim strokes. He also enjoys practicing them.

______________________________

**3.** Jack thanked his father. His father had taught him the sidestroke.

______________________________

**4.** The favored swimmer took third place in the 200-meter backstroke. She had struggled.

______________________________

Name ______________________________ Date ____________

## Grammar: Revising Sentences by Combining With Gerunds and Participles

### Assess

**A** Combine each pair of sentences using a gerund.

1. Teresa practices basketball a lot. That is just about all Teresa does.

___

2. Juan's plans for the weekend include cleaning his room. He also plans to read.

___

3. The team gets to their away games. They ride on the bus to get there.

___

4. Some tourists take stones from the Indian ruins. This practice is illegal.

___

5. Playing soccer is good exercise. It is good to hike for exercise too.

___

**B** Combine each pair of sentences using a participle. Circle the word your participle modifies.

1. "The Tortoise and the Hare" is a fable about a race. It is well known.

___

2. The hare becomes too sure of himself. He stops to take a nap.

___

3. The tortoise plods along steadily. He eventually passes the hare.

___

4. The hare watches his opponent cross the finish line. The hare is stunned.

___

5. The tortoise goes on his way. He is pleased by his victory.

___

Name ______________________ Date __________

# Writing: Scene With Dialogue

## Practice

Drama is literature that is written to be performed. Most dramas, or plays, contain the following elements:

- **Acts and Scenes:** Acts are the main units of action in a drama. Acts are often divided into smaller parts, called scenes.
- **Characters:** Like short stories, dramas contain characters. When a drama is performed on stage, the characters are played by actors.
- **Dialogue:** The action in a play is revealed through the dialogue, or conversations, among the various characters.
- **Stage Directions:** Stage directions appear as bracketed information that indicates how the characters should move and speak.

**A** Read this example of a scene with dialogue. Then, answer the questions that follow.

Scene 2. Harry's apartment
HARRY. [*stands in living room and opens door to hallway as Charlie strolls in*] Where have you been, Charlie? I've been looking all over for you.
CHARLIE. Oh, I'm sorry. I stopped off at the video store on the way home.
HARRY. [*clearly angry*] Well, that's just great. Now we'll be late for the game!
CHARLIE. Okay, okay. Calm down. Quit yelling.
HARRY. [*grabs his jacket and opens the door*] Let's go!

1. Where does this scene take place? ______________________

2. Who are the characters? ______________________

3. In the first line of dialogue, what do the stage directions indicate? __________

______________________

______________________

4. What is the conflict that exists between the characters in this scene? ______

______________________

______________________

**B** On a separate sheet of paper, write a brief dramatic scene that contains a dialogue between two or more characters. Be sure to indicate where the scene takes place, and use the correct dramatic form, showing who is speaking each line. Include bracketed stage directions to indicate how the characters should move and speak.

Name ____________________ Date __________

# Writing: Scene with Dialogue

## Assess

**A** Read this example of a scene with dialogue. Then, answer the questions that follow.

Scene 1. A school bus stop
RHONDA. [*looking at her watch*] Wow, it's already 7:45. The bus should have been here by now.
GREG. [*yawning*] Another boring day, another late bus. What's the difference?
RAMON. [*stooping down to pick up a crumpled piece of paper on the ground*] Look at this messy litter. [*tone brightens as he unfolds paper*] Hey, look at this! It's a treasure map!
RHONDA. [*tries to grab the paper*] Let me see that!
RAMON. [*pulls away, speaking sharply*] Hey! Hold on! Don't rip it!
GREG. [*suddenly interested*] What's the map show, Ramon?
RAMON. [*turning the paper this way and that, trying to make sense of it*] Hmmm. [*suddenly excited*] It looks like your back yard, Greg! This might be our lucky day!

1. Where and when does this scene take place? ____________________

2. Who are the characters? ____________________

3. Give an example of a stage direction that tells an actor how to move.

____________________

4. Give an example of a stage direction that tells an actor how to use tone of voice to show feelings.

____________________

5. Summarize the action that takes place in this scene. ____________________

____________________

____________________

____________________

**B** On a separate sheet of paper, write a brief dramatic scene that might take place after school that day, as Rhonda, Greg, and Ramon get off the bus. Use your scene to describe what happens when they try to follow the treasure map. Be sure to indicate where the scene takes place, and use the correct dramatic form, showing who is speaking each line. Include bracketed stage directions to help readers and actors understand how the characters should move and speak.

Name ______________________________ Date __________

# Writing: Business Letter

## Practice

A **business letter** is a letter concerning a business or a professional matter. For example, you would write a business letter to report a problem with a purchase or to apply for a job. A business letter should include the following:

- **heading**—the writer's address and date
- **inside address**—address where the letter will be sent
- **greeting**—a salutation to the person receiving the letter
- **body**—brief, clear presentation of the writer's purpose
- **closing**—appropriate farewell
- **signature**—signed name of the sender
- formal, polite **language**
- standard **formatting**—either **block style** (all parts of the letter lined up on the left margin) or **semiblock/modified block style** (heading, closing, and signature lined up on the right side of the page)

**A** Label each part of this business letter on the numbered line next to it.

New Inventions, Inc.
**3.** ____________ 416 Main Street
Smalltown, CA 95030
January 31, 2007

Tyler Randall
Amazing Things, Inc. **1.** ____________
614 Central Boulevard
Bigtown, NY 10101

Dear Ms. Randall: **4.** ____________

We would like to meet with you soon to discuss merging our two companies. What time would be convenient for you?

**2.** ____________ Sincerely,

Rand Marshall
President, New Inventions

**B** On a separate sheet of paper, write a business letter to someone you know asking for a letter of recommendation to attend a special summer program in an area in which you have some talent or skill.

Name ______________________ Date __________

# Writing: Business Letter

## Assess

**A** Answer the questions that follow about the business letter shown here.

531 First Street
A Suburb, PA 16901
January 31, 2007

The Right Stuff
B 72 West Street
Middle City, NM 95011

C To Whom It May Concern:

I am returning the widget that I received from you last week. When I opened
D the package, the product was dented. Could you please refund my payment
of $24.67? Please send it to the above address. Thank you.

E Sincerely,

F Madison Bellton

**1.** Which letter identifies the inside address? ______

**2.** Which letter identifies the close? ______

**3.** What format does this letter follow? ______________________

**4.** What is the purpose of this business letter? ______________________

______________________________________________

**B** Write a business letter to a store owner to complain about or praise an employee who served you at his or her store. Use your own address but invent an address for the store owner. Use the modified block style. Use the back of this page if you need more space.

______________________________________________

______________________________________________

______________________________________________

______________________________________________

______________________________________________

______________________________________________

______________________________________________

Name ______________________________ Date ____________

# Reading: Cause and Effect

## Practice

A **cause** is an event, an action, or a feeling that produces a result, or **effect.**

- *Sometimes one cause has several effects.* For example, a snowstorm can cause traffic accidents, school closings, and power failures. As you read, think about all the possible effects that might result from one cause.
- *Sometimes several causes come together to create one effect.* For example, you may fall on the sidewalk because it snowed, nobody shoveled it, and you forgot to wear your boots. Causes and effects can also occur in a chain: one event causes another, which causes the next, and so on.
- Keep in mind that *events may occur in order but not be connected.* As you read, ask yourself whether two events are related or just coincidental.

Read the following selection. Then, answer the questions.

The night of the big basketball game, Tim ate pizza for dinner and then rushed to catch the team bus. Traffic was backed up on the highway because of an accident, so the team arrived late, which meant they had very little practice time before the game. Nevertheless, they were ahead at half time, thanks to Zach's hot shooting arm and Tim's five rebounds. However, Zach fouled out in the fourth quarter, so the rest of the team had to step up their defense and also pass the ball more to maintain their lead.

**1.** What is the relationship between Tim's having pizza and the other events?

**A.** It is a cause with one effect.
**B.** It is one event in a cause-effect chain.
**C.** It is a cause with two effects.
**D.** It has no relationship to the other events.

**2.** What is the relationship between the highway accident and other events?

**A.** It is a cause with one effect.
**B.** It is one event in a cause-effect chain.
**C.** It is an effect with one cause.
**D.** It has no relationship to the other events.

**3.** What causes the team to be ahead at half time?

**A.** Zach's shots **B.** Tim's rebounds **C.** both A and B **D.** neither A nor B

**4.** What is the relationship between Zach's fouling out and other events?

**A.** It is a cause with one important effect.
**B.** It is a cause with two important effects.
**C.** It is an effect with one cause.
**D.** It has no relationship to other events.

 

Name ______________________________ Date ____________

# Reading: Cause and Effect

## Assess

**A** Write whether each statement is *true* or *false*.

**1.** ____________ When one event follows another, the two events are always related.

**2.** ____________ Most effects have only one cause.

**3.** ____________ A single cause may have several effects.

**4.** ____________ An effect of one event may then become the cause of another event.

**B** Read the selection below. Then, answer the question.

The United States acquired the Louisiana Purchase in 1803. The next year, Lewis and Clark began exploring the new American territory. They wrote glowing reports of the vast prairies rich with wildlife. People who wanted their own land read the reports and decided to journey west to the frontier. These settlers came into conflict with Plains Indians who had freely wandered the prairies as their homeland for centuries.

How would you describe the relationships between the events described in the passage?

**A.** They describe one cause with several effects.
**B.** They describe one effect with two causes.
**C.** They describe a chain of causes and effects.
**D.** They describe events that occurred in sequence but are unrelated.

Name ______________________ Date __________

# Reading: Evaluate Unity and Coherence

## Practice

When you evaluate a text for unity and coherence, you examine it for a consistent point of view and logical organization. You look at details to see how they are arranged. Then, you decide whether the writer has effectively used the details to communicate a main idea. Ask yourself if the author has conveyed a solid message and whether there is a good reason for people to read the text.

The web page below provides information and links. Use the chart to analyze the parts of a website. Then, answer the questions that follow.

| Where to Look | What It Is | What it Does |
|---|---|---|
| Banner or Navigation Bar | a panel at the top of an electronic page | It shows links to other pages. |
| Body | the main part of the web page | It provides highlighted or underlined links to other pages of interest. |
| Visuals | small images | They may lead to maps, photos, or other text pages. |

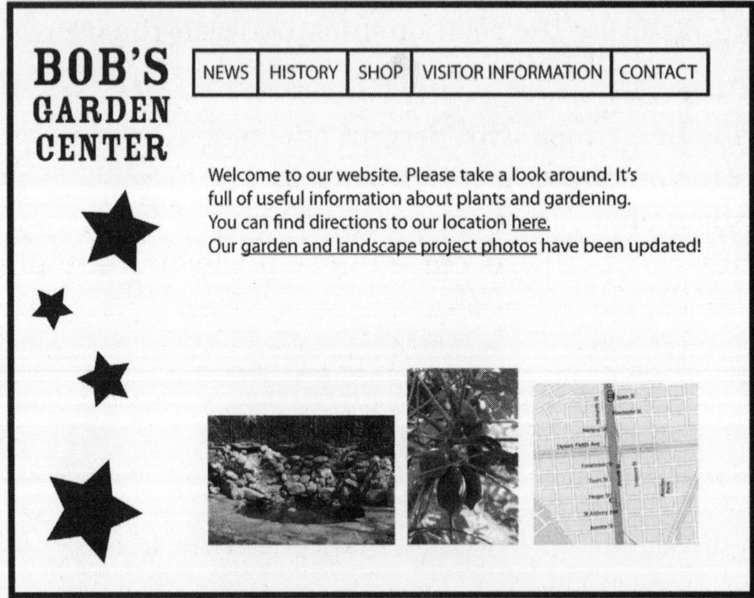


1. What links are provided in the banner or navigation bar?

2. What links are provided in the body? How can you tell they are links?

3. Is there a link to directions to the garden center? Where?

 

Name ______________________ Date ____________

# Reading: Evaluate Unity and Coherence

## Assess

The website below provides information and links. Use the chart to analyze the parts of a website. Then, answer the questions that follow.

**1.** Where is the link you would follow to look for sale items?

**A.** banner/navigation bar **B.** body **C.** visuals

**2.** Where is the link to follow if you are looking for a pet to adopt?

**A.** banner/navigation bar **B.** body **C.** visuals

**3.** Where are the links that provide access to information about products for specific types of pets?

**A.** banner/navigation bar **B.** body **C.** visuals

**4.** Where is the link to find out where the store is located?

**A.** banner/navigation bar **B.** body **C.** visuals

Name ______________________ Date ____________

# Literary Analysis: Dialogue

## Practice

**Dialogue** is a conversation between or among characters. In the script, or text, of a play, lines of dialogue follow the name of each speaker. Dialogue reveals character traits and relationships, advances the plot, and shows conflicts that exist between characters or between a character and an outside force.

Read the following dialogue. Notice what it shows about the characters and the conflict between them.

> Mike. Who took my CD? Everyone's always taking my stuff.
> Ben. Nobody took it. You left it in the car again, the way you always do. Stop blaming everyone else for your own carelessness.

Read the following selection. Then, answer the questions.

> Grasshopper. [*knocking on Ant's door*] Mr. Ant! I'm freezing and starving to death out here in the cold, while you have a warm home and plenty to eat. Can you spare a grain of corn for me?
> Ant. I warned you about this, Mr. Grasshopper, but you wouldn't listen. All summer, you played and sang, while I was working hard, storing food for winter.
> Grasshopper. Come on, Mr. Ant, have a heart. Take me in, and I'll sing and dance for you all winter. We'll have fun.
> Ant. I'm truly sorry, but I have no food to spare. If I share with you, I may not survive the winter myself. Goodbye. [*slams his door*]

**1.** Which is the best description of the selection?

**A.** narration
**B.** nonfiction
**C.** dialogue
**D.** monologue

**2.** What does the selection reveal about the character of Grasshopper?

**A.** He is fun-loving but impractical.
**B.** He is hard-working but heartless.
**C.** He is kind and compassionate.
**D.** He is sneaky and dishonest.

**3.** What does the selection reveal about the character of Ant?

**A.** He is fun-loving but impractical.
**B.** He is hard-working but heartless.
**C.** He is kind and compassionate.
**D.** He is sneaky and dishonest

**4.** What conflict is revealed in the selection?

**A.** a struggle for power
**B.** a struggle for popularity
**C.** a struggle for love
**D.** a struggle for survival

Name ______________________________ Date ____________

# Literary Analysis: Dialogue

## Assess

**Read the selection below. Then, answer the questions.**

**Beggar.** Who can spare a bowl of water, so I can wash my feet? That's all I ask.
**Rich Woman.** Go away, you disgusting creature. You're not fit to darken my doorstep.
**Beggar.** I beg your pardon, ma'am. [*continues to the next door*] Who can spare a bowl of water, so I can wash my feet? That's all I ask.
**Auntie Lily.** Come here, poor man. A bowl of water is all you ask?
**Rich Woman.** Send him away, or he'll be back for more. It's your fault these beggars come around.
**Auntie Lily.** Who knows, my luck may change some day, and I may be desperate for a bowl of water. Come here, my poor man, and wash the dust from your feet.
**Beggar.** Thank you, ma'am. Your kindness will be rewarded.

**1.** Which is the best description of the selection?

**A.** monologue
**B.** dialogue
**C.** narration
**D.** nonfiction

**2.** What does the selection reveal about the Rich Woman?

**A.** She lacks friends.
**B.** She lacks compassion.
**C.** She is generous and caring.
**D.** She is weak and stupid.

**3.** What does the selection reveal about Auntie Lily?

**A.** She lacks friends.
**B.** She lacks compassion.
**C.** She is generous and caring.
**D.** She is weak and stupid.

**4.** Why is there a conflict between the Rich Woman and Auntie Lily?

**A.** One is rich, and one is poor.
**B.** One is lonely, and one is not.
**C.** One is hard-working, and one is lazy.
**D.** One is generous, and one is selfish.

Name ______________________________ Date ____________

# Literary Analysis: Character's Motivation

## Practice

A **character's motivation** is the reason he or she takes a particular action. It may be internal, external, or both.

- **Internal motivations** are based on emotions such as loneliness or jealousy: *To ease her loneliness, Kate began volunteering at the hospital.*
- **External motivations** are sparked by events or situations like a fire or poverty: *Dale looked for a new home after a flood gutted his house.*

**A** Circle the letter of the best answer. Then, explain your choice.

1. Members of the rain forest project have been working for months to design a method for harvesting spider silk. Every time they think they have it figured out, something goes wrong. Still, they refuse to give up. What motivates the project members?

   **A.** frustration **B.** fear **C.** determination **D.** kindness

   **Explain:** ______________________________

2. Robbie is tired of coming home to an empty house. When a hungry-looking dog shows up on his front porch, he takes him in and feeds him. After no one claims the dog, Robbie decides to keep him. What sparks Robbie's decision to keep the dog?

   **A.** internal motivation **B.** external motivation **C.** both motivations

   **Explain:** ______________________________

**B** Read each passage, and circle the motivation(s) for the underlined action. Write *I* if the motivation is internal, *E* if it is external, or *B* if it is both.

**1.** ______ Mara saw the three-car pileup in her rearview mirror. She <u>pulled over immediately</u> and ran down the road to see if anyone needed help.

**2.** ______ Cati was afraid to stay home alone at night. She turned on all the lights and clicked on the TV. She heard a rustling noise outside and <u>peered anxiously through the blinds into the darkness</u>.

**3.** ______ Gemma <u>sat at the bus station</u> for the fifth day in a row. All day, she watched passengers come and go. Her brother had promised he would be home soon. She adored her brother and couldn't wait to see him.

Name ______________________ Date ____________

# Literary Analysis: Character's Motivation

## Assess

**Read the passage. Then, answer the questions that follow.**

Niles felt fast and strong. He easily cleared hurdle after hurdle in the 300-meter race. Today was the final track meet of the season. After this, the championship meets would begin. All season, Niles had fought hard to maintain his place on the varsity team. It hadn't been easy. A sophomore runner, he'd had fierce competition from Cal, a freshman, and Mike, a senior. They always started out strong, but Niles usually overtook them both just before the end of the race. He knew his place on varsity was secure.

In addition to being the final meet, it was also Senior Day. It was the last time seniors would run in a home meet as part of the team. As Niles headed into the final stretch off the race, he quickly passed Cal. Then, he closed in on Mike. Fifty feet from the finish line, Niles and Mike were neck and neck. Niles could hear Mike breathing hard. He knew Mike had worked just as hard as he had this season. It would mean a lot to him to win this race today. Niles crossed the finish line a fraction behind him.

**1.** Why has Niles been running hard all season?

**A.** He does not like Cal and Mike.
**B.** He wants to stay on varsity.
**C.** He wants to be the best runner on the team.
**D.** He will graduate this year.

**2.** What emotion best describes Niles's motivation for working so hard?

**A.** annoyance **B.** fear **C.** determination **D.** kindness

**3.** Why does Niles slow down in the end?

**A.** He wants Mike to finish before him.
**B.** He is not very competitive.
**C.** He feels tired.
**D.** He wants Cal to catch up.

**4.** Which internal motivation prompts Niles to finish in second place?

**A.** kindness **B.** fatigue **C.** guilt **D.** pity

**5.** Which external motivation prompts Niles to finish in second place?

**A.** It is the last meet of the season.
**B.** It is Senior Day.
**C.** His legs hurt.
**D.** The championship meets are coming up.

Name ______________________________ Date __________

Literary Analysis: Comparing a Primary Source With a Dramatization

## Practice

A **primary source** is a firsthand account in which the writer describes real events he or she experienced, such as a diary written by George Washington during the American Revolution. A **dramatization** is a play that has been adapted from another work. For example, a playwright might adapt George Washington's diary, creating a script in which Washington appears as a character, experiencing or discussing the events in his diary.

Read this primary source and the dramatization based on it. Then, answer the questions.

| Primary Source | Dramatization |
|---|---|
| Dear Mother,<br>My internship in Washington, D.C., is going well, and this week brought an amazing experience. Senator Ross sent me to the White House to pick up some documents. In the main hall, I saw Secretary of State Carson. I have always admired her, so I introduced myself and told her how I felt. She asked me if I worked in Washington. I told her about my summer internship. Then, she did an incredible thing. She asked me if I would join her for lunch to talk about career possibilities in the State Department. She said she was always looking for young people with interests in diplomacy. Wow!<br>See you soon,<br>Kate | Scene 2. Main hall in the White House<br>**KATE.** [*shyly*] Secretary Carson! I so admire what you've accomplished at the State Department.<br>**SEC. CARSON.** [*reaches out to shake hands*] Why, thank you. Do you have a summer job here?<br>**KATE.** [*showing badge*] Yes, I'm working for Senator Ross on an environmental project, but I'd rather work in diplomacy or foreign service.<br>**SEC. CARSON.** Well! [*looks at watch*] I'm free for lunch today. Would you join me? Maybe I could suggest ways for you to work on that goal. I'm always on the lookout for new young staff members with lots of talent! |

**1.** How are the primary source and the dramatization alike? ______________________________

______________________________________________________________

**2.** How are they different? ______________________________

______________________________________________________________

Name ______________________________ Date ______________

Literary Analysis: Comparing a Primary Source With a Dramatization

## Assess

Read this primary source and the dramatization based on it. Then, answer the questions. If you need additional space, use a separate sheet of paper.

| Primary Source | Dramatization |
|---|---|
| **July 25:** I'm nervous about the rafting trip tomorrow. Ralph says not to worry, but I can't help it.<br>**July 26:** The rafting trip was awesome. At the start, the water was very calm, and that let me build up some confidence. But then we went around a bend, and the water looked like it was a boiling pot of spaghetti! The raft shimmied and shuddered, and I almost fell out. Hal was sitting in front of me, and he DID fall out! Somehow I reached out the oar to him, and he grabbed on while Ralph steered the raft out of the rapids. Hal was OK, just a little shaken. He said that I saved his life. That felt good, but I knew that I was just lucky—REALLY lucky! | Scene 2. On a rubber raft in the river, in the midst of calm water<br>**RALPH.** That was fun, right, Pete?<br>**PETE.** [*trying to look and sound brave*] Sure. This seems easy.<br>**HAL.** [*pointing ahead, as raft turns bend*] Wow! Check out those rapids. Yikes! I'm falling! [*falls out of raft into churning, dangerous rapids*]<br>**PETE.** [*extends oar to Hal*] Hal, Hal! Grab on, Hal! Grab on!<br>**RALPH.** [*steering raft to safe water*] Good move, Pete! Fast thinking!<br>**HAL.** [*gasping for breath*] Pete! You saved my life!<br>**RALPH.** [*with great relief*] We were lucky, Hal. We were really, really lucky! |

**1.** How are the primary source and the dramatization alike? ______________________________

______________________________________________________________

**2.** How are they different? ______________________________

______________________________________________________________

**3.** What device in the dramatization helps convey the characters' feelings?

______________________________________________________________

**4.** Which version do you feel is more exciting? Explain. ______________________________

______________________________________________________________

Name ______________________________ Date __________

# Grammar: Prefix *in-*; Suffix *-ory*

## Practice

A **prefix** is added to the beginning of a word or word root to change its meaning. As you learned in Unit 4, the prefix *in-* sometimes means "not." If you add it to the word *considerate*, meaning "polite," you get a new word, *inconsiderate*, meaning "not polite."

A **suffix** is added to the end of a word or word root to change its meaning. Often it changes its parts of speech as well. The suffix *-ory* means "of," "relating to," or "characterized by."

Examples:

insight: the ability to see into a situation
Her years working with young children gave her *insight* into their behavior.

explanatory: having the characteristic of explaining
Because I wanted my boss to understand my decision, I wrote an *explanatory* e-mail.

**A** Circle the letter of the correct answer to each question.

**1.** How do you dress if you dress informally?

**A.** You dress in formal wear, such as a tuxedo.
**B.** You dress in clothing that is not formal, such as jeans.

**2.** What might you do to get a sensory experience?

**A.** read a book about nature and natural events
**B.** watch, smell, and listen to things around you

**3.** What kind of work could be described as satisfactory?

**A.** work that satisfies a requirement
**B.** work that fulfills a life-long goal

**4.** What kind of behavior is instinctive?

**A.** behavior that is based on reason
**B.** behavior that is built in,or that you do without thinking about it

**5.** What kind of person might be called ambulatory?

**A.** someone who is characterized by the ability to walk
**B.** someone who helps others

Name ________________ Date ________

# Grammar: Prefix *in-*; Suffix *-ory*

## Assess

**A** Think about whether each sentence below makes sense, given the meaning of the underlined word. Circle "Y" if it makes sense and "N" if it does not. Then, explain your answer. If the sentence does not make sense, write a new sentence using the word correctly.

1. **Y/N** The students <u>included</u> the new girl by refusing to let her play with them.

   ________________

2. **Y/N** The mad scientist experimented with all kinds of rare and unknown chemicals in his secret <u>laboratory</u>.

   ________________

3. **Y/N** He took antibiotics to treat a skin <u>infection</u>.

   ________________

4. **Y/N** The <u>introductory</u> passage appeared at the end of the long narrative.

   ________________

5. **Y/N** The air rushed out of my lungs as I <u>inhaled</u>.

   ________________

6. **Y/N** Store workers took an <u>inventory</u> to learn how many canned goods were on hand.

   ________________

**B** Match each word with the sentence in which it fits best.

| | Word Bank |
|---|---|
| 1. I ________ the plug into the outlet. | advisory |
| 2. The student lived in a ________ during his freshman year. | infer |
| 3. I'm trying to reduce my ________ of sugar. | inserted |
| 4. The weather ________ urged people to seek shelter from the storm. | dormitory |
| 5. I was able to ________ the answer from the clues. | intake |

Name ______________________________ Date __________

# Grammar: Independent and Subordinate Clauses

## Practice

A **clause** is a group of words that has a subject and a verb. An **independent clause** expresses a complete thought and can stand by itself as a complete sentence. A **subordinate clause** cannot stand by itself as a sentence because it does not express a complete thought. Subordinate clauses begin with words such as *since, that, until, which, because, although, when, as if, after, unless, before, if,* and *as though.*

In the following examples, the subjects are underlined once, and the verbs are underlined twice.

| | |
|---|---|
| Independent Clause | the letters were old and dusty [complete thought]<br>The letters were old and dusty. [stands alone as a sentence] |
| Subordinate Clauses | that Judy found in the attic [incomplete thought]<br>if they had been written by her grandfather [incomplete thought]<br>when he was courting her grandmother [incomplete thought] |

Each of the following sentences has both an independent clause and a subordinate clause. The subordinate clauses are in bold.

The letters **that Judy found in the attic** were old and dusty.
She wondered **if they had been written by her grandfather.**
**When he was courting her grandmother,** he had sent her some love letters.

Identify each word group by writing *IND* for *independent clause, SUB* for *subordinate clause,* or *NC* for *not a clause.*

1. ______ because she wants to become a champion figure skater
2. ______ gets good advice from her coach
3. ______ she appreciates the new skates
4. ______ that her mother bought her for her birthday
5. ______ unless she can make the Olympic trials
6. ______ mornings are the best time to practice
7. ______ which can lead to injuries

Name ______________________ Date __________

# Grammar: Independent and Subordinate Clauses

## Assess

**A** *Identify each underlined clause by writing IND for independent clause or SUB for subordinate clause.*

1. ______ Until the Spanish came along, the Inca had a large empire.
2. ______ The Inca were skilled engineers who built vast networks of roads.
3. ______ If they cooperated with the Inca, local leaders could stay in power.
4. ______ Inca children began working before they turned six years old.
5. ______ The empire fell when Spanish forces conquered it in 1532.

**B** Underline each independent clause once and each subordinate clause twice.

1. Mammals that bear extremely underdeveloped offspring are called marsupials.
2. Kangaroos are in the macropod family, which also includes wallabies.
3. Although rat-kangaroos are related to kangaroos, they do not belong to the same family of marsupials.
4. Kangaroos usually search for food in the late evening and early morning.
5. Baby kangaroos are only about one inch long when they are born.

**C** Add an independent clause to each subordinate clause to make a complete sentence.

**Example:** Miguel spends time with horses whenever he gets a chance.

1. ______________________ where he works as a stable boy.
2. Although he does not get paid much, ______________________.
3. ______________________ because he wants to become a veterinarian.
4. ______________________ which can be a rewarding career.
5. If you love animals, ______________________.

Name ______________________________ Date ____________

## Grammar: Revising to Combine Sentences With Subordinate Clauses

### Practice

Writing that has mostly short sentences sounds choppy and dull. You can **combine short sentences into longer ones** to make your writing smoother and more interesting.

One way to combine sentences is by using a subordinate clause. A **subordinate clause** is a word group with a subject and verb that cannot stand by itself as a sentence. Subordinate clauses begin with words such as *after, although, as long as, as soon as, because, before, since, than, that, unless, when, where,* and *which.* These words help you show the connections between your ideas.

First, make sure the two sentences are related. Then, rewrite the less important idea as a subordinate clause, and add it to the other sentence. Make sure the word you use to begin your subordinate clause shows the correct relationship between the two ideas.

| | |
|---|---|
| ORIGINAL | Nathan finished his homework. Then, he took a bike ride. |
| COMBINED | **After Nathan finished his homework,** he took a bike ride. [The subordinate clause shows a time relationship.] |
| ORIGINAL | The bicycle is broken. Nathan has been riding it for years. |
| COMBINED | The bicycle **that Nathan has been riding for years** is broken. [The subordinate clause tells which bicycle is broken.] |

Combine each pair of sentences by changing one sentence into a subordinate clause and adding it to the other.

**1.** Susan B. Anthony published a journal. It demanded equal rights for women.

______________________________

**2.** Anthony voted in the presidential election of 1872. She was arrested and fined.

______________________________

**3.** She never paid the fine. The authorities did not take further action.

______________________________

**4.** Susan B. Anthony died. Women got the right to vote later.

______________________________

Name ______________________ Date __________

## Grammar: Revising to Combine Sentences With Subordinate Clauses

### Assess

**A** Underline the subordinate clause in each sentence.

**1.** Crickets are known for their songs, which usually consist of series of trills and chirps.

**2.** They make these sounds when they rub their two front legs together.

**3.** Because they help male and female crickets find each other, the songs are important.

**4.** Some crickets live in ants' nests, where they feed on the baby ants.

**5.** Although crickets are related to grasshoppers, these two insects differ in many ways.

**B** Combine each pair of sentences by changing one sentence into a subordinate clause and adding it to the other. Use the word in parentheses to begin your subordinate clause.

**Example:** My family visited Philadelphia. It is a historic city. (which)

My family visited Philadelphia, which is a historic city.

**1.** William Penn was an English Quaker. Penn founded Philadelphia in 1682. (who)

______________________

**2.** Many of the early settlers were Quakers. The city became known as the Quaker City. (because)

______________________

**3.** It was located near trade routes. Philadelphia became an important shipping center. (Since)

______________________

**4.** We toured Independence Hall. The U.S. Constitution was signed there. (where)

______________________

**5.** The Delaware Indians lived in this area. The Europeans arrived. (before)

______________________

Name ______________________ Date __________

# Spelling: Plurals

## Practice

To form the plurals of most nouns, follow these rules:

- Add *s* to the noun. This is the "regular" way to form plurals of nouns. **Examples:** book/books, paper/papers, chore/chores.
- Add *es* to nouns that end in *s, sh, ch,* or *x.* **Examples:** glass/glasses, leash/leashes, peach/peaches, fax/faxes.
- If a noun ends in a *y* that follows a consonant, form the plural by changing the *y* to *i* and adding *es.* **Examples:** pantry/pantries; spy/spies; ferry/ferries.
- For some words ending in f, just add *s.* **Example:** chief/chiefs; For others, change the *f* to *v* and add *es.* **Example:** loaf/loaves.
- If a noun ends in an *o* that follows a vowel, add *s.* **Examples:** radio/radios; studio/studios. If, however, the final *o* follows a consonant, add *es.* **Examples:** mango/mangoes; tomato/tomatoes.

Note these exceptions and irregular plurals:

- Some nouns have the same spelling in both the singular and plural. **Example:** fish/fish.
- Some nouns have irregular plurals. **Examples:** mouse/mice; woman/women; child/children.

**A** Write the singular form of each of these plural words.

**1.** halves ______________ **4.** patches ______________

**2.** fish ______________ **5.** reasons ______________

**3.** properties ______________ **6.** tomatoes ______________

**B** State the rule that applies to the spelling of the plural form shown.

**1.** reasons ______________________________

**2.** studios ______________________________

**3.** patches ______________________________

Name ______________________________ Date ____________

# Spelling: Plurals

## Assess

Circle the letter of the sentence in which the italicized word is spelled correctly.

**1.** **A.** Some *studioes* are devoted to television productions.
**B.** Artists often locate their *studioze* in large lofts.
**C.** The college radio *studioses* do not have the latest equipment.
**D.** Real-estate agents sometimes call one-room apartments *studios.*

**2.** **A.** Give me four good *reasones* your team will win the game.
**B.** My *reasonies* for declining the invitation are personal.
**C.** The *reasonnes* for some illnesses remain unknown.
**D.** Investigators were looking into the *reasons* for the accident.

**3.** **A.** The pond was well stocked with *fish.*
**B.** The variety of *fishs* at the aquarium was truly amazing.
**C.** *Fishes* are an important source of protein.
**D.** The *fishess* in this area are threatened by water pollution.

**4.** **A.** You should cut that large portion into *halfes.*
**B.** Dividing the money into *halfs* will not do if there are three people.
**C.** Usually the first fraction students learn are *halvies.*
**D.** Football games are divided into *halves.*

**5.** **A.** *Tomatose* are the basis for many dishes.
**B.** *Tomatoes* are rich in nutrients.
**C.** Cold sliced *tomatos* are an excellent addition to salads.
**D.** My sister prefers fresh vine-ripened *tomatoze.*

**6.** **A.** *Theorees* are not as reliable as facts.
**B.** There are a number of *theoreez* about the origin of the universe.
**C.** The prosecutor presented several *theories* about the motives for the crime.
**D.** Scientists test their *theores* with experiments.

**7.** **A.** Today the sky has only *patchez* of blue.
**B.** Some consider it very fashionable to have *patchies* on their jeans.
**C.** Because of his multicolored coat, we named our dog *Patches.*
**D.** The museum guide pointed out the *patchess* of green in the painting.

Name ______________________________ Date __________

# Writing: Diary Entry

## Practice

A **diary** is a written account of daily events that includes personal thoughts and feelings. A person might make a **diary entry** every day, once a week, or at irregular intervals. Diaries are not written for publication, but sometimes interesting diaries or diaries of famous people are published after the writer's death. Diary entries usually include these features:

- The date of the entry, and sometimes even the time and place
- First-person point of view, with the writer using the pronoun *I*
- Chronological order, with the writer discussing events in order of time
- The writer's thoughts and feelings about the events

Read the following diary entry. Then, answer the questions and complete the activities.

December 15, 11:30 p.m., Seaside

I went to see a production of *A Christmas Carol* at the high-school auditorium tonight with my friend Sally. It was excellent! I think that is my very favorite Charles Dickens work. The costumes were really spectacular. The scene where Mr. Fezziwig gives the party for his employees and their families was really fun. The colorful costumes added to the festive atmosphere. Sally was telling me that her mom worked on the costumes for this show—I'll have to tell her she did a great job.

1. What event does the writer describe in this diary entry? ______________

______________________________________________

2. How does the writer feel about the occasion? ______________

______________________________________________

3. Name a recent event in your community that you could write about in a diary entry. ______________

______________________________________________

4. What are your strongest thoughts or feelings about the event? ______________

______________________________________________

______________________________________________

______________________________________________

Name ______________________________ Date ____________

# Writing: Diary Entry

## Assess

For a series of diary entries, choose an event from your life that took at least several days to experience, such as planning a surprise party or practicing for a big swim meet. Then, complete the following activities.

1. What event did you choose? ______________________________

______________________________

2. Write the details of the event in the order in which they happened.

First, ______________________________

Next, ______________________________

After that, ______________________________

Finally, ______________________________

3. Write two brief journal entries about the event. Tell what happened, and then tell how you felt about it.

Journal Entry #1 Date ____________

______________________________

______________________________

______________________________

______________________________

______________________________

Journal Entry #2 Date ____________

______________________________

______________________________

______________________________

______________________________

______________________________

Name ______________________________ Date ____________

# Writing: Letter

## Practice

A **letter** can be written to convince the reader of a point of view, to get the reader to agree to do something, or to encourage the reader to take some action. An effective letter will include these features:

- A statement that identifies the issue or situation
- A thesis statement, or topic sentence, giving the writer's point of view
- Supporting facts and ideas, such as appeals to authority ("doctors everywhere agree"), emotion ("you will be proud you participated"), and reason ("statistics prove")
- A strong conclusion

Read the following letter. Then, complete the activities that follow.

Dear Mom and Dad,

I would like you to start allowing me to baby-sit for the neighbors. I think I am responsible enough to do a good job, and I know that my grades would not suffer. I would be able to study when the children are sleeping, earning money at the same time. Grandma agrees with me, and she thinks baby-sitting is an excellent job for a girl my age. Now that I am thirteen years old, I would like to start saving for a car. Baby-sitting for just six hours a week will enable me to save enough money in three years for a good used car. I know that you would be proud of me if I could buy my own car when I am sixteen. What do you think?

Sincerely,
Carla

**1.** What is Carla trying to get her parents to do? ______________________________

______________________________________________________________

**2.** Circle one point that is an appeal to authority.

**3.** Underline one point that is an appeal to reason.

**4.** Bracket one point that is an appeal to emotion.

**5.** On a separate sheet of paper, write a brief, effective letter asking your parents for permission to take lessons or instruction of some kind, such as piano lessons or martial arts classes.

Name ______________________________ Date ____________

# Writing: Letter

## Assess

Circle one of the following topics for a letter. Fill in a specific choice if necessary. Then, answer the questions and complete the activities.

Best place for a vacation: ______________________________

Highly recommended book: ______________________________

Best movie of the year: ______________________________

The dangers of heavy backpacks for students

The need for more healthful cafeteria food

Cell phones at school

1. Identify your audience. ______________________________

2. Write a thesis statement (topic sentence) that expresses your opinion.

______________________________

______________________________

3. List three facts, examples, or appeals to support your point of view.

______________________________

______________________________

______________________________

4. Write a brief, effective letter below. Use the back of this page if you need more space to write.

______________________________

______________________________

______________________________

______________________________

______________________________

______________________________

______________________________

Name ______________________________ Date __________

# Writing: Research Report

## Practice

A **research report** presents facts and information. Select a topic that interests you. Then, gather information from books, magazines, interviews, and the Internet. A research report includes a bibliography or a Works Cited list that shows where you got your information.

To write a research report, you should complete the following steps:

- Choose a suitable topic, one that is not too narrow or too broad.
- Express your main idea in a thesis statement—a topic sentence that clearly states the main idea of your report.
- Gather information, and take notes.
- Write an outline. Organize how you will present your information.
- Write a draft and then a final version. Include a Works Cited list.

**A** Read one student's plan for a research report. Then, respond to each item.

Mori plans to write a research report on the history of his state, Ohio. He wants to cover the natural resources, major land formations, climate, history, famous people from the state, and important statistics. He is especially interested in his hometown and thinks that he could possibly do some research at the town historical society and library.

Mori has already done a lot of research on the Internet and at the library. He has been taking notes and keeping track of sources and works cited.

1. Mori's topic is too broad for a research report at his level. Suggest a better topic for Mori's research report, based on what you have read in his plan.

______________________________

2. What would be a good thesis statement for Mori's new topic?

______________________________

**B** Think of an ancient civilization that interests you. Then, fill in the numbered items.

1. Name the ancient civilization that interests you. __________

2. Choose a topic that is narrow enough to cover in a short paper. __________

______________________________

3. Create a thesis statement that states your main idea. __________

______________________________

Name ______________________ Date __________

# Writing: Research Report

## Assess

**A** Read one student's plan for a research report. Then, answer the questions.

Mara is very interested in television news shows. She has decided to write a research report that examines television news broadcasting today. She wants to know how opinions shape the news and how ratings determine what stories are covered in nightly news broadcasts. She has done research in the library and on the Internet. She has also contacted her local television station and arranged to interview one of the local news anchors.

As part of her report, Mara is also going to trace the history of broadcast news, going back to the 1950s.

1. What is Mara's thesis? ______________________

2. What are some questions Mara might ask as part of her research? ______________________

3. What is a problem with the focus of Mara's research report, and what would you suggest as a solution? ______________________

**B** Think of a topic in the field of art, music, or entertainment that interests you. Then, begin a research report by filling in the numbered items.

1. A topic that is narrow enough to cover in a short paper: ______________________

2. A thesis that states my main idea: ______________________

3. Three sources where I might find information ______________________

Name ____________________ Date ________

# Reading: Summary

## Practice

A **summary** is a short statement that presents the main ideas and most important points in a piece of writing. Follow these steps to summarize a section of text or a whole work:

- **Read** the piece of writing all the way through.
- **Reread** to identify main events or ideas. Jot them down.
- **Organize your notes** by putting the main events or ideas in order and crossing out minor details that are not important for an overall understanding of the work.
- **Summarize** by restating the main ideas *briefly* in your own words.

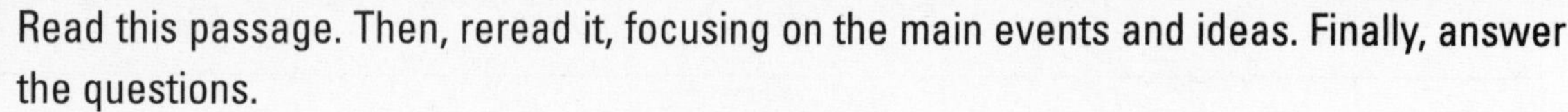

Read this passage. Then, reread it, focusing on the main events and ideas. Finally, answer the questions.

(1) The eighth grade at Ward Middle School has created a community garden on the old soccer field, facing Marshall St. (2) Class President Wanda Reed said, "Once the school completed the new soccer field, we saw a terrific opportunity to put the old field to good use. (3) Our goal is to grow enough tomatoes, beans, and other vegetables to supply the Grant Avenue Soup Kitchen with as much fresh produce as possible." (4) With the help of Ms. Sanchez, their social studies teacher, and several parent volunteers, the students were able to clear a large plot of approximately 12 feet by 20 feet.

**1.** What is the main idea of this passage?

**A.** Wanda Reed is president of the eighth-grade class at Ward Middle School.
**B.** A teacher and several parent volunteers helped the class create a garden.
**C.** The eighth grade made a garden to supply a soup kitchen with vegetables.
**D.** The eighth grade plans to grow tomatoes, beans, and other vegetables.

**2.** Which sentence gives the most important information?

**A.** Sentence 1 **B.** Sentence 2 **C.** Sentence 3 **D.** Sentence 4

**3.** Which is a main idea that should appear in a summary of this passage?

**A.** Mrs. Sanchez teaches social studies.
**B.** Among the vegetables the students will grow are tomatoes.
**C.** The garden is about 12 feet by 20 feet.
**D.** The students created their garden on the old soccer field.

Name ______________________ Date __________

# Reading: Summary

## Assess

**A** Read this passage. Then, reread it, focusing on the main ideas. Finally, answer the questions.

(1) Many paleontologists, the scientists who study dinosaurs, believe that the smallest dinosaur of all time was probably *Compsognathus.* (2) It was a slender, flesh-eating dinosaur that lived during the last part of the Jurassic period. (3) Fossils and skeletal remains have been found in southern Germany. (4) This dinosaur was only about 2 feet long, and most of its length was in the form of a long, whip-like tail. (5) About the size of a turkey, *Compsognathus* probably weighed no more than 22 pounds.

1. What is the main idea of this passage?
   - **A.** *Compsognathus* was a dinosaur that lived in southern Germany.
   - **B.** *Compsognathus* was about the size of a turkey.
   - **C.** *Compsognathus* was probably the smallest dinosaur of all time.
   - **D.** *Compsognathus* is one of the dinosaurs that scientists study.

2. Which sentence gives the most important information?
   - **A.** Sentence 1 **B.** Sentence 2 **C.** Sentence 3 **D.** Sentence 4

3. Which is a main idea that should appear in a summary of this passage?
   - **A.** It was a flesh-eating dinosaur.
   - **B.** It was only about two feet long.
   - **C.** It had a long, whip-like tail.
   - **D.** Its remains have been found in Germany.

4. Which is a minor detail that should *not* appear in a summary of this passage?
   - **A.** The dinosaur has been studied by paleontologists.
   - **B.** The dinosaur was about the size of a turkey.
   - **C.** The dinosaur probably weighed no more than 22 pounds.
   - **D.** Most of the length of its short body was in the form of a long, whip-like tail.

**B** On a separate sheet of paper, write a brief summary of the passage. Include only the main ideas, expressed in your own words.

Name ______________________________ Date __________

# Reading: Use Text Features to Analyze Information

## Practice

Structural patterns in texts organize information. They provide internal consistency so readers can easily follow an author's logic. Book reviews and books typically include text features that reinforce the structural patterns of a text. As you examine the book review and the book features, evaluate whether the author has successfully used structural patterns.

### Happy All the Time

*How To Live A Happy Life* by Regina Stewart is the latest in a never-ending series of books that seek to teach people how to be happy. The author and her gullible readers seem to believe that happiness is just a matter of finding the right formula. Then, once that magic formula is found, it's just a matter of applying it. They lose sight of the fact that, perhaps, people aren't meant to be happy all the time. Certainly Regina Stewart seems to believe you should be. And she obviously thinks that she knows best. Ms. Stewart must be very happy. She is making lots of money publishing this drivel. There is absolutely nothing new or useful in this book. You would be better off spending your money on a box of chocolates. Now that will make you happy!

—*Marian Williams*

**1.** Does the reviewer have a positive or negative opinion about this book? ______

______________________________

**2.** Give two examples of words or phrases that the reviewer uses to convey her feelings. ______________________________

______________________________

**3.** Does the reviewer indicate who might enjoy this book? ______________________________

______________________________

**4.** Summarize what the reviewer says about the book: ______________________________

______________________________

Name ______________________________ Date ____________

# Reading: Use Text Features to Analyze Information

## Assess

**Read the two reviews of the same book below. Then, answer the questions.**

### Home Sweet Home

When I reached the end of Merle Winston's latest book, *Homeward,* I wanted to cry. It wasn't because the book was sad. It was because I was so entranced that I didn't want to reach the end! This is one of the most engrossing and enjoyable books that I have read in a long time. Winston makes the characters come alive in a way that few authors do. You want to spend more time with them. Even those characters who may not be admirable are always interesting and believable. I think that that is what makes Winston such an excellent writer: his characters seem like real people, only more interesting. I only hope that there will be a sequel to *Homeward,* and soon!

### Style is Not Enough

I couldn't reach the end of *Homeward* soon enough. Yes, Merle Winston's characters were, as usual, unusual. That is not enough. The plot was weak, to say the least. "The least" is the only way to describe the amount of effort Winston seems to have put into this book. Riding the success of his previous bestseller, it seems as though he cranked this one out on auto-pilot. The man can write; I'll give him that. But there is no thought or compelling plot behind the lovely words and interesting characters. Take more time, Mr. Winston. Don't send us another book until you have something to say and a more interesting plot through which you say it.

1. Does the first reviewer have a positive or negative opinion about this book?

   ______________________________

2. Give two examples of words that the first reviewer uses to convey his feelings. ______________________________

3. Does the second reviewer have a positive or negative opinion about this book? ______________________________

4. Give two examples of words that the second reviewer uses to convey her feelings.

   ______________________________

Name ____________________ Date __________

# Literary Analysis: Mythology

## Practice

A **myth** is an ancient tale that presents the beliefs or customs of a culture. Every culture has its own **mythology,** or collection of myths. Here are some purposes of ancient myths:

- *to explain events in nature,* such as why thunder occurs
- *to explain events in a culture's history,* such as why two kingdoms went to war
- *to describe the actions of gods and goddesses,* such as how a god punished a man for being too greedy
- *to present animals or natural forces with human qualities,* such as a kind tree that offers shade to a weary hiker, or a brave raven that leads a lost child to safety
- *to celebrate a great hero or heroine,* such as the brave warrior who saved his people from a terrible dragon
- *to teach a lesson,* such as the importance of loyalty and honesty

Read this myth. Then, answer the questions.

When the village of Mort was threatened by a terrible sea monster, a brave sailor named Goar sailed out to sea to kill the beast. On the way, he ran into a bad storm, and his boat almost sank. The North Wind felt sorry for him and blew icy breezes into the storm, calming it by freezing its power. Goar thanked the North Wind, who replied, "Do not fear, for as long as you respect my power, I will guide and protect your boat." Goar then continued on his voyage and killed the monster. Then, as the North Wind promised, he guided Goar's boat back to shore. The people celebrated Goar's great strength and courage. And to this day, the people of Mort pray to the North Wind before sailing out to sea.

**1.** Who is the hero in this myth? ____________________

**2.** What qualities make this character a hero? ____________________

**3.** What animal or natural force has human qualities? ____________________

**4.** What element of cultural history or tradition does this myth explain? __________

____________________

**5.** What lesson regarding nature does the myth contain? ____________________

____________________

Name ______________________ Date __________

# Literary Analysis: Mythology

## Assess

**A** Circle the letter of the best answer to each question.

1. A *myth* is an ancient story. Which statement is most accurate about its subject matter?

   **A.** It is about the birth of nature.
   **B.** It is about ancient animals and plants.
   **C.** It is about ancient beliefs and customs.
   **D.** It is about ancient humans who act like gods.

2. Which is *not* among the main purposes of ancient mythology?

   **A.** to teach an important life lesson
   **B.** to entertain through humor and music
   **C.** to explain how the gods punished a thief
   **D.** to explain how the leopard got its spots

**B** Read this myth. Then, answer the questions.

The people of Goran were weak because there was no water to drink. A brave young woman named Ida crossed over the high mountains to find Rain Cloud. "Please, Rain Cloud," she pleaded, "send water to my people." Rain Cloud was very proud, and he was surprised that Ida would have the courage to speak to him directly. No one else had ever dared.

"Your courage is rare," he said, "and so is your willingness to help your people. I will send water in a storm for your people. And I will do something else. I will send a lightning bolt to the River Koo. The bolt will shatter the river's banks and cause water to flow to Goran."

Ida thanked Rain Cloud and ran back to Goran in the midst of the great rainstorm. Lightning suddenly hit the banks of the River Koo, splitting the river in half. Today, the village of Goran sits on the banks of the mighty River KooToo.

1. Who is the hero in this myth? ______________________
2. What qualities make this character a hero? ______________________
3. What animal or natural force has human qualities? ______________________
4. What element of cultural history or tradition does this myth explain? ______________________
5. What lesson regarding human behavior does the myth contain? ______________________

Name ____________________ Date __________

# Literary Analysis: Oral Tradition—Dialect

## Practice

Throughout history, people have told stories through the **oral tradition**—passing down many myths, legends, and folk tales through the spoken word. Often, when these stories were written down, they contained **dialect**—the language and grammar of a particular region. Here are two sentences with similar meanings. One is in formal English, and the other, from "Davy Crockett's Dream," is in dialect.

- **Formal English:** I had a troubling dream that I was floating down the Mississippi River in a hollow tree.
- **Dialect:** I had a pesky dream that I was floating down the Massassippy in a holler tree.

**A** Read this passage from "Davy Crockett's Dream." Then, answer the questions.

(1) One day when it was so cold that I was afeard to open my mouth, lest I should freeze my tongue, I took my little dog named Grizzle and cut out for Salt River Bay to kill something for dinner. (2) I got a good ways from home afore I knowed where I was, and as I had swetted some before I left the house my hat froze fast to my head, and I like to have put my neck out of joint in order to pull it off. (3) When I sneezed the icicles crackled all up and down the inside of my nose, like when you walk over a bog in winter time. (4) The varmints was so scarce that I couldn't find one. . . .

1. In Sentence 1, what is the meaning of *afeard*? ____________________
2. In Sentence 1, what is the meaning of *cut out for*? ____________________
3. In Sentence 2, what is the meaning of *afore*? ____________________
4. Translate the clause *I like to have put my neck out of joint in order to pull it off* from Sentence 2. ____________________

   ____________________
5. In Sentence 4, what is the meaning of *varmints*? ____________________

   ____________________

**B** On a separate sheet of paper or on the back of this sheet, rewrite this passage from "Davy Crockett's Dream" in your own words. Use formal English and spelling.

Name ______________________ Date ____________

# Literary Analysis: Oral Tradition—Dialect

## Assess

**A** Read this passage from "The King of Mazy May" by Jack London. It takes place as a group of men sit around a campfire in Canada's icy Klondike region. They want to get rich by finding a very valuable source of gold hidden in the bed of a creek. They have traveled to this place by dog sled, rested, and eaten by the campfire. Now, they are talking about resuming their search for gold.

Once you have read the passage, answer the questions.

"The creek is all right, boys," a large, black-bearded man, evidently the leader, said, "and I think the best thing we can do is to pull out tonight. The dogs can follow the trail; besides, it's going to be moonlight. What say you?"

"But it's going to be beastly cold," objected one of the party. "It's forty below zero now."

"An' sure, can't ye keep warm by jumpin' off the sleds an' runnin' after the dogs?" cried an Irishman. "An' who wouldn't? The creek's as rich as a United States mint! Faith, it's an ilegant chanst to be gettin' a run fer your money! An' if ye don't run, it's mebbe you'll not get the money at all, at all."

1. In Paragraph 1, what does the speaker mean by "The creek is all right"?

_______________________________________________

2. Give another example of dialect in Paragraph 1, and tell what it means.

_______________________________________________

3. In Paragraph 2, what does the speaker mean by "beastly cold"?

_______________________________________________

**B** Rewrite Paragraph 3 in your own words. Use formal English and spelling.

_______________________________________________

_______________________________________________

_______________________________________________

_______________________________________________

_______________________________________________

_______________________________________________

_______________________________________________

Name ______________________ Date __________

# Literary Analysis: Comparing Heroic Characters

## Practice

**Heroic characters** show great courage and overcome difficult challenges. A heroic character can be fictional or real. Often, the hero in a tall tale or legend is a combination of both—a real historical figure whose actions have become so exaggerated over time that he or she has become a legend.

When **comparing heroic characters** in literature, ask the following questions about each character:

- Was this person an actual historical figure? (For example, the stories of King Arthur are probably based on an actual ancient king.)
- What heroic qualities does this person have? (For example: courage, honesty)
- Which actions make the character heroic? (For example, King Arthur defended Britain against serious threats.)

**Read the selections. Then, answer the questions.**

A Geronimo was a powerful Apache warrior born in 1829. He fought against the U.S. government, which was attempting to destroy his culture. Guided by visions, he led successful raids and avoided capture for years at a time. Geronimo was said to walk without leaving footprints, and he could hold off the dawn so his people would be safe. His magical powers protected him from death. Guns and bullets could not harm him.

B Johnny Appleseed was born John Chapman on September 26, 1774. As a young man he roamed the country planting apple trees. He dreamed of a land so full of apples that no one would ever be hungry again. During his travels, Johnny made friends with humans and animals alike. Once he wandered into a cave where a bear and her cubs were hibernating. Unfazed, Johnny curled up beside them and slept through the night.

1. Is either of the characters described above an actual historical figure? Explain.

______________________________________________

2. List the heroic qualities of each character. Then, underline a heroic action in each selection that demonstrates one of these qualities.

   Geronimo: ______________________________________________

   Johnny Appleseed: ______________________________________________

3. Circle an example of an exaggerated action performed by each character.

Name ______________________ Date __________

# Literary Analysis: Comparing Heroic Characters

## Assess

**Read the selections. Then, complete the chart.**

A John Henry was a steel-driving man. Folks say he was born with a hammer in his hand. As a boy, John Henry dreamed he would one day work on the C. & O. Railroad, and he made that dream come true. John Henry was so strong he could do the work of six men. When he swung his hammer, lightning flashed and thunder cracked. One day John Henry agreed to race a steam drill through a mountain. He won the race; then, he lay down and died.

B Paul Bunyan was a giant of a man. When he was born, it took five storks to deliver him to his parents. As a baby, Paul uprooted saplings to use as rattles. One year, when Paul was grown, it rained four months in a row. Paul got fed up, so he swam up the biggest waterfall he could find. After an hour, the rain finally stopped, and Paul splashed back down the waterfall. "I jus' had to turn that thing off," he said. Later, with the help of Babe, his blue ox, Paul pulled the kinks out of crooked logging roads. When the roads were pulled straight, there were an extra five miles of road left over, which Paul rolled up and gave to the town.

| | John Henry | Paul Bunyan |
|---|---|---|
| 1. Do you think he is a historical figure? Why? | | |
| 2. What are his heroic qualities? | | |
| 3. What heroic actions does he perform? | | |
| 4. What exaggerated actions are described? | | |

Name ______________________ Date __________

# Vocabulary: Word Root *-sacr-* and Suffixes *-eer* and *-ful*

## Practice

A **root** is the basic unit of meaning of a word. The word root *-sacr-* means "holy." Consider these examples:

sacr + ed = sacred: "dedicated to religious purposes; holy"

sacr + ament = sacrament: "a religious ritual"

A **suffix** is added to the end of a word to change its meaning or part of speech. The suffix *-eer* means "one who does something." It is sometimes used to change other word parts to nouns. The suffix *-ful* means "full of." It can be used to change nouns to adjectives.

auction + eer = auctioneer: "the person in charge at an auction"

grace + ful = graceful: "moving with grace"

**A** Circle the letter of the correct answer to each question.

**1.** What are you doing if you make a sacrifice?

**A.** gaining something valuable

**B.** giving something up for a holy purpose

**2.** Which kind of behavior would be considered sacrilegious?

**A.** treating ordinary things with respect

**B.** treating holy things with disrespect

**3.** What does it mean to consecrate a place?

**A.** to set it aside for holy purposes

**B.** to set it aside for business purposes

**B** Add *-eer* or *-ful* to each underlined word to form a new word that fits the meaning of the sentence.

**1.** ________________ I felt regret about missing my grandmother's birthday.

**2.** ________________ The mountain was determined to reach the summit.

**3.** ________________ The musket was responsible for guarding the French king.

**4.** ________________ When I found out he had lied to me, I accused him of being deceit.

Name ______________________________ Date ____________

# Vocabulary: Word Root *-sacr-* and Suffixes *-eer* and *-ful*

## Assess

**A** Circle T if the statement is true or F if the statement is false. Then, write a sentence to explain your answer.

**1.** T/F A musketeer is a person who carries a musket, or old-fashioned gun.

______________________________

**2.** T/F If something is sacrosanct, people are not allowed to interfere with it.

______________________________

**3.** T/F A person who has been harmed might feel vengeful.

______________________________

**4.** T/F A ship's captain would be pleased to have mutineers as part of the crew.

______________________________

**B** Add the suffix indicated to each underlined word to form a new word. Write this word on the line. Then rewrite the original sentence to use the new word.

**1.** ____________ The mother and daughter shed many tears at their parting. (add *-ful*)

______________________________

______________________________

**2.** ____________ The singer was best known for performing ballads. (add *-eer*)

______________________________

______________________________

**3.** ____________ I have great hope that I will get into the college of my choice. (add *-ful*)

______________________________

______________________________

Name ______________________________ Date ____________

# Grammar: Sentence Structure

## Practice

The chart shows examples of the four basic **sentence structures.**

| Sentence Structures | Examples |
|---|---|
| A **simple sentence** has a single independent clause and at least one subject and verb. | **We visited Grandma last Saturday.** (1 subject, 1 verb) |
| A **compound sentence** consists of two or more independent clauses usually joined by a comma and a conjunction. | **Nicole likes popular songs**, but **I prefer classical music**. (2 subjects, 2 verbs) |
| A **complex sentence** consists of one independent clause and one or more subordinate clauses. | **Mom and Dad will take us to a movie** when we finish our homework. |
| A **compound-complex sentence** consists of two or more independent clauses and one or more subordinate clauses. | **I can reach my father on the phone**, or **I will go to his office** if I have enough time. |

Identify each sentence as *simple, compound, complex,* or *compound-complex.*

1. ______________ Mr. Griffin runs a pet store, and his children help him.

2. ______________ My brother and sister will arrive tomorrow.

3. ______________ The company that contacted me by phone has a bad reputation.

4. ______________ When I get to London, I will try to buy you a present, but I can't really promise since I may be very busy.

5. ______________ The hunters and bird watchers followed the birds' flight.

6. ______________ Laura is in charge because she is an expert camper.

7. ______________ Lions live in Africa, but most of them are in national parks.

8. ______________ Since the blizzard ended, the schools have remained closed, but shops in town have reopened.

Name ______________________________ Date __________

# Grammar: Sentence Structure

## Assess

**A** Identify each sentence as *compound, complex,* or *compound-complex.*

**1.** ____________ After the game was over, we ordered a pizza.

**2.** ____________ The situation is confusing, but I hope to have more news soon.

**3.** ____________ Your argument is weak, for you have no proof to support your ideas.

**4.** ____________ I am interested in going into politics when I finish college.

**5.** ____________ The mountain areas are barren, but the valleys are fertile since they are irrigated daily.

**6.** ____________ Wild cats often hunt at night, but some prefer dawn or dusk.

**B** Write a compound sentence for each pair of shorter sentences below. Use an appropriate conjunction and correct punctuation.

**1.** The article was interesting. It did not have the information I needed.

______________________________

**2.** Cats vary in size. Many have wild colorings.

______________________________

**3.** We had been traveling for ten hours. We were happy to reach the motel.

______________________________

**C** Rewrite each sentence by adding a dependent clause to form a complex sentence. Use the word in parentheses to introduce the dependent clause.

**1.** School closings were announced on TV and radio. (because)

______________________________

**2.** Do your homework first. (if)

______________________________

Name ______________________ Date __________

# Grammar: Commas

## Practice

A **comma** is a punctuation mark that signals a brief pause.

Use a comma

- before a conjunction to separate two independent clauses in a compound sentence.

  They had been working very hard**, but** they didn't seem especially tired.

- between items in a series.

  **December, January,** and **February** are summer months in the Southern Hemisphere.

- between adjectives in a series.

  The man had a **long, narrow,** and **sad** face.

- after introductory material.

  **Sparkling in the light of the sun,** the ocean looked beautiful.

- with parenthetical expressions.

  **To tell the truth,** history is my favorite subject.

- to set off appositives, participial phrases, or adjective clauses.

  Mars, **one of the closest planets,** can be seen without a telescope.

Insert commas as needed in the following sentences.

**1.** After they built a sand castle they had a picnic.

**2.** Baseball basketball and soccer are my favorite sports.

**3.** She was tired yet she was determined to finish the race.

**4.** Red blue and silver fish flashed in the lagoon.

**5.** After the brief rain shower had ended the sun began to shine.

**6.** Sarah stop talking and listen to me.

**7.** Wind rattled the windows of the cabin yet the campers slept soundly.

**8.** His words I believe struck home.

Name ____________________ Date __________

# Grammar: Commas

## Assess

**A** Insert commas as needed in the following sentences.

1. If you are easily frightened don't see that movie.
2. I've called the guests bought the food and warned the neighbors.
3. Do you want to bring pretzels salad or soda to the picnic?
4. Goodness no one could lift this rock without help.
5. The praying mantis on the other hand kills many harmful insects.
6. Mowing the lawn on such a hazy hot humid day was no fun.
7. Lost and frightened the child began to cry.
8. Claire saw two of her friends in the grandstand so she went to sit with them.
9. Mrs. Whitman I am happy to say will be back in the classroom soon.
10. If Mr. Wilson complains we'll invite him for a snack.

**B** Read the sentences. Write *C* if the sentence is correctly punctuated. Write *I* if the sentence is incorrectly punctuated. Then, rewrite any incorrect sentences correctly, adding a comma or commas as necessary.

1. ______ The road ran around the mountain across the river and into the town.

____________________

2. ______ Apply the paint smoothly and evenly and steadily.

____________________

3. ______ Jimmy Carter, the former president was also governor of Georgia.

____________________

4. ______ By the way, can you bring knives and forks?

____________________

5. ______ Ernest Hemingway the famous author wrote *The Old Man and the Sea*.

____________________

Name ______________________ Date __________

# Grammar: Using Language to Maintain Interest

## Practice

When giving a presentation, you should **use language to maintain interest** in what you are saying. You can keep the audience actively engaged by doing the following as you use make your points:

- **Vary sentence length:** Alternate short sentences with long ones.
- **Vary sentence type:** Combine simple, compound, complex, and compound-complex sentences in an interesting way.

  **Simple**

  Objects from space like meteors fall into the atmosphere.

  **Compound**

  Friction makes meteors incredibly hot, and they burn up miles above

  **Complex**

  the earth's surface. When some large meteors do not burn up completely, they are called meteorites.
- **Use transitions:** To smooth sudden shifts in topics, use common transitions to show relationships between ideas.

**Examples:** again, also, in the same way, likewise, although, however, for example, for instance, all in all, in conclusion, as a result, consequently

Read the paragraph. Then, make the changes indicated.

1) America was always a country of immigrants. 2) Immigrants came to America for different reasons. 3) Some of them wanted to own land or find work. 4) Others wanted religious freedom or self-government. 5) Immigrants from the same country often settled together in their own neighborhoods. 6) These neighborhoods were often poor and crowded. 7) Immigrants who lived together in one neighborhood were slow to adapt and change to new ways. 8) Prejudice against the new immigrants was not uncommon.

**1.** Combine sentences 3 and 4 to make a longer, compound sentence.

______________________________________

**2.** Combine sentences 5 and 6 to make a complex sentence.

______________________________________

**3.** Add a transition to the beginning of sentence 8 to show that sentence 7 caused sentence 8.

______________________________________

Name ______________________________ Date __________

# Grammar: Using Language to Maintain Interest

## Assess

**A** Write the transition that best completes each sentence.

However   For example   All in all   Finally   In a like manner

1. Animals have had to adjust to the desert. ____________________, the camel can store water.

2. Most people think that a camel stores water in its hump. ____________________, it actually stores the water in its stomach

3. The Pilgrims sailed aboard the *Mayflower* for six weeks. ____________________, the sailors sighted land.

4. Alligators usually attack other animals in the water. ____________________, crocodiles will pull an animal under water and hold it there until it drowns.

5. Our science fair had many successes and a few problems. ____________________, it was a great day.

**B** Read the paragraph. Then, make the changes indicated.

1) Harriet Tubman was a great woman. 2) Tubman escaped from slavery in Maryland. 3) She returned nineteen times to help other slaves escape. 4) The Underground Railroad was a system by which the opponents of slavery secretly helped fugitive slaves escape to the free states or to Canada. 5) Harriet Tubman had the support of many Americans. 6) They provided hiding places, or stations, along the "railroad." 7) Harriet Tubman never lost one of her passengers. 8) Many other runaway slaves were not so lucky.

1. Combine sentences 2 and 3 to make a longer, compound sentence.

_____________________________________________

2. Combine sentences 5 and 6 to make a complex sentence.

_____________________________________________

3. Add a transition to the beginning of sentence 8 to show that it is in contrast to sentence 7.

_____________________________________________

Name ______________________________ Date ____________

# Writing: Myth

## Practice

**Myths** are ancient tales that present the beliefs or customs of a culture. Many myths began as ways to explain natural occurrences, such as why the sky is blue. The characters in myths include animals, gods, humans, and forces of nature, such as the sea. Myths usually convey a lesson that is valued by the culture that created the myth, such as *bravery is rewarded.* When writing a myth of your own, keep these major elements of myths in mind.

Read this myth. Then, respond to each item below.

Ages ago, giraffes had short necks. They lazed about, nibbling tender grass and leafy bushes. Then the Great Dry Year began. Day after day, Old Man Sun burned the grass and scorched the bushes. A young giraffe named Nika went to Old Man Sun and said, "Please, sir, stop burning our food! I fear that old Nona Giraffe may die of hunger."

"Silly child," said Old Man Sun. "There are plenty of green leaves high up in the trees. You just have to stop lazing about and work harder!" Indeed, Nika saw many delicious leaves high in the tall trees. She stretched and stretched to reach them. It was very tiring, but she knew she had to work hard to get food for Nona Giraffe. As she stretched, her neck grew and grew until finally she reached the leaves. From that day on, giraffes have had long necks.

**1.** What natural occurrence does this myth explain? (Phrase it as a question.)

______________________________

**2.** In your own words, briefly describe the myth's explanation of this natural occurrence. ______________________________

______________________________

______________________________

______________________________

______________________________

**3.** Who are the characters? ______________________________

______________________________

**4.** What lesson does the myth teach? ______________________________

______________________________

Name ______________________________ Date ______________

# Writing: Myth

## Assess

**A** Complete the activities to begin writing a myth.

**1.** Choose a natural occurrence that you would like to explain creatively, phrasing it as a question.

______________________________

**2.** Devise a creative answer to your question. ______________________________

______________________________

______________________________

**3.** List your characters. ______________________________

______________________________

______________________________

**4.** Plan your action, the events that will provide the answer to your central question. ______________________________

______________________________

______________________________

**5.** Include a lesson. ______________________________

**B** On the lines provided, write the first paragraph of your myth.

______________________________

______________________________

______________________________

______________________________

______________________________

______________________________

______________________________

______________________________

______________________________

Name ______________________________ Date ______________

# Writing: Critical Analysis

## Practice

A **critical analysis** is an evaluation of how well an author achieves his or her purpose. Often, a critical analysis focuses on one element of a literary work, such as the plot, the main character, or the author's use of language. Usually, you will write a critical analysis in response to a specific assignment from your teacher or to a writing prompt in your textbook or on a test. Use these tips to write a critical analysis:

- Read the writing assignment carefully. Note which literary element you should evaluate and what standards you should use to evaluate the element.
- Reread the literary work, and take notes on the element you are evaluating.
- Write a topic sentence that expresses your evaluation of how well the author uses the literary element.
- Use details from the literary work to support your main idea.

Read this beginning of a critical analysis of the character Pecos Bill in "Pecos Bill: The Cyclone." Then, complete the activities that follow.

Pecos Bill is a superhero who saves the day by using his skills as a cowboy to defeat one of the cowboy's greatest enemies, the cyclone. Cyclones are storms that can destroy property, animals, and human life in the Southwest. In his battle with the cyclone, Bill demonstrates all the qualities of a good cowboy: riding ability, courage, humor, and pride in his accomplishments.

1. What main idea about Pecos Bill does this critical analysis express?

______________________________

______________________________

2. What qualities of Pecos Bill does this critical analysis point out?

______________________________

______________________________

3. What kinds of details from the story should the writer include in further paragraphs of this critical analysis? ______________________________

______________________________

______________________________

Name ______________________________ Date ____________

# Writing: Critical Analysis

## Assess

Use the following steps to write a critical analysis.

1. Choose a heroic character from a story or movie. Write the character's name and the name of the work in which he or she appears.

_______________________________________________

2. What main idea would you like to express about this character's achievements in the story or movie?

_______________________________________________

3. What qualities about this hero do you admire most?

_______________________________________________

_______________________________________________

4. Describe three scenes in the story or movie in which the hero demonstrates these qualities.

_______________________________________________

_______________________________________________

_______________________________________________

5. On the lines below, write a critical analysis of the character you chose in Step 1. Use the sentence you wrote in Step 2 as your topic sentence. Use the qualities and scenes you listed in Steps 3 and 4 as details to support the main idea in your topic sentence.

_______________________________________________

_______________________________________________

_______________________________________________

_______________________________________________

_______________________________________________

_______________________________________________

_______________________________________________

_______________________________________________

Name ______________________________ Date ____________

# Writing: Multimedia Report

## Practice

If you enhance an oral or written report with other media, you will have a **multimedia report.** The other media may include any of the following: music, artwork, charts, maps, posters, live performance, slides, or video. A multimedia report should include these elements:

- A topic that can be covered thoroughly in the time allowed
- A main idea that shows a clear focus
- Facts, details, examples, and explanations to support the main idea
- Media that effectively support the topic and main idea
- Careful and accurate research

Read this plan for a multimedia report. Then, answer the questions.

Sara wants to do a multimedia report on animals of Africa. She wants to cover mammals, birds, fish, reptiles, and insects. She went to the library and consulted several encyclopedias and about twenty books. She plans to include video of the animals, recordings of the animals' sounds, and charts showing genus and species relationships. She is hoping to get a zoo worker to present some live animals for members of her audience to observe and pet.

**1.** What is the problem with Sara's topic? ______________________________

______________________________

**2.** How could Sara change her topic to improve its focus? ______________________________

______________________________

**3.** Give at least two examples of how Sara could change her plan so she would have a more effective presentation.

______________________________

______________________________

______________________________

______________________________

______________________________

______________________________

Name ______________________ Date __________

# Writing: Multimedia Report

## Assess

**A** Read this description of a plan for a multimedia report. Then, complete the activities.

Kevin is creating a multimedia report on the great athletes of the twentieth century. He plans to include a slide show, accompanied by appropriate music to add excitement. He has started to do some research on the Internet. He is not sure where else to look, but his uncle has an extensive collection of sports magazines and memorabilia in his rec room.

1. Explain the problem with Kevin's topic and how you would change it.

______________________

2. Explain where Kevin could go to get help with the research on his topic.

______________________

3. Give at least two examples of how Kevin might improve the way he plans to present information on the topic.

______________________

______________________

**B** Suppose you are planning a multimedia report about a topic of interest from science, social studies, literature, or another school subject. Fill in the information below. Then, write a description of the multimedia report you will present.

My topic: ______________________

My main idea: ______________________

Two examples of media I can use to support my ideas: ______________________

______________________

Brief description of my multimedia report:

______________________

______________________

______________________

______________________

______________________

Name ______________________ Date __________

# Reading: Setting a Purpose for Reading

## Practice

When you **set a purpose for reading,** you decide on a specific reason for reading a selection. Setting a purpose for reading helps you focus your attention as you read. One way to set a purpose for reading is to ask questions about the topic of the work using a ***K-W-L*** chart, as below.

**Topic** ______________________

| What I Already Know | What I Want to Know | What I Learned |
|---|---|---|
| | | |

Fill in the first two columns of your chart before you begin to read. The second column identifies your purpose for reading.

Circle the letter of the best answer.

**1.** When should you set a purpose for reading?

**A.** after you finish reading
**B.** only when you have an assignment
**C.** before you begin reading
**D.** only when you are reading for enjoyment

**2.** Imagine that you have been given a research assignment: investigate the history of something we use every day. You decide to find out about the history of glass. You make a K-W-L chart and write in the "K" column facts you already know about glass. Which of the following would you probably *not* include in the "W" column of your chart?

**A.** When were the first man-made glass objects made?
**B.** What culture first made glass?
**C.** Was the first glass clear?
**D.** Why does glass break?

**3.** What is your most likely purpose for reading?

**A.** to learn more about the origins of glass
**B.** to learn about how to make stained glass
**C.** to find amusing stories about glass
**D.** to find life stories of scientists who developed new kinds of glass

Name ______________________________ Date ____________

# Reading: Setting a Purpose for Reading

## Assess

**A** Circle the letter of the best answer.

1. What is the best definition of *a purpose for reading*?
   - **A.** a reason for opening a book
   - **B.** a specific reason for reading a selection
   - **C.** to be entertained
   - **D.** to be informed

2. How is setting a purpose for reading helpful to the reader?
   - **A.** It sets a time frame for reading.
   - **B.** It improves reading skills overall.
   - **C.** It helps the reader focus his or her attention.
   - **D.** It helps readers with scheduling problems.

3. Which of the following would be most helpful in setting a purpose for reading a specific work?
   - **A.** understanding where to locate the work
   - **B.** asking questions about the topic of the work
   - **C.** hoping to have a positive response to the work
   - **D.** knowing what the author's purpose was in writing the work

**B** Look at the K-W-L chart, and complete the activities.

**Topic** ______________________________

| What I Already Know | ________ W ________ | What I Learned |
|---|---|---|
| | ____________________<br>____________________<br>____________________ | |

1. Fill in the title for the **W** column.

2. In the **W** column, indicate what you should write down here.

3. What does the information that you enter into a **W** column of a K-W-L chart help you identify? ______________________________

Name ______________________ Date __________

# Reading: Analyze Treatment, Scope, and Organization of Ideas

## Practice

Any subject can be explored through multiple forms of media, such as the written word, television, radio, and the visual arts. Transcripts are complete written records of what people said in a TV show, a trial, an interview, a debate, or a speech. They contain the exact words of the speakers.

**Heading** This feature contains important information such as the date, topic, and time of the event.

**Formatting** Each speaker is identified at the beginning of each line with capital letters, spacing, or special typefaces and colors.

**Organization** An interviewer's or reporter's questions and comments identify the topics covered in the transcript. The text that follows each question or comment provides detailed information.

**Brackets or Parentheses** These identify information that is not part of what was said. This can include source information or background information.

Circle the letter of the best answer.

1. What is a transcript?

   **A.** a brief summary of what people said
   **B.** a critical review of what people said
   **C.** a complete and accurate record of what people said.
   **D.** a simplified paraphrase of what people said

2. For what would you most likely use a transcript for research?

   **A.** a TV interview
   **B.** a TV football game
   **C.** a concert shown on TV
   **D.** a TV commercial

3. What part of a transcript tells you when the event took place?

   **A.** the heading
   **B.** the formatting
   **C.** the information in brackets/parentheses
   **D.** the organization

Name ______________________________ Date ____________

# Reading: Analyze Treatment, Scope, and Organization of Ideas

## Assess

**Read the transcript below. Then, answer the questions that follow.**

Partial transcript of radio interview with Art Nathan, legendary creator of the cartoon SillyBoy, January 13, 2008

INTERVIEWER: How did you get the idea for this cartoon?

ART NATHAN: (laughs) I think that the idea was always there, even when I was a child. I had drawn versions of the character that would become SillyBoy. I made those flip books, where you draw the same character in a slightly different way on each page, and then when you flip them with your thumb, it looks like a cartoon. Now, of course, it's all done with computers.

INTERVIEWER: Do you use computers now?

ART NATHAN: I mess around with them. But when I have an idea for something, I still draw or at least sketch it by hand. I have been doing it for so long that I can draw by hand much faster than I can do anything on the computer.

INTERVIEWER: So, is the character really a cartoon version of you?

ART NATHAN: (sighs) People always ask me that. Strictly speaking, no. But of course, any work that you do always has some of yourself in it. In this case, I have tried to make him the opposite of me—to give him characteristics I don't have, but maybe wish I did.

INTERVIEWER: Why do you think he became so popular?

ART NATHAN: Perhaps because he does what people wish they had the nerve to do. He speaks his mind.

1. Name the two people taking part in this interview. ______________________________

______________________________

2. Give two examples of information given that is not the words of either person.

______________________________

3. How does the information in item two help you understand the interview better?

______________________________

4. How is this interview transcript organized? ______________________________

______________________________

Name ______________________ Date ____________

# Literary Analysis: Cultural Context

## Practice

The **cultural context** of a literary work is the social and historical environment in which the characters live. Major historical events, such as bad economic times or the outbreak of war, can shape people's lives in important ways. Understanding the effects of such events can give you insight into characters' attitudes and actions.

Read the following portion of a letter written by a young teen living in Virginia in 1970, when men between the ages of 18 and 35 were being drafted for the war at the rate of 50,000 each month. Then, answer the questions about cultural context.

Charlie and I had been planning to drive to Texas this summer to visit our sister. We'd been looking forward to it all year. It was our big chance to spend some real time together before he left for college in the fall. But all that changed when Charlie received his draft letter. Now he's in a ditch somewhere fighting off the Vietcong. I worry every day that he won't make it back home alive. I don't understand why Charlie had to go. I told him he should run away to Canada, but he said the people who run away are traitors. He said it was his duty to serve his country.

1. What historical event is most significant in this letter's cultural context?

   A. the Gulf War
   B. the Vietnam War
   C. the American Revolution
   D. the presidential election

2. How are Charlie's plans affected by the draft of the 1960s and 1970s?

   A. His sister will not be able to come visit him as planned.
   B. He will not be able to go to college in the fall as planned.
   C. He will have to begin a new life in Canada.
   D. He will have to move in with his sister in Texas.

3. How does the writer react to these changes?

   A. She welcomes the change and looks forward to moving to Canada.
   B. She is unhappy that Charlie is moving to Canada.
   C. She is unhappy that Charlie was drafted and worries about him.
   D. She is upset with Charlie for not driving to Texas with her.

4. What does the letter tell you about the social environment during this time?

   A. The draft was controversial; some people chose to evade it.
   B. All men called to serve went willingly and enthusiastically.
   C. Men who went to Canada had the support of their communities.
   D. Friends and family of draftees felt sure that they would return safely.

Name ______________________ Date __________

# Literary Analysis: Cultural Context

## Assess

**Read the following portion of a fictional journal, and then answer the questions below.**

My family arrived here five years ago during the Second Wave, just two years after the Great Exodus of 2100, when the air on Earth was becoming too toxic to breathe. The most exciting part of life on this new planet is that people here can fly. They have discovered how to make their bodies lighter than air. That means there is no need for cars or other vehicles that pollute the planet. Humans are a minority here, but we live in a supportive, immigrant community, and we coexist peacefully with the natives. One day soon I hope to learn their ways and fly as they do.

**1.** What conclusion can you draw about the social environment in which the journal's author lives?

**A.** He lives on a planet more advanced than Earth.
**B.** He lives on a new planet dominated by humans.
**C.** He lives on Earth, the cleanest, most advanced planet in space.
**D.** He lives on a planet in which humans are not welcome.

**2.** What does the author mean when he refers to a "supportive immigrant community"?

**A.** an ethnic community of Italian Americans
**B.** an ethnic community of Asian Americans
**C.** a human community of Earthlings
**D.** a community of aliens who can fly on their own

**3.** How is the author affected by the Second Wave?

**A.** He is uprooted from his childhood planet.
**B.** He is forced to live on a toxic planet.
**C.** He is forced to live in a hostile community.
**D.** He is suddenly able to fly.

**4.** How is the journal author's cultural context different from our own? ______

______

______

______

______

______

Name ______________________ Date ____________

# Literary Analysis: Identify Author's Influences

## Practice

An **author's influences** are the cultural and historical factors that affect his or her writing. These factors may include the time and place of an author's birth, the author's cultural and educational background, or world events during the author's lifetime.

**Read the following portion of a fictional letter by an Englishman living in London in 1778, when the American colonies were fighting for their independence from England. Then, circle the letter of the answer that best completes each statement.**

I had expected to sail next year to the colony of Virginia to visit my brother. It is a difficult trip at any time. However, now the ridiculous "war of independence" has made the voyage impossible. I do not understand why the American colonies wish to separate from us. They are Englishmen, as we are. Our armies protect them from their enemies. They complain of paying taxes, but the taxes we charge them are payment for that protection. I wonder how my brother can bear to live among such people. Surely he cannot have taken up their cause.

**1.** One *historical* factor that influenced the author was

**A.** the Civil War.
**B.** the age of Discovery.
**C.** the first Thanksgiving.
**D.** the American War of Independence.

**2.** According to this passage, one *cultural* factor that affected the author was

**A.** brotherly love toward his Virginian brother.
**B.** loyalty to his homeland, England.
**C.** fear of America.
**D.** dislike of unfair taxation.

**3.** The fact that the author states that the voyage to America is "a difficult trip at any time" shows

**A.** the state of sea travel at the time.
**B.** the author's personal fear of the sea.
**C.** the historical facts of war.
**D.** the psychological effects of a long trip.

Name ______________________________ Date __________

# Literary Analysis: Identify Author's Influences

## Assess

**Read the following passage from "Marigolds" by Eugenia W. Collier (born 1928). Then, circle the letter of the answer that best completes each statement.**

The Depression that gripped the nation was no new thing to us, for the black workers of rural Maryland had always been depressed. I don't know what it was that we were waiting for; certainly not for the prosperity that was "just around the corner," for those were white folks' words, which we never believed. Nor did we wait for hard work and thrift to pay off in shining success as the American Dream promised, for we knew better than that, too. . . .

We children, of course, were only vaguely aware of the extent of our poverty. . . . In those days everybody we knew was just as hungry and ill-clad as we were. Poverty was the cage in which we were trapped. . . .

**1.** One *historical* factor that influenced the author was

**A.** the growth of industry.
**B.** the migration of African Americans to Northern states.
**C.** the poverty of African Americans in Maryland.
**D.** the admission of Maryland to the Union.

**2.** A *cultural* factor that the author responds to is

**A.** the freedom of life in the big city.
**B.** the American Dream.
**C.** the lack of better schools for rural children.
**D.** the strength of community.

**3.** The author's attitude toward white people's words shows the cultural influence of

**A.** segregation and prejudice.
**B.** books and magazines.
**C.** poverty and deprivation.
**D.** hard work and thrift.

Name ________________________________ Date ____________

## Literary Analysis: Comparing Works on a Similar Theme

### Practice

The **theme** of a literary work is the central idea, underlying message, or insight that it reveals. For example, the theme of a short story about a boy who finds a wallet, turns it into the police, and gets a large reward might be *Honesty often brings rewards.* Many pieces of literature—short stories, poems, nonfiction articles, dramas—can share the same theme. However, the ways in which each writer reveals and develops that theme are often quite different.

Read these two pieces of literature. Then, answer the questions.

**MARGARET,**
**a poem by Carl Sandburg**

Many birds and the beating of wings
Make a flinging reckless hum
In the early morning at the rocks
Above the blue pool
Where the gray shadows swim lazy.
In your blue eyes, O reckless child,
I saw today many little wild wishes,
Eager as the great morning.

**JOAN, a narrative essay**

I often go walking in the park in the early morning. But there are many things that I don't tend to notice any more. I guess I'm so used to the sights and sounds. However, when I walk with my little sister Joan, I'm always struck by the delight she takes in even the smallest details—a chirping bird, a pale white flower. To Joan, that flower is a jewel; to me, it is just a weed. But when I experience such sights with Joan, I'm able once again to see the jewels and to be filled with wonder, eagerness, and hope.

**1.** Which statement best expresses the theme that these two pieces share?

**A.** Early morning walks often bring discoveries.
**B.** Nature is filled with color, form, and movement.
**C.** A child can rely on play and imagination to make a walk interesting.
**D.** Children are better than adults at appreciating nature's beauty.

**2.** How are the sights and sounds mentioned in each piece alike and different?

________________________________________________________________

________________________________________________________________

**3.** How are the ways in which the writer develops the theme alike and different? ____________________________________________

________________________________________________________________

Name ______________________________ Date __________

## Literary Analysis: Comparing Works on a Similar Theme

### Assess

Read these two pieces of literature. Then, answer the questions.

**THEY WILL SAY,**
**a poem by Carl Sandburg**

OF my city the worst that men will ever say is this:
You took little children away from the sun and the dew,
And the glimmers that played in the grass under the great sky,
And the reckless rain; you put them between walls
To work, broken and smothered, for bread and wages,
To eat dust in their throats and die empty-hearted
For a little handful of pay on a few Saturday nights.

**A TERRIBLE SITUATION,**
**a newspaper editorial**

Our city has a terrible secret. Hidden in farmers' markets in the Blethwith area are vegetable stalls being managed illegally. To stock them, children work long hours, planting, tending, and harvesting vegetables. These children are not protected by our laws because they are invisible—the sons and daughters of unregistered immigrants. They do not go to school. They do not play. All they do is toil in dusty fields from dawn until dusk, working for terribly low wages. These children need our protection!

**1.** Which statement best expresses the theme that these two pieces share?

**A.** Many factory workers are not paid fairly and are forced to work long hours.
**B.** It is shameful that children are forced to work in terrible conditions.
**C.** People who work in clothing factories often die empty-hearted.
**D.** We must protect children and immigrants with new laws.

**2.** How are the children's situations in each piece alike and different?

______________________________

______________________________

**3.** How are the writer's purposes for writing alike and different? __________

______________________________

**4.** How are the ways in which the writer develops the theme alike and different? __________

______________________________

Name ______________________________ Date __________

# Vocabulary: Word Roots *-nat-*, *-grat-*, *-her-*, and *-aud-*

## Practice

A **root** is the basic unit of meaning of a word. Knowing the meanings of word roots can help you figure out the meanings of many new words. Study these examples.

| Root | Meaning | Words with the Root |
|---|---|---|
| -nat- | to be born | native, national, international, natural |
| -grat- | thanks; pleasing | grateful, congratulate, gratify, gratitude |
| -her- | heir, inheritor | heiress, heritable, heritage, inherit |
| -aud- | to hear | audio, audience, inaudible, auditorium |

**A** Replace each underlined word or phrase with the most appropriate word from the chart above.

**1.** ______________ I felt thankful for all the help she had given me.

**2.** ______________ She enjoyed celebrating her Scandinavian background on holidays.

**3.** ______________ The crowd applauded wildly when the rock star appeared on stage.

**4.** ______________ Our team may get to take part in a countrywide competition.

**B** Circle the letter of the word that best completes each sentence.

**1.** The wealthy ______________ had many suitors

**A.** audience **B.** heiress **C.** native

**2.** Both my parents are ______________ of New York.

**A.** heirs **B.** ingrates **C.** natives

Name ______________________ Date __________

# Vocabulary: Word Roots *-nat-*, *-grat-*, *-her-*, and *-aud-*

## Assess

**A** Revise each sentence so that the underlined vocabulary word is used logically. Be sure not to change the vocabulary word.

1. The worker tried to ingratiate himself with his boss by insulting her.

_______________________________________________

2. I like to go to the mall to spend time in a natural setting.

_______________________________________________

3. I like to download and watch audio files on my computer.

_______________________________________________

4. My father inherited his blue eyes from me.

_______________________________________________

5. Prenatal care is very important after childbirth.

_______________________________________________

**B** Circle the root in each word, and think about its meaning. Then, write the word's meaning on the first line. Use a dictionary to check the meaning. Finally, use each word in a new sentence.

1. audition _______________________________________________

_______________________________________________

2. innate _______________________________________________

_______________________________________________

3. gratitude _______________________________________________

_______________________________________________

4. hereditary _______________________________________________

_______________________________________________

Name ______________________________ Date ____________

# Grammar: Semicolons and Colons

## Practice

Use a **semicolon** (;) to join independent clauses that are not already joined by the conjunctions *and, but, or, nor, for, so,* or *yet*. Use a **colon** (:) before a list of items that follows an independent clause.

> **Example:** Christine is eight years older than her brothers; she often baby-sits for them.
> These cookies contain the following ingredients: flour, brown sugar, butter, eggs, and nuts.

Rewrite these sentences, adding semicolons and colons where needed.

1. Gradually the water evaporates the salt forms crystals.

   ______________________________

2. The basic unit consists of three rooms a living room, bedroom, and kitchen.

   ______________________________

3. They decided not to go shopping instead, they went walking in the park.

   ______________________________

4. Four states border Mexico California, Arizona, New Mexico, and Texas.

   ______________________________

5. Some cheeses are made from cow's milk others are made from goat's milk.

   ______________________________

6. Becky is fascinated by sharks however, she has not yet met one close up.

   ______________________________

7. Their new home is beautiful no one would guess it was once a barn.

   ______________________________

8. Add these things to your list soap, bread, eggs, and milk then, come back as soon as you can.

   ______________________________

Name ______________________ Date ____________

# Grammar: Semicolons and Colons

## Assess

**A** In each sentence, put a semicolon where it is needed.

1. We expect to win easily nevertheless, we are still practicing very hard.
2. Running through the park, Gail tripped she scraped her knee badly.
3. The man did not show up for his appointment that morning instead, he left town.
4. Steve sent the hamburger back it was too rare.
5. Kerrie had a cast on her leg nevertheless, she was the first one on the dance floor.
6. This was the heaviest snowfall in years it broke all records.
7. I love tennis in fact, I play four times a week.
8. If I am not awake by five o'clock, call me otherwise, I will be late for work.

**B** In each sentence, put a colon where it is needed.

1. This semester we are studying several civilizations Egyptian, Greek, and Roman.
2. My list for camp includes the following items of clothing shirts, shorts, sneakers, socks, sweatshirts, and swimming suits.
3. We saw many types of dogs at the show collies, setters, poodles, beagles, and boxers.
4. Four team sports are popular in U.S. schools basketball, baseball, football, and soccer.
5. Campers should bring the following items sheets, blankets, and towels.
6. Nick chose three poets to study Dickinson, Frost, and Sandburg.
7. In this wallet are my life's savings six dollar bills, eight quarters, and two nickels.
8. Their birthdays were all in the summer June 23, July 11, and August 9.

Name ______________________ Date __________

# Grammar: Capitalization

## Practice

A **capital letter** is used at the beginning of a sentence and for the first letter of proper nouns and adjectives.

| Capitalize | Examples |
| --- | --- |
| the first word in a sentence | **T**he museum is open to the public daily. **H**ave you seen the most recent exhibit? |
| the first word in a quotation that is a complete sentence | Richard Lovelace wrote, "**S**tone walls do not a prison make." |
| the pronoun *I* | This summer **I** am going to camp for six weeks. |
| proper nouns, geographical names, and organizations | The largest country in **S**outh **A**merica is **B**razil. |
| titles of people | We went to visit **M**r. Donohue in the hospital. |

Rewrite these sentences, substituting capital letters where appropriate.

**1.** wow! these fireworks are spectacular!

______________________________

**2.** whenever i see andrea, she is with rachael.

______________________________

**3.** the city of cleveland lies on the shore of lake erie.

______________________________

**4.** my brother will enter the university of wisconsin in september.

______________________________

**5.** george washington fought on the side of the british in the french and indian war.

______________________________

______________________________

Name ______________________ Date __________

# Grammar: Capitalization

## Assess

**A** Underline the words in each sentence that should begin with a capital letter.

1. as soon as i met janet scott, i knew we would be friends.
2. it was emma lazarus who wrote, "give me your tired, your poor."
3. the yellow sea separates south korea from china.
4. the matterhorn is one of the mountains in the alps.
5. my brother jason is going to a class reunion at the university of chicago.
6. she asked, "have you ever appeared on late-night TV?"
7. hoover dam is in nevada, southeast of las vegas.
8. the rose bowl parade is televised every new year's day.
9. how could the owner have said, "my dog is friendly?"
10. my whole family went to visit aunt cecilia.

**B** Each numbered pair contains a two-word proper noun and a proper adjective modifying a common noun. Capitalize each item correctly.

**Example:** **A.** english channel **B.** english silverware
**A.** English Channel **B.** English silverware

1. **A.** korean war ______________ **B.** korean soldier ______________

2. **A.** roman empire ______________ **B.** roman architecture ______________

3. **A.** italian renaissance ______________ **B.** italian pastries ______________

4. **A.** kentucky derby ______________ **B.** kentucky people ______________

5. **A.** french revolution ______________ **B.** french dressing ______________

Name ______________________________ Date __________

## Grammar: Revising Run-on Sentences and Sentence Fragments

### Practice

Sentence errors such as run-on sentences and sentence fragments can make writing difficult to understand. A **run-on sentence** is two or more complete sentences that are not properly joined or separated. This sentence error can be corrected by breaking the sentence into two, or by adding punctuation or words to clarify the meaning of a single sentence.

| Run-on | Corrected |
|---|---|
| The pilot landed the plane in Chicago it had been a bumpy flight. | **Separate sentences:** The pilot landed the plane in Chicago. It had been a bumpy flight.<br>*or*<br>**Add comma and coordinating conjunction:** The pilot landed the plane in Chicago, but it had been a bumpy flight.<br>*or*<br>**Use a semicolon:** The pilot landed the plane in Chicago; it had been a bumpy flight. |

A **sentence fragment** is a group of words that does not express a complete thought. You can fix a fragment by either adding it to a nearby sentence or adding more information to complete the idea.

Fragment: When I finished my homework.
Corrected: It was nine o'clock when I finished my homework.

Identify each of the following as a *complete sentence,* a *run-on,* or a *fragment.*

**1.** ____________ As I gazed at the tree.

**2.** ____________ In the afternoon, we had a picnic.

**3.** ____________ Have you seen my new costume it looks terrific?

**4.** ____________ After graduation, Paul is joining the army.

**5.** ____________ Which opened last week on Broadway.

**6.** ____________ Kevin is the best football player on the team.

**7.** ____________ Rain forests thrive in tropical weather not all rain forests are in the Tropics.

Name ______________________ Date ____________

## Grammar: Revising Run-on Sentences and Sentence Fragments

### Assess

**A** Correct each of the run-ons in the following sentences.

**Example:** We began to shovel the snow it was very deep.
We began to shovel the snow. It was very deep.

1. We expected the senator to arrive tonight she has just returned from Africa.

___

2. Here is the package you ordered, it was delivered this morning.

___

3. Karen writes music she is a fine pianist.

___

4. The storm flooded major highways, motorists were warned to stay at home.

___

5. A trip to the state park seemed like a good idea everyone agreed to go next Sunday.

___

**B** Use each of the following fragments in a sentence.

1. when the delivery man rang the bell

___

2. on top of the hill

___

3. a policeman standing on the corner

___

4. since my last visit to Los Angeles

___

5. between you and me

___

Name ________________________________ Date ____________

# Spelling: Vowel Sounds in Unstressed Syllables

## Practice

In many words, the vowel sounds in one or more certain syllables is not clear. Because these unclear vowel sounds occur in syllables that are not stressed or accented, they can lead to spelling mistakes. The *i* in *episode*, for example, sounds the same as the *e* in *competent*. This "uh" sound may be spelled by any vowel, and it may occur in more than one syllable, as in ***a**ccomp**a**ny*. Study the word list, and note the spelling of vowels in unstressed syllables.

| pleasant | bargain | desperate | buoyant | hesitate |
|---|---|---|---|---|
| syllable | anonymous | benefit | adjourn | epilogue |

**A** In each word below, underline the unstressed syllable or syllables that represent the "uh" sound.

**1.** buoyant

**2.** epilogue

**3.** benefit

**4.** hesitate

**5.** anonymous

**B** Underline the five misspelled words in the following paragraph. Give the correct spelling for each on the lines below.

The jurors were desparate to get to the end of the trial. They were so bored by the prosecutor's remarks that they hoped that the judge would edjourn the trial so they could leave. Nevertheless, they did their duty by listening to every syllible of the presentation. They even hoped that the defense lawyer would try to plea bargan to cut the trial short. It was a pleasunt surprise when the prosecutor finally ended his remarks.

**1.** ____________________ **4.** ____________________

**2.** ____________________ **5.** ____________________

**3.** ____________________

Name ______________________________ Date __________

# Spelling: Vowel Sounds in Unstressed Syllables

## Assess

**A** Circle the letter of the sentence in which the underlined word is spelled correctly.

1. **A.** The donor to the hospital wanted to remain anonamous.
   **B.** We were buoyunt over the enthusiastic applause we received.
   **C.** The epilogue was longer than the rest of the book.
   **D.** Everyone loves a bargin.

2. **A.** Our dog does not hesitate when offered fresh meat.
   **B.** It was so noisy in the theater that I could not hear one sylluble of dialogue.
   **C.** I saw no benifit in renting movies I could borrow for free from the library.
   **D.** There is nothing more pleasent than a long walk in the country at sunrise.

3. **A.** The defendant made a last desparate plea to the judge.
   **B.** The host said, "Let us ajourn to the living room."
   **C.** The ball was buoyent and thus easy to recover from the pond.
   **D.** There are many anonymous heroes that we never hear about.

4. **A.** Free public education is our country's greatest bargen.
   **B.** The movie was plesant but not outstanding.
   **C.** She was desperite for a glass of water after running the marathon.
   **D.** Someone once said that old age is the epilogue of our lives.

**B** Circle the letter of the correctly spelled word to fill in the blank.

1. The speech was so fascinating that I took in every ______________.

   **A.** syllible **B.** syllable **C.** sylluble **D.** sylleble

2. There is a new prescription-drug ______________ for senior citizens.

   **A.** benafit **B.** benifit **C.** benefit **D.** benufit

3. The plot centered on who had written the ______________ note.

   **A.** anonamous **B.** anonmous **C.** anonimous **D.** anonymous

4. One should never ______________ to greet a new student in class.

   **A.** hesatate **B.** hesitate **C.** hesutate **D.** hesetate

5. The holiday shoppers were ______________ to find the hot new toy.

   **A.** desprate **B.** desprit **C.** desparate **D.** desperate

Name ______________________________ Date ____________

# Writing: Research Proposal

## Practice

A **research report** is a piece of expository writing that presents information about a topic you have researched. A **research proposal** is a brief overview of the paper you plan to write. It identifies your topic and explains what you want to learn about the topic. A well-written research proposal should include:

- a statement identifying the topic of your report: *My report will discuss how bridges are built.*
- the questions that your research report will answer: *How do bridge builders get the foundation set into water?*
- the specific sources you will use to find the answer to each question: *interviews with engineers, Internet search, encyclopedia*
- an explanation of why these sources would be useful: *Interviews with engineers will help me understand some principles of physics.*

Respond to each item below.

**1.** Which group of questions would be most useful to ask when researching a report on the Black Plague that ravaged Europe in the 1300s and 1400s?

**A.** Why was there an outbreak of the Black Plague in London in 1665? How likely is it that the Black Plague will return again? What similar epidemics have we had in America?

**B.** What were the symptoms of the Black Plague? How quickly did it spread? What effects did the Black Plague have on European society?

**C.** What was life like in medieval Europe? How many people were killed by the Black Plague? What other diseases threatened the population then?

**2.** Which sources would best answer questions about the Black Plague?

**A.** magazine articles, a book on American history, interviews with survivors

**B.** a biology textbook, the local newspaper, an encyclopedia

**C.** historical documents, an atlas, a dictionary

**D.** a book on European history, an encyclopedia, an Internet search

**3.** Explain why the sources you chose would be useful. ____________________

______________________________________________

______________________________________________

**4.** On a separate sheet of paper, write a brief proposal for a report on the Black Plague.

Name ______________________________ Date ____________

# Writing: Research Proposal

## Assess

**Complete these activities to help you write a research proposal.**

**1.** Choose one of the following research topics:

The Effects of Hurricane Katrina on the City of New Orleans

The Perceived Threat of an Avian Flu Epidemic

The Civil Rights Movement of the mid-1900s

The History of Baseball in America

Alternative Sources of Energy

Homeland Security in the 21st Century

Other: ______________________________

**2.** List three questions that you would like to answer about your topic.

______________________________

______________________________

______________________________

**3.** List at least three sources that might contain the information you need to answer your questions, and explain why each source would be useful.

______________________________

______________________________

______________________________

**4.** Present and support your research proposal for this topic in a few paragraphs, using the information above.

______________________________

______________________________

______________________________

______________________________

______________________________

Name ______________________________ Date ____________

# Writing: Speech

## Practice

A **speech** is an oral presentation before an audience. A good speech begins with an acknowledgment of the audience, an introduction of the topic, adequate development of the topic, and an effective conclusion. To make the speech more powerful when it is read aloud, add the following elements:

- Repetition of words or phrases
- Dramatic pauses
- Vivid language

**A** Read the following part of a speech given on April 4, 1931, by the Reverend Father Charles L. O'Donnell at the funeral of the legendary football coach Knute Rockne. Then, respond to each item below.

In this Holy Week a tragic event has occurred which accounts for our presence here today. Knute Rockne is dead. And who was he?

Ask the President of the United States, who dispatched a personal message of tribute to his memory and comfort to his bereaved family. Ask the King of Norway, who sends a special delegation as his personal representative to this solemn service. Ask the several state legislatures now sitting that have passed resolutions of sympathy and condolence. Ask the thousands of newspapermen, whose labor of love in his memory has stirred a reading public of 125 million Americans. Ask men and women from every walk of life. Ask the children, the boys of America. Ask any and all of these, who was this man whose death has struck the nation with dismay and has everywhere bowed heads in grief?

1. Circle the passage that serves as the introduction.
2. Underline an example of the use of repetition in this speech.
3. Give an example of vivid language that makes this speech more powerful.

______________________________

4. What do you think would be a good place to pause for dramatic effect?

______________________________

**B** Imagine that you have been asked to write a speech in honor of your personal hero. On a separate sheet of paper, write the introduction to this speech.

Name ____________________ Date ____________

# Writing: Speech

## Assess

**A** Imagine that you have been asked to speak at an awards ceremony honoring your best friend. It might be an athletic award, a scholastic award, or a service award. What would you say? Answer these questions.

**1.** For what accomplishment is your friend being given this award?

____________________

**2.** Who is in the audience?

____________________

**3.** What will be the main point of your speech?

____________________

**4.** How will you support your main point?

____________________

____________________

**5.** What phrase will you repeat for effect?

____________________

**6.** Where might you pause for effect?

____________________

**7.** Write three phrases with vivid language that will add power to your speech.

____________________

**B** Write the first two paragraphs of your speech below. Indicate where you might pause for effect by leaving a space of about one inch.

____________________

____________________

____________________

____________________

____________________

Name ______________________ Date ____________

# Writing: Cause-and-Effect Essay

## Practice

When you write a **cause-and-effect essay,** you analyze the reasons something happened or you consider its results. You should use facts, evidence, and reason to support your explanation. A cause-and-effect essay can have several possible organizations:

- **Many Causes / Single Effect:** If your topic has several causes of a single effect—such as good health being caused by good nutrition, plenty of rest, and exercise—*develop a paragraph to discuss each cause.*
- **Single Cause / Many Effects:** For one cause with several effects—such as breaking a leg leading to missing track season but also to more time spent practicing guitar and writing short stories—*devote a paragraph to each effect.*
- **Chain of Causes and Effects.** If you are presenting a chain of causes and effects—such as the snowstorm caused a power outage, which caused the heat to go off, which resulted in everyone huddling around the wood stove—*present them in chronological order with transitions to show the connections.*

**A** Decide which organization best suits each topic. Circle the letter of the best answer.

1. Topic: What major events led up to the Civil War?

   A. Many Causes / Single Effect
   B. Single Cause / Many Effects
   C. Chain of Causes and Effects

2. Topic: Discuss the impact of the Internet on our society.

   A. Many Causes / Single Effect
   B. Single Cause / Many Effects
   C. Chain of Causes and Effects

3. Topic: Describe the plight of the farmers in the Dust Bowl during the 1930s.

   A. Many Causes / Single Effect
   B. Single Cause / Many Effects
   C. Chain of Causes and Effects

**B** Imagine that you have been asked to write a cause-and-effect essay on this topic: "Discuss the possible effects of not using sunscreen." Decide which sort of organization best suits the topic. Then, using that type of organization, write a brief cause-and-effect essay. Use a separate sheet of paper.

Type of organization: ______________________

Name ______________________ Date __________

# Writing: Cause-and-Effect Essay

## Assess

**A** Read the list of topics. Then, answer the questions that follow.

How poor air quality can affect people's health

How cell phones have changed the way we live

How natural disasters, like hurricanes, change people's lives

The effects of practicing a musical instrument every day

1. All of the above topics can be described as the same type of cause-and-effect topic. What type of topic are they?

   A. Many Causes / Single Effect
   B. Single Cause / Many Effects
   C. Chain of Causes and Effects

2. Based on your answer to question 1, how would you organize your essay?

   A. I would develop a paragraph to discuss each cause.
   B. I would write a paragraph to discuss each effect.
   C. I would discuss events, both causes and effects, in the order they happened.

**B** Now, select one of the topics. Begin a cause-and-effect essay by completing the graphic organizer.

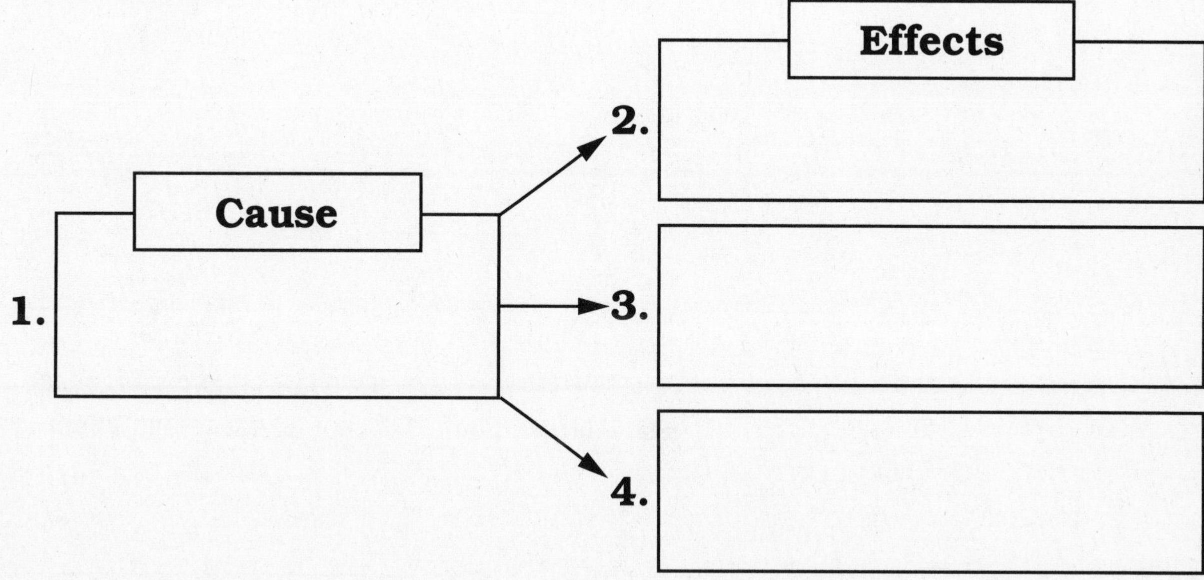

# Literature-Based Strategies

# **Predictogram** Relating Words

## About the Strategy

Predictograms ask students to use what they know about words and phrases from a selection to make predictions about its content and structure. Prediction activities involve students in the text, engage their attention, and give them a stake in the outcome of a story.

A sample predictogram is provided using the story "Seventh Grade."

*A relating words predictogram works well with any fictional piece in which the words, phrases, and quotations selected can show associations between characters and concepts.*

**Predictogram** Relating Words

(Title) Seventh Grade **2**

Look at the words below. Draw lines between any items you think might be connected. Explain your connection on the line you draw. You might choose several connections with some words and none with others.

**1** **embarrassed**

**rosebushes of shame**

**a new year, new experiences**

**confusing, like the inside of a watch**

**Victor** (the main character)

**bouquets of love**

**bluff**

**3**

*Victor is trying to impress someone.*

**impress**

**with greater conviction**

**Step 1**

*Choose nine words, phrases, or quotations from the selection that will help students predict what a story will be about.*

**Step 2**

*Encourage students to use the title as they make their predictions.*

**Step 3**

*Remind students to think about what they already know about the words and phrases.*

**Skills and Strategies:** *predict outcomes, activate prior knowledge, draw conclusions*

### Keep in Mind

- Choose appropriate words, phrases, quotations, and topical cues, such as titles or key words, to help students make associations.
- Model one prediction before individuals begin.
- Be sure students return to their predictograms after reading to confirm their predictions.

### All Together Now

You might use the relating words predictogram to begin a class discussion. Students could state their predictions rather than writing them down.

# **Predictogram** Relating Words

(Title) ___________________________________________

**Look at the words below. Draw lines between any items you think might be connected. Explain your connection on the line you draw. You might choose several connections with some words and none with others.**

# **Predictogram** Literary Features

## About the Strategy

Predictograms ask students to use what they know about words and phrases from a selection to make predictions about its content and structure. Prediction activities involve students in the text, engage their attention, and give them a stake in the outcome of a story.

The following model is based on "All Summer in a Day."

*A literary features predictogram works well with any fictional piece in which the words or phrases selected can help students identify specific features of a story.*

**Predictogram** Literary Features

(Title) All Summer in a Day ❷

Look at the selection title above and this list of words and phrases to write sentences that predict who and what this story might be about.

❶

| | | |
|---|---|---|
| **teacher** | **silence was so immense** | **jungle** |
| **solemn and pale** | **remembered a warmness** | **Margot** |
| **muffled cries** | **turning their faces up** | **Venus** |
| **9 years old** | **rocket men and women** | **a closet** |
| **then looked away** | **raining for seven years** | **soon** |
| **It's stopping.** | **very frail** | **running** |

**Characters:** ______

**Setting:** ______

❸

**Problem:** ______

**Events:** ______

**Outcome:** ______

**Mystery Words or Phrases:** ______

**Step ❶**

*Choose five to ten words or phrases from the selection that will help students predict what the story will be about.*

**Step ❷**

*Encourage students to use the title as they make their predictions.*

**Step ❸**

*Remind students to think about what they already know about the words and phrases.*

**Skills and Strategies:** *predict outcomes, activate prior knowledge, draw conclusions*

### Keep in Mind

- Choose appropriate words, phrases, and topical cues, such as titles or key words, to help students make associations.
- Model one prediction before individuals begin.
- Be sure students return to their predictograms after reading to confirm their predictions.

### Solo Exploration

Encourage students to use this predictogram to plan their own writing. They can collect their ideas in the box and sort them according to literary feature as a prewriting strategy. **(writing)**

# **Predictogram** Literary Features

(Title) ____________________________________________

Look at the selection title above and this list of words and phrases to write sentences that predict who and what this story might be about.

**Characters:** ____________________________________________

____________________________________________

**Setting:** ____________________________________________

____________________________________________

**Problem:** ____________________________________________

____________________________________________

**Events:** ____________________________________________

____________________________________________

____________________________________________

**Outcome:** ____________________________________________

____________________________________________

**Mystery Words or Phrases:** ____________________________________________

____________________________________________

# **Predictogram** Asking Questions

## About the Strategy

Predictograms ask students to use what they know about words and phrases from a selection to make predictions about its content and structure. Prediction activities involve students in the text, engage their attention, and give them a stake in the outcome of a story.

Look at the following example.

*An asking questions predictogram works well with any fictional piece in which the words and phrases selected suggest questions to the reader.*

**Predictogram** Asking Questions

(Title) A Ribbon for Baldy ❷

Look at the title of the selection above and the words or phrases below. Can you think of any questions to ask about this selection?

❶

| **project** | Why is a project important in this story? |
|---|---|
| **posture** | |
| **Little Baldy** | |
| **cone-shaped** | |
| **broom-sedge** | |
| **fire** | |
| **corn row** | |
| **corkscrew** | |

❸ Choose one of your questions and write a paragraph answering it.

**Question:** ____________________

**Answer:** ____________________

**Step ❶**

*Choose eight words or phrases from the selection that will help students write questions to predict what a story will be about.*

**Step ❷**

*Encourage students to use the title as they make their predictions.*

**Step ❸**

*Remind students to think about what they already know about the words and phrases as they answer the question.*

**Skills and Strategies:** *predict outcomes, activate prior knowledge, draw conclusions*

### Keep in Mind

- Choose appropriate words, phrases, and topical cues, such as titles or key words, to help students write their questions.
- Model one prediction before individuals begin.
- Be sure students return to their predictograms after reading to confirm their predictions.

### Buddywork

Suggest to students that they use the glossary at the end of a chapter in their social studies book to create an asking questions predictogram. They can use their predictograms to help them set purposes for reading the chapter. **(cross-curricular connection)**

# **Predictogram** Asking Questions

(Title) ______________________________________________

Look at the title of the selection above and the words or phrases below. Can you think of any questions to ask about this selection?

| | |
|---|---|
| | |
| | |
| | |
| | |
| | |
| | |
| | |

Choose one of your questions and write a paragraph answering it.

**Question:** ______________________________________________

______________________________________________

**Answer:** ______________________________________________

______________________________________________

______________________________________________

______________________________________________

______________________________________________

______________________________________________

______________________________________________

# **Predictogram** Using Quotations

## About the Strategy

Predictograms ask students to use what they know about words and phrases from a selection to make predictions about its content and structure. Prediction activities involve students in the text, engage their attention, and give them a stake in the outcome of a story.

Look at the following example.

*A using quotations predictogram works well with any fictional piece in which characters can be identified by their words.*

### **Predictogram** Using Quotations

(Title) Becky and the Wheels-and-Brake Boys

Look at the title above and the descriptions of each character below. Can you predict who might have said each of the following? Write the quotation next to the character who might have said it.

1

"D'you think you're a boy?"

"I can't get rid of it, mam.

"What am I going to do?"

2

| Character | Quotation |
|---|---|
| **Becky:** a young girl who wants a bike | 3 |
| **Mum:** Becky's mother | |

Now write a paragraph about one of the characters using the quotations above.

______________________________

______________________________

______________________________

______________________________

**Step 1**

*Choose three to ten quotations from the selection that will help students predict what a story will be about.*

**Step 2**

*Choose two main characters and write a brief description of each.*

**Step 3**

*Ask students to match the quotations with the characters who might say them.*

**Skills and Strategies:** *predict outcomes, activate prior knowledge, draw conclusions*

### Keep in Mind

- Choose identifying quotations and topical cues, such as titles or key words, to help students make associations.
- Model one prediction before individuals begin.
- Be sure students return to their predictograms after reading to confirm their predictions.

### All Together Now

Students could take turns reading the quotations with differing inflections. The class could predict how each sentence might be said in the context of the story. While reading they can check their predictions.

# **Predictogram** Using Quotations

(Title) ____________________________________________

Look at the title above and the descriptions of each character below. Can you predict who might have said each of the following? Write the quotation next to the character who might have said it.

| **Character** | **Quotation** |
| --- | --- |
| | |
| | |

Now write a paragraph about one of the characters using the quotations above.

____________________________________________

____________________________________________

____________________________________________

____________________________________________

# K-W-L Chart

## About the Strategy

K-W-L is a strategy for reading expository text that helps students use their prior knowledge to generate interest in a selection. K-W-L also helps students set purposes for reading by encouraging them to express their curiosity for the topic they will be reading about. K-W-L encourages group members to share and discuss what they know, what they want to know, and what they learn about a topic.

*List selections for which you would like to use a K-W-L chart.*

**Step 1**
*Students brainstorm what they know or think they know about the topic.*

**Step 2**
*Students list questions they hope to have answered as they read.*

**Step 3**
*Students list what they learn as they read.*

**K-W-L Chart**

**Topic:** Abraham Lincoln

| What We Know | What We Want to Know | What We Learned |
|---|---|---|
| Lincoln was president of the United States. | What was Lincoln's childhood like? | Lincoln was born in a log cabin and was poor as a child. |
| Lincoln grew up poor. | How was Lincoln educated? | Lincoln went to school when he could and read everything he could find. |
| | What kind of person was Lincoln? | Lincoln was a good wrestler and runner and loved to tell jokes and stories. |
| 1 | 2 | 3 |

**Skills and Strategies:** *activate prior knowledge, generate questions, set purpose, summarize facts*

### Keep in Mind

- If students are unsure of a fact they listed in column one, they can turn it into a question in column two.
- Encourage students to find out the answers to any unanswered questions.

### Solo Exploration

Students can use a K-W-L chart to set purposes for reading a daily newspaper. Before reading, students should think about what they know (e.g., the weather forecast from listening to the radio) and what they want to know. **(cross-curricular connection)**

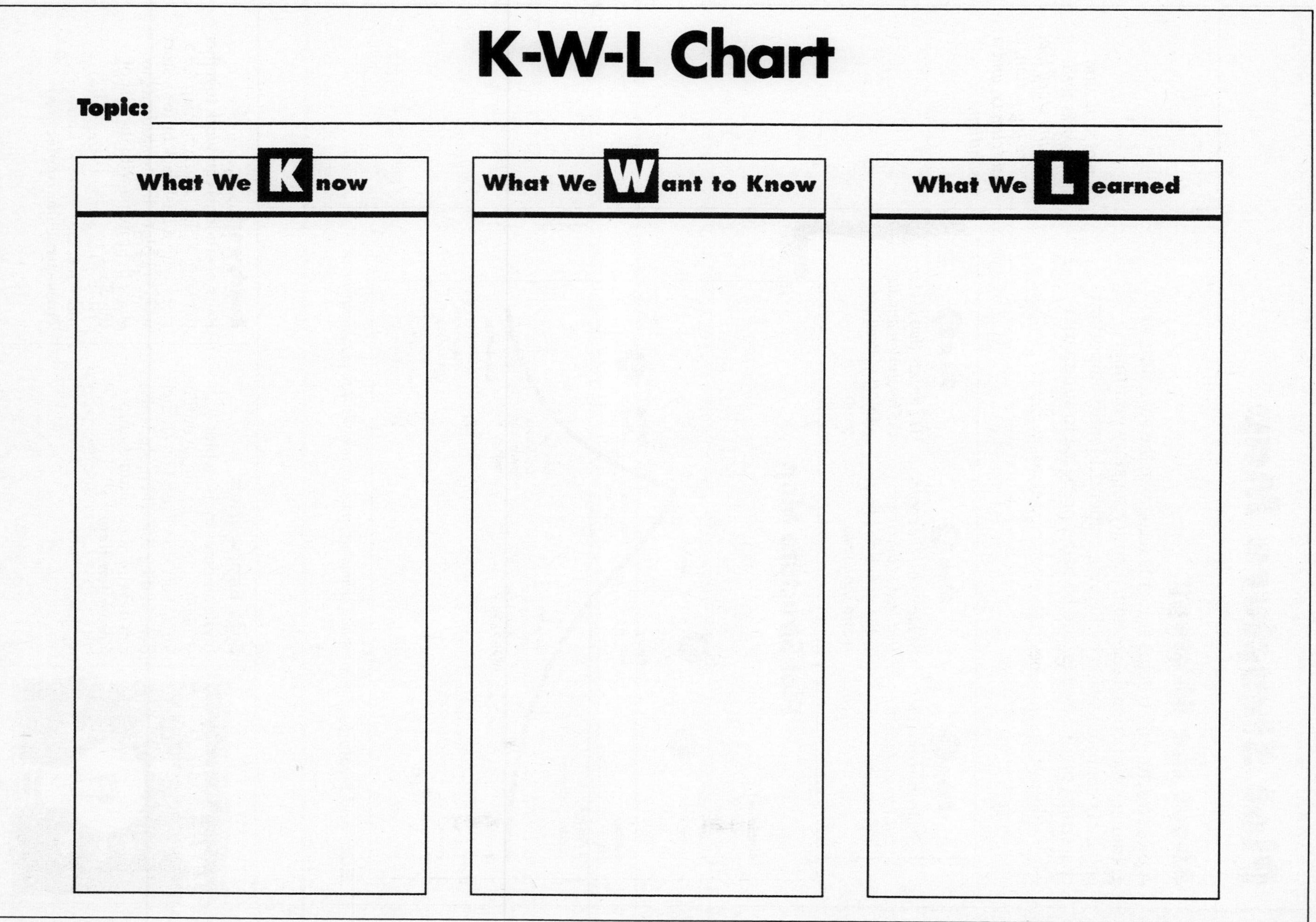
K-W-L Chart
Topic:
What We Know
What We Want to Know
What We Learned

# Plot Structure Map

## About the Strategy

A plot structure map helps students recognize the structure, or grammar, of a fictional selection. Identifying story grammar enhances comprehension by helping students identify important characters, predict events, and be better prepared to summarize a selection.

*A plot structure map works well with any story that has rising action, a clear climax, and a resolution.*

**Step 1**

*Students record the setting, characters, and problem.*

**Step 2**

*Students list the events that lead to the climax of the story before they record the climax.*

**Step 3**

*The events that lead to the resolution and the resolution itself are recorded.*

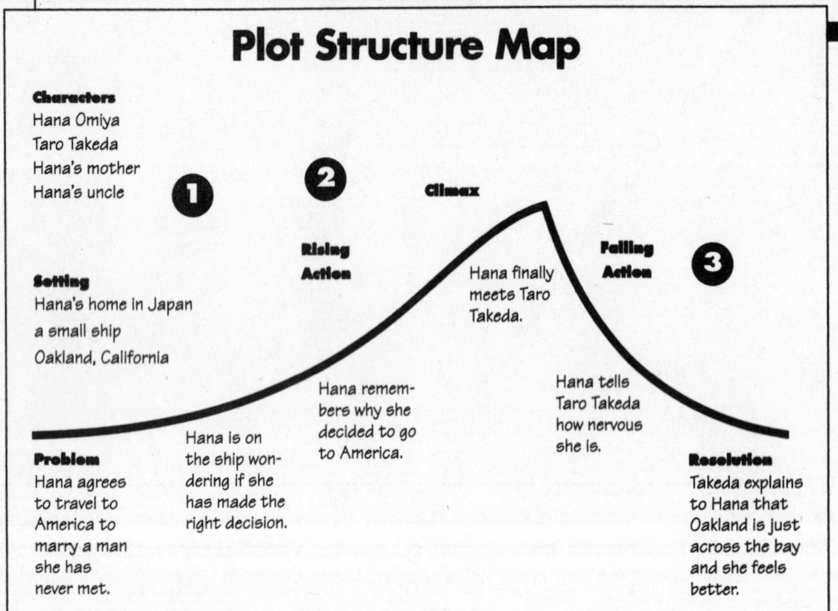


**Skills and Strategies:** *understand characters, note setting, identify plot, summarize*

**Idea Exchange**

### Solo Exploration

Invite students to use a plot structure map to create an outline for a short story based on an incident in their life. Then, students can develop their outlines into stories. **(writing)**

### Buddywork

Pairs of students can work together to create a plot structure map for a story with a flashback or for a story with subplots. Invite students to share their maps with the rest of the class.

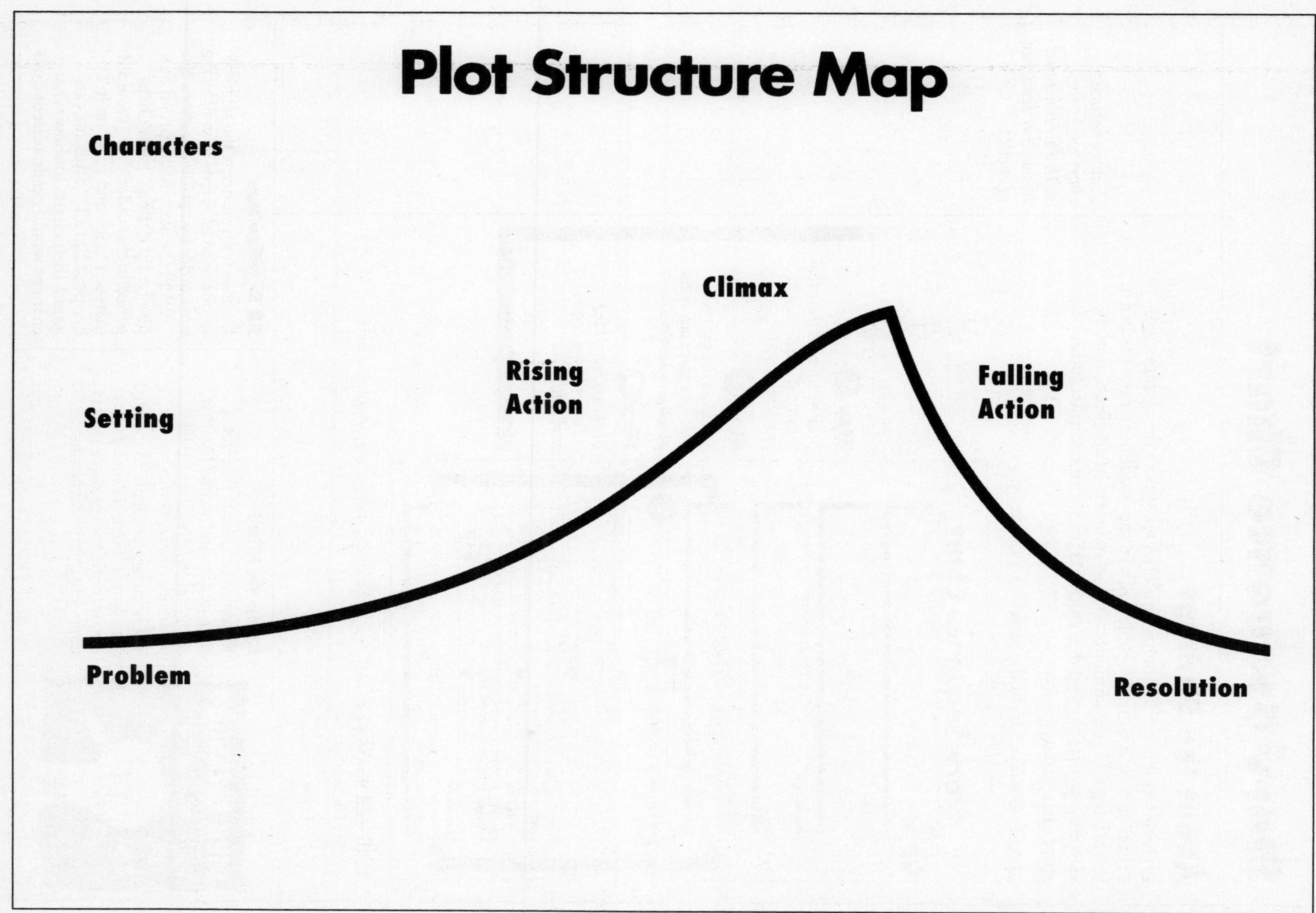
Plot Structure Map
Characters
Setting
Rising Action
Climax
Falling Action
Problem
Resolution

# Story Sequence Chart

## About the Strategy

A story sequence chart helps students recognize the sequence of events in a selection. Keeping track of the sequence of events is a simple way to give students a sense of story. In addition, understanding sequence prepares students for more complex types of story structures.

Modify the chart to fit the specifics of a story.

*A story sequence chart works well with any story that has a clear sequence of events.*

**Story Sequence Chart**

1. **Title:** Zlateh the Goat

**Setting:** a village and the road to town

**Characters:** Aaron, a boy; Reuven, his father; Zlateh, their goat

**Problem:** The family needs money and Reuven decides to sell the goat.

**Events** (2)

- The butcher offers money for the goat.
- Aaron and Zlateh leave for the butcher.
- On their way, a huge snowstorm develops and they get lost.
- Zlateh and Aaron take shelter in a haystack, where Zlateh provides warmth and milk.

(3) **Solution:** The family is grateful to Zlateh and decides never to sell the goat.

**Step 1**
*Students record the title, setting, characters, and problem.*

**Step 2**
*Students list the events that take place before the problem is resolved.*

**Step 3**
*Students record the solution to the central problem.*

**Skills and Strategies:** *understand characters, note setting, sequence events, identify plot, summarize*

### Keep in Mind

- Remind students that dates, time of day, and words like *first*, *next*, and *last* are clues to the sequence of events in a story.
- Encourage students to look for clue words like *while* and *during* that indicate two or more events happening at the same time.

### All Together Now

Discuss with students the relative importance of events as well as the time order by asking questions like "Would the story have turned out differently if things hadn't happened in this order?" or "Would it matter if 'such and such' hadn't happened at all?" Students can adjust their charts to show what changes would occur. **(discussion)**

# Story Sequence Chart

**Title:**

**Setting:**

**Characters:**

**Problem:**

**Events**

**Solution:**

# Story Triangle

## About the Strategy

A story triangle is a creative way to think about and summarize a story. Like a traditional story map, the story triangle helps students recognize story elements. However, a story triangle allows students to respond personally to a story since students must describe rather than just list characters, events, and problems.

The following model is based on the story "Seventh Grade."

*Story triangles work well with all types of fiction, including realistic and historical fiction.*

### Story Triangle

1. Name of main character
2. Two words describing main character
3. Three words describing setting
4. Four words stating main problem
5. Five words relating one event
6. Six words relating second event
7. Seven words relating third event
8. Eight words reporting solution

❶

1. Victor
2. friendly shy
3. Fresno school warm
4. Victor's shyness with Theresa
5. Victor tries talking to Theresa.
6. Victor looks for Theresa during lunch.
7. Victor fakes knowing French and embarrasses himself.
8. Theresa, impressed by Victor's "French," requests his help.

❷

**Step ❶**

*Students follow the directions at the top of the page to fill in the story triangle.*

**Step ❷**

*Encourage students to be creative as they choose words, phrases, and sentences.*

**Skills and Strategies:** *understand characters, note setting, identify plot, summarize*

### Keep in Mind

- If students get stuck in the middle, encourage them to start with the last line and work backward.
- When using a story triangle with another story, be sure to change the guidelines to match the story.

### Solo Exploration

After students complete their story triangles, they can circle any vague words they used. Encourage students to choose synonyms that are more interesting and specific to replace the vague words.

# Story Triangle

1. Name of main character
2. Two words describing main character
3. Three words describing setting
4. Four words stating main problem
5. Five words relating one event
6. Six words relating second event
7. Seven words relating third event
8. Eight words reporting solution

1. ______________

2. __________ __________

3. _________ _________ _________

4. ________ ________ ________ ________

5. _______ _______ _______ _______ _______

6. ______ ______ ______ ______ ______ ______

7. ______ ______ ______ ______ ______ ______ ______

8. ______ ______ ______ ______ ______ ______ ______ ______

# Story-Within-a-Story Map

## About the Strategy

A story-within-a-story map helps students identify the plot events of this complex text structure. Keeping track of plot events enhances comprehension by helping students recognize the change in narrative that is part of this structure.

*Story-within-a-story maps work well with fiction in which the plot includes a story within the story.*

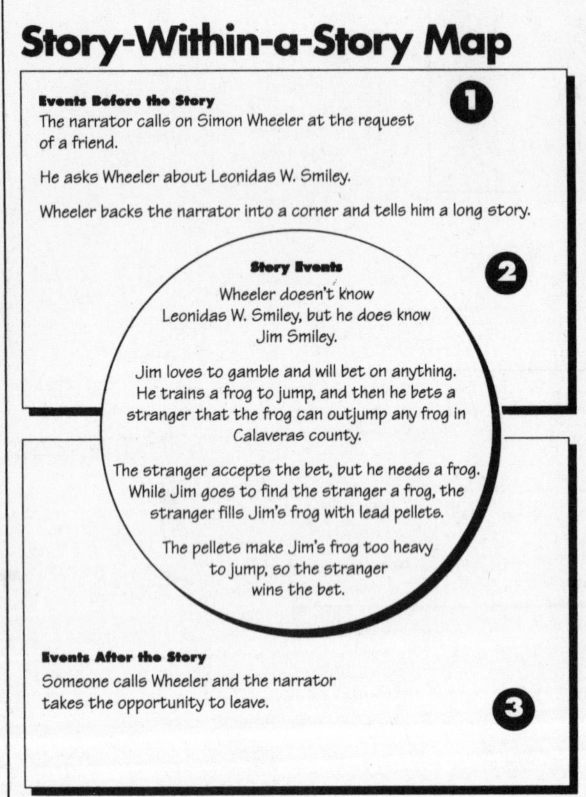


**Step 1**

*At the top, students write the plot events that take place before the story is told.*

**Step 2**

*In the inner circle, students list the plot events of the story.*

**Step 3**

*At the bottom, students write the events that happen after the story is told.*

**Skills and Strategies:** *use story elements, use text structure/genre, sequence*

### Keep in Mind

If students are having difficulty recognizing this text structure, have them reread to look for the point in the story when the narrative shifts.

### Solo Exploration

Suggest that students do a story-comparison map for the story and the story within the story to look for similarities and differences between them.

# Story-Within-a-Story Map

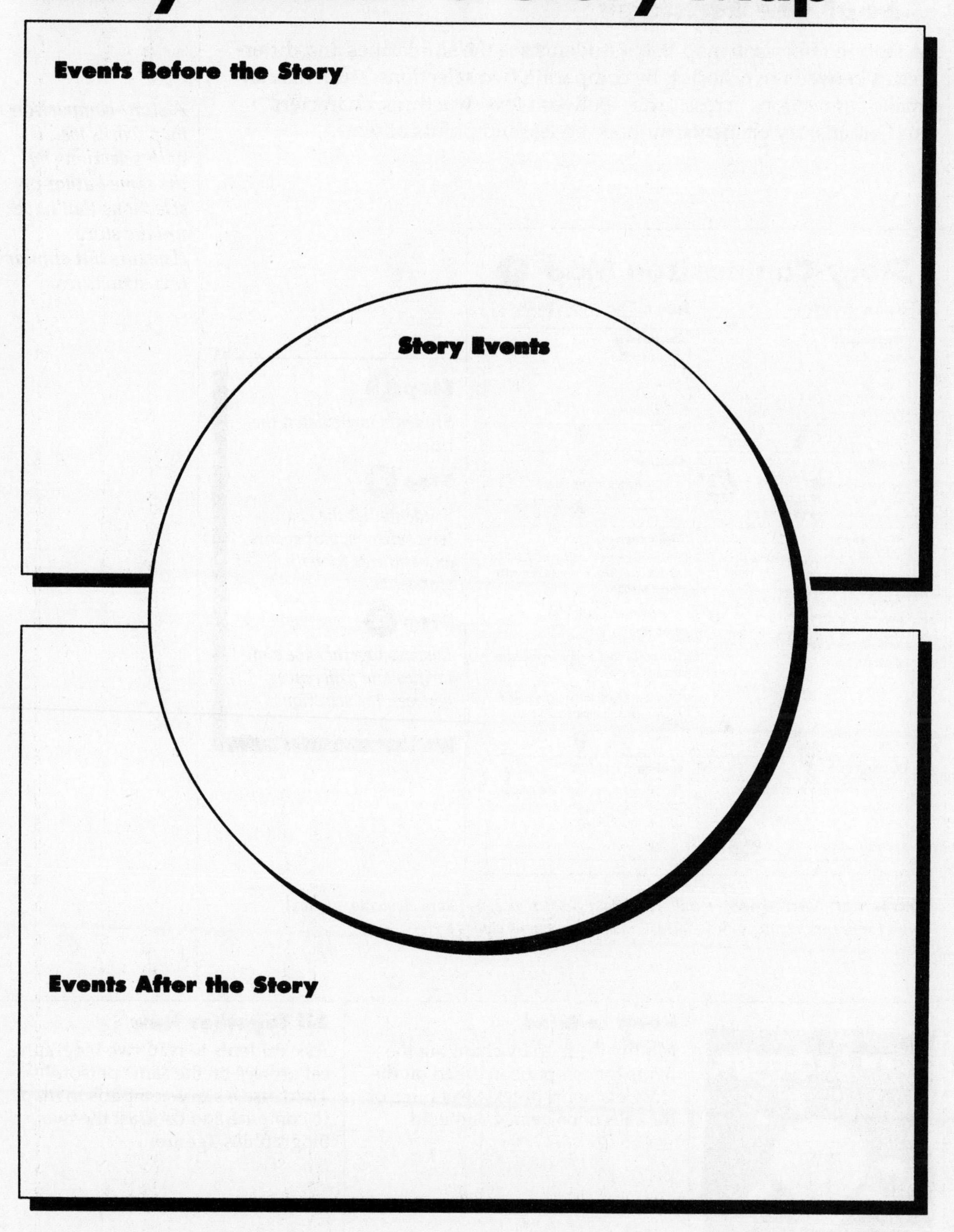

# Story-Comparison Map

## About the Strategy

A story-comparison map helps students see the similarities and differences between two stories. By comparing two selections, students can make connections across texts—between text structures, characters and other story elements, authors' styles, and points of view.

*A story-comparison map works well with selections by the same author or selections that have unique story elements but similar text structures.*

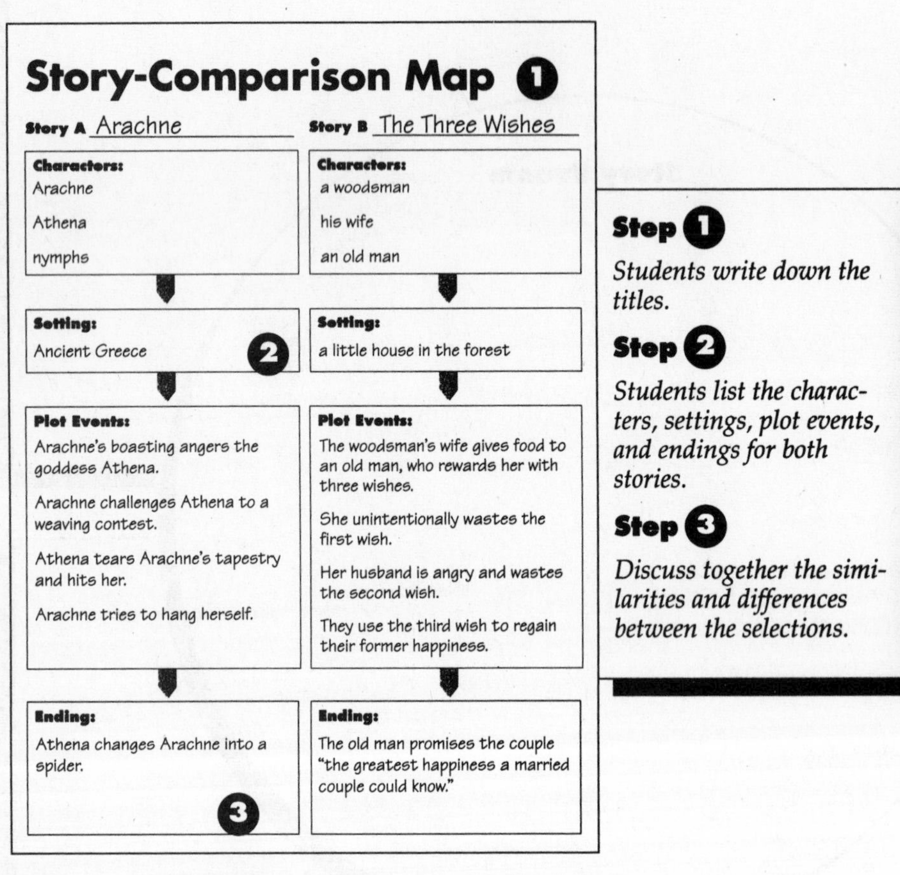


**Skills and Strategies:** *recall prior reading experience, use story elements, use text structure/genre, compare and contrast, make connections across texts*

**Keep in Mind**

Modify the map by changing the items for comparison based on the story elements or text structures of the selections being compared.

**All Together Now**

Ask students to read two biographical articles on the same person. Then, use a story-comparison map to compare and contrast the two biographies. **(genre)**

# Story-Comparison Map

**Story A** ______________________ **Story B** ______________________

| Story A | Story B |
| --- | --- |
| **Characters:** | **Characters:** |
| **Setting:** | **Setting:** |
| **Plot Events:** | **Plot Events:** |
| **Ending:** | **Ending:** |

# Cause-Effect Frame

## About the Strategy

A cause-effect frame helps students identify what happened and why it happened in both fictional and nonfictional texts. When students can see that there are causal relationships between events or ideas in text, they can make generalizations about other causal relationships in new texts and in life situations.

*Cause-effect frames work well with any selection that has clear cause-and-effect relationships.*

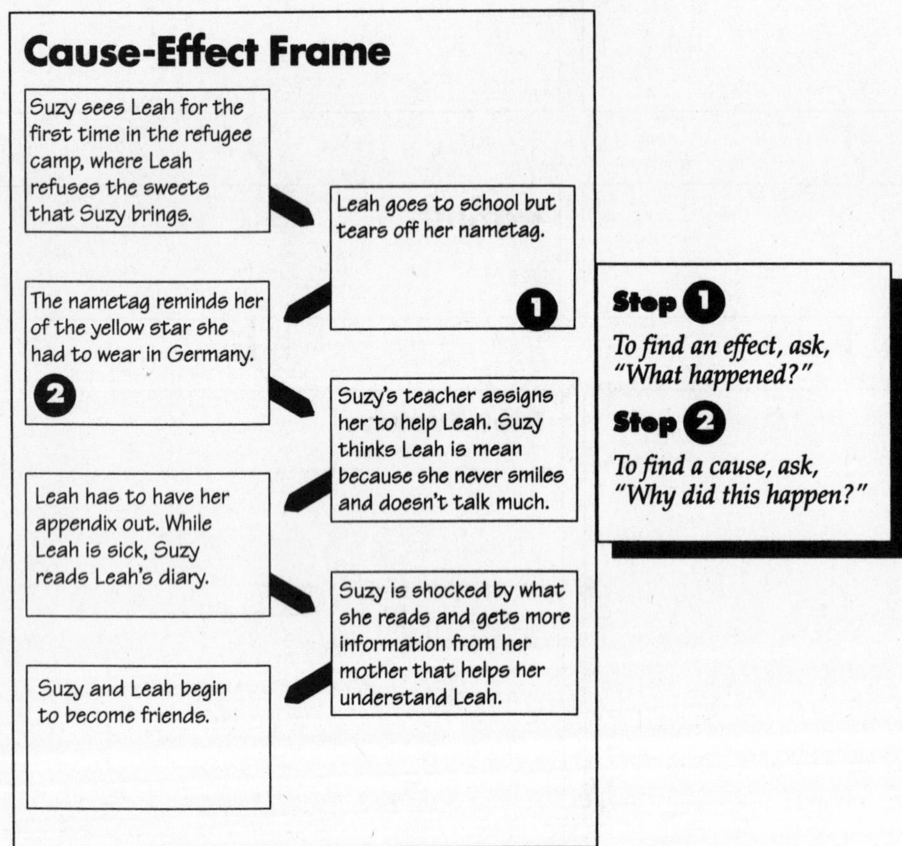


**Skills and Strategies:** *summarize, sequence, cause-effect, make inferences*

### Keep in Mind

- Suggest that students look for clue words, such as *since, as a result, consequently, therefore,* and *thus.*
- Remind students that some causes are not stated in the text. Students will have to figure out the cause by looking at what happened and asking themselves, "Why might this have happened?"

### Solo Exploration

Help students see that they can use cause-effect frames as a way to organize their writing. Students can choose an important school issue and use a cause-effect frame to outline the main point. Ask students to place the outlines in their portfolios to use for future writing. **(portfolio)**

# Cause-Effect Frame

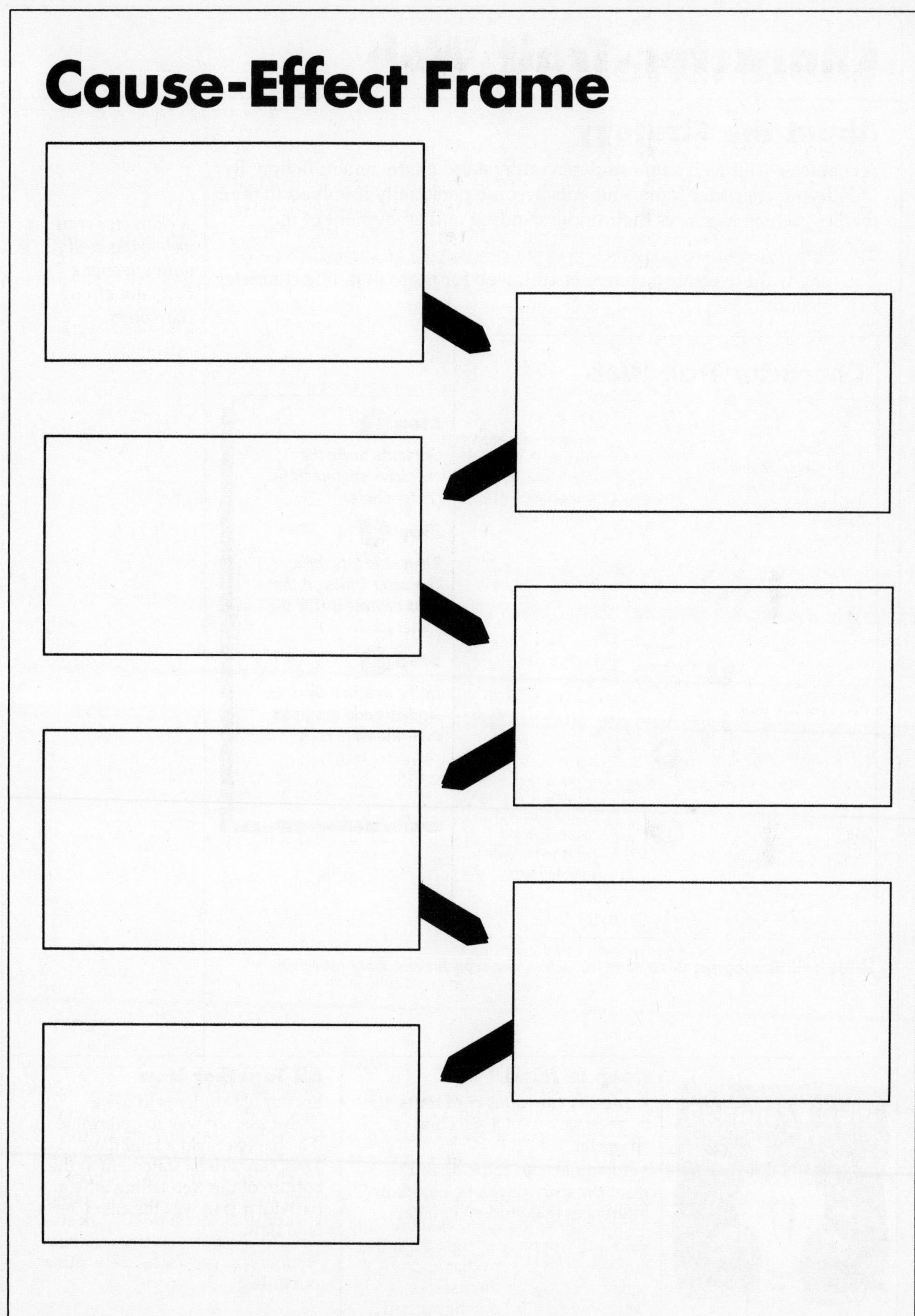

# Character-Trait Web

## About the Strategy

A character-trait web helps students understand characters in fiction. By identifying character traits, students become personally involved in their reading, which increases their understanding and enjoyment of the selection.

You may want to create a character-trait web for more than one character in a selection.

*A character-trait web works well with selections that have strong characters.*

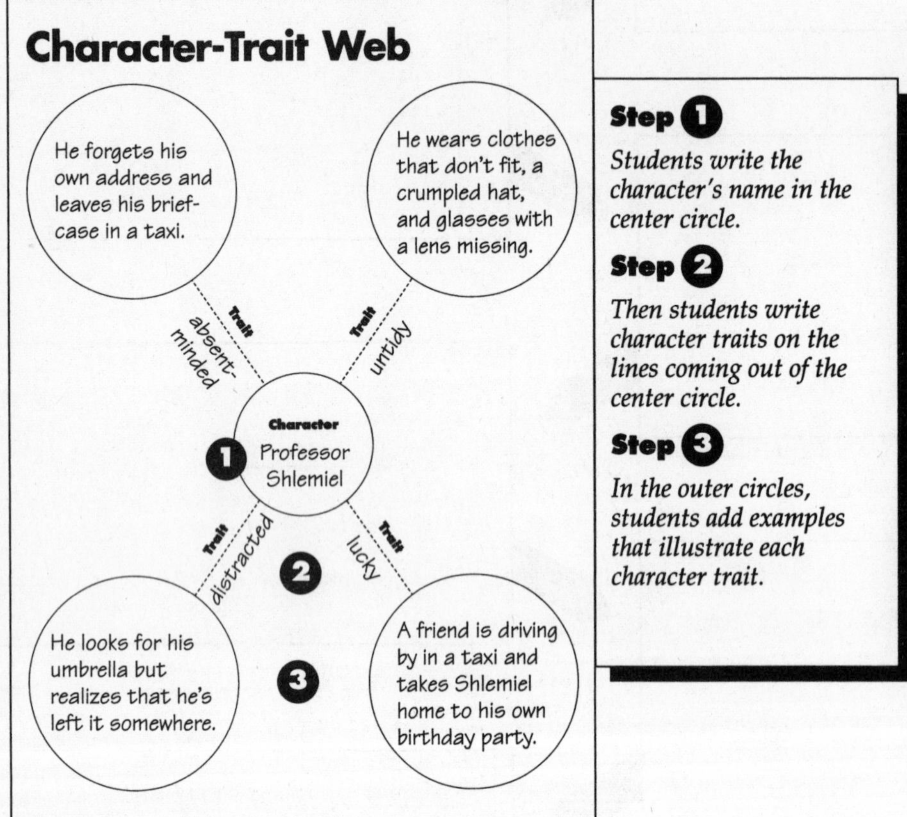


**Skills and Strategies:** *understand characters, draw conclusions, make inferences*

### Keep in Mind

- Modify the number of traits as necessary to fit a selection or character.
- Examples can come directly from the story or can be based on inferences that students make.

### All Together Now

Encourage students to use a character-trait web to determine if a character had a fatal flaw. They can write a statement at the bottom of the web telling why a particular trait was the character's fatal flaw.

# Character-Trait Web

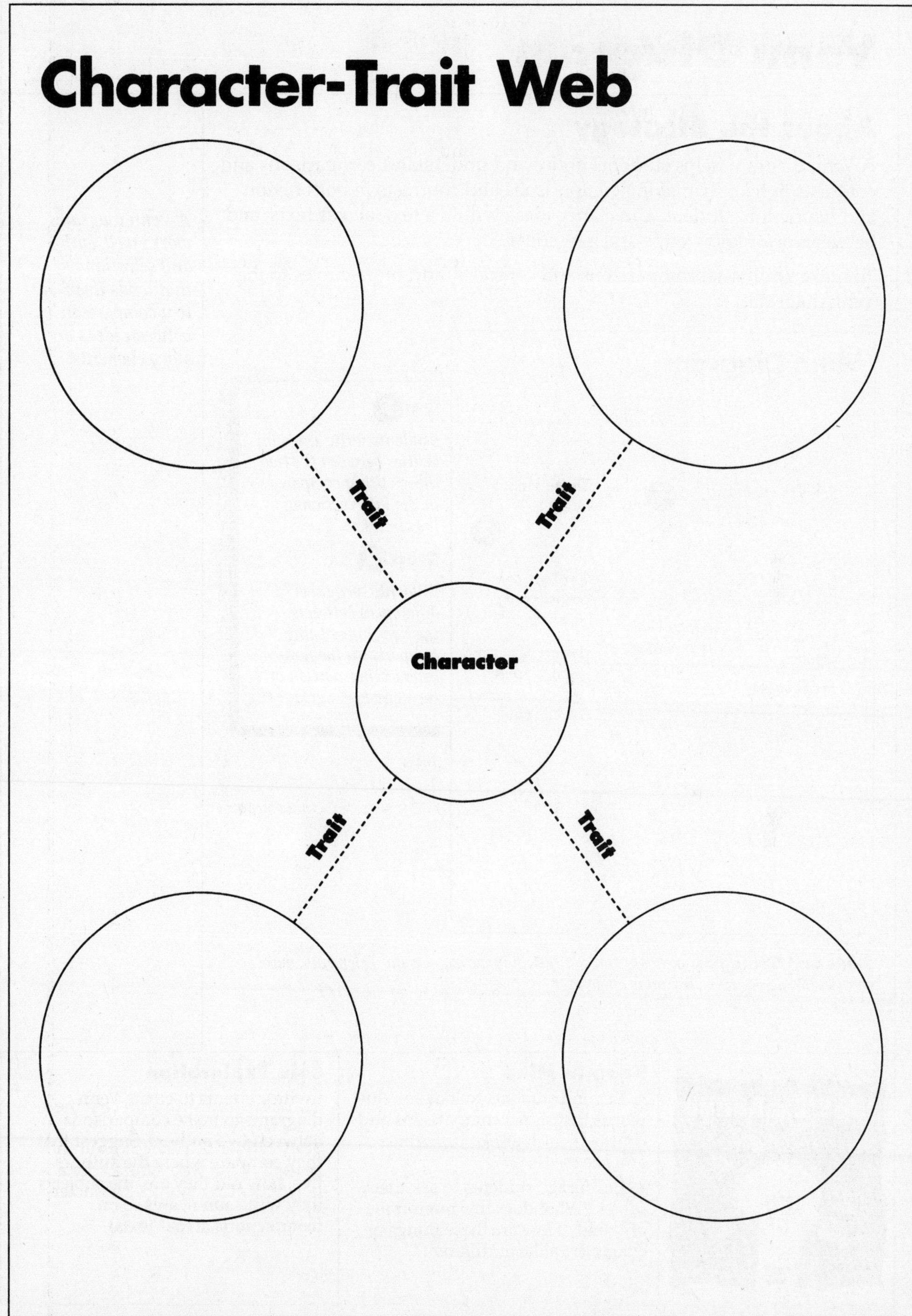

# Venn Diagram

## About the Strategy

A Venn diagram helps students notice and understand comparisons and contrasts in text. By making comparisons and contrasts in both fiction and nonfiction, students can clarify ideas within a text, across texts, and between prior knowledge and new ideas.

To make additional comparisons and contrasts, add more circles to the Venn diagram.

*A Venn diagram works well with any selection that lends itself to a comparison between ideas or story elements.*

### Venn Diagram

Lion | ❶ | Three bulls | ❷

| Lion | Both | Three bulls |
|---|---|---|
| tries to attack bulls<br>spreads evil reports<br>attacks the bulls | spend time in a pasture | protect one another at first<br>believe the evil reports and withdraw from one another |

*Step* ❶

*Students write any similarities between the two things being compared in the intersection of the circles.*

**Step** ❷

*Students write the differences between the two things being compared in the non-intersecting portion of each circle.*

**Skills and Strategies:** *compare and contrast, summarize, use story elements, make connections across texts, use prior knowledge*

### Keep in Mind

- Remind students to look for clue words that signal comparisons and contrasts, such as *like, different,* and *however.*
- Encourage students to ask themselves "What does this remind me of?" and "How are these things or characters alike or different?"

### Solo Exploration

Invite students to create Venn diagrams to make comparisons between two authors. Suggest that they compare where the authors live, how old they are, the subjects they write about, and so on. **(connections across texts)**

# Venn Diagram

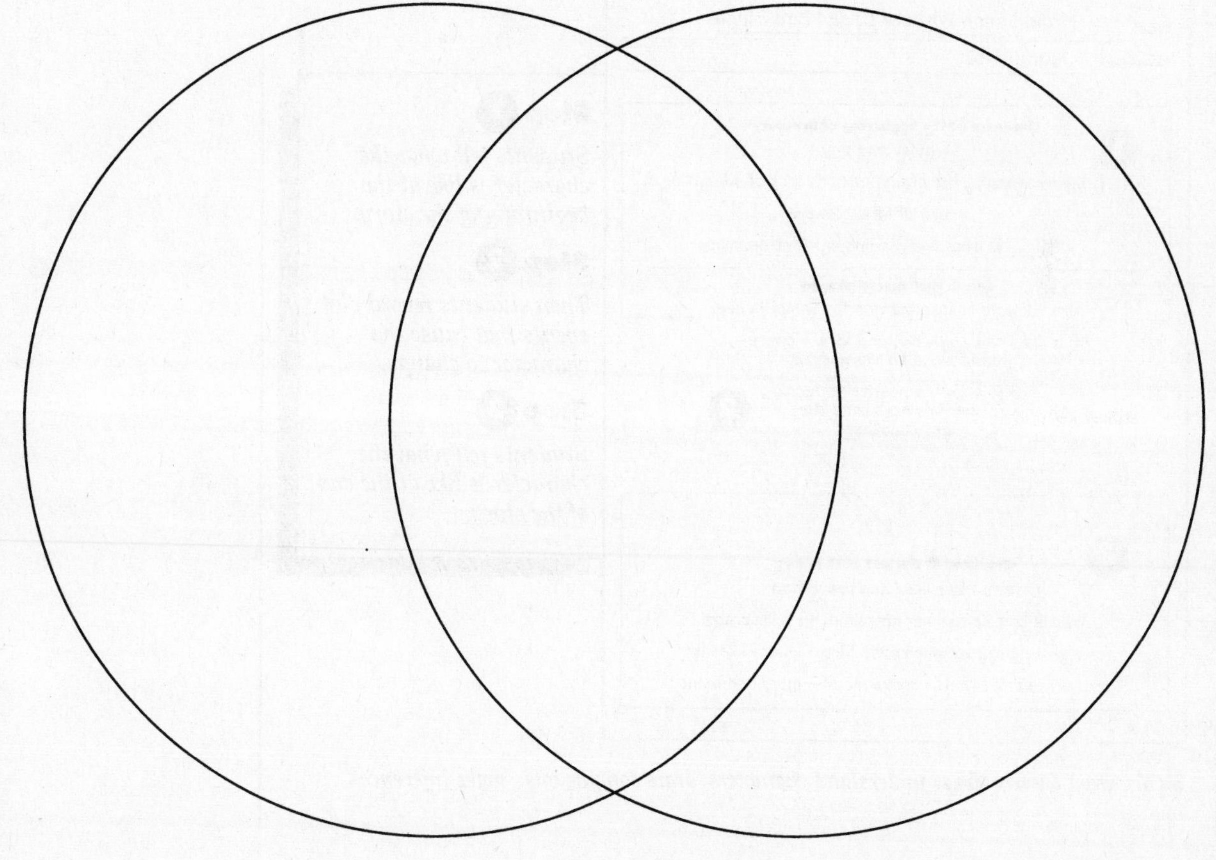

# Character-Change Map

## About the Strategy

A character-change map helps students understand characters in fiction. By analyzing a character over the course of a story, students can see how a character changes in response to plot events.

The following character-change map is modeled using an excerpt from *I Know Why the Caged Bird Sings.*

*A character-change map works well with selections that have dynamic characters.*

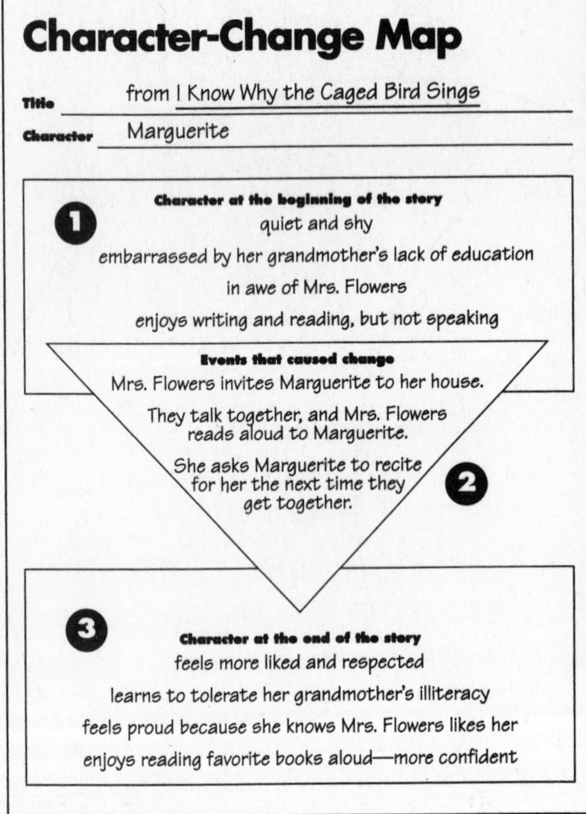

**Character-Change Map**

Title: from I Know Why the Caged Bird Sings

Character: Marguerite

1 **Character at the beginning of the story**
quiet and shy
embarrassed by her grandmother's lack of education
in awe of Mrs. Flowers
enjoys writing and reading, but not speaking

2 **Events that caused change**
Mrs. Flowers invites Marguerite to her house.
They talk together, and Mrs. Flowers reads aloud to Marguerite.
She asks Marguerite to recite for her the next time they get together.

3 **Character at the end of the story**
feels more liked and respected
learns to tolerate her grandmother's illiteracy
feels proud because she knows Mrs. Flowers likes her
enjoys reading favorite books aloud—more confident

**Step 1**

*Students tell what the character is like at the beginning of the story.*

**Step 2**

*Then students record plot events that cause the character to change.*

**Step 3**

*Students tell what the character is like at the end of the story.*

**Skills and Strategies:** *understand characters, draw conclusions, make inferences*

### Keep in Mind

You may want to ask students to map the changes in more than one character in a selection.

### Solo Exploration

To help students see that cause-and-effect relationships are often a part of change, suggest that they create a cause-and-effect map for the changes a character goes through in a story.

# Character-Change Map

**Title** ______________________________

**Character** ______________________________

**Character at the beginning of the story**

**Events that caused change**

**Character at the end of the story**

# Details Web

## About the Strategy

A details web helps students organize information in fictional or nonfictional text when many details are centered around one key or main idea. By completing the web, students see the relationship between the key or main idea and the details that support it.

*A details web works well with informational selections.*

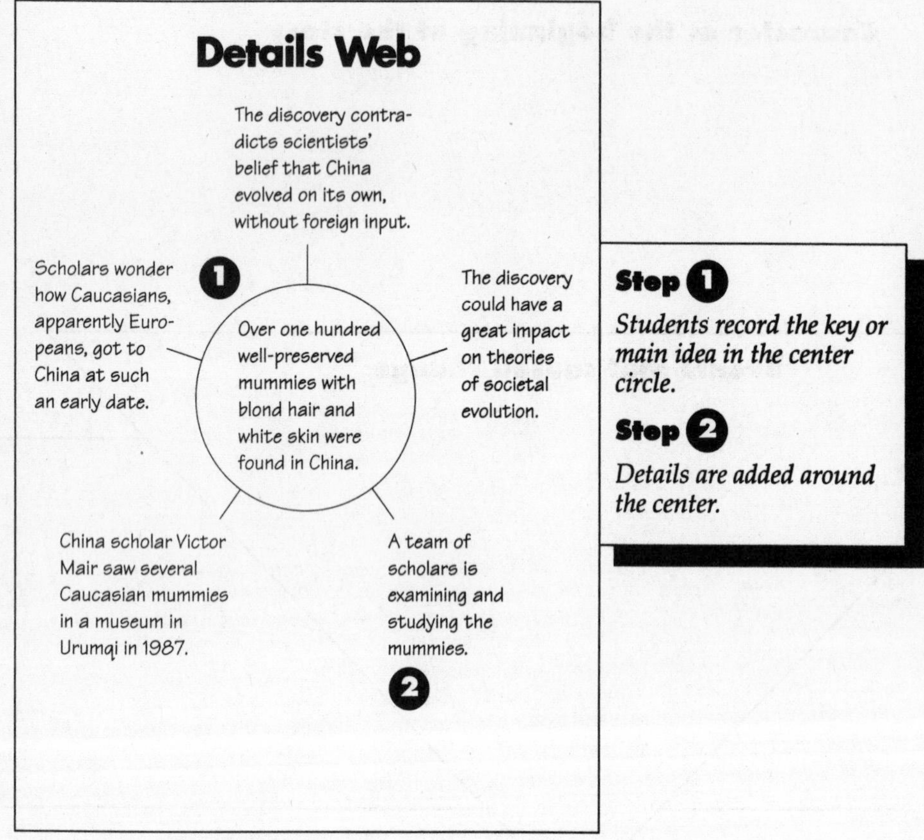


**Skills and Strategies:** *main idea/supporting details, summarize*

**Keep in Mind**

- If there is more than one key or main idea in a selection, create a separate details web for each idea.
- Help students identify the main idea of a nonfictional selection by asking "What is the most important idea in the selection?"

**Solo Exploration**

Encourage students to create details webs to help organize their thoughts for a panel discussion or debate. Students can write the discussion/debate topic in the center of the web and brainstorm ideas in support or opposition. **(discussion)**

# Details Web

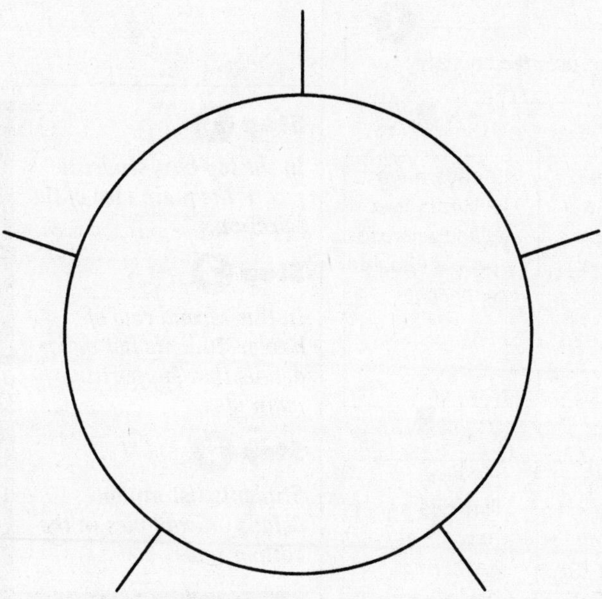

# Main Idea Map

## About the Strategy

A main idea map helps students recognize the main idea of a nonfictional selection and distinguish between the main idea and supporting details. Students determine the relative importance of what they read by organizing and reorganizing information from the text.

*Main idea maps work well with any nonfictional selection that is organized around one main idea supported by major and minor details.*

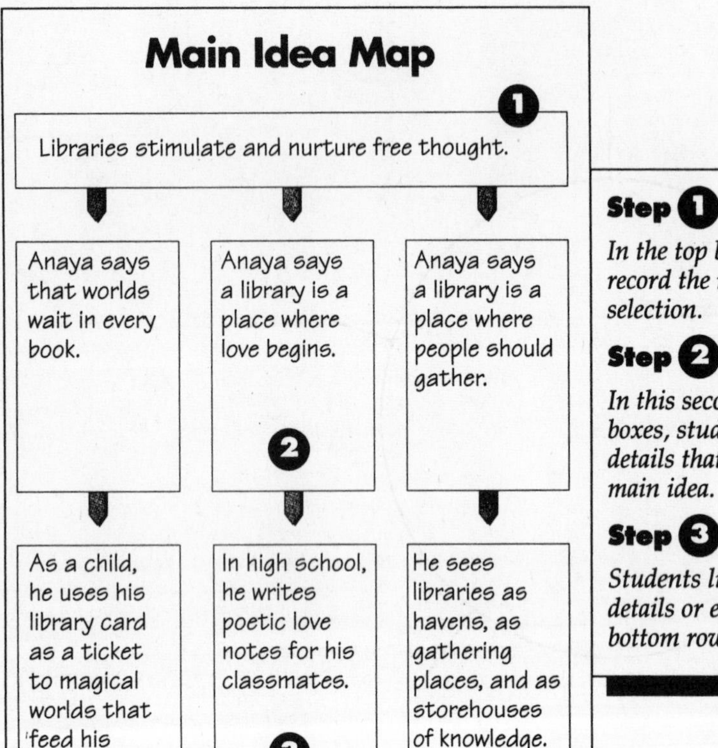


**Step 1**
*In the top box, students record the main idea of the selection.*

**Step 2**
*In this second row of boxes, students list major details that support the main idea.*

**Step 3**
*Students list minor details or examples in the bottom row.*

**Skills and Strategies:** *main idea/supporting details, summarize, analyze information*

**Keep in Mind**

- Encourage students to think about the most important idea in the selection to figure out the main idea.
- Remind students that the main idea is not always stated in the text. Sometimes students will have to state the main idea in their own words.
- Sometimes it's easier to see a main idea *after* listing the details.

**Solo Exploration**

Invite students to use the information in a main idea map to create a pie chart showing the importance of the details. Each detail becomes a slice of the pie, with more important details making up the larger slices. **(cross-curricular connection)**

# Main Idea Map

# Time Line

## About the Strategy

A time line helps students organize both fictional and nonfictional events in sequential order along a continuum. Not only do students see the events in order, but they are also exposed to the overall time frame in which the events occurred.

*Time lines work well with any fictional or nonfictional selection in which understanding the order of events would help comprehension.*

**Step 1**
*Students record the first event.*

**Step 2**
*Students add the remaining events, placing them on the time line relative to the other events.*

### Time Line

| After church, Pepys goes to a meeting to talk about ways to keep the plague from growing. (1) | Alderman Hooker tells the story of a man and his wife who took their last surviving child from an infected house in London. | Pepys mentions the good news that there has been a decrease of over five hundred in the number of new cases of the plague. | Pepys is very sad to hear of the people he knows who have lost someone to the plague or are sick themselves. | Jane, one of Pepys' maids, wakes him and his wife in the middle of the night to tell them about a great fire in the city. (2) | Pepys goes out to track the progress of the fire, then goes to Whitehall to make a report. | As the fire continues to burn, Pepys and his family are forced to pack up their belongings and evacuate their home. |
|---|---|---|---|---|---|---|
| Sept. 3, 1665 | | Sept. 14, 1665 | | Sept. 2, 1666 | | |

**Skills and Strategies:** *summarize, sequence*

**Buddywork**

Invite pairs of students to create time lines into the future. They can list events that they imagine will occur before people live on the moon. Students might place their time lines in their portfolios to use for future writing. **(portfolio)**

**All Together Now**

As a class, make a list of the clue words in a selection organized by chronological, or time, order. You can add to the list as you read other selections organized by time order. Remind students to include clue words that indicate simultaneous order (*meanwhile*, *during*, etc.).

# Time Line

# Enumerative Text Frame

## About the Strategy

An enumerative article states a main idea and lists examples to support the main idea. Students can use an enumerative text frame to help them recognize this type of expository text structure. Becoming aware of this and other expository text structures improves students' reading, particularly in the content areas.

*An enumerative text frame works with selections that are organized according to this text structure.*

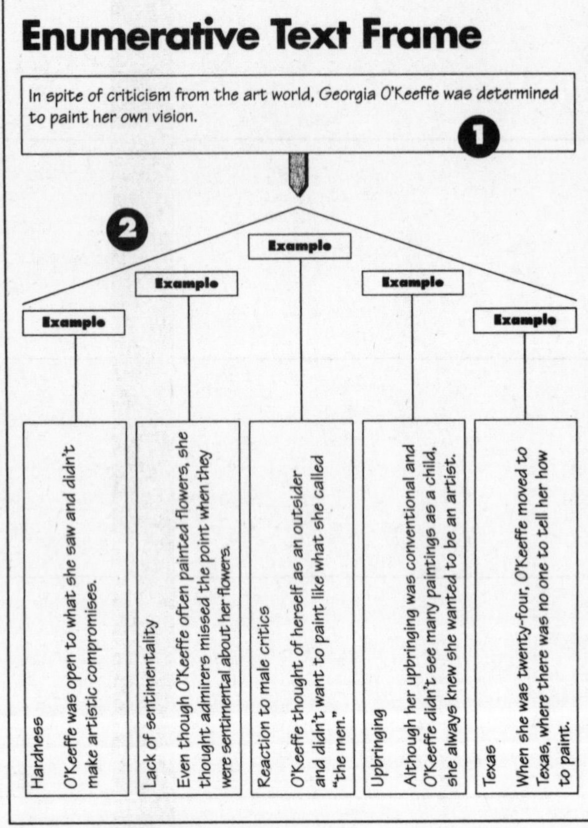


**Step 1**

*Students fill in the main idea at the top of the graphic organizer.*

**Step 2**

*Students list examples that support the main idea.*

**Skills and Strategies:** *main idea/supporting details, use text structure/genre, use text features, analyze information*

### Keep in Mind

If students are having difficulty recognizing this text structure, suggest they look for clue words such as *first*, *next*, and *finally*.

### Solo Exploration

Try using this graphic organizer to help students make predictions. After telling students the main idea of an enumerative article, suggest that they fill in examples they predict will be used to support the main idea. Remember to have students return to their predictions after reading.

# Enumerative Text Frame

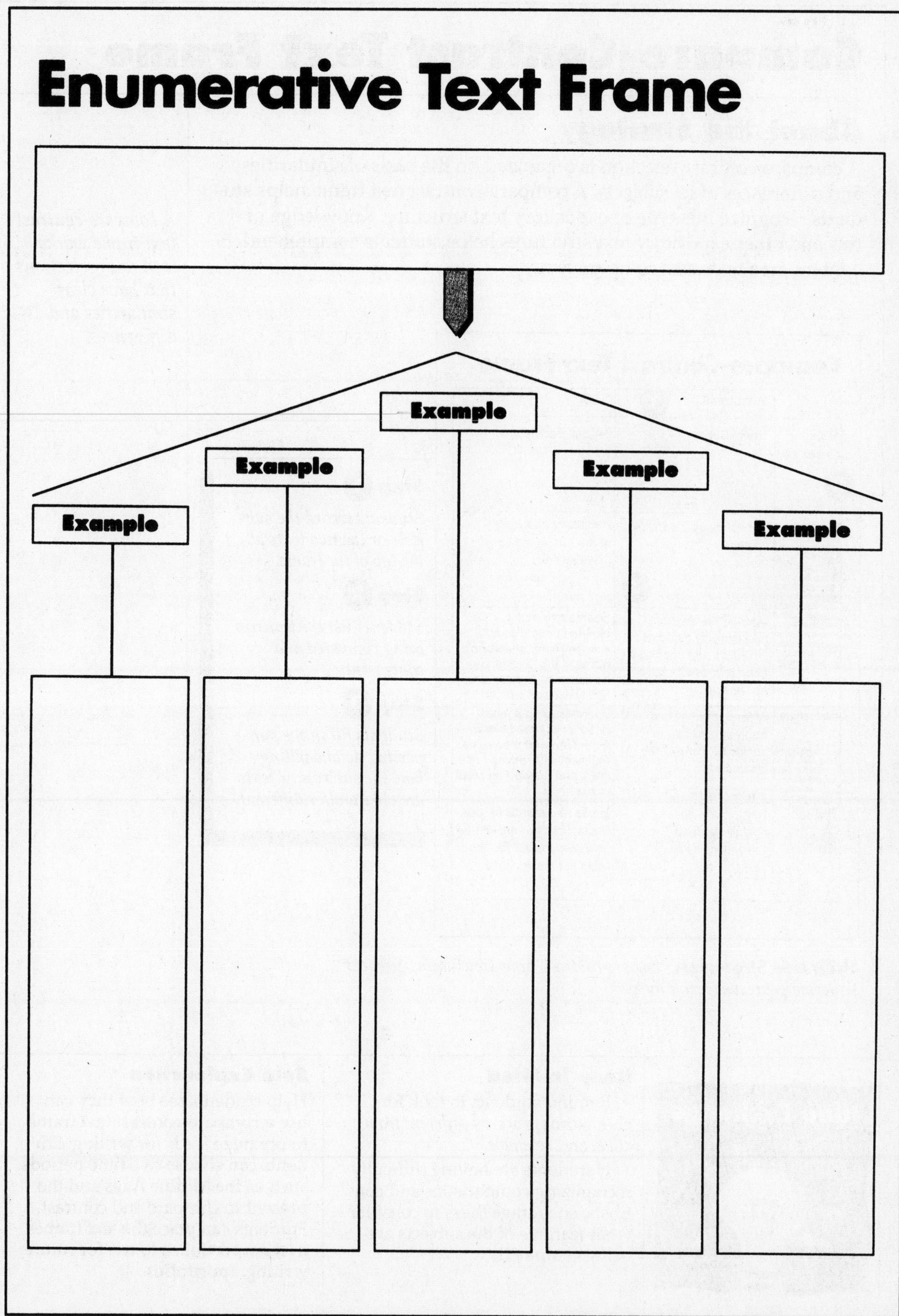

# Compare-Contrast Text Frame

## About the Strategy

A compare-contrast selection is organized on the basis of similarities and differences of its subjects. A compare-contrast text frame helps students recognize this type of expository text structure. Knowledge of this and other expository text structures helps students comprehend content-area texts and compare texts.

*A compare-contrast text frame works well with selections that have clear similarities and differences.*

### Compare-Contrast Text Frame

| | "A Problem" ❶ | "Luck" |
|---|---|---|
| Main Character ❷ | Sasha Uskov | Arthur Scoresby |
| Setting | The study of the Uskov home ❸ | A military academy and a battle in the Crimean War |
| Conflict | Sasha has disgraced his family by getting into debt and cashing a false promissory note at the bank. | Scoresby is really a blundering soldier, but every military situation works in his favor and he becomes famous and highly decorated. |
| Denouement | After his family has forgiven him, Sasha demands money from his uncle. | Scoresby wins a great victory because he makes a mistake and moves his regiment left instead of right and forward instead of back. |
| Theme | Forgiveness does not always lead to responsibility. | Those who create heroes, like the clergyman, can be held responsible for the false heroes' actions. |

**Step ❶**

*Students record the subjects or the two texts at the top of the frame.*

**Step ❷**

*Students list the features being compared and contrasted.*

**Step ❸**

*Students fill in the supporting details telling how the subjects or texts are alike and/or different.*

**Skills and Strategies:** *compare-contrast, draw conclusions, use text structure/genre, use text features*

**Keep in Mind**

- Remind students to look for clue words, such as *different from*, *alike*, and *resemble*.
- If students are having difficulty recognizing comparisons and contrasts, encourage them to consider what features of the subjects are being compared.

**Solo Exploration**

Help students see how they can use a compare-contrast text frame to organize ideas for writing. Students can choose two time periods such as the Middle Ages and the present to compare and contrast. Students can place the text frames in their portfolios to use for future writing. **(portfolio)**

# Compare-Contrast Text Frame

| | | |
|---|---|---|
| | | |
| | | |
| | | |
| | | |
| | | |

# **Cause-Effect Frame** Multiple Causes

## About the Strategy

This type of cause-effect frame helps students identify what happened and multiple reasons why it happened in both fictional and nonfictional texts. When students can see that there are causal relationships between events or ideas in text, they can make generalizations about other causal relationships in new texts and in life situations.

*This cause-effect frame works well with any selection that has clear cause-and-effect relationships with multiple causes.*

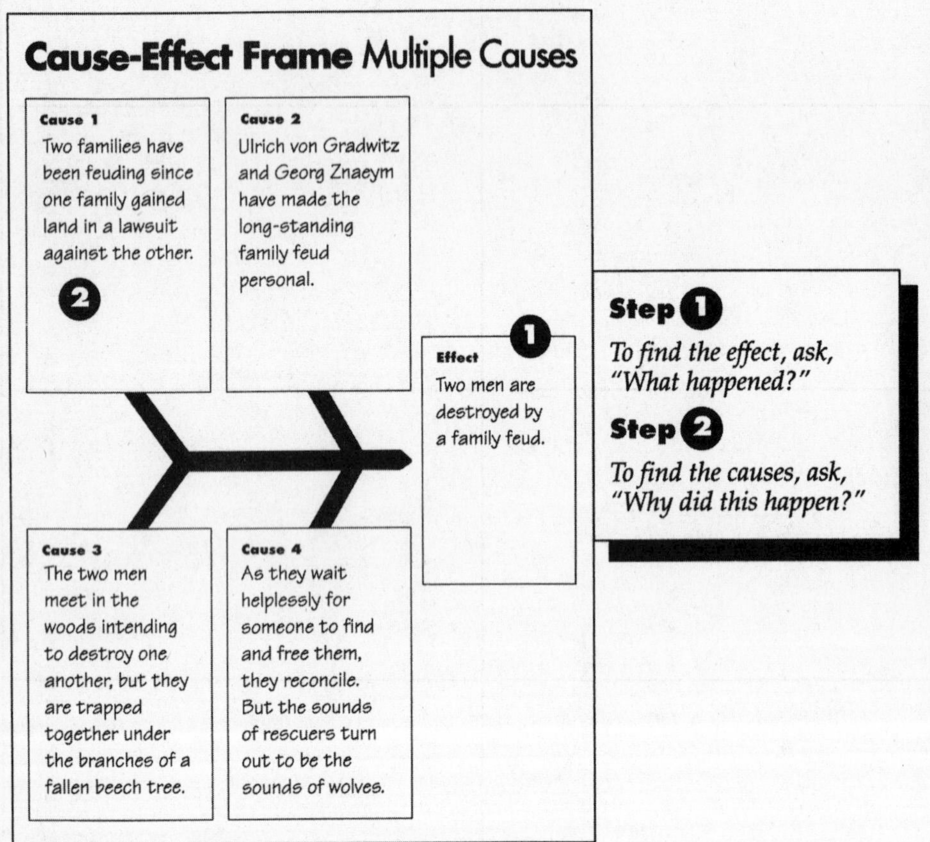


**Step 1**
*To find the effect, ask, "What happened?"*

**Step 2**
*To find the causes, ask, "Why did this happen?"*

**Skills and Strategies:** *summarize, sequence, cause-effect, make inferences*

### Keep in Mind

- If students have trouble identifying cause-and-effect relationships, suggest they look for clue words, such as *since, as a result, consequently, therefore,* and *thus.*
- Remind them that not all causes are stated directly in the text.

### All Together Now

Try posing a question for students, such as "What would life be like if freedom of the press were not guaranteed under the First Amendment?" Ask students to suggest possible effects. **(cross-curricular connection)**

# **Cause-Effect Frame** Multiple Causes

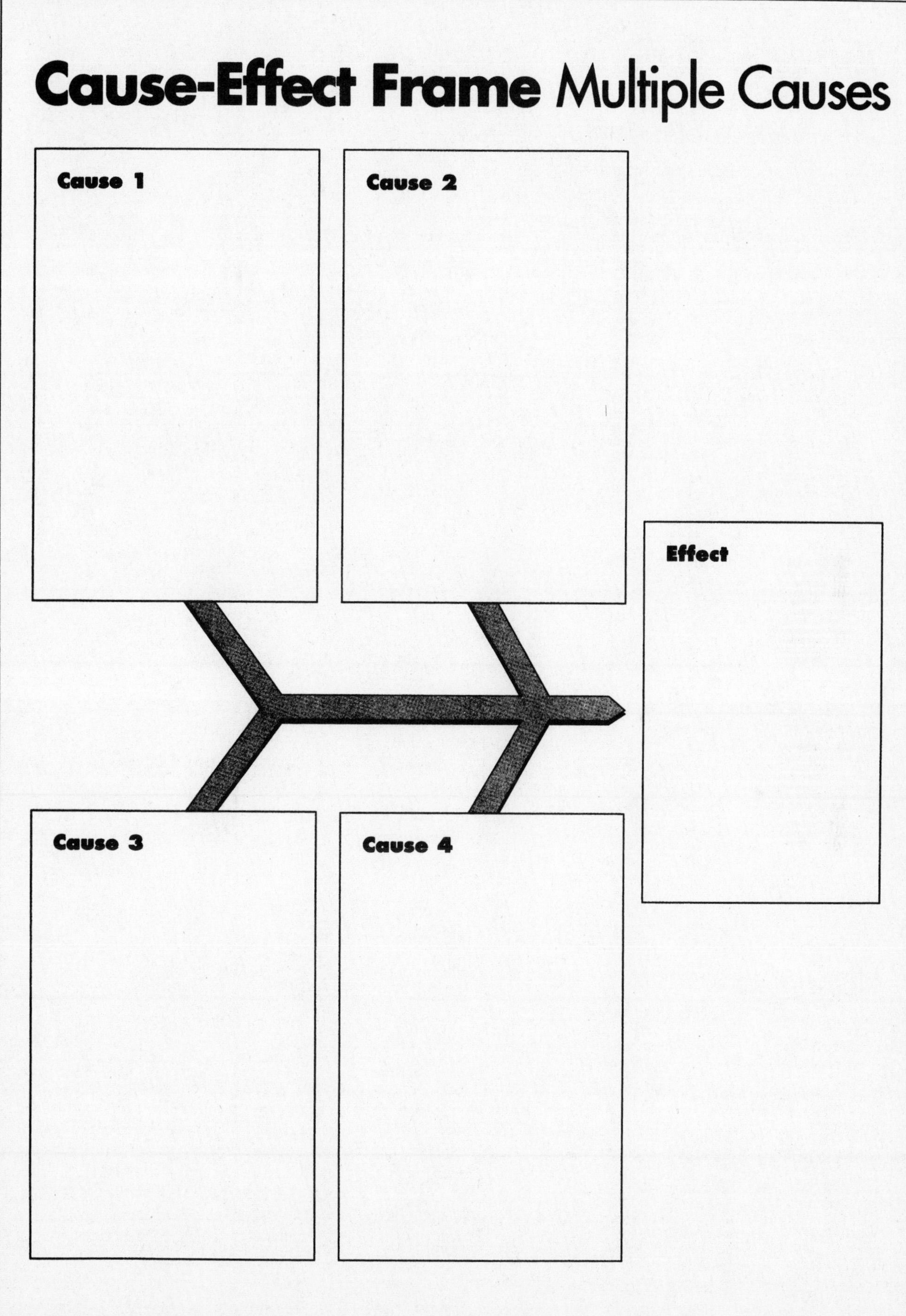

# Classroom Management Strategies

# Teacher-Mediated Classroom Reading Strategies

## Introduction

### The Challenge of Academic Text Reading

Most students enter classrooms woefully underprepared to independently navigate their reading assignments across the subject areas. While they may be able to tackle recreational reading of teen novels and magazines with relative ease, they often lack the academic language and strategic knowledge necessary for comprehending and studying concept and data rich texts. The challenging narrative and non-fiction selections students will be assigned in the course of an academic year are meant to be approached as learning tasks, not recreational activities. As such, these texts must be read multiple times with a clear learning purpose in mind.

Such an approach to reading is far from typical of adolescents engaging today's standards-driven Language Arts curricula. It is absolutely essential for teachers to assume an active instructional role, responsibly preparing students with the linguistic and strategic tools necessary for this potentially daunting task.

### Strategies for Structuring Reading

The worksheets that follow offer strategies a teacher can draw on in taking this active role. The following worksheets give concrete formats for structuring students reading:

- Choral Reading
- Oral Cloze
- Silent Independent Rereading
- Structured Partner Reading

Sophisticated texts require rereading, and scaffolding the types of reading students do on each pass is essential to bringing them into a more sophisticated engagement with the text. Here is one recommended way of using these strategies to scaffold readings:

**First Reading**—Oral Cloze with broad task
**Second Reading**—Silent rereading with detailed task
**Conclude**—Class discussion/debriefing

### Strategic Questioning

In traditional content-area reading instruction, the teacher assigns independent reading followed by an end-of-text question and answer session, in which the teacher and a handful of students dominate the discussion, leaving struggling readers disengaged and confused. Research suggests that struggling readers need explicit guidance in emulating the behaviors of competent readers.

This guidance must include breaking the reading into manageable chunks, approaching each section of text with a concrete question or purpose, and rereading sections for different levels of details. Teachers should pose increasingly complex questions while modeling a more active and strategic approach to reading.

The following worksheets give strategies to assist struggling readers in formulating appropriate reading questions and in connecting their guide questions to concrete tasks.

- Preparing-to-Read Questions
- Reading Guide Questions
- A Range of Appropriate Questions
- Question Frames

# Choral Reading

## Strategy

A common primary-grade practice, choral reading can also work very well with older readers. Choral reading is effective because it requires that each student, regardless of level or proficiency in English, actively engage in attending to the text while it provides a nonthreatening atmosphere in which to practice. Many teachers find it helpful to use choral reading one row or group at a time. This modification tends to be less demanding and more manageable for diverse learners.

**Tips to ensure success with choral reading:**

- Request students to "Keep your voice with mine" to discourage them from racing ahead.
- Choose relatively short passages (e.g., 300–500 words).
- Follow with a silent rereading. Now that all students have basic access to the text, a second reading can elicit deeper understanding, supply an opportunity to apply previously taught strategies, answer inductive questions, and so on, while reinforcing the message that "constructing meaning is your job. I am here to help, not to do it for you."

# Oral Cloze

## Strategy

The oral cloze is a choral reading adaptation of a commonly used reading-comprehension assessment process, in which words are selectively deleted from a brief passage, and students are prompted to fill-in reasonable word choices. In the oral cloze, the teacher reads aloud while students follow along silently. The teacher occasionally omits selected words, which the students chime in and read aloud together. The oral cloze is useful in guiding students in an initial read of a difficult passage, thereby insuring that struggling readers will have access to the text. Often during teacher read-alouds, students listen passively, read ahead, or remain off-task. This strategy keeps students on their "reading toes" by giving them a concrete job while allowing teachers to check participation.

**Tips to ensure success with cloze reading:**

- To begin, demonstrate the oral cloze by contrasting it with a traditional read-aloud. Read a few sentences aloud without assigning students a role or task. Clarify the importance of being an active, thoughtful reader when the goal is accountable reading to learn, often with an assessment (e.g., quiz or paper). Explain that you will be reading aloud, and their job is to follow along, reading at the same pace and chorally chiming in when a word is occasionally omitted. Then reread the same sentences leaving out 2–3 words so that students see the contrast and grasp their active role.
- Choose to leave out meaningful words (e.g., nouns, verbs, adjectives) that most students can easily pronounce (prepositions and other connecting words do not work well).
- Take care to not distract students by leaving out too many words, not more than one per sentence (e.g., in a 50-word paragraph, delete 2–3 words).
- Pick words that come at a natural pause.
- Pick words (if any) that you have pretaught, providing students with a meaningful context for the new word.
- Provide students with an additional concrete active-reading task or question directing their attention to the content of the passage. On the first read, this task should be fairly broad and easy (e.g., Circle two adjectives describing how the character felt).
- In a mixed-ability class with many struggling readers, consider guiding students' reading with two rounds of the oral cloze before assigning a silent reading task. On the second reading, omit different words and pick up the pace a bit while providing an additional focus question or task.

# Silent Independent Rereading

## Strategy

After facilitating students in their first reading of a challenging passage using the oral cloze, prepare them for an active independent rereading of the passage.

The essential element here, as with both choral and cloze reading, is to make sure the students have a job, a task during reading that increases their attentiveness, cognitive focus, and accountability. Rereading silently to answer a question previously posed to the class as a whole efficiently meets this goal. Teachers may pose useful questions that the class reads silently to answer. Over time, students are taught to construct a range of questions themselves before such class reading (moving from literal to inferential).

After each section is read, engage students in a brief discussion to clarify questions and vocabulary and to ensure common understanding of essential big ideas in the text. You may choose to guide students in mapping or note-taking from the text at this point as well.

### Tips to Get the Most From Structured Silent Rereading

- Chunk the text into 1–4 paragraph sections within which students silently reread and actively identify information necessary to respond to the teacher's focus question.
- Request that anyone who finishes before you convene the discussion go back and reread the section to look for additional details in the text.
- The first few times, model how one thinks while reading to find answers to a question. Think aloud to give students a "window" on this sophisticated cognitive task.
- Encourage students to discuss their thinking, as well as their answers, during whole-class discussion. For example, focus on such issues as *"How did you know?"* or *"Why did you think that?"*

# Structured Partner Reading

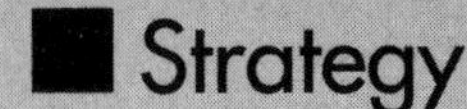

## Strategy

Research has consistently pointed to partner reading as a potent strategy to increase the amount of actual reading students engage in, while providing access for all students to key ideas in the text. Partner reading is an excellent way to ensure that all students are actively engaged in the text and accountable for doing their jobs.

**Tips to get the most from structured partner reading:**

- Rank-order students by overall literacy and proficiency in English. In a group of 30 students, for example, students #1 and #15 are the first readers and #16 and #30 are the first coaches.
- Ensure that activities are fully reciprocal—students should spend equal time in the roles of reader and coach.
- Provide specific directions and demonstrate the roles of reader and coach (e.g., "First reader: Whisper-read the first paragraph, coaches follow along, fix mistakes, and ask the comprehension questions.").

**The Reader**

The reader reads a paragraph or a page or reads for a given amount of time. Touching under the words may be helpful if the students have extremely limited literacy.

**The Coach**

The coach encourages and supports the reader.

1. If the reader asks for a word, the coach will say the word.
2. If the reader makes a mistake, the coach will correct the error using the following steps:
   **a.** Point to the word and say, *"Can you figure out this word?"*
   **b.** If the reader cannot figure out the word in five seconds, say *"This word is __."*
   **c.** Have the reader repeat the word and then reread the sentence.

   Why reread the entire sentence?
   - Improve comprehension.
   - Practice the word again—read it fluently in context.
   - Hold students accountable for reading more carefully.

After students have mastered the basic sequence, add various comprehension strategies, such as retelling main ideas after each page or section.

**Summarize/paraphrase.** State the main idea in ten words or less. (Using only ten words prompts students to use their own words.)

**Predict and monitor.** Reader predicts what will happen next, reads a paragraph/section and then determines if the prediction was accurate, revises as needed, summarizes, and predicts again, continuing for a set amount of time.

# Preparing-to-Read Questions

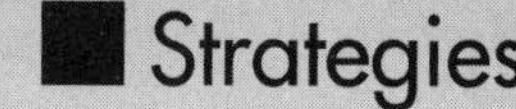

## Strategies

**Provide focused questions to guide students before reading.**
If students have background knowledge regarding the subject, it is very helpful to pose a few open-ended questions to elicit a lively brainstorming session prior to reading. Cueing students to examine any related visual support, as well as the title, can assist students in focusing their thinking more productively.

What are the possible effects of eating too much junk food?
Take a look at this school lunch menu in the photograph and identify with your partner two healthy and two unhealthy foods.

***Instructional Tip**: Guide students to share answers with a teacher-selected partner; take care to designate roles (1s and 2s) to insure ALL are active participants.*

When students lack critical background knowledge related to a topic, brainstorming alone is often insufficient. Students will benefit from carefully formulated questions before and during each reading segment to focus their attention on the most important information. Without a concrete purpose when tackling each segment of a text, less proficient readers are apt to get mired in confusing details and distracted by unfamiliar yet non-essential vocabulary. Thus, it is essential to provide students a very specific question to guide their initial reading.

What are the three most important reasons cited by the author in favor of recycling? How can recycling actually save money?

**Provide questions during the reading process.**
It is critical that teachers guide less proficient students in reading each segment of text at least twice, providing a clear task each time. Posing a thoughtful question before students read challenging text will help them understand the active and focused approach necessary for reading to learn. Global questions are most appropriate for initial reading, followed by questions that require more careful analysis and attention to detail in subsequent reading.

**1st read:** What is this section in our article on teen health mainly about?
**Task:** Identify a word or phrase that names our topic (e.g., *teen diet*).

**2nd read:** Why is the author so concerned about adolescent diet?
**Task:** Identify two reasons stated by the author.

**3rd read:** Since the snack foods provided at school are a major cause of poor adolescent health, why do you think schools continue to sell them?
**Task:** Write down a specific reason you think schools still make candy, sodas, and chips so easily available in vending machines.

***Instructional Tip:** Complement the guide question with a concrete task to increase student accountability and increase focus and attention.*

# Reading Guide Questions

## Strategies

There are common text elements that teachers can utilize to frame reading guide questions and model an alert and strategic reading process for students.

**Use headings and topic sentences to generate reading guide questions.**
Model for students how to turn a heading into a reading guide question for the initial reading of a passage. Be sure to prompt them to translate the question into a concrete task for which they will be held accountable in subsequent class discussion.

Subheading: Recycling Saves Money

Guide question: How does recycling save money?

Task: "I need to identify two ways that recycling helps people save money."

Students need to approach each paragraph within a section of text with a clear sense of what they need to attend to in and extract from their reading. While a heading often provides the overall topic for a section of text, topic sentences provide a more specific focus for developing reading guide questions for discrete paragraphs.

Subheading: Recycling Saves Money

Topic sentence, paragraph one: "Because of the recent downturn in the auto industry, Smithville has come up with a creative recycling program to support their cash-strapped schools."

Guide Question: What is Smithville's recycling program?

Task: I need to identify the key features of Smithville's recycling program.

Helping struggling students develop genuine competence in formulating and applying reading guide questions is rather labor intensive. Students who are accustomed to approach all forms of reading material in a generic, unfocused manner will require considerable hand-holding through a gradual release process that moves systematically from "I'll do it" (teacher modeling) to "We'll do it" (unified class with teacher guidance) to "You'll do it" (partner practice) to "You do it on your own" (independent practice).

**Provide questions after reading a passage.**
After students have navigated a demanding text and achieved basic comprehension, they are well positioned to extend their thinking by responding to higher-order questions requiring greater reflection and application. These questions are the interesting and provocative ones that teachers long to pose but that fall flat unless students have been prepared.

How could we set up a viable recycling program in our school community?

If you had two minutes to address the school board, what are the three best arguments you would provide to support the development of a district wide recycling program?

# A Range of Appropriate Questions

## Strategies

**Begin with "on the surface" questions.**

**Why?** Struggling readers must be able to identify the most essential information in the reading *before* they are guided in grappling with more abstract analysis/interpretation. Otherwise, many students will not have the cognitive tools to benefit from the discussion.

**What?** Ask questions that require literal, factual recall and text-based answers that students can point to, underline, or circle.

> What is an endangered species? What are two examples of endangered species mentioned in this article? How are environmentalists working with oil companies to protect the red-tailed hawk?

**Include "under the surface" questions.**

**Why?** To comprehend challenging reading material, students must go beyond the factual basics of the text. Getting the gist certainly is no small feat for many struggling readers. However, it is important to help less proficient students acquire a more in-depth understanding and the strategic know-how required for mature comprehension.

**What?** Ask questions that require students to make inferences from or to analyze and synthesize text-based information, as well as to make inferences connecting new ideas from the text with prior knowledge.

> Why has it been difficult for environmentalist and oil companies to work together in protecting the red-tailed hawk? What environmental factors are placing some animal species in danger in your community?

**Teach students the questions for reading to learn.**

**Why?** Less proficient readers have often spent their early literacy development with relatively undemanding stories. In the classroom, they have largely responded to the "who, where, and when" questions appropriate for stories, leaving them ill equipped to reply to the "why, how, and what" demands of information text comprehension.

**What?** Teachers need to teach specific tasks involved in responding to questions associated with informational texts. Students need to understand that when asked a "why question" (e.g., Why have many schools outlawed soft drink sales?), they need to read, looking for specific reasons. It is not enough simply to model the questions; students must understand what prompted you to ask that specific question and the kind of information the question suggests.

> Why? = For what reasons? What are the reasons?
> How? = What was the process? What was the sequence?
> What? = Definition (What is ______?)
> What? + signal word  What are the <u>benefits</u> of ___________?
> What was the <u>reaction</u> to ___________?

# Question Frames

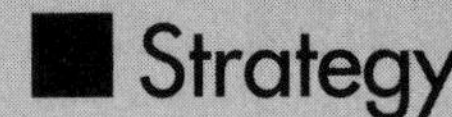


Teaching students how to generate their own questions is an important comprehension-enhancing element of structured silent reading. Underprepared readers are often overly dependent on teachers and have not learned to self-question as they read. According to the research of Taffy Raphael,[1] students who understand how questions are written are more capable of analyzing and answering them than students who lack this understanding. One useful model, derived from Bloom's *Taxonomy*,[2] was developed by Stiggins[3] using Question Frames for different levels of questions to provide initial support for students during self-questioning:

**Recall (Literal)** ("I can put my finger on the answer in the text.")
- What is the name of ____________?
- Define ____________.
- Identify the ____________.
- Who did ____________?

**Analysis (Inferential)** ("I combine my knowledge with the author's information to understand.")
- What is the main idea?
- The most important part of ______ is ______ because ______.
- The essential parts are ____________.

**Compare/Contrast** ("I analyze similarities and differences.")
- Compare the motives of ________ to those of ________.
- What are the most important differences/similarities between ____________ and ____________?

**Prediction** ("I predict based on the evidence so far.")
- What do you think will happen in the next ____________?
- Predict what you think ____________ will do. Why?
- What would happen if ____________?

**Evaluation** ("I make and defend judgments.")
- What is your opinion of ____________?
- What is the best solution to the problem of ____________?
- Defend why ________ is a better solution than ________.

Question Frames are helpful when teaching diverse learners to ask questions beyond simple recall/literal questions. Teacher modeling and well-supported initial practice are key to assisting all students in generating different types of questions.

---

1. Raphael, T. "Teaching Learners About Sources of Information for Answering Questions." *Journal of Reading* (1984), vol. 28(4), 303–311.
2. Bloom, B. *Taxonomy of Educational Objectives.* New York: Longmans, Green, 1956.
3. Stiggins, R. "Improving Assessment Where It Means the Most: In the Classroom." *Educational Leadership* (1985), 43, 69–74.

**Vocabulary**

To succeed in narrowing the language divide, a school-wide comprehensive academic vocabulary program must include the following four components:

1. **Fluent, wide reading.** Vocabulary for academic purposes grows as a consequence of independent reading of a variety of texts (in particular, informational texts) and increasing reading volume.
2. **Direct scaffolded teaching of critical words.** Students learn new words via various explicit, teacher-directed instructional strategies.
3. **Teaching word-learning strategies.** When taught the tools to exploit context, analyze prefixes, and various other strategies, students can independently learn new word meanings while reading independently.
4. **Daily participation in structured, accountable contexts for daily speaking and writing.** Academic language develops when students are engaged in rigorous and meaningful application of newly acquired vocabulary and syntax in structured speaking and writing tasks.

The following group of worksheets, marked with the triangle icon, provide concrete strategies for addressing many of these objectives for vocabulary development:

- Preteaching Vocabulary: Convey Meaning
- Preteaching Vocabulary: Check Understanding
- Vocabulary Development
- Choosing Vocabulary Words
- Possible Sentences
- Word Analysis/Teaching Word Parts
- Assessing Vocabulary Mastery

Concept development goes hand in hand with vocabulary enrichment. The following worksheets, also labeled with the triangle icon, provide strategies for concept development:

- List-Group-Label
- Concept Mapping/Clarifying Routine
- Using Concept Maps

The remaining worksheets in Part 3, marked with the circle icon, offer strategies for structuring academic discussion and writing.

# Preteaching Vocabulary: Convey Meaning

## ▼ Strategy

- If your goal is simply to familiarize students with a word to help them recognize and comprehend it in a reading, follow steps 1–4.

  **1.** Pronounce the word (and give the part of speech).

  This article focuses on an *ecstatic* moment in a high school student's life.

  **2.** Ask students to all repeat the word.

  Say the word *ecstatic* after me. (ec stat' ic)

  **3.** Provide an accessible synonym and/or a brief explanation.

  *Ecstatic* means "extremely happy."

  **4.** Rephrase the simple definition/explanation, asking students to complete the statement by substituting aloud the new word.

  If you are extremely happy about something, you are ____ (students say *ecstatic*).

- If your goal is to familiarize students with a word that is central to comprehending the reading and that you also want them to learn, continue with step 5, then check for understanding.

  **5.** Provide a visual "nonlinguistic representation" of the word (if possible) and/or an illustrative "showing" sentence.

  Showing image: a picture of a man happily in love.
  Showing sentence: Julio was *ecstatic* when Melissa agreed to marry him.

  Have students fill out a vocabulary worksheet as you preteach the words; doing so involves them more directly and provides them with a focused word list for later study and practice.

**Sample Vocabulary Note-Taking**

| Term | Synonym | Definition/ Example | Image |
|---|---|---|---|
| **ecstatic,** *adj.* | extremely happy | feeling very happy, excited, or joyful<br>*Julio was ecstatic when Melissa agreed to marry him.* | |
| **distraught,** *adj.* | extremely worried and upset | feeling very worried, unhappy, or distressed<br>*Mark was distraught to learn that the camp bus had left without him.* | |

# Preteaching Vocabulary: Check Understanding

## ▼ Strategies

**1. Focused Questions**

Ask focused questions to see if students seem to grasp the word's meaning (as opposed to questions such as *Any questions? Do you understand?* or *Is that clear?*). Questions may be initially directed to the unified group for a thumbs-up or thumbs-down response; to teams using Numbered Heads; or to pairs using Think-Pair-Share, followed by questions to individuals.

- Would you be ecstatic if you won the lottery?
- Would you be ecstatic if you were assigned a 20-page report to complete over the Spring break?
- Would you be ecstatic if you won two front-row tickets to a concert given by your favorite band?
- Would you be ecstatic if your mother bought your favorite brand of breakfast cereal?

**2. Images**

If the word is crucial (for the lesson and their academic vocabulary tool kit), consider asking students to generate their own relevant images or examples.

- Turn to your partner and ask what has happened recently that made him/her ecstatic. Or ask what would make him/her ecstatic. Be prepared to share one example with the class.
- What other images might we associate with *ecstatic?* Think of one or two, turn to your partner and discuss, and then be prepared to share one of your images with the class.

Words that are new to students but that represent familiar concepts can be addressed using a number of relatively quick instructional tactics. Many of these (e.g., synonyms, antonyms, examples) are optimal for prereading and oral reading, which call for more expedient approaches.

**Brief Strategies for Vocabulary Development (Stahl[4])**

- **Teach synonyms.** Provide a synonym that students know (e.g., link *stringent* to the known word *strict*).
- **Teach antonyms.** Not all words have antonyms, but for those that do, thinking about their opposites requires students to evaluate the critical attributes of the words in question.
- **Paraphrase definitions.** Requiring students to use their own words increases connection-making and provides the teacher with useful informal assessment—"Do they really get it?"
- **Provide examples.** The more personalized the example, the better. An example for the new word *egregious* might be *Ms. Kinsella's 110-page reading assignment was egregious indeed!*
- **Provide nonexamples.** Similar to using antonyms, providing nonexamples requires students to evaluate a word's attributes. Invite students to explain why it is not an example.
- **Ask for sentences that "show you know."** Students construct novel sentences confirming their understanding of a new word, using more than one new word per sentence to show that connections can also be useful.
- **Teach word sorting.** Provide a list of vocabulary words from a reading selection and have students sort them into various categories (e.g., parts of speech, branches of government). Students can re-sort words into "guess my sort" using categories of their own choosing.

---

4. Stahl, S. A. *Vocabulary Development.* Cambridge, MA: Brookline Books, 1999.

# Choosing Vocabulary Words

## ▼ Strategies

Restrict your selections to approximately six to eight words that are critical to comprehending the reading passage/segment you intend to cover in one lesson (e.g., one Science chapter section; a three-page passage from a six-page short story.)

- Choose **"big idea"** words that name or relate to the central concepts addressed in the passage (in subject areas outside of English Language Arts, these central lesson terms are typically highlighted by the publisher).
- Choose high-use, widely applicable **"academic tool kit"** words that student are likely to encounter in diverse materials across subject areas and grade levels (e.g., *aspect, compare, similar, subsequently*).
- Choose high-use **"disciplinary tool kit"** words for your subject area that you consider vital for students to master at this age and proficiency level (e.g., *metaphor, policy, economic, application, species*).
- Choose **"polysemous"** (multiple meaning) words that have a new academic meaning in a reading in addition to a more general, familiar meaning (e.g., "wave of immigrants" in U.S. History vs. a greeting or an ocean wave).
- Identify additional academic words, not included in the reading selection, that students will need to know in order to engage in **academic discourse** about the central characters, issues, and themes (especially for literary selections).
- Be careful not to overload students with low-frequency words that they are unlikely to encounter in many academic reading contexts, especially words that are not essential to comprehend the gist of the text.

# Possible Sentences

Possible Sentences (Moore and Moore[6]) is a relatively simple strategy for teaching word meanings and generating considerable class discussion.

1. The teacher chooses six to eight words from the text that may pose difficulty for students. These words are usually key concepts in the text.
2. Next, the teacher chooses four to six words that students are more likely to know something about.
3. The list of ten to twelve words is put on the chalkboard or overhead projector. The teacher provides brief definitions as needed.
4. Students are challenged to devise sentences that contain two or more words from the list.
5. All sentences that students come up with, both accurate and inaccurate, are listed and discussed.
6. Students now read the selection.
7. After reading, revisit the Possible Sentences and discuss whether they could be true based on the passage or how they could be modified to be true.

Stahl[7] reported that Possible Sentences significantly improved both students' overall recall of word meanings and their comprehension of text containing those words. Interestingly, this was true when compared with a control group and when compared with Semantic Mapping.

---

6. Moore, P. W., and S. A. Moore. "Possible Sentences." In E. K. Dishner, T. W. Bean, J. E. Readence, and P. W. Moore (eds.). *Reading in the Content Areas: Improving Classroom Instruction,* 2nd ed. Dubuque, IA: Kendall/Hunt, 1986, pp. 174–179.
7. Stahl, op. cit.

# Word Analysis/Teaching Word Parts

▼ Strategy

Word Analysis/Teaching Word Parts helps many underprepared readers who lack basic knowledge of word origins or etymology, such as Latin and Greek roots, as well as discrete understanding of how a prefix or suffix can alter the meaning of a word. Learning clusters of words that share a common origin can help students understand content-area texts and connect new words to those already known. For example, a secondary teacher (Allen[8]) reported reading about a character who suffered from amnesia. Teaching students that the prefix *a-* derives from Greek and means "not," while the base *-mne-* means "memory," reveals the meaning. After judicious teacher scaffolding, students were making connections to various words in which the prefix *a-* changed the meaning of a base word (e.g., *amoral, atypical*).

The charts below summarize some of the affixes worth considering, depending on your students' prior knowledge and English proficiency.

| **Prefix** | **Meaning** | **Percentage of All Prefixed Words** | **Example** |
|---|---|---|---|
| *un-* | not; reversal of | 26 | uncover |
| *re-* | again, back, really | 14 | review |
| *in-/im-* | in, into, not | 11 | insert |
| *dis-* | away, apart, negative | 7 | discover |
| *en-/em-* | in; within; on | 4 | entail |
| *mis-* | wrong | 3 | mistaken |
| *pre-* | before | 3 | prevent |
| *a-* | not; in, on, without | 1 | atypical |

| **Suffix** | **Meaning** | **Percentage of All Suffixed Words** | **Example** |
|---|---|---|---|
| *-s, -es* | more than one; verb marker | 31 | characters, reads, reaches |
| *-ed* | in the past; quality, state | 20 | walked |
| *-ing* | when you do something; quality, state | 14 | walking |
| *-ly* | how something is | 7 | safely |
| *-er, -or* | one who, what, that, which | 4 | drummer |
| *-tion, -sion* | state, quality; act | 4 | action, mission |
| *-able, -ible* | able to be | 2 | disposable, reversible |
| *-al, -ial* | related to, like | 1 | final, partial |

**8.** Allen, J. *Words, Words, Words: Teaching Vocabulary in Grades 4–12.* York, ME: Stenhouse, 1999.

## ▼ Strategies

Following are three meaningful and alternative assessment formats that require relatively little preparation time:

1. Select only four to six important words and embed each in an accessible and contextualized sentence followed by a semicolon. Ask students to add another sentence after the semicolon that clearly demonstrates their understanding of the underlined word as it is used in this context. This assessment format will discourage students from rote memorization and mere recycling of a sample sentence covered during a lesson.

   Example: Mr. Lamont had the most eclectic wardrobe of any teacher on the high-school staff.

2. Present four to six sentences, each containing an underlined word from the study list, and ask students to decide whether each word makes sense in this context. If yes, the student must justify why the sentence makes sense. If no, the student must explain why it is illogical and change the part of the sentence that doesn't make sense.

   Example: Mr. Lamont had the most eclectic wardrobe of any teacher on the high-school staff; rain or shine, he wore the same predictable brown loafers, a pair of black or brown pants, a white shirt, and a beige sweater vest.

3. Write a relatively brief passage (one detailed paragraph) that includes six to ten words from the study list. Then, delete these words and leave blanks for students to complete. This modified cloze assessment will force students to scrutinize the context and draw upon a deeper understanding of the words' meanings. Advise students to first read the entire passage and to then complete the blanks by drawing from their study list. As an incentive for students to prepare study cards or more detailed notes, they can be permitted to use these personal references during the quiz.

Because these qualitative and authentic assessments require more rigorous analysis and application than most objective test formats, it seems fair to allow students to first practice with the format as a class exercise and even complete occasional tests in a cooperative group.

# List-Group-Label

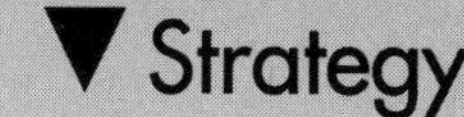


List-Group-Label (Taba[5]) is a form of structured brainstorming designed to help students identify what they know about a concept and the words related to the concept while provoking a degree of analysis and critical thinking. These are the directions to students:

| |
|---|
| 1. Think of all the words related to ________________. (a key "big idea" in the text) |
| 2. Group the words listed by some shared characteristics or commonalities. |
| 3. Decide on a label for each group. |
| 4. Try to add words to the categories on the organized lists. |

Working in small groups or pairs, each group shares with the class its method of categorization and the thinking behind its choices, while adding words from other class members. Teachers can extend this activity by having students convert their organized concepts into a Semantic Map that becomes a visual expression of their thinking.

List-Group-Label is an excellent prereading activity to build on prior knowledge, introduce critical concepts, and ensure attention during selection reading.

---

**5.** Taba, H. *Teacher's Handbook for Elementary Social Studies.* Reading, MA: Addison-Wesley, 1988.

# Concept Mapping/Clarifying Routine

## ▼ Strategies

Research by Frayer et al.[9] supports the strategy of teaching by Concept Mapping:

1. identifying the critical attributes of the word.
2. giving the category to which the word belongs.
3. discussing examples of the concept.
4. discussing nonexamples.

Others have had success extending this approach by guiding students through representation of the concept in a visual map or graphic organizer. The Clarifying Routine, designed and researched by Ellis,[10] is a particularly effective example:

1. Select a critical concept/word to teach. Enter it on a graphic clarifying map like the sample for *satire.*
2. List the clarifiers or critical attributes that explicate the concept.
3. List the core idea—a summary statement or brief definition.
4. Brainstorm for knowledge connections—personal links from students' world views/prior knowledge (encourage idiosyncratic/personal links).
5. Give an example of the concept; link to clarifiers: "Why is this an example of ________________?"
6. List nonexamples: "How do you know ________________ is not an example of ________________?"
7. Construct a sentence that "shows you know."

**Term: SATIRE**

**Core Idea: Any Work That Uses Wit to Attack Foolishness**

| Example | Clarifiers | Knowledge Connections |
|---|---|---|
| • A story that exposes the acts of corrupt politicians by making fun of them<br>**Nonexample**<br>• A story that exposes the acts of corrupt politicians through factual reporting<br>**Example sentence**<br>• Charles Dickens used satire to expose the problems of common folks in England. | • Can be oral or written.<br>• Ridicule or expose vice in a clever way.<br>• Can include irony, exaggeration, name-calling, understatement.<br>• Are usually based on a real person or event. | • Political cartoons on the editorial pages of our paper<br>• Stories TV comics tell to make fun of the President—as on *Saturday Night Live*<br>• My mom's humor at dinner time! |

---

9. Frayer, D. A., W. C. Frederick, and H. J. Klausmeier. *A Schema for Testing the Level of Concept Mastery* (Technical Report No. 16). Madison, WI: University of Wisconsin Research and Development Center for Cognitive Learning, 1969.
10. Ellis, E. *The Clarifying Routine.* Lawrence, KS: Edge Enterprises, 1997.

# Using Concept Maps

## Strategies

Students benefit from graphic presentations of the connections between the ideas they are learning. Each Unit Resources booklet includes Concept Maps—graphic organizers that illustrate the logical relationship among the skills taught in a Part or a Unit. In Grades 6 through 10, the Concept Maps focus on the Literary Analysis, Reading Skill, and Academic Vocabulary skills in each Part. In Grades 11 and 12 and in *World Masterpieces*, each Map connects the Literary Analysis skills in a Unit to the trends and themes of the period covered.

**Steps**

1. Review the Concept Map and identify the skills you will cover.

2. Distribute copies of the Concept Map to students. Identify those skills and concepts you will teach and have students circle or otherwise note them. Elicit from students any prior knowledge they may have about the ideas you have introduced. In addition, you may wish to ask them about their own interests in connection with the ideas. In later classes, you can make connections to students' prior knowledge and interests as relevant.

3. Briefly note the connections between ideas on the Concept Map. For example, you might explain that the "Big Picture" or "Main Idea" in the Part is the short story. Using the Concept Map, explain that a plot is an important part of a short story.

4. Emphasize for students that the skills you have identified represent a goal for the class: Everyone will be working toward mastery of those skills.

5. In succeeding lessons, refer students to their Concept Maps at appropriate junctures. As you introduce a selection, review the relevant portion of the Concept Map with students so that they clearly grasp the goals you are setting.

6. As you conclude teaching the selection, review the Concept Map with students to see how the skills are connected with other concepts they have learned. Have students add the name of the selections they have completed to the appropriate blanks. Have students log the additional assignments they complete, such as Extension Activities, in the Learning Log on the chart.

7. As you conclude instruction for a Part or for a Unit, review with students the skills they have covered and the logical connections among the skills.

Grateful acknowledgment for the idea of the Concept Map is made to B. Keith Lenz and Donald D. Deshler, who develop the idea in their book *Teaching Content to All: Evidence-Based Inclusive Practices in Middle and Secondary Schools* (New York: Pearson Education, Inc., 2004).

# Idea Wave

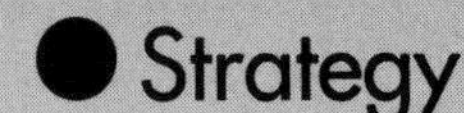

- Students listen while the teacher poses a question or task.
- Students are given quiet time to consider what they know about the topic and record a number of possible responses. This may be a simple list of words and phrases or a focused quick-write. It is also helpful to provide students with a series of response prompts to complete prior to being asked to share aloud. In this way, less proficient academic language users will have a linguistic scaffold to bolster their linguistic output along with their confidence in sharing aloud.

  For example, if students are being asked to make predictions about what will happen in the next chapter of *The Joy Luck Club,* they might be provided with these sentence prompts to complete:

  I predict that Waverly's mother will be (disappointed in / proud of) her daughter's behavior because . . .

  Based on Waverly's relationship with her mother, I assume that her mother will react very (positively / negatively) because . . .
- The teacher whips around the class in a relatively fast-paced and structured manner (e.g., down rows, around tables), allowing as many students as possible to share an idea in 15 seconds or less.
- After several contributions, there tends to be some repetition. Students point out similarities in responses using appropriate language strategies (e.g., *My idea is similar to / related to . . .*), rather than simply stating that their ideas have already been mentioned. This fosters active listening and validation of ideas.
- The teacher can record these ideas for subsequent review or have students do a quick-write summarizing some of the more interesting contributions they heard during the discussion.

# Numbered Heads and Think-Write-Pair-Share

## Strategies

**Numbered Heads**

- Students number off in teams, one through four.
- The teacher asks a series of questions, one at a time.
- Students discuss possible answers to each question for an established amount of time (about 30 seconds to 90 seconds, depending on the complexity of the task).
- The teacher calls a number (1–4), and all students with that number raise their hand, ready to respond.
- The teacher randomly calls on students with the specified number to answer on behalf of their team.
- Students are encouraged to acknowledge similarities and differences between their team's response and that of other teams (e.g., *We predicted a very different outcome. Our reaction was similar to that of Ana's group.*).
- The teacher continues posing questions and soliciting responses in this manner until the brainstorming or review session is finished.

**Think-Write-Pair-Share**

- Students listen while the teacher poses a question or a task.
- Students are given quiet time to first answer the question individually in writing.
- Students are then cued to pair with a neighbor to discuss their responses, noting similarities and differences. Students encourage their partners to clarify and justify responses using appropriate language strategies:

  How did you decide that?

  In other words, you think that . . .
- It is often helpful to structure the roles (first speaker, first listener) and designate the time frames:

  First speakers, you have 90 seconds to share your answers with your partner.
- After rehearsing responses with a partner, students are invited to share with the class.
- The teacher asks a series of questions, one at a time.
- Students discuss possible answers to each question for an established amount of time (about 30 seconds to 90 seconds, depending on the complexity of the task).

# Clear Assignment Guidelines

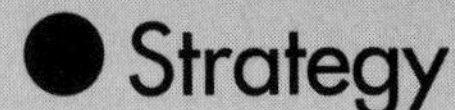
Strategy

Students who bring special learning needs to the writing process are more likely to internalize the assignment expectations if the task is first clearly outlined on the board or in a handout. They must, in turn, hear the assignment described and, subsequently, have the opportunity to paraphrase what they understand the actual assignment expectations to be—ideally, orally to a partner and in writing to the teacher. If all students are then encouraged to turn in two clarification questions about the assignment, less proficient writers will have a safe and structured venue for monitoring their comprehension and articulating instructional needs. In so doing, passive or apprehensive students are more likely to vocalize any misunderstandings about the task in a timely and responsible manner, rather than realizing the night before the paper is due that they are unsure how to proceed.

**Sample Description of a Writing Assignment**

**Writing Assignment Guidelines:**
***A Color That Has Special Significance***

Write a detailed expository paragraph providing specific reasons that your chosen color has special meaning in your life. Your justification paragraph must include these qualities of effective expository writing:

- An appropriate title (e.g., *Jade Green: A Link to My Heritage*)
- A topic sentence that lets the reader know that you will be discussing the relevance of a particular color to specific aspects of your life
- Transition words that introduce each of your new points about your chosen color (e.g., *first of all, in addition, furthermore, moreover*)
- Specific reasons for selecting this color, including details and relevant commentary that help the reader easily understand the color's special significance
- A visible effort to include new vocabulary from this unit
- An effort to use subordinating conjunctions to join related ideas
- A concluding statement that thoughtfully wraps up your paragraph
- Proofreading goals for the final draft:
  - –complete sentences (no fragments or run-on sentences)
  - –correct verb tenses
  - –correct spelling

Your first draft is due on ________________. Please bring two copies of your draft for a peer-response session

# Using Sentence Starters

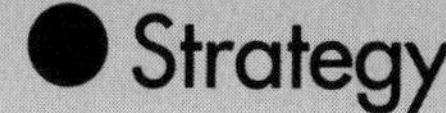

● Strategy

As demonstrated in your *Prentice Hall Literature* Teacher's Edition, one concrete way to structure linguistic equity and to scaffold the vocabulary demands of a challenging writing assignment is to provide students with an array of sentence starters, including practical vocabulary options relevant to the specific writing task and topic. Another equally important scaffold for students writing in a second language or second dialect is a word-form chart that highlights important forms of a base word germane to the assignment.

Following is a list of sentence starters and a relevant word-form chart for a writing assignment on a personally significant color.

**Sentence Starters to Discuss a Color You Value**

__________ is my favorite color because I associate it with __________. (my future career, my love of nature, my personality, my hobby)

This color reflects/represents/is associated with my interest in __________. (salsa dancing, R & B music, physical fitness, environmental protection)

This color symbolizes/is a symbol of __________. (my culture, my ethnicity)

I have included/selected/chosen the color __________ because __________.

The color __________ is meaningful/valuable/significant to me because __________.

I appreciate/value/like/am fond of the color __________ because/since __________.

**Sample Word-Form Chart**

| Noun | Adjective | Verb | Adverb |
|---|---|---|---|
| symbol | symbolic | symbolize | symbolically |
| meaning | meaningful | | meaningfully |
| value | valuable | value | valuably |
| relevance | relevant | | relevantly |
| importance | important | | importantly |
| relationship | related | relate | |
| association | associated | associate | |
| significance | significant | signify | significantly |
| preference | preferred; preferable | prefer | preferably |
| fondness | fond | | fondly |

# Professional Development Articles

# The Literacy Challenge of Diverse Learners

## Introduction

> The number of children in the country who can be classified as diverse learners because of the special circumstances they bring to public education is growing at a pace that currently outstrips educators' abilities to keep up. Unless significant educational changes are made in response to the dramatic changes occurring in classrooms throughout the country, including the development and utilization of instructional strategies that address the needs of diverse learners, the number of children who "fall through the cracks" in public education will continue to rise.[1]

The 2000 census confirmed what demographers had been documenting for the previous decade: America is more diverse than ever. Certainly, the diversity of our population is a significant asset to our nation in many ways; however, it also places considerable stress on our educational system to effectively accommodate the range of learning needs found in students today. A typical high-school classroom includes students who are diverse in terms of their experiential, linguistic, cultural, socioeconomic, and psychological backgrounds. The range of student needs, interests, motivation, and skill levels often presents heightened challenges to both curriculum and instruction. It should be clearly acknowledged that the individual needs of some students require additional specialized support in basic reading skills, English language development, study skills, and behavioral/emotional/social domains. However, the goal of a comprehensive Language Arts program remains the provision of "universal access" for all students to an intellectually rich and challenging language arts curriculum and instruction, in addition to whatever specialized intervention may be required.

Universal access exists when teachers provide curriculum and instruction in ways that allow all learners in the classroom to participate and to achieve the instructional and behavioral goals of general education, as well as of the core curriculum. Teachers will succeed in providing universal access if they teach in heterogeneous, inclusive classrooms and consistently

1. Kame'enui, Edward, and Douglas Carnine. *Effective Teaching Strategies That Accommodate Diverse Learners.* Upper Saddle River, NJ: Prentice Hall, 1998.

and systematically integrate instructional strategies that are responsive to the needs of typical learners, gifted learners, less proficient readers, English language learners, and students who are eligible for and receiving special education services.

Although each student population represented in the classroom may require specific interventions and supports, these learner populations also share many common characteristics, such as the need to build on prior knowledge, the need for systematic vocabulary development, and the need for systematic instruction in strategic reading approaches, to name a few key curricular and instructional areas. Through identification of these shared needs and the implementation of teaching and learning strategies responsive to these needs, the general education teacher, with the support of specialists and other staff, can make significant inroads in designing inclusive lessons that are responsive to the learning and behavioral needs of all learners.

This book provides numerous suggestions to assist teachers in designing English Language Arts lessons that strive for universal access. The suggestions focus specifically on the instructional needs of students who are less proficient readers, students who are English language learners, and students with identified special education needs. The next section describes the reading process and what it takes to be a proficient reader. The remaining sections explore the specific needs of the three focus student populations: English language learners, less proficient readers, and students with special education needs.

# The Reading Process

A clear consensus has emerged in the field of reading education supporting the notion that reading is a complex process of constructing meaning from text. Successful readers must bring an array of interrelated skills, knowledge, and strategies together in order to understand written English. Skillful readers are able to decode the words accurately and fluently, connect their meanings to prior knowledge, and continually monitor their emerging understanding as they read. In other words, successful readers are active, thoughtful, and strategic learners able to make meaning from what they are reading.

### Factors That Affect Reading Success

Successful reading is largely determined by the elaborate interaction of four factors: learner characteristics, skill and instructional variables, demands of the text, and nature of the classroom environment. To better understand these elements, we will examine each in turn, as well as the way they interact to affect successful reading.

### Learner Characteristics

Each learner brings unique characteristics to the learning experience. For example, students who are less proficient readers may experience attention and memory issues that make reading especially challenging. English language learners may be highly capable students who, because of limited vocabulary or experiences in their new country, lack the schema for understanding the ideas encountered in text. Students with disabilities may experience cognitive, behavioral/social, and/or physical challenges that make the development of reading skill more challenging.

### Skill and Instructional Factors

Reading success is largely determined by the particular skills an individual reader brings to the reading act. For example, the ability to fluently and accurately decode the words in a given reading selection is a necessary but not sufficient condition for successful reading. In addition, the ability to activate and build prior knowledge along with the related ability to connect what one is reading to existing knowledge are essential for proficient comprehension. Moreover, comprehension is significantly determined by a student's level of English acquisition, vocabulary, and skillful use of various reading comprehension strategies such as summarization or self-questioning.

An essential personal aspect of successful reading is the extent to which a reader is actively engaged in the reading, has a clear purpose for reading, and is interested in the content being explored. Skillful readers have learned helpful mental habits such as perseverance, managing and directing attention, being aware of and monitoring their thoughts and feelings as they read. Skilled readers are active participants in the reading act—reading is not a spectator sport.

Instructional interventions provided in the classroom play a significant role in students' development of these skills. Explicit, systematic instruction in decoding and fluency, the incorporation of activities that build and enhance prior knowledge, the provision of explicit vocabulary instruction, and the direct teaching, modeling, and practicing of comprehension strategies will lead to students' skill development and their enhanced engagement and interest in the complexities of the reading act.

### Text-Based Factors

It is immediately apparent that the types of texts encountered by students vary widely and create different levels of challenge for different readers. Just as the make and model distinguish one automobile from another, text-based factors differentiate one text from another. While some of these factors may be largely cosmetic in nature, others, such as sentence length, novel vocabulary, density of the concepts, or clarity of the organizational pattern, can have a significant influence on reader comprehension. For example, the presence of well-designed reader aids, including pictures, charts, graphs, and focus questions, can provide additional support to naive readers.

Perhaps the most fundamental distinction in text-based factors affecting reading success is that of narrative (story) reading vs. expository (informational) reading. Expository texts are generally written to inform or persuade the reader using very different organizational patterns from those typically utilized in narratives. For example, information in content-area reading, such as in science and social studies, is often arranged according to structures such as chronological sequence, comparison and contrast, cause and effect, main idea and supporting details, and so forth. Many students are quite comfortable reading stories but find themselves ill equipped to deal with the demands of informational content-area texts.

### Classroom Environment

The classroom environment affects everything and everyone within it, including the nature of the reading/literacy program. Specifically, the classroom environment can be viewed as composed of both physical and social-psychological dimensions.

Research suggests that students learn best in a friendly, respectful setting where

- they feel a sense of safety/order and are comfortable taking risks.
- they understand the purpose of and value the tasks at hand.
- they have high expectations/goals for learning.
- they feel accepted by their teacher and peers.

These general factors are of particular import when thinking about what accounts for successful reading. Students will often have significant gaps in their skill, knowledge, proficiency in English, and be self-conscious concerning their lagging literacy.

It is important to be respectful and truthful with students about what it will take to significantly improve their abilities in the Language Arts: It takes PRACTICE, and lots of it. Literacy cannot be "done to" students—it is a collaborative enterprise that is "done with" students. To be sure, teachers provide excellent direct instruction, guided practice, specific feedback, coaching, and more, yet students must understand their roles as active self-directed learners. The intentional design of a caring yet "on purpose" classroom climate creates the condition within which the hard work of improving literacy can take place.

**Summary**

Understanding that successful reading comprises a complex interaction of factors—learner, skills and instruction, text, and environment—provides a template for thinking about how classrooms can provide universal access to a rich core curriculum for the diverse range of learners in today's high-school classrooms. Secondary students need a balanced Language Arts program based on their individual needs. All students require a firm foundation in fluent/automatic decoding, broad background knowledge of various subjects, ever-expanding vocabularies, all coupled with an array of comprehension strategies to fit the purpose for reading as well as the type of text being read.

In the following section, we examine strategies for developing lesson plans that support diverse learners in meeting rigorous grade-level standards in the Language Arts.

# English Language Learners

The number of immigrant, migrant, and refugee students in the United States who have little knowledge of the English language is growing exponentially. In fact, students who are learning English as an additional language are the fastest-growing segment of the school-age population. While the number of English language learners (ELLs) nationwide has skyrocketed, their academic achievement trails behind that of their native English-speaking peers. National studies of English language learners have shown that they are likely to come from disadvantaged socioeconomic backgrounds, attend low-income schools, and have parents with limited English proficiency. These students are also judged by their teachers to have weaker academic abilities, receive lower grades, and score well below their classmates on standardized tests of mathematics and reading.[1] Moreover, in a large-scale California study, secondary schools reported that even long-term resident ELLs entered high school with only fourth to sixth grade academic competencies.[2]

**Differential Preparation for Second-Language Schooling**

Secondary-school curricula are based on assumptions about basic reading and writing skills and elementary subject matter foundations. However, the growing population of secondary English language learners is tremendously diverse, particularly with regard to their educational backgrounds. These students enter U.S. schools with varying degrees of curricular preparation and a vast range of language proficiencies, in English and their native language. At times, it may seem that the one thing these diverse students have in common is the need to accelerate their English language and literacy acquisition in order to participate more fully in their secondary schooling.

Although some have parents with impressive levels of formal education and professional job experiences, many come from less privileged families, challenged by limited functional literacy even in their native language. Newcomers from war-torn regions and rural areas of developing countries are apt to arrive severely under-schooled, with fragmented native language literacy training and weak subject matter foundations.

---

1. Moss, M., and M. Puma. *Prospects: The Congressionally Mandated Study of Educational Growth and Opportunity.* Washington, DC: U.S. Department of Education, 1995.
2. Minicucci, C., and L. Olsen. "Programs for Secondary Limited English Proficiency Students: A California Study." *Focus,* Vol. 5. Washington, DC: National Clearinghouse for Bilingual Education, 1992.

These youths predictably require compassion, considerable time, and patient modeling simply to adjust to basic school routines and expectations before they can ever begin to concentrate on phonemic awareness lessons, let alone literary analysis.

On the other hand, more fortunate immigrant youths have benefited from rigorous and sustained elementary schooling in their native country and make the transition to American classrooms more effortlessly. Literate in their home language, these second-language learners have already internalized critical scripts for schooling and often function above equivalent grade levels in math or science. However, these traditionally educated newcomers still face a daunting transition to daily instruction in a language they have only begun to study, along with curriculum content, teaching practices, and skills that may not have been emphasized in their native schooling.

Our secondary schools also serve increasing numbers of students who have been raised and educated entirely in the United States but who speak a language other than English at home. These continuing English language learners were either born in the United States or arrived here as very small children. Many of these long-term U.S. residents are not literate in their home language and remain struggling English readers well into the upper grades and beyond. They may demonstrate a comfortable handle on the social domain of both languages but flounder with grade-level reading and writing tasks.

In summary, with regard to prior schooling, secondary English language learners tend to fall into one of three general and frequently overlapping categories:

1. Recent adolescent immigrants who have received continuous native language schooling prior to immigration to the United States and are prepared with relatively strong academic and study skills to apply to new subject matter

2. Language minority students continuing into secondary schools from U.S. elementary schools with insufficient English fluency and literacy to compete in challenging academic areas

3. Immigrant, refugee, and migrant students with sporadic or no prior schooling who consequently enter lacking basic literacy and elementary curricular foundations.

### Second-Language Literacy Development

Statistics on the academic achievement of English language learners demonstrate a dire need for informed attention devoted to literacy, the cornerstone of all academic abilities.

Nonetheless, given the extreme variability in these students' educational histories, they must be offered different pathways to eventual academic success. One approach to literacy instruction will not fit all English language learners. However, the instructional practices outlined in this chapter and throughout this manual should greatly assist them in participating more fully in a heterogeneous secondary Language Arts classroom.

Those with significant gaps in their elementary educational backgrounds will require a thoughtful and sustained literacy intervention program, complemented by a substantive and protracted English language development program. Their acute and compelling academic needs cannot be accommodated solely within the confines of the general education Language Arts classroom, an after-school tutorial, or a reading intervention program.

Similarly, literate and academically prepared newcomers will still need a viable English language development program to enable them to transfer the knowledge and skills they acquired in their native language schooling to the curricula they are studying in the United States. Literate adolescents who are virtual beginners in English will also benefit from a separate reading support class, to help them readily acquire the basic phonology, morphology, and syntax of English and to more efficiently transfer the reading skills they have already mastered in their native language. Students who can already read relatively fluently in their first language will make an easier transition to English decoding than bilingual classmates who are nonreaders. These literate second-language learners will therefore need to move more rapidly than struggling ELL readers, from initial skill-building lessons that focus on decoding, word recognition, and pronunciation to explicit instruction in comprehension strategies such as prediction, questioning, and summarizing that will help them deal more productively with the reading demands of content-area classrooms.

## Reading in a Second Language

Research findings suggest that reading processes in a second language are not significantly different from those in a first language.[3] For example, both rely on the reader's background knowledge regarding the topic and text structure to construct meaning, and both make use of cueing systems (graphic,

**3.** Grabe, W. "Current Developments in Second Language Reading." *TESOL Quarterly* (1991), 25, 375–406.

syntactic, phonological, semantic) to allow the reader to predict and confirm meaning.

While literacy processes in first and second languages may be quite similar, two crucial areas of difference must be addressed. First, initial reading and writing in English will be slower and more painstaking for second-language learners because of their lack of overall fluency. The second-language learner is often in the process of acquiring basic oral language while simultaneously developing literacy skills in English. Limited proficiency in a second language can cause a proficient reader in the native language to revert to poor reading strategies, such as reading word by word. Also, some students may not even have the native language literacy skills to transfer concepts about print and strategies to the second language.

Secondly, ELL students are likely to have less prior knowledge and relevant vocabulary to process new information while reading academic English assignments. Furthermore, readers' background knowledge is often culture-bound and may not match the content needed for a given reading text. ELL students with a limited range of personal and educational experiences on a reading topic will therefore have little to draw upon to construct meaning from a selection even if they are able to accurately decode.

### Academic Language Development

Many adolescent ELL students come to school with sufficient social language for everyday classroom interactions yet are severely lacking in the academic English foundations to tackle a poem or follow the instructions on a standardized test. This is because academic vocabulary is primarily developed through school-based reading and repeated exposure during content-based classroom activities.

The average native English-speaking student enters elementary school with an internalized understanding of the syntax and phonology of English, plus a working vocabulary of several thousand words. This vocabulary base is enhanced each year through new school experiences and reinforced in home and community settings. In striking contrast, the language minority student enters U.S. schooling with a tenuous grasp of the phonology and syntax of the English language, a scant working English vocabulary, and rare opportunities for practice and expansion of this knowledge outside the classroom. As a consequence, they must develop content-specific language and literacy skills along with conceptual foundations, all the while competing with native English-speaking classmates who may also be challenged by grade-level Language Arts curricula, but who at least operate from a relatively firm foundation in basic academic English and years of exposure to high-frequency social English vocabulary.

**Implications for English Language Arts Instruction**

A number of implications for instruction can be drawn from these descriptions of the academic language and literacy challenges of ELL students. Novice English readers will require extensive and dynamic instructional "front-loading" in order to effectively grapple with challenging literacy tasks. Teachers all too often concentrate their energies on the damage-control phase, when it becomes clear that students either failed to comprehend or felt too overwhelmed to even try to tackle a reading task. Explaining critical concepts and language after the fact does little to engender reader confidence or competence for the next task. The students may walk away with a better grasp of the plot development in *The Joy Luck Club* but have no sense of how to proceed with the next chapter. Instead, conscientious literacy mentors essentially "teach the text backwards" by devoting far more instructional time to the preparation and guidance phases of lessons. Since a second-language reader may be approaching an assignment with impoverished background knowledge and weak English vocabulary, it makes sense to concentrate on classroom activities that build strong conceptual and linguistic foundations, guide them into the text organization, model appropriate comprehension strategies, and provide a clear purpose for reading. This responsible preparation will in turn help to create the kind of nurturing affective and cognitive arena that communicates high expectations for their literacy development and encourages them to persist and take risks.

**Instructional Considerations When Preparing Lessons to Support English Language Learners**

All of the instructional practices detailed in Part 3 of this booklet will support ELL students in making strides in their second-language literacy development and in becoming vibrant members of the classroom community of learners. Following are some additional reminders of ways in which you can support ELL students at various stages of your lesson planning to deal more productively with the reading and writing demands of English Language Arts curricula.

## Phase 1: Preteach

- Pull out a manageable number of key concepts.
- Identify vocabulary most critical to talking and learning about the central concepts. Don't attempt to cover all of the vocabulary words you anticipate they will not know. Do more than provide synonyms and definitions. Introduce the essential words in more meaningful contexts, through simple sentences drawing on familiar issues, people, scenarios, and vocabulary. Guide students in articulating the meanings of essential terms through these familiar contexts and hold them responsible for writing the definitions in their own words.
- Present key words when they occur within the context of the reading selection or activity. Make the words as concrete as possible by linking each to an object, photo, drawing, or movement.
- Post the new essential vocabulary in a prominent place in the classroom to create a word bank of organized lesson terminology.
- Examine your lesson to see what types of language functions students will need to participate in various activities. For example, if they are being asked to make predictions about upcoming paragraph content in an essay based on transition words (e.g., *therefore, in addition, consequently*), students will need to be taught some basic sentence patterns and verbs to express opinions (e.g., "I predict that . . ."; "Based on this transition word, I conclude that . . ."). If being asked to agree or disagree with the arguments in a persuasive article, students will need to learn some sentence patterns and verbs to convey agreement or disagreement (e.g., "I don't agree with the author's argument that adolescents don't have a work ethic because . . .").
- Engage students in prereading activities that spark their curiosity and involve them in all four language modes.
- Assess students' prior knowledge related to key concepts through participation structures and collaborative group discussions with realia (e.g., photographs, objects) serving as a visual trigger.
- Utilize realia and visuals needed to make the concepts less abstract.
- Use multimedia presentations such as CD-ROM and videos to

familiarize students with the plot, characters, and themes of a narrative text prior to reading, but don't use it as a replacement for reading.

- Provide a written and oral synopsis of the key content prior to actually asking students to read a selection if the sentence structures and vocabulary are particularly demanding.
- Use graphic organizers and semantic maps to help students grasp the central content in an accessible manner prior to reading.
- Lead a quick text prereading, or "text tour," focusing student attention on illustrations; chapter title and subtopics; boldface words; summary sections; and connection of chapter to theme, previous chapters, activities, and concepts.
- When possible, build in opportunities for "narrow reading," allowing students to read more than one selection on the same topic, to build concept and vocabulary recognition that will support their reading more fluently and confidently.

**Phase 2: Teach**

- Clearly establish a reading purpose for students prior to assigning a manageable amount of text.
- Describe and model strategies for navigating different kinds of text. Provide a convincing rationale for each new strategy and regularly review both the purpose and process.
- Familiarize students with a manageable tool kit of reading comprehension and study strategies and continue practicing these selective strategies. In this way, students end the school year with a viable approach unattainable through sporadic practice with a confusing array of new reading behaviors.
- Introduce a new strategy using a text that isn't too difficult in order to build credibility for the strategy and ensure student success. Otherwise, if a selection is too difficult and the strategy fails to deliver for students, they will have little faith in experimenting with the new strategy on future texts.
- Whenever possible, get students physically involved with the page, using highlighters, self-sticking notes, and a small piece of cardboard or heavy construction paper to focus and guide their reading from one paragraph or column to the next.

- Alternate between teacher-facilitated and student-dominated reading activities.
- Do "think-aloud" reading to model your cognitive and metacognitive strategies and thought processes.
- Assign brief amounts of text at a time and alternate between oral, paired, and silent reading.
- Guide students through the process of reading and comprehending a passage by reading aloud to them and assisting them in identifying the text organization and establishing a clear reading purpose.
- Allow students to read a passage while listening to an audiotape recorded by a classmate, cross-age tutor, or parent volunteer.
- Have students engage in "repeated readings" of the same brief passage to build word recognition, fluency, and reading rate.
- Provide some form of study guide in order to focus their reading on the critical content and prevent them from getting bogged down with nonessential details and unfamiliar vocabulary. A partially completed outline or graphic organizer is more task based and manageable than a list of questions to answer, which often results in simple scanning for content without really reading and comprehending material.
- Demonstrate your note-taking process and provide models of effective study notes for students to emulate.

**Phase 3: Assess**

- Prepare both text-based and experientially based questions, which lead students from simply getting the gist of a selection to establishing a personal connection to the lesson content.
- Build in task-based and authentic assessment during every lesson to ensure that ELL students are actually developing greater proficiency with new content and strategies. Quick writes, drawings, oral and written summaries, and collaborative tasks are generally more productive indicators of lesson comprehension than a closing question/answer session.
- Provide safe opportunities for students to alert you to any learning challenges they are experiencing. Have them submit

anonymous written questions (formulated either independently or with a partner) about confusing lesson content and process, and then follow up on these points of confusion at the end of class or in the subsequent class session.

- Ask students to end the class session by writing 3–5 outcome statements about their experience in the day's lesson, expressing both new understandings and needs for clarification.
- Make sure that assessment mirrors the lesson objectives. For example, if you are teaching students how to preread expository text, it isn't relevant to assess using comprehension questions. A more authentic assessment of their ability to apply this strategy would be to provide them with a photocopy of an expository selection and ask them to highlight and label the parts one would read during the actual prereading process. It would be relevant, however, to ask them to identify two reasons for engaging in a text prereading before tackling the entire selection.
- Build in opportunities for students to demonstrate their understandings of texts that draw upon different language and literacy skills: formal and informal writing assignments, posters, small-group tasks, oral presentations, and so on.
- Don't assign ELLs tasks that require little or no reading or lesson comprehension. For example, don't allow them to simply draw a picture while other students are writing a paragraph. Instead, make sure that you have adequately scaffolded the task and equipped them with a writing frame and model to guide them through the process. While one might argue that this is multimodal and tapping into multiple intelligences, it is actually conveying expectations for their development of academic competence in English.
- Make sure that students understand your assessment criteria in advance. Whenever possible, provide models of student work for them to emulate, along with a nonmodel that fails to meet the specified assessment criteria. Do not provide exemplars that are clearly outside their developmental range. While this may be an enriching reading task, it will not serve as a viable model. Save student work that can later serve as a model for ELLs with different levels of academic preparation.

- Develop accessible and relevant rubrics for various tasks and products that are customized to the task rather than generic assessment tools. Introduce a rubric in tandem with exemplars of successful and less productive work to help them internalize the assessment criteria. Guide students in identifying the ways in which sample work does or does not meet established grading criteria.

### Phase 4: Extend

- Consider ways in which students can transfer knowledge and skills gleaned from one assignment/lesson to a subsequent lesson.
- Build in opportunities for students to read a more detailed or challenging selection on the same topic in order to allow them to apply familiar concepts and vocabulary and stretch their literacy muscles.
- Recycle pre- and postreading tasks regularly, so students can become more familiar with the task process and improve their performance. If they are assailed with curricular novelty, ELLs never have the opportunity to refine their skills and demonstrate improved competence. For example, if you ask them to identify a personality trait of an essential character in a story and then support this observation with relevant details in an expository paragraph, it would make sense to have them shortly afterwards write an identical paragraph about another character.
- Discuss with students ways in which they can apply new vocabulary and language strategies outside the classroom.
- Praise students' efforts to experiment with new language in class, both in writing and in speaking.
- Demonstrate the applicability of new reading and writing strategies to real-world literacy tasks. Bring in potentially more engaging reading selections that will pique their interest and provide a more compelling rationale for applying a new strategic repertoire. Design periodic writing tasks for an authentic audience other than the teacher: another class, fellow classmates, and so on.

# Less Proficient Learners

## Characteristics of Less Proficient Learners

Every classroom has a number of less proficient students, individuals who begin the year one, two, or more years below grade level yet who do not qualify for special education services and may not be English language learners. It is important to keep in mind that most accommodations made for English learners and special needs students will be helpful for all kinds of diverse learners, including less proficient learners. However, it is worthwhile to briefly examine some of the learner characteristics of less proficient students in comparison with their average achieving peers. An appreciation of these distinctions will provide a useful foundation for understanding the importance of using the various "universal access" strategies described throughout this section and incorporated into the Prentice Hall Literature program.

## Attention and Memory

Research suggests that underachieving students have difficulty in organizing and categorizing new information during instruction. Typically, less skillful students do not effectively order, classify, and arrange information in meaningful ways during learning, frequently leaving them confused and missing the "big picture." Long-term memory is often adversely affected due to the lack of meaningful connections established and difficulty with noticing how new information relates to prior knowledge. In addition, underprepared students frequently do not know how to focus their attention on the important aspects of a classroom presentation, demonstration, or reading selection. In either case, the intentional use of explicit strategies coupled with interactive review and extension activities can make a significant difference in providing poorly prepared students full access to the Language Arts curriculum.

## Lesson Planning and Instructional Accommodations for Attention and Memory

### Phase 1: Preteach

- Gain attention requesting a simple physical response (e.g., "Everyone, eyes on me please," "Touch number one," and so forth). Students need to show you they are ready.
- Keep the lesson pace moving along briskly—a "perky not pokey" pace is helpful.
- Clarify or introduce critical "big ideas" or conceptual anchors that the reading or lesson or activity is built around (e.g., an example, a metaphor, a demonstration).
- Use brief choral responses when the answer is short and identical (e.g. "Everyone, the answer to number one is ______.").
- Use brief partner responses when the answer is open-ended and longer (e.g., "Ones, tell twos the most important new information revealed in the last paragraph.").
- After students have had a chance to rehearse or practice with a partner, randomly call upon them to build prior knowledge or raise questions the text may answer.
- Use graphic organizers, charts, and concept maps to assist students with focusing on critical concepts as well as categorizing and organizing information to be studied/learned.

### Phase 2: Teach

- Engage students in a "read/reflect/discuss/note" cycle of filling out the graphic organizers/concept maps collaboratively as you progress through the reading or lesson.
- Do a brief oral review using partners (e.g., think-write-pair-share) to ensure that all students are firm on the big ideas/critical concepts.
- Cue students to take special note of crucial information and explore why this information is so critical.
- Engage students in the active use or processing of the new information (e.g., paraphrase, give an example, write a response).
- Emphasize connections between new and known information.
- Connect new learning to student's personal experience (e.g., coach students to create analogies or metaphors using prior knowledge).

### Phase 3: Assess

- Ask students to explain their graphic organizer/concept map to a partner. Monitor selected students and determine their level of understanding—reteach/provide additional examples as necessary.
- Provide students the opportunity to reorganize, prioritize, and otherwise reflect on the key aspects of the lesson.
- Systematically monitor retention of key information or "big ideas" over time using "quick writes" (brief written summaries to a prompt), random questioning, observing student interactions, written assignments, and so on. Reteach, provide additional examples, invite students to elaborate, and so on, as necessary.

### Phase 4: Extend

- Have students design investigations or projects using the information in new ways.
- Design homework assignments that require students to go beyond the text to apply lessons learned to their lives or to other circumstances.
- Challenge students to organize information in novel ways, come up with different categories, and otherwise elaborate the information being studied.
- Draw explicit connections and prompt students to induce connections between information studied earlier in the term and new ideas encountered in the current reading selection.

## Learning Strategies and Use

Perhaps the most ubiquitous characteristic of less proficient students is their lack of effective and efficient strategies for accomplishing various academic tasks, from writing a persuasive essay to taking notes during a lecture to responding to a piece of literature. Less skillful students tend to have a very limited repertoire of learning strategies and have little awareness of how to monitor the use of learning strategies during reading, writing, and other academic activities. In contrast, successful learners are active, "strategic," and flexible in their employment of appropriate learning strategies tailored to the demands of a particular academic task or assignment.

Kame'enui and Carnine[4] suggest three critical design principles teachers need to keep in mind when addressing the issue of learning strategies with underprepared or diverse learners.

4. Kame'enui, Edward and Douglas Carnine, op. cit.

1. Important learning strategies must be made overt, explicit, and conspicuous.

2. Strong verbal and visual support, or "scaffolding," should be provided to ensure that diverse learners understand when, where, and how to use the strategies.

3. Judicious review of new learning strategies is required to allow less prepared students enough practice to incorporate the new strategy into their learning routines.

It is important to note that differences between less proficient students and average achievers in their use of learning strategies is not based on organic or biological differences. In other words, it is their lack of experience and preparation that is the critical difference. Fortunately, less proficient learners are quite capable of acquiring effective learning strategies and significantly improving their academic performance when provided with direct instruction in the "what-why-how-when" of strategy use in a highly focused educational setting.

## Lesson Planning and Instructional Accommodations for Learning Strategies

### Phase 1: Preteach

- Clarify the rationale for learning the new strategy in terms, examples, and results the students value (e.g., "Where in school or life would it be useful to know how to write a persuasive essay?").
- Brainstorm for examples of successful strategy usage with interactive tactics such as "give one, get one" to involve all students (e.g., each student lists as many ideas as possible in 3–4 minutes and then has 3–5 minutes to compare with a peer and "give one" idea to them as well as "get one" from them to extend their brainstormed list).
- Provide personal examples of how you have used this strategy to your academic advantage.
- Directly teach any "pre-skills," or prerequisite skills, students need to perform the strategy.

### Phase 2: Teach

Explicitly model the use of the strategy, including a significant focus on thinking aloud during the execution of each step in the strategy.

- Provide students with a brief summary of the strategy steps or an acronym to facilitate retention of the strategy.

  **Example:**

  **POWER: P**repare, **O**rganize, **W**rite, **E**dit, **R**evise

  (Archer & Gleason 2000)
- Guide students in practicing the strategy using less demanding content that allows students to focus on the new strategy. Gradually transition to more difficult content.
- Break the strategy down into explicit steps, ensuring that students are able to perform each step and combine steps to use the whole strategy.
- Structure partner-mediated practice in which students take turns practicing the strategy and providing feedback to one another (e.g., taking turns reading a paragraph or page and paraphrasing the gist in 12 words or less).

### Phase 3: Assess

- Monitor partners during strategy practice to observe competence, areas for review, and so forth.
- Randomly call on students to informally demonstrate their strategy knowledge.
- Include explicit use of strategies taught as part of the quiz, paper, report, project, and other formal assessments.

### Phase 4: Extend

- Discuss with students where else in or out of school they could use the strategy.
- Provide extra credit or some other incentive to encourage the use of the strategy in other content area classes.
- After they have gained some degree of mastery, encourage students to modify and otherwise personalize the strategy to better fit their learning style or needs.

### Vocabulary and Reading Fluency

Vocabulary differences between struggling and average students are apparent from the primary years in school and tend to get worse over time. It is not surprising that less prepared learners engage in far less reading in and out of school, resulting in substantially impoverished vocabularies.

In addition, their ability to read fluently and accurately is often diminished, further compounding the issue and rendering reading a frustrating and defeating experience.

There is no shortcut, or "quick fix," for vocabulary building, but teachers can make a tremendous difference by sustained attention to the following practices:

- Directly teaching key conceptual vocabulary using strategies that take students beyond simple memorization
- Teaching students how to learn words and concepts from context
- Encouraging wide reading in and out of school; students who have serious fluency problems (e.g., reading below 100 words per minute in grade-level text) will require sustained practice daily in repeated reading of instructional level/age-appropriate texts

## Lesson Planning and Instructional Accommodations for Vocabulary and Fluency

### Phase 1: Preteach

- Select conceptually rich, critical vocabulary for more detailed instruction before reading.
- Choose age- and level-appropriate passages for students to use repeated reading strategies (e.g., on prerecorded tapes, partner reading, choral reading with small groups).

### Phase 2: Teach

- Directly teach the meanings of critical, conceptually rich vocabulary required for full understanding of the passage or lesson.
- Pick vocabulary strategies that take students beyond simple repetition of the definition to prompt active construction of new connections between the concept and their prior knowledge. Such strategies include
  —creating semantic maps showing how words are related
  —using the words in sentences that "show you know" the meaning
- Define the critical attributes of the concept in short bulleted phrases and create examples and nonexamples of the concept, prompting students to explain why the exemplar does or does not have the attributes of the concept under consideration (a graphic organizer showing the attributes and examples/nonexamples can be very useful).

- Engage students in word sorts: Provide 10–20 vocabulary words for students to place into preset categories (e.g., parts of speech, words descriptive of the character or not, and so on).
- Pair students at similar instructional levels for repeated reading practice; have the more proficient student read a paragraph or a page and then have the less proficient student reread the same section.
- Practice repeated reading of instructional-level passages of 150–200 words in length with prerecorded tapes, set goals, and individually graph and monitor fluency daily, finishing with a written retelling of the passage.
- Teach students important generative word roots (e.g., Latin and Greek) and common affixes. Practice sorting and combining to examine how they work (e.g., *-spec-*: *spectrum, spectacle, inspection, speculation*).
- Model and practice the use of context in predicting word meanings during reading, thinking aloud to demonstrate to students how textual cues direct your thinking.

### Phase 3: Assess

- Randomly call on students to provide examples of the vocabulary word under examination.
- Monitor students during partner discussion of selected critical vocabulary words.
- Evaluate students during small-group discussion, written products, and so on.
- Directly monitor the fluency of selected students via one-minute timings. Note rate, accuracy, and expression.

### Phase 4: Extend

- Encourage students to informally use recently taught vocabulary words in "show you know" sentences during classroom conversations, written products, and so on.
- Intentionally revisit newly acquired vocabulary during discussion, while thinking aloud during demonstrations, and so on.
- Encourage students to practice fluency building via repeated reading at home, appropriate CD-ROM technology, and cross-age tutoring of younger students, in which the target student must prepare a story to read fluently with his or her tutee.

### Motivation and Academic Identity

Motivation is complex and difficult to define, but most experts agree that it is significantly related to how much success or failure one has experienced relative to the activity in question. Less proficient secondary students typically do not see themselves as capable of sustained reading, inquiry, or writing in a challenging academic setting. The old cliché "Nothing succeeds like success" is relevant to this discussion. To build motivation and encourage the development of a productive "academic identity," it is important to engage less proficient students in challenging lessons while simultaneously incorporating adequate support or instructional scaffolding to increase the likelihood students will experience success. In addition, helping students to explore their thinking as they read and write through structured dialogues and thinking aloud can be very helpful. Noted reading researcher David Pearson calls this process a "metacognitive conversation," allowing less proficient students to gain an understanding of how successful readers and writers think as they work. In a manner of speaking, teachers can provide less proficient students with an academic or cognitive role model. For example, modeling a simple self-monitoring strategy during writing such as "remember your audience" can assist students in keeping multiple perspectives in mind as they compose.

### Lesson Planning and Instructional Accommodations for Motivation and Academic Identity

Motivation and academic identity do not lend themselves to the Preteach, Teach, Assess, and Extend lesson format. In a sense, motivation is more "caught than taught" and will be the result of successfully engaging students in the curriculum. However, there are a number of general strategies that are useful to consider including:

- **Self-selected reading** Allow less proficient students regular opportunities to read material they are interested in, at their instructional level.
- **Goal setting** Engage students in setting personal goals for various academic tasks, such as pages/chapters read per week, strategy usage, words read per minute during fluency practice, and so forth.

- **Metacognitive dialogues** Ask students to informally share their perceptions, approaches, and fears regarding various school-related challenges. Students and teachers then share their thoughts and feelings about how they used various strategies to become more successful.
- **Book clubs, book reviews, newsletter reviews, e-mail postings** These provide an audience for students' opinions about books they have read.
- **Partnerships** Have students build partnerships with peers and with younger students, community members, and business personnel.
- **Negotiated choices** As appropriate, involve students in negotiating alternative assignments, options, and novel ideas to reach common goals.
- **Model an "academic identity"** Invite teachers/students/ other adults into the classroom to share how they developed as literate citizens.

### Summary

Less proficient high-school students are underprepared for the academic challenges of a rigorous grade-level Language Arts program in a variety of ways. Many of their difficulties can be linked to difficulties with attention and memory, learning strategies, vocabulary and reading fluency, and motivation/academic identity. Secondary Language Arts teachers can have an extremely beneficial effect on the learning of less proficient students by the sustained focus on appropriate strategies for preteaching, teaching, assessment, and extension beyond the lesson.

# Students With Special Needs

Students with special education needs are a highly diverse student group. Although their learning needs vary greatly, a majority of children identified as special education students will experience mild to severe difficulties in becoming proficient and independent readers and writers. Through instruction that incorporates adaptations and modifications and is delivered in collaborative ways, students with disabilities can gain literacy skills and be active participants in general education Language Arts curricula and instruction.

## Characteristics of Special Education Learners

### Eligibility for Special Education

Federal law IDEA '97 (Individuals with Disabilities Education Act, P.L. 105–17) specifies the disabling conditions under which students are found eligible to receive special education services. These disabling conditions may be clustered into the two broad categories of high incidence and low incidence disabilities (see chart on the following pages for descriptions of disabling conditions). Each student with a disability may experience specific cognitive, communicative, behavioral/social/emotional, physical, and learning issues. Students may exhibit all, or some combination, of the characteristics listed for their particular disability and, in the case of some students, have more than one disability (e.g., a student identified as having a learning disability may also have a communicative disorder). Because of the heterogeneity of the special education student population, even within categories of disability, an Individualized Education Program (IEP) is created for each student found eligible to receive special education services.

| Disabling Conditions | | |
|---|---|---|
| **High Incidence Disabilities** | **Descriptors** | **Reading Instruction Consideration** |
| • *Speech or Language Impairment* | • Speech disorders include difficulties in articulation, voice, and fluency.<br>• Language impairments may include difficulties in phonology, morphology, syntax, semantics, and pragmatics. | • When possible, provide opportunities for intensive instruction in decoding and word-recognition skills (e.g., computer drill and practice programs; flash cards of frequently encountered words).<br>• Provide time for students to read the text multiple times to gain fluency (e.g., repeated readings; paired reading).<br>• Explicitly teach vocabulary and provide strategies for dealing with unknown words (e.g., teaching syllabification skills; teaching meaning of prefixes and suffixes).<br>• Explicitly teach more complex language patterns (e.g., compound sentences) and literary elements (e.g., idioms; metaphors). |
| • *Learning Disabilities* | • Students exhibit average to above-average intelligence combined with uneven academic performance patterns (i.e., perform at an average to above-average level in some academic subjects, while experiencing significant difficulties in others).<br>• Students experience processing difficulties (e.g., have difficulty taking in oral and print information and in expressing ideas orally and in writing).<br>• Students may experience attention and social/behavioral challenges. | • Preteach "big ideas" and vocabulary.<br>• Provide multiple opportunities for students to read text to gain fluency.<br>• Explicitly teach vocabulary using activities that are multisensory and require active participation (e.g., acting out meanings of words; drawing images to represent word meanings; tape-recording words and word meanings; using computer software programs).<br>• Explicitly teach comprehension strategies by modeling the steps, guiding the students through the steps, and monitoring for implementation (e.g., webbing and outlining; predicting; summarizing).<br>• Provide multiple avenues for demonstrating comprehension of text (e.g., writing, drawing, speaking, acting out scenes). |
| • *Emotional Disturbance* | • Students experience difficulty learning that is not due to cognitive, sensory, or health factors.<br>• Students may have difficulty forging and maintaining interpersonal relationships. | • Make students accountable during large-group, small-group, and paired reading (e.g., have them take notes and make and check predictions; ask questions of all group members, not just a spokesperson; have students complete individual quizzes to check for understanding). |

*continued*

| | | |
|---|---|---|
| | • Students may display inappropriate behaviors or feelings under normal circumstances.<br>• Students may experience feelings of unhappiness or depression.<br>• Students may have physical symptoms or fears associated with personal or school problems. | • Explicitly teach skills for working in groups (e.g., how to ask questions; how to state an opinion; how to disagree with another person's ideas).<br>• Provide structure and establish routines for reading activities and transitions (e.g., specify expectations during large-group reading; establish routines for how students are to complete comprehension activities).<br>• Become familiar with the student's behavior plan and systematically implement it in the classroom (e.g., use the reinforcers and consequences identified in the plan to build consistency for the student). |
| • *Mental Retardation* | • Students will demonstrate subaverage (in students with mild/moderate mental retardation) to significantly subaverage (in students with severe mental retardation) intellectual functioning.<br>• Students will demonstrate overall low performance in adaptive behavior domains (e.g., taking care of personal health needs). | • Preteach and reteach vocabulary and concepts as needed.<br>• Make concepts concrete by linking concepts to the students' daily lives.<br>• Explicitly model what is expected, and when able, provide examples of completed projects.<br>• Provide multiple avenues for students to engage with text (e.g., books on tape, paired reading, passages in hypertext format).<br>• Provide multiple exposures to the same text and its key vocabulary.<br>• Provide multiple ways for students to demonstrate understanding of text. |
| • *Low Incidence Disabilities* | **Note:** Students with low incidence disabilities may have average to above-average intelligence or may experience cognitive impairments ranging from mild to severe. | **Note:** Students with low incidence disabilities may have average to above-average intelligence or may experience cognitive impairments ranging from mild to severe. |
| • *Deaf/Hard of Hearing* | • Students who are deaf or who have some degree of hearing loss | • Present ideas visually.<br>• Capture key ideas from discussions in written form on the overhead or chalkboard.<br>• Use FMI systems when available.<br>• When orally reading text, reduce background noise as much as possible; when conducting small-group or paired reading activities, consider having the groups move to other rooms or spaces.<br>• Work with the interpreter or special education staff to identify adaptations and modifications. |

*continued*

| | | |
|---|---|---|
| • *Blind/Low Vision* | • Students who are blind or who have some vision | • Present ideas auditorially and through tactile modes to support student access.<br>• Work with the special education teacher to secure large-print text, Braille text, books on tape, and AAC reading devices.<br>• Work with the special education staff to identify specific adaptations and modifications. |
| • *Deaf/Blindness* | • Students who have concomitant hearing and visual impairments | • Work with the special education staff to identify specific adaptations and modifications.<br>• Gain understanding and a level of comfort in using the AAC devices the student is using in the classroom. |
| • *Other Health Impaired* | • Students with health conditions that limit strength, vitality, or alertness (e.g., heart condition, sickle cell anemia, epilepsy, AIDS) | • Work with the special education staff to identify adaptations and modifications.<br>• Gain understanding of the child's condition and day-to-day and emergency medical needs.<br>• Develop plans for dealing with students' absences. |
| • *Orthopedic Disabilities* | • Students with physical disabilities (e.g., club-foot, bone tuberculosis, cerebral palsy) | • Work with the special education staff to identify specific adaptations and modifications.<br>• Work with the special education staff to secure adapted materials and AAC devices, as appropriate (e.g., book holder; computer voice-recognition system that allows student to dictate written assignments).<br>• Adapt routines and activities to take into consideration the student's physical needs (e.g., room arrangement that allows for mobility in a wheelchair; procedures for distributing and collecting materials; procedures for forming work groups.) |
| • *Autism* | • Students experience difficulty in verbal and nonverbal communication<br>• Students experience difficulties in social interactions<br>• Is commonly referred to as a "spectrum disorder" because of the heterogeneity of the group | • Work with the special education staff to identify specific adaptations and modifications.<br>• Structure group and paired activities to take into consideration the child's needs; teach social skills and supports for working in small group and paired situations.<br>• Connect concepts and vocabulary to the interests of the student.<br>• Work with the special education staff to implement behavioral/social plans to provide consistency.<br>• Establish and maintain routines to ensure predictability within the classroom. |

*continued*

| | | |
|---|---|---|
| • *Traumatic Brain Injury* | • Students who experience an acquired injury to the brain<br>• Injury results in total or partial functional disability or psychological impairment (e.g., cognition, language, memory, attention, reasoning) | • Work with the special education staff to identify specific adaptations and modifications.<br>• Adapt routines and activities to take into consideration the student's physical needs (e.g., room arrangement that allows for mobility in a wheelchair).<br>• Take into consideration student's language, memory, and attention skill needs when constructing class assignments and activities.<br>• Preteach and reteach concepts and vocabulary as appropriate. |

## Individualized Education Plan

The IEP serves to guide general and special education teachers, related service providers, and parents in designing and delivering educational programs that maximize students' school participation and learning. The IEP includes goals, objectives, and benchmarks that outline what an individual student is expected to learn and achieve during the course of the academic year, as well as the types of services and special adaptations and modifications that are to be put into place to support the educational achievement of the student. For example, in the area of Language Arts instruction, a student's IEP may include the following goal and objectives:

*Goal:* Jamal will improve in reading comprehension skills as measured by the district-adopted standardized test.

*Objective:* Given narrative passages written at the seventh-grade level, Jamal will correctly write the name(s) of the main character(s) and outline, in writing, the main events of the passages in correct sequence for three out of four passages by December.

*Objective:* Given expository passages written at the seventh-grade level, Jamal will correctly write the main idea of the passages and at least three supporting details for three out of four passages by February.

The IEP goes on to identify specific services the student will need in order to achieve these goals and objectives. A range of services is available to students with disabilities through their IEP. Services fall along a continuum and include the option of students receiving instruction in general education classrooms with special education supports and participating in specialized instruction delivered by special education teachers in special education classrooms for one or more periods a day. The type of service delivery to be provided is determined individually for each student through the IEP meeting. The general education teacher, in partnership with the special education staff and the student's parents and, when appropriate, the student, determine the type of service delivery that is most appropriate for a student based on his or her learning needs.

Many students with disabilities are educated in general education classrooms alongside their general education peers. Service-delivery models that support student participation in general education classrooms go by various names, including mainstreaming, integration, and inclusion. All have the underlying same intent—to provide for the needs of students with disabilities in the least restrictive environment, alongside their general education peers.

In the case of Jamal, the service delivery option selected and specified in his IEP may look something like this:

> Student will participate in the general education Language Arts class and in one period of special education reading resource support each day. The special education teacher will team with the general education Language Arts teacher at least two days per week to provide instruction in the general education Language Arts class.

IEPs also specify the types of curricular, instructional, and behavioral adaptations and modifications that are to be put into place to support the student's achievement. For Jamal, the following adaptations and modifications may be specified in the IEP:

> The student will receive instruction in learning strategies to identify characters, story sequence, and main ideas and supporting details. The student will be provided a story map for identifying the main character(s) and for sequencing story events. The student will be provided a main idea/supporting details map when working with expository passages.

The IEP is a guide that details the types of goals, educational program, and adaptations and modifications a special education student is to receive. The IEP is developed by a team and is reviewed at least annually. General education teachers, special education professionals, administrators, parents, and students all have a voice in the development of the individual IEP.

## Lesson Planning and Instructional Accommodations

When developing Language Arts lesson plans for inclusive classrooms of general and special education learners, teachers will want to consider the addition of teaching and learning strategies that will support universal access to the content. Teachers will need to be familiar with the unique learning needs and requirements of the students and their goals, objectives, and benchmarks and, through collaboration with other IEP team members, incorporate those needs and strategies into the classroom.

This process does not need to be as intimidating as it sounds because there are some common, relatively unintrusive teaching and learning strategies that can be implemented in the classroom to address students' specific needs, as well as support the learning of the other students present in the classroom. For example, students with disabilities can greatly benefit from activities that preteach and reteach concepts, that explicitly link lesson content with prior experience and knowledge, that directly teach the meaning of critical vocabulary words, and that explicitly model how tasks are to be completed. This is true for other learners as well, including less proficient readers and students who are English language learners. Lesson plans that include explicit instruction in behavioral and social expectations also help to ensure student participation and learning. Pacing is also an issue. Some students with disabilities will require a somewhat slower pace or an ongoing review of key concepts if they are to grasp key understandings and skills. Also, activities need to be considered in light of the students' disabilities. For example, will special materials be needed (such as materials with enlarged print for students with low vision or adapted manipulatives that can be used by a student with a physical disability)? If participating in student-mediated instruction (e.g., small-group learning), what type of preparation will students receive for participating in these activities? Will the activities provide necessary supports to ensure student participation (e.g., will directions be explicit and in writing as well as presented verbally)?

There are a number of other simple adaptations and modifications general education teachers can implement in the classroom to directly address the literacy learning needs of students with disabilities. In fact, in many cases, these adaptations and modifications will assist all learners in the classroom, including typically developing readers, English learners, and less proficient readers. A beginning list of suggestions for meaningfully including students with disabilities in the general education Language Arts curriculum is presented in the chart at the end of this section. Although presented in terms of disabling conditions, the suggestions apply across conditions.

It is also helpful to think of instructional considerations that specifically apply to the four phases of instruction: Preteach, Teach, Assess, and Extend. A beginning list of suggestions is provided below.

### Phase 1: Preteach

- Identify the most critical and high-utility vocabulary words for comprehension of the passage. Provide explicit instruction in the meaning of these words that incorporates instruction in the understanding of prefixes, suffixes, word roots, synonyms, and antonyms.
- Provide an overview of key ideas and concepts presented in the text using study guides, outlines, or maps.
- Explicitly connect text content with the students' lives.
- Preteach key concepts.

### Phase 2: Teach

- Present all ideas orally and visually and, when possible, incorporate tactile and kinesthetic experiences as well.
- Stop often to discuss key ideas and check for understanding.
- Limit the presentation of information or discussion of key topics to short periods of time (no more than ten minutes) to enhance attention.
- Require students to demonstrate that they are listening and following along (e.g., taking notes, running a finger along the text).
- Incorporate active reading strategies (e.g., choral reading, paired reading) to assist students in maintaining attention.
- Provide necessary adaptive materials as appropriate (e.g., enlarged print).
- Incorporate the same comprehension and learning strategies over extended periods to allow for mastery. This will provide students with multiple opportunities to practice a strategy and to become comfortable in its application. This will also prevent "strategy clutter," which can occur when a student has too many strategies to draw from and is not facile enough with any to allow for ease of use.

- Provide specific and step-by-step instructions. Model what the students are to do, step-by-step.

### Phase 3: Assess

- Go beyond questioning techniques to assess students' understanding by having them write questions about what they have learned, identify those sections they find are unclear or confusing, or complete short writes of the key points.
- When having students work in groups or pairs, set up procedures that maintain individual student accountability (e.g., students each having to write, draw, or state a response).
- When appropriate, have students self-manage and chart their performance. Academic performance, homework and assignment completion, and behavior could be charted.

### Phase 4: Extend

- Provide examples of completed projects.
- Allow students to work in pairs or small groups.
- Provide outlines of what is to be done, with suggested dates and timelines for project completion.

### Collaboration as a Key to Student Achievement

One of the most critical things a general education teacher can do is to collaborate with the special education teachers and staff. Special education staff have extensive expertise in working with students with disabilities and are there to support each student with an IEP. These professionals are available as support systems for general education teachers and parents. The chart that follows presents a brief list of potential special educators that you may want to contact when working with students with disabilities in your general education classroom.

General education teachers can do a great deal to ensure that students with disabilities are meaningfully included in the life of the classroom. The attributes listed on the next page are important to all classrooms, but they play a key role in the creation of a classroom culture and climate that supports the participation and achievement of students with disabilities.

- Exploring differences and the importance of the acceptance of differences
- Setting clear expectations for all students that take into consideration students' learning styles and needs
- Providing students with reasonable choices
- Setting up instructional activities that foster the development of relationships between students and between students and teachers
- Demonstrating mutual respect, fairness, and trust

For example, in the case of Jamal, you could work with the special education teacher to identify those learning strategies you are already teaching in the classroom that will assist Jamal. You may want to invite the special education teacher into the classroom to provide instruction in other critical learning strategies that would assist all of your students in becoming better readers and writers, including Jamal. Because Jamal is receiving resource-room support one period per day, you may want to discuss with the special education teacher the type of instruction he is receiving during the support period and together work to develop a plan that links the curriculum of the two learning environments. You will most likely be involved in assessing whether Jamal is achieving his goals and objectives and in providing instruction to support their achievement.

### Summary

Students with disabilities are a highly heterogeneous group of learners. Their cognitive and behavioral, social, and physical needs can present unique challenges in the classroom, but through careful and strategic planning and collaboration among professionals and parents, these students can be contributing and vital members of the classroom community, as well as readers and writers. It is the professionals' responsibility, in consultation with the parents, to ensure universal access to the curriculum for these students. Lesson planning and the inclusion of adaptations and modifications within lessons are beginning points for achieving the goal of universal access for students with disabilities.

| Special Education Teachers and Service Providers | | |
|---|---|---|
| **Support Provider** | **Roles** | **How They Can Support the General Education Teacher** |
| Special Education Teacher<br>• resource teacher<br>• itinerant teacher<br>• special-day class teacher<br>• inclusion specialist | • Is intimately familiar with students' IEP goals, objectives/benchmarks, and the students' academic, communicative, and behavioral/emotional needs<br>• Has expertise in how to adapt and modify curriculum and instruction to meaningfully include students with disabilities in general education classrooms and curriculum<br>• Has expertise for providing remedial support and intensive intervention services for students with disabilities | • Can answer questions about students' learning needs<br>• Can explain the students' IEP and what can be done in the general education class to support student achievement of IEP goals and objectives/benchmarks<br>• Can help you develop ways to adapt and modify instruction that will help students learn<br>• Can work with you in the classroom to support the students' participation and achievement |
| Para-professional | • May be assigned to "shadow" a student in the general education classroom<br>• Can assist in adapting and modifying curriculum and instruction for the particular student(s)<br>• May serve to monitor students' academic and behavioral/ emotional needs and intervention plans<br>• May assist students in meeting physical, mobility, and health needs | • Can assist you in addressing the student's needs (e.g., can provide a one-on-one explanation that you may not be able to furnish because of the other students in the classroom)<br>• Can be responsible for adapting and modifying instructional activities and assignments, with guidance from you and the special education teachers<br>• Can oversee the implementation of specialized intervention plans<br>• Can be responsible for the student's physical, mobility, and health needs |
| Audiologist | • Expertise in measuring students' hearing levels and evaluating hearing loss | • Can give you suggestions for how to work with students who have partial or total hearing loss<br>• Can give you suggestions for how to deal with a student who refuses to wear his or her hearing aids in class |

*continued*

| | | |
|---|---|---|
| Physical and Occupational Therapist | • Physical therapist generally focuses on gross motor development (e.g., walking, running)<br>• Occupational therapist generally focuses on fine motor development (e.g., using writing tools) | • Can give you suggestions for how to modify requirements to take into consideration students' motor and physical needs |
| School or Educational Psychologist | • Expertise in educational testing administration and interpretation<br>• May also have training in counseling and working with students in crisis situations | • Can help you understand testing results and may be able to come into the classroom to observe and give you suggestions for working with a particular student<br>• Can help you work with a student who is in crisis (e.g., divorce, death) |
| Augmentative and Alternative Communicative Specialist | • Expertise in assessing students' AAC needs<br>• Expertise in developing programs that assist students in using alternative means for communicating verbally and in writing (e.g., communication boards; using speech synthesizer software) | • Can explain to you how a student's AAC device works<br>• Can give you suggestions for how to make adaptations and modifications that support the student's use of the AAC device in the classroom (e.g., physical arrangement of the learning environment; assignment adjustments) |
| Educational Therapist | • Expertise in assessment and remediation for students experiencing learning problems<br>• May serve as a case manager and build communicative links between school, home, and related service providers | • Can give you suggestions for how to adapt instruction to meet the student's needs<br>• Can give you suggestions for communicating with parents and for working with the special education staff |

# ANSWERS

## Unit 1

### Reading: Make Predictions

**Practice,** p. 2

1. Students will most likely predict that the story will be about a dog that surfs. Other predictions are acceptable as long as they are based on some prior knowledge—"surf" could be used in the context of surfing the Internet, for example.
2. C
3. Students will revise their predictions using new information. Knowing that the main character, the dog named Milo, fell off a fishing boat gives more details for forming predictions.
4. **Sample answer:** chunk of driftwood (this detail would support a prediction that Milo will use something as a surfboard); driftwood caught a wave (this detail would support a prediction that Milo would actually surf); rode it in to shore (this detail supports a prediction that Milo will surf).

**Assess,** p. 3

**A** 1. B
2. Students will predict that something will go wrong with the project.
3. Students will base their predictions on the title, which indicates that something will go wrong, or on the details of the hamster and the car, which indicate that the project will be unpredictable.

**B** 1. With the new information in the second paragraph, students will be able to predict that the hamster will escape or crash the car. Some students may make more detailed predictions involving specific characters.
2. Students should underline details that support their predictions.

### Reading: Use Information to Solve a Problem

**Practice,** p. 4

1. Thursday, Friday, Saturday, Sunday
2. No. Yes.
3. No.

**Assess,** p. 5

1. 7
2. Yes, 3.
3. You will fall into the reservoir.
4. They are closer to the Rest Station.
5. No.

### Literary Analysis: Plot

**Practice,** p. 6

1. B; 2. C; 3. A; 4. C; 5. D

**Assess,** p. 7

1. C; 2. A; 3. D; 4. B; 5. D

### Literary Analysis: Conflict and Resolution

**Practice,** p. 8

**A** **Sample answers:**
1. E; The racers are in conflict with each other; it is an external force.
2. E; The woman is in conflict with the rising water; it is an external force.
3. I; Adam is struggling with his conscience; it is an internal force.

**B** **Sample answers:**
1. Both racers end up tying for the winning position.
2. The woman manages to escape the flooding waters.
3. Adam decides to go to Angela and tell her to talk to Steven about the secret.

**Assess,** p. 9

**A** **Sample answers:**
1. E; The children are sunburned; it is an external force.
2. E; The scientist is concerned about global warming; it is an external force.
3. I; Paula is struggling with her feelings; they are an internal force.

**B** **Sample answers:**
1. This is not a resolution. They are still sunburned and in pain.
2. This is a resolution. The machine may help with the problem of global warming.
3. This is a resolution. Paula and Gina work on the project together and repair their relationship.

### Literary Analysis: Comparing Narrative Structure

**Practice,** p. 10

**Sample answers:**
1. Flashback; the story moves to a scene from the character's childhood.

2. Foreshadowing; the hikers will probably meet a bear.
3. Chronological order; the events are told in time order.

### Assess, p. 11

**A** **Sample answers:**

1. Chronological order; the events are told in time order.
2. Flashback; the old man remembers his first meeting with his wife.
3. Foreshadowing; the sounds suggest a frightening event about to happen.

**B** **Flashback:** (The scores go up. The fans roar. The announcer's voice echoes over the ice, "Miss Janelle Ames, the youngest winner of the Ice Castle Tournament.")
**Foreshadowing:** From the corner of her eye, she sees 15-year-old Mei Lee, the challenger, watching her and smiling calmly.

## Vocabulary: Word Roots *-trib-, -scop-, -limin-, -jud-*

### Practice, p. 12

**A** 1. tribute; 2. eliminate; 3. judge; 4. contribution
**B** 1. telescope; 2. tributary; 3. judgment; 4. preliminary

### Assess, p. 13

**A** Sample answers:

1. F A microscope is a tool for seeing things that are very small.
2. T Someone who is judicious uses good judgment.
3. F Prejudice means judging people unfairly.
4. F If you sought retribution, you would want the person to pay for hurting you.

**B** Sample answers:

1. jud; the act of judging; He showed good judgment by choosing friends who had the same interests.
2. trib; to spread something around; The teacher distributed the quizzes to the students.
3. scop; a tool for listening to body sounds; The doctor listened to the patient's heart with a stethoscope.
4. jud; the court system; A Supreme Court justice is part of the judiciary.

## Grammar: Common and Proper Nouns

### Practice, p. 14

1. proper—Ernest Hemingway, Oak Park, Illinois
2. common—volunteer; proper—World War I, Hemingway, Red Cross, Italy
3. common—weeks, ambulance, canteen
4. common—writer; proper—Pulitzer Prize
5. common—heroes, violence, destruction, courage
6. common—years; proper—Hemingway, Paris, United States
7. common—time; proper—Spain
8. common—setting, novel; proper—Spanish Civil War, *For Whom the Bell Tolls*
9. common—stories; proper—"A Clean, Well-Lighted Place"
10. common—years, illnesses; proper—Hemingway

### Assess, p. 15

**A** **Sample answers:**

1. Montgomery Avenue; 2. Springdale Senior High School; 3. May Swenson; 4. Tom Hanks; 5. Eiffel Tower

**B** 1. B; 2. D; 3. A; 4. B

## Grammar: Plural Nouns

### Practice, p. 16

1. knifes—knives; 2. hobbys—hobbies; 3. hilles—hills; 4. gooses—geese; 5. churchs—churches; 6. highwais—highways; 7. gentlemans—gentlemen; 8. elfs—elves

### Assess, p. 17

**A** 1. shelves; 2. brushes; 3. submarines; 4. galleries; 5. beliefs; 6. turkeys; 7. countries; 8. branches; 9. foxes; 10. paintings

**B**

1. Both men and women can become astronauts.
2. Exhibits at zoos often include giraffes, wolves, and monkeys.
3. Children like to make wishes on their birthdays.
4. Older houses often have many narrow hallways.
5. Grand displays of artwork decorated all the lobbies in the county courthouse.
6. Sheriffs and deputies usually carry handcuffs with them.
7. In some cities, food banks collect boxes of food for citizens who are struggling.
8. Most plants have broad leaves, but narrow leaves are found on grasses.

## Grammar: Concrete, Abstract, and Possessive Nouns

### Practice, p. 18

1. abstract; 2. possessive; 3. concrete; 4. abstract; 5. concrete

## Assess, p. 19

**A** 1. concrete—Italy; abstract—heritage
2. concrete—Visitors, beaches, vineyards, mountains; abstract—beauty
3. concrete—Cities, Florence, Rome, Venice, tourists
4. concrete—People, artworks, museums; abstract—inspiration
5. concrete—countryside; abstract—relaxation

**B** 1. abstract; 2. concrete; 3. concrete; 4. abstract; 5. concrete; 6. abstract; 7. abstract; 8. concrete; 9. abstract; 10. concrete

**C** 1. Teresa's; 2. Joneses'; 3. bloodhound's; 4. children's; 5. artist's; 6. parents'; 7. men's; 8. teachers'

### Writing: New Ending

## Practice, p. 20

1. **Sample answer:** The narrator, an old farmer, wants to stay on his farm, but his son wants to sell the farm for the money.
2. first-person point of view
3. **Sample answer:** The farmer could decide to sell after all.
4. **Sample answer:** [sample maintains point of view and voice of character] Finally I agreed to it. Just couldn't bear to see Mike be so angry and upset. So we sold the farm. Earned more money than I'd ever seen or even imagined. I bought a nice little fishing cabin by the lake, and I'm just as happy as I ever was. Just no aching back. Mike comes up now and then, too. It's a nice way to retire, I tell ya.

## Assess, p. 21

1. **Sample answer:** Dr. Marina Hall keeps her amazing alien children safe and hidden.
2. third-person point of view
3. **Sample answer:** A reporter could find out about Zone 1.
4. **Sample answer:** [sample maintains point of view and tone of story] When Dr. Hall wakes up one morning, she hears helicopters whirring overhead. She rushes to the tower to see what is happening. A cameraman is dangling from a rope ladder, taking pictures. She waves at him to leave. A second helicopter is not far behind. She rushes downstairs and tells the children to pack their things. They will have to leave.

### Writing: Letter

## Practice, p. 22

1. friendly letter; 2. B
3. Students should list three people with whom they have personal relationships.
4. **Sample answers:** a recent movie or concert; family news; an invitation to an upcoming event.

## Assess, p. 23

1. Students should name a person with whom they have a personal relationship.
2. **Sample answers:** an expression of thanks for a gift; news about mutual friends; a description of a recent event in the writer's life.
3. Students should follow the standard format and write in the appropriate tone for the type of letter they choose to write.

### Writing: Descriptive Essay

## Practice, p. 24

**A** **Sample answers:**
1. The writer's grandfather is much weaker than he used to be when he was younger.
2. Lila is very friendly and cares about other people.

**B** 1. Students should give a main impression of the family member.
2. Students should provide an example or anecdote about the family member that supports the main impression.
3. Students should provide two details about appearance, behavior, or speech that are characteristic of their subject.
4. Students should explain how the family member has affected him or her.

## Assess, p. 25

**A** Students should select someone they wish to write about.
1. Students should write four sensory details about the person.
2. Students should give an overall impression of the person.
3. Students should list at least two details about the appearance, behavior, or speech of the person.
4. Students should describe the present and future impact of the person on them.

**B** Students should write a short paragraph about a person who has had an impact on them. The paragraph should include a main impression of the person; concrete examples or anecdotes that describe the person; details about the person's appearance, behavior, and speech; and a statement about the person's effect on the writer.

### Reading: Author's Purpose

**Practice,** p. 26

1. to inform
2. Students should list any two details that are informative.
3. to entertain
4. Students should list any two details from the paragraph that are entertaining.

**Assess,** p. 27

**A** 1. to persuade

2. Students should list persuasive language, such as "wherever and whenever . . . you should wear a helmet," and the use of statistics, or other details that they found persuasive.

**B** 1. B; students should explain why the article is informative.

2. D; students should understand that this writer is trying to persuade, to inform, and to entertain all at once in his negative review of the movie.
3. D; students should state that though this author has the opposite opinion, he does have the same purpose—to persuade, to inform, and to entertain all at once.

### Reading: Identify Main Idea and Details

**Practice,** p. 28

1. Strength training can benefit teens if it is done correctly.
2. don't do it too often; don't do it for too long; don't lift too much weight

**Assess,** p. 29

1. It is important to understand complicated medical reports so you can make good decisions about the information they contain.
2. Stated. The first sentences state it.
3. Complicated information is difficult to present in a short period of time. Sometimes a report about a new health danger can cause unnecessary fears.
4. analyze, investigate
5. Analyze the information you hear but focusing on the details that explain it. Investigate by consulting your doctor or other reliable sources if you think the report applies to you.

### Literary Analysis: Mood

**Practice,** p. 30

**A** 1. C; 2. B

3. **Sample answer:** Yes, the setting of the deserted roadway at night contributes to the mood of fearfulness.

**B** **Sample answers:**
bright; joy; field of daisies smiles; The mood is joyful.

**Assess,** p. 31

**A** 1. A

2. **Sample answers:** As we kayaked along, ducks followed us; A fish leaped out of the water right in front of me.
3. Yes, the beautiful setting of the lake contributes to the mood of delight.
4. C

**B** **Sample answers:**
empty; every wall blank; a dusty toy soldier is stuck in the radiator's coils; The mood is nostalgia, or regret.

### Literary Analysis: Author's Style

**Practice,** p. 32

1. B; 2. A; 3. A; 4. C

**Assess,** p. 33

**A** 1. A; 2. D

**B** **Sample answers:**

1. Paragraph 1
2. **Answers include:** Believe it or not; totally worth it; awesome
3. **Answers include:** surprisingly emotional; it was a long and draining trip; I was reminded of
4. enthusiastic; impressed; excited
5. Paragraph 2

### Literary Analysis: Comparing Characters of Different Eras

**Practice,** p. 34

**Sample answers:**

1. It is set on a prairie in 1861, as a wagon train proceeds west to Oregon. Daniel must find firewood to build up a fire to keep his sick mother warm.
2. There is no electricity, so Daniel's only source of warmth is a wood-burning fire.
3. It is set in Chicago in modern times (sometime after 2002). Bob must get help because the furnace in his home is broken, and his mother is sick and needs warmth.

4. Bob is dependent on a modern furnace for heat and can use the telephone to call for help.
5. Both need to find a source of heat to care for their sick mothers. Daniel, in historic times, must search for firewood. Bob, in modern times, must seek help to repair his home furnace.

## Assess, p. 35

**Sample answers:**

1. It is 1902 in a town called Acton. Chief Adams must lead the efforts to put out a fire in Will Fischer's barn.
2. He lives in an era before gasoline engines, so the firetruck is driven by horses. He also is helped by volunteers from neighboring farms. The firefighting method is primitive—a bucket brigade.
3. It is set in Detroit in modern times (2006 or slightly thereafter). The firefighters must fight a fire that resulted when lightning struck an office building.
4. They have modern protective suits and gas-powered firetrucks. They will also have the help of firefighting helicopters, which can drop both water and firefighting chemicals onto the blaze.
5. Both involve the fighting of a major fire. In Passage A, the firefighting equipment is primitive, due to the historical era. By contrast, the firefighters in Passage B have modern equipment.

# Vocabulary: Word Roots *-duc-*, *-lum-*, *-sol-*, *-equi-*

## Practice, p. 36

**A** 1. D; 2. A; 3. B; 4. C

**B** 1. luminous; 2. desolate; 3. equitable; 4. reduce

## Assess, p. 37

**A Sample answers:**

1. I turned on the lights to illuminate the room.
2. I spent a solitary evening at home by myself.
3. Electricity travels easily through water because it is a good conductor.
4. The two sides of an equation should have the same value.
5. The introduction to a book comes at the beginning.
6. I fell down the stairs because I lost my equilibrium.

**B Sample answers:**

1. Neither trip is longer. *Equidistant* means "an equal distance."
2. No. A soliloquy is a speech made while alone.
3. No. *Abducted* means "kidnapped."
4. At night. *Illumination* means "lighting."

# Grammar: Personal Pronouns

## Practice, p. 38

1. me—objective; 2. his—possessive; 3. it—nominative; 4. they—nominative; 5. them—objective

## Assess, p. 39

**A Sample answers:**

1. him; 2. mine; 3. we; 4. your; 5. she; 6. us; 7. them; 8. She

**B** 1. possessive; 2. nominative; 3. objective; 4. objective; 5. possessive

# Grammar: Reflexive Pronouns

## Practice, p. 40

1. themselves—(Viewers); 2. himself—(producer); 3. ourselves—(sisters and I); 4. itself—(TV); 5. yourself—(You)

## Assess, p. 41

**A**

1. herself—<u>chimp</u>
2. ourselves—<u>teammates and I</u>
3. yourself—<u>you</u>
4. itself—<u>jenny wren</u>
5. himself—<u>Mr. Hannigan</u>
6. themselves—<u>Dr. Jane Goodall and Dr. Louis S. B. Leakey</u>
7. myself—I

**B** 1. B; 2. B; 3. A; 4. B; 5. A

# Grammar: Revising for Pronoun-Antecedent Agreement

## Practice, p. 42

1. it—<u>moon</u>; 2. me—I; 3. its—<u>Neither</u>; 4. they—<u>children</u>; 5. his or her (*or* his *or* her)—<u>Everyone</u>

## Assess, p. 43

**A** 1. <u>Several</u>—(their); 2. <u>Anyone</u>—(he or she); 3. <u>one</u>—(it); 4. <u>Everyone</u>—(his or her); 5. <u>Each</u>—(its)

**B**

1. The ladies in the card club have postponed their next meeting.
2. Ask someone on the girls' swim team to show you her technique.
3. Nobody on the boys' soccer team ever forgets his cleats.
4. The drawer had two pencils and a notepad inside it.
5. Correct

## Spelling: Commonly Misspelled Words

### Practice, p. 44

**A** 1. recommend; 2. occasion; 3. really; 4. aggravate; 5. parallel

**B** I once thought about pursuing a carreer in bussiness. My parents always reccommend this as a sure path to financial security. But I am not sure that this is what I realy want to do. I guess I won't know for sure untill I graduate from college.

1. career; 2. business; 3. recommend; 4. really; 5. until

### Assess, p. 45

**A** 1. Correct; 2. Correct; 3. occasion; 4. really; 5. until; 6. business; 7. aggravate; 8. always; 9. Correct; 10. parallel

**B** My math teacher told me that there is a special kind of geometry in which paralell lines meet at some point. I said to her, "This idea realy sounds crazy to me! In fact, I clearly remember the occassion when you told the class that such lines never meet." She then offered to reccommend a book that might explain this idea. I answered, "Untill I read this book, I won't believe that it is possible." I have now read this book and have begun to understand this other kind of geometry. I have even begun to consider a carreer in advanced mathematics, even though my parents want me to get a degree in bussiness administration.

1. parallel; 2. really; 3. occasion; 4. recommend; 5. until; 6. career; 7. business

## Writing: Personal Narrative

### Practice, p. 46

**A** My family and I drove to the Grand Canyon this summer. (At first I didn't want to go.) Slowly, though, I changed my mind. We drove through the incredible scenery of the desert. The sunsets were astonishing, coloring the faraway mountains with shades of gold and orange. Even before we got to the Grand Canyon, (I realized that I would not have wanted to miss this for the world.)

**B** 1. Students should name a personal experience suitable for a personal narrative.

2. Students should give a descriptive detail from the experience.

3. Students should give one of their reactions to the experience, such as a thought or feeling they had at the time.

### Assess, p. 47

**A** 1. Students should list two personal experiences to write about.

2. Students should list three or four events that were part of the experience, in chronological order.

3. Students should give three descriptive details about the event.

4. Students should give two thoughts or feelings they had at the time, especially realizations, solutions to problems, or changes in thinking.

**B** Students' personal narratives should tell the events they have listed in Activity A in the order of their occurrence. Students should incorporate into their narratives the descriptive details and reactions they listed in Activity A.

## Writing: Observations Journal

### Practice, p. 48

Students should complete the sample observations journal, using complete sentences to describe two possible solutions to the problem of overcrowding in a school cafeteria and explaining how the proposed solutions would improve the situation.

### Assess, p. 49

Students should fill in the sample observations journal by describing the problem they selected in Step 1, proposing two possible solutions, and explaining how the solutions might improve the situation.

## Writing: Autobiographical Essay

### Practice, p. 50

**A** Sample answers:

1. The narrative covers a few hours, from early morning until mid to late morning. Details: the writer leaves home early in the morning; his stomach begins to rumble because he is hungry for breakfast.
2. (summer); (ocean); (warm and foggy)
3. I was nine years old; I decided to explore the ocean; The more I walked, the more frightened I became.
4. The writer faces the problem of being lost on a tidal basin on a foggy morning during low tide.

**B** Sample answer:

When Dad, Josh, and I got home, my mom was waiting for us. She was really happy to see me. I think she was scared, too. She made me some scrambled eggs, toast, and bacon and gave me a big hug. Then, my mom and dad showed me the tide chart and explained what might have happened if they had not found me.

## Assess, p. 51

**Sample answers:**

1. I will tell about the last soccer game I ever played.
2. the new soccer fields at my school
3. The characters include myself, my teammates, and members of the opposing team.
4. I was playing on the soccer team against another school; during the game, I became flustered and kicked the ball into the wrong goal; our team lost the game, and my teammates were angry.
5. The events include beginning the game; sitting on the bench for most of the game; being put in the game during the last two minutes; becoming flustered; kicking the ball into the wrong goal; the horn blowing; the other team winning the game; my teammates not speaking to me. The problem is solved by my withdrawing from the soccer team and giving up sports.
6. Details include the slippery grass of the wet soccer field; the colors of the team uniforms; the fans huddled under umbrellas.
7. The stern expression of the coach; the bright red uniforms of the opposing team; the incredulous, then jubilant, faces of the opposing team; the angry looks of my teammates

# Unit 2

### Reading: Compare and Contrast

## Practice, p. 52

**Sample answers:**

1. **A.** two athletes; **B.** comparison; **C.** The word *both* is a clue, and the writer describes their hard work.
2. **A.** two cities; **B.** contrast; **C.** The word *however* is a clue, and the writer describes two different climates.

## Assess, p. 53

**Sample answers:**

**A** 1. **A.** two states; **B.** contrast; **C.** The word *but* is a clue, and the writer also describes different geographical features.

2. **A.** a mine and a cave; **B.** comparison; **C.** The word *like* is a clue, and the writer describes how both places are deep and dark.

**B** Jeanine was the talker. However, her twin sister Janet was quiet and shy. (They were both outstanding musicians.) Jeanine called herself "the noisemaker of the orchestra." She played percussion instruments, while Janet played the flute with a lovely, gentle touch. They had different musical styles, (but they were alike in that they appreciated each other's talents).

### Reading: Comparing an Original Text With Its Summary

## Practice, p. 54

**Sample answers:**

1. The most important information is that Mr. Cesar's carnival project is working well but that his dog could be a problem.
2. Children and adults are participating in an outdoor fair or carnival to raise money for a playground project. The small children are able to win prizes, and there are many activities. But Rusty might eat some of the food.

## Assess, p. 55

**Sample answers:**

1. Mr. and Mrs. Anders are caring parents.
2. The Anders family has been traveling for a while and is trying to locate the home of their relatives.
3. The name of the horse does not need to be included in a summary of the story.
4. When the family finally arrives at their relatives' house, the father knows things will get better after difficult times.

### Literary Analysis: Setting

## Practice, p. 56

**Sample answers:**

1. Boston Harbor, in 1773 ; 2. excited and hopeful

## Assess, p. 57

**Sample answers:**

1. in a fictional future time
2. Students might underline references to going to work in a Jetstar; landing on a pod; the unusual time reference; the blue-and-white shower.
3. on the planet Andaron
4. Students might circle the name Andaron in one or both of the places it is mentioned.
5. The mood varies; the narrator seems a little annoyed by the weather and by hurrying to get to work, but he or she is also amused by Commander Voss. The rain and the traffic contribute to a rushed mood; the last paragraph suggests that Commander Voss shouldn't be taken too seriously.

### Literary Analysis: Character Traits

**Practice,** p. 58

1. B
2. Leonard: creativity, loyalty, insensitivity; Ginger: humor, thoughtfulness, sensitivity, creativity, leadership; Mr. Cruthers: unfriendliness
3. Flat characters would include Simon, Leonard, and Mr. Cruthers. The boys are portrayed only as insensitive jokesters, while Mr. Cruthers is portrayed as nothing but a grumpy, unfriendly man.
4. Ginger would be described as round. She likes to laugh at a good joke, but she is also thoughtful and kind. She also shows creativity and leadership in coming up with a plan to teach the boys a lesson and getting her neighbors to play along.

**Assess,** p. 59

**A** 1. confidence, shyness, adventurousness

2. Round characters are complex, with many different character traits, whereas flat characters are one-sided, with just a single character trait.
3. Round. He is portrayed as confident and adventuresome, yet shy around girls.

**B** Passage 1 Liah is a round character. She has many positive character traits: popular, charming, hardworking, athletically gifted. She also has a few negative ones: moody, insensitive.
Passage 2 Frankie is a flat character. He is portrayed as a gluttonous slob who leaves a trail of chaos behind as he moves through the house.

### Literary Analysis: Comparing Types of Narratives

**Practice,** p. 60

1. C; 2. A; 3. C; 4. B

**Assess,** p. 61

1. B; 2. A; 3. C; 4. C

### Vocabulary: Prefixes and Suffixes *de-, -ee, -ity*

**Practice,** p. 62

**A** 1. A; 2. B; 3. A

**B** 1. appointee; 2. insensitivity; 3. timidity

**Assess,** p. 63

**A** Sample answers:

1. away; She got sick because of a vitamin *deficiency*.
2. down; I am one of my grandfather's *descendants*.
3. away; He *denied* that he had cheated on the quiz.
4. away; The train will *depart* the station at noon.
5. down; I felt *depressed* after my grandmother died.
6. away; She *deducted* her business expenses on her taxes.

**B** Sample answers:

1. honoree; He will be the *honoree* at the banquet tonight.
2. complexity; The problem is hard to solve because of its *complexity*.
3. purity; The best thing about this brand of soap is its *purity*.
4. nominee: She was her party's *nominee* for the Senate seat.
5. futility: The *futility* of his three attempts to solve the problem led him to call in an expert.

### Grammar: Action and Linking Verbs

**Practice,** p. 64

**A** 1. A; tasted; 2. L; seemed; 3. L; became;
4. A; sounded; 5. L; is; 6. A; looked

**B** 1. Her rug is too (small) for her room.

2. Television is an important (tool) of education.
3. Dana may be the most likely (choice) for the office.
4. The girls were (hoarse) from cheering.
5. The aroma of freshly baked bread smells (wonderful) to me.

**Assess,** p. 65

**A** 1. A; remained; 2. A; felt; 3. L; smells;
4. A; tasted; 5. L; is; 6. L; is; 7. L; looks;
8. A; grew; 9. L; is; 10. L; was

**B** 1. *Frankenstein* is a famous (novel.)

2. The dinosaur is a prehistoric (animal.)
3. The afternoon speaker appears very (confident.)
4. After their swim, the boys felt very (refreshed.)
5. Jerry has been (president) of his class for three years.
6. A good dictionary is a valuable (tool) for writing assignments.
7. The plant grew (sturdy) in the hothouse.
8. The new chorus sounds even (better) than the old.
9. Rhode Island is the smallest (state) in the Union.
10. The visitor became more and more (demanding.)

## Grammar: Principal Parts of Regular Verbs

### Practice, p. 66

1. present, lives; 2. past, waited; 3. present participle, is visiting; 4. present participle, are listening; 5. past participle, had paused; 6. past participle, has drawn; 7. past, coached; 8. past participle, had remembered; 9. present participle, are planning; 10. present, play

### Assess, p. 67

**A** 1. past, filled; 2. present participle, is holding; 3. present participle, is enrolling; 4. past participle, have announced; 5. present; shrinks; 6. present, prepares; 7. past participle, had arrived; 8. present participle, are planning; 9. present, drives; 10. present participle, am calling

**B** 1. lived; 2. discussing; 3. exercise; 4. agreed; 5. smiled; 6. performed; 7. attempting; 8. promised; 9. practicing; 10. suggesting

## Grammar: Revising Irregular Verbs

### Practice, p. 68

1. rise; 2. did; 3. gone; 4. saw; 5. did; 6. did; 7. went; 8. brought; 9. drunk; 10. chosen

### Assess, p. 69

**A** 1. blown; 2. threw; 3. sprung; 4. began; 5. become; 6. ran; 7. seen; 8. gone; 9. flown; 10. known

**B**
1. I had grown to love my car.
2. I had sworn never to get rid of it.
3. Now its engine has worn out somewhat.
4. The seat belt buzzer has rung its last warnings.
5. Among my friends I have sung its praises.

## Writing: Description of an Imagined Setting

### Practice, p. 70

**Sample answers:**

**A**
1. window frame, tires, table
2. heavy oak, screeching, folding
3. sound: "jarring sounds of honking horns and screeching tires"; smell: "pungent smells of exhaust and uncollected trash"; sight: "colorful assortment of milk crates"; touch: "welcome current of cool September air"

**B** Students' descriptions should provide an overview of the scene through the use of concrete language, vivid descriptions, and language that appeals to the senses.

### Assess, p. 71

Student answers should reflect an understanding of how to describe an imagined scene. Students should choose a scene, use concrete language to describe the contents of the scene, and include vivid descriptions and sensory details that bring the scene to life.

## Writing: Character Profile

### Practice, p. 72

**A** 1. B; 2. A

**B** Students should select a fictional character or someone they know and list at least four character traits of that person.

### Assess, p. 73

1. Students should select a character about whom to write.
2. Students should list at least four character traits of that character.
3. Students should write one sentence about how the character deals with conflict.
4. Students should write one sentence about how the character has solved a problem.
5. Students should write a character profile of their chosen character using the information from the first four items.

## Writing: Critical Review

### Practice, p. 74

**A** **Sample answers:**
1. Both poems have winter settings, but they are very different in tone and content.
2. The reviewer feels that the poem has powerful imagery that appeals to the reader's senses.
3. The reviewer includes a line from the poem that describes the feel of the icy sleet.
4. The reviewer thinks that the poem is songlike and childish.
5. The reviewer includes two rhyming lines in which the speaker in the poem talks to a snowman.

**B** Students should write a critical review of two pieces of literature that are similar in some way. The pieces should be clearly identified and the similarity clearly stated. The review should contain the writer's opinions, supported by facts, details, or examples from each work.

### Assess, p. 75

**A** **Sample answers:**
1. Both stories are about pioneer families traveling to the American West.
2. The reviewer thought the book was very exciting. The reviewer felt suspense as the

family encountered challenges and was thrilled when they were ultimately successful.

3. The family had to deal with diseases, lack of food and water, and an attack by a pack of wolves. The narrator was a 15-year-old girl, close in age to the reviewer.
4. The reviewer thought that the book was dull and the characters were disagreeable.
5. Unlike the characters in "Westward Ho!," these characters did not face exciting or suspenseful challenges. Instead, they argued with each other about the trail and their ultimate goals.

**B** Students should write a critical review of two pieces of literature that are similar in some way. The pieces should be clearly identified and the similarity clearly stated. The review should contain the writer's opinions, supported by facts, details, or examples from each work.

## Reading: Make Inferences

### Practice, p. 76

**Sample answers:**

**A** 1. Lana probably feels impatient.

2. Students might underline paced back and forth; flipping through pages impatiently; sighed and slumped down on the sofa; or other details that show Lana's impatience.

**B Sample answers:**

1. Your brother had a bad day at his new job.
2. Your friend does not want you to use her skates.
3. Students should underline details such as she forgets to bring them; Maybe some other day; she looks away, or other details that support their inference.

### Assess, p. 77

**A** 1. A

2. Students should underline two details such as Tom had gotten lost; he made his way to the back of the room; Some of the kids stared.
3. A
4. Students should underline two details such as Tom bit his thumbnail; Tom looked at the floor.

**B** 1. A

2. Students should underline two details such as Paula loved writing her own music; she planned to write every note of it; She jotted down melodies and chords.
3. A
4. Students should underline the detail just fooling with your musical doodles again?

## Reading: Evaluate Persuasive

### Practice, p. 78

**Sample answers:**

1. "I urge you to join your neighbors" suggests that the listener's neighbors are all voting for the speaker.
2. The words "dangerous, wild policies" are claims that may or may not be true, but the speaker is not using facts to back up his words.
3. "Mr. Yuri Jackson of the Clarksville lumber mill is supporting my candidacy" offers a testimonial from a member of the community who is obviously liked and respected.
4. "Life will be better here in Clarksville" is a generalization that cannot be proved.

### Assess, p. 79

**Sample answers:**

1. The use of "friends and family" suggests that everyone except the listener is buying Triple Flex, and it appeals to the desire to belong.
2. "Huffing and puffing" suggests that if the listener does not buy Triple Flex, he will be tired and out of shape.
3. A doctor is quoted as saying that Triple Flex is a good product, but it is not clear whether the Life Fitness Center is a reputable organization.
4. The generalizations that say "you'll feel ten years younger" and that the listener will have "a better life" cannot be proved.
5. It may be true that the supply is limited, and the offer of three bottles for the price of two is a fact. Both appeals are persuasive because they combine the attractive idea of a special price with the threat that the product may soon be unavailable.

## Literary Analysis: Point of View

### Practice, p. 80

1. T-P; **2.** F-P; **3.** F-P; **4.** T-P; **5.** T-P

### Assess, p. 81

**A** 1. A; **2.** B; **3.** B; **4.** A

**B** 1. First-person point of view. The narrator is part of the story and uses the pronouns "I" and "me" when talking about himself or herself.

2. Third-person point of view. The narrator is outside the story. The pronoun "they" is used when talking about the characters.

## Literary Analysis: Theme

### Practice, p. 82

1. A ; laziness does not lead to success.
2. **Sample answers:** People who play tricks on others often get caught; People are smarter

than you think; Don't trick a trickster; Pride often leads to defeat.

3. **Sample answers:** If opportunity knocks, open the door; Make the most of what life offers.

## Assess, p. 83

**A** 1. D; 2. A

**B** 1. unstated; 2. A; 3. D

### Literary Analysis: Comparing Symbols

## Practice, p. 84

**A** **Sample answers:**

1. a choice; two different opportunities
2. a barrier that prevents freedom of choice or direction

**B** 1. the crow and its call

2. **Sample answer:** Although it isn't a beautiful voice, like that of many birds, the crow is not shy to use it to call to its friends. Its friends respond with similar calls.
3. **Sample answer:** Be comfortable and use the voice ("qualities") you have. Others have similar traits and similar fears.
4. butterfly emerging from cocoon
5. **Sample answer:** Although it wobbled a little bit at first, the butterfly flew off into its new life.
6. **Sample answer:** Try to be confident that you will do all right when faced with change, even though you might wobble a little bit at first.

## Assess, p. 85

**A** **Sample answers:**

1. something that can't be straightened out
2. rainbow = hope, peace, prosperity; storm = trouble, problems, violence
3. progress; technological advance; triumph

**B** 1. the embroidery thread and colorful stitches

2. **Sample answer:** Like Grandma's plain shirt, Larry might "embroider" the true experiences of his life, using imaginative details and events to make an exciting short story.
3. **Sample answer:** Every "real" event has the makings for a good story.
4. the perseverance of the squirrel
5. **Sample answer:** The squirrel kept trying, even though it was a struggle. He finally succeeded.
6. **Sample answer:** Keep trying and practicing, and never give up.

### Vocabulary: Word Roots and Prefixes *-spec-, -nounc-/-nunc-, mis-, per-*

## Practice, p. 86

**A** 1. spectators; 2. announced; 3. inspected; 4. enunciate

**B** 1. B; 2. A; 3. B

## Assess, p. 87

**A** 1. C; 2. D; 3. C; 4. B; 5. B; 6. C

**B** **Sample answers:**

1. I wear spectacles because I am nearsighted.
2. The mayor was upset about being misquoted in the local paper.
3. She was so persuasive that people always did as she suggested.
4. I could always understand him because his pronunciation was excellent.

### Grammar: Verbs—Simple Tenses

## Practice, p. 88

**A** 1. <u>landed</u>, past; 2. <u>started</u>, past; 3. <u>will travel</u>, future; 4. <u>explain</u>, present; 5. <u>launched</u>, past; 6. <u>continue</u>, present; 7. <u>measures</u>, present

**B** 1. Jon and Tina studied their parts alone and together.

2. They still need a few more hours of practice.
3. Jon will accompany Tina on the piano.

## Assess, p. 89

**A** 1. <u>are</u>, present; 2. <u>climb</u>, present; 3. <u>climbed</u>, past; 4. <u>will scale</u>, future; 5. <u>trained</u>, past; 6. <u>completes</u>, present; 7. <u>conditioned</u>, past; 8. <u>departed</u>, past; 9. <u>will wait</u>, future; 10. <u>shopped</u>, past

**B** 1. The band stopped their rehearsal.

2. By next week, the workers will finish the job.
3. Only one train stops at this station.
4. The audience listened closely to the speaker.

### Grammar: Verbs—Perfect Tenses

## Practice, p. 90

1. present perfect, <u>have heard</u>; 2. past perfect, <u>had thought</u>; 3. future perfect, <u>will have read</u>; 4. past perfect, <u>had been</u>; 5. present perfect, <u>have been</u>; 6. past perfect, <u>had sunk</u>; 7. present perfect, <u>have looked</u>; 8. future perfect, <u>will have searched</u>; 9. future perfect, <u>will have discovered</u>; 10. present perfect, <u>has found</u>

## Assess, p. 91

**A** 1. present perfect, <u>have taken</u>; 2. future perfect, <u>will have attended</u>; 3. present perfect, <u>has complimented</u>; 4. present perfect, <u>has improved</u>; 5. present perfect, <u>have practiced</u>; 6. future perfect, <u>will have raced</u>; 7. past perfect, <u>had swum</u>; 8. future perfect, <u>will have taken</u>

**B** 1. I have wondered about a life without friends.

2. Now I have concluded it is no life at all.
3. Until yesterday, I had talked to no one for thirty days.
4. I had visited no one.

5. I finally have learned what friendship means.

### Grammar: Revising for Subject/Verb Agreement

**Practice,** p. 92

1. live; 2. are; 3. take; 4. want; 5. have; 6. has; 7. expects

**Assess,** p. 93

**A** 1. stands; 2. were; 3. grows; 4. were; 5. are; 6. was; 7. belong; 8. was; 9. sail; 10. are

**B** 1. The mail carrier delivers mail about noon.

2. The cities close the beaches in September.
3. The toy soldier and the stuffed dog were thrown away in the trash.
4. My brother and sister have been very cooperative lately.
5. A box of cookies is in the cupboard.

### Spelling: Tricky or Difficult Words

**Practice,** p. 94

**A** 1. 3; 2. 3; 3. 2; 4. 3; 5. 3

**B** In a <u>mischievious</u> move, my parents told us we were going someplace special. We ended up going to see an <u>opra</u>! So we traveled twenty miles in <u>blustry, wintery</u> weather to see four hours of loud, old-fashioned singing. Luckily, the theater sold <u>choclate</u> candy between acts, so all was not lost.

1. mischievous; 2. opera; 3. blustery; 4. wintry; 5. chocolate

**Assess,** p. 95

**A** 1. C; 2. D; 3. B; 4. D

**B** 1. C; 2. A; 3. D; 4. B

### Writing: Dialogue

**Practice,** p. 96

**Sample answers:**

**A** 1. They are outside a castle during a time long, long ago.

2. Ian seems to be a good friend to Hector. He encourages and supports him.

**B** Students should write at least four lines of dialogue based on a story or situation concerning events that took place a time long ago. The characters' words should seem natural, and the dialogue should be written in proper script format.

**Assess,** p. 97

**Sample answers:**

1. They are on a farm; it is toward evening, and a bad storm is brewing.
2. Aunt Molly is a strong woman who cares about her niece.
3. They will spend the night in the storm cellar.
4. Aunt Molly's expression, "Lands' sakes," seems natural because she lives on a farm. Donna's words also seem natural. She uses the expression "ma'am" to show respect.

**B** Students should write at least six lines of dialogue based on a story or situation having to do with an event that involves older people. The characters' words should seem natural, and the dialogue should be written in proper script format.

### Writing: Personal Essay

**Practice,** p. 98

**A** 1. an appearance on a TV quiz show.

2. The writer is nervous about the performance of his or her team.
3. The writer learns that he or she should put forth a good effort, whether the team wins or loses.

**B** Students should give the main theme or idea behind a personal essay they would write about a team or group in which they helped accomplish a particular task.

**Assess,** p. 99

1. Students should choose events or experiences from their own lives.
2. Students should list descriptive details that relate to the event.
3. Students should describe their thoughts and feelings.
4. Students should describe insights or lessons they learned as a direct result of the event.
5. Students' paragraphs should be written in the first person. Students should use specific details, thoughts, and feelings to describe an event or something they have read and their reaction to it.

### Writing: Narration—Short Story

**Practice,** p. 100

**Sample answers:**

**A** 1. Mrs. Sampson, her family, and the Thomas family

2. There is something wrong with the Sampsons' heat.

**B** Students should add to the passage to develop it with additional characters and dialogue.

**Assess,** p. 101

**A** 1. Students should summarize their ideas for a story.

2. Students should identify the characters in the story, along with a detail about each of them.

3. Students should identify at least two setting details.
4. Students should identify a problem or conflict.
5. Students should write brief dialogue that uses words and phrases fitting each character's personality and moves the story forward.
6. Students should identify the theme of their stories.

**B** Students should write the first few paragraphs of a story with one or more characters; a clear setting; a conflict; a plot that develops the conflict, leads to a climax, and resolves the conflict; a theme; and dialogue.

# Unit 3

## Reading: Main Idea

### Practice, p. 102

1. Alaska is a good place to fish; **2.** The main idea is stated in the first sentence; **3.** Details: over 600 kinds of fish in Alaska; over 3 million lakes, 3,000 rivers, and numerous streams.

### Assess, p. 103

**A** 1. Dark chocolate can help lower blood pressure; **2.** The main idea is stated in the first sentence; **3.** Details: Dark chocolate is better for you than milk or white chocolate; dark chocolate is an antioxidant.

**B** **Sample answer:** Main idea: I am enjoying myself on a beautiful spring day; Explanation: All of the details could support this main idea.

## Reading: Analyze Treatment, Scope, and Organization of Ideas

### Practice, p. 104

1. Primary source. The tone is youthful, bubbly, enthusiastic.
2. The purpose is to convey information and excitement to a friend.

### Assess, p. 105

1. The first passage is a primary source because a person witnessed the event he was writing about.
2. The second passage is a secondary source, because it was written about an event in the past that the writer didn't witness or participate in.
3. The first passage is excited and enthusiastic. The second passage is clam and reflective.
4. [the student's opinion of which passage is more interesting to read]

## Literary Analysis: Narrative Essay

### Practice, p. 106

1. D; **2.** A; **3.** C; **4.** C

### Assess, p. 107

1. C; **2.** D; **3.** D; **4.** B; **5.** B

## Literary Analysis: Biographical and Autobiographical Essay

### Practice, p. 108

**A** 1. A; **2.** B; **3.** B and A; **4.** B

**B**
1. autobiographical—uses the pronoun *I* and describes the writer's experience
2. biographical—uses the pronoun *he* and describes someone else's experience

### Assess, p. 109

**A** 1. T; **2.** T; **3.** F; **4.** T; **5.** F; **6.** T; **7.** F; **8.** T

**B** 1. biographical—describes someone else's experience; **2.** autobiographical—uses the pronoun *I* and describes the writer's experience; **3.** biographical—uses the pronoun *he* and describes someone else's life

## Literary Analysis: Comparing Types of Organization

### Practice, p. 110

**Sample answers:** 1. like, however; **2.** because, as a result; **3.** first, finally

### Assess, p. 111

**A**
1. cause-and-effect order—the writer shows all of the causes that can result in an avalanche;
2. chronological order—the writer shows the steps that lead to an avalanche in chronological order, with one event happening after another

**B** **Sample answers:** The two paragraphs are alike in that they both cover the same topic, which is the development of an avalanche. However, they are different in how the writer organized information in each paragraph. The first paragraph uses cause-and-effect order, showing that every change that happens in the snow causes another. The second paragraph uses chronological order, showing each change in the snow in sequence.

## Vocabulary: Suffixes and Word Roots *-ly, -ance, -val-, -nym-*

### Practice, p. 112

**A** 1. appearance; 2. thoughtfully; 3. comfortably; 4. variance

**B** 1. valid; 2. synonym; 3. anonymously; 4. valor

## Assess, p. 113

**A** 1. horrible; horribly
2. allied; alliance
3. immediately; immediate

**B** Sample answers:
1. -val-; having value, or worth; The jewelry was very *valuable.*
2. -nym-; an assumed name; He used a *pseudonym* instead of his real name.
3. -nym-; nameless; The police got an *anonymous* tip.
4. -val-; to measure something's worth; The teacher will *evaluate* the student's work.

### Grammar: Adjectives and Articles

## Practice, p. 114

**A** 1. The older man stopped us on the street.
2. Did you speak to the newspaper reporter?
3. He flew in a supersonic jet to the airport.
4. The weary citizens sought out the shadiest spots.
5. The long, hot day drew to a close in a fiery sunset.

**B** 1. The sleek gray horse galloped across the pasture.
2. This fine novel was written by a friend of mine.
3. The long, narrow column of soldiers marched through the pass.
4. Every qualified person can enter the contest.
5. Bob loaded the plate with four large sandwiches.
6. Make one special wish and blow out the candles.
7. The car was a powerful and efficient vehicle.
8. During the winter, we had little snow and no temperatures below zero.
9. Our history teacher gave us a special assignment.
10. Great flocks of large birds migrate here in the spring.

## Assess, p. 115

**A** 1. Laura bought a blue blouse with white trim.
2. Each one in the class will develop an original project.
3. I made three attempts to reach the local representative.
4. A gracious hostess greeted us at the flower show.
5. We packed the fragile glassware in a reinforced container.
6. The investigator hopes to get some answers from the lone witness.
7. The decorator suggested using three large paintings to cover the bare wall.
8. My foreign car is equipped with radial tires.
9. The many rings of Saturn glowed in the blurry photograph.
10. Several athletes complained about the old stadium.

**B** 1. C; 2. A; 3. A; 4. B; 5. B; 6. B; 7. C; 8. B; 9. A; 10. C

### Grammar: Adverbs

## Practice, p. 116

**A** 1. watched—today; 2. competed—enthusiastically; 3. glistened—brightly; 4. flapped—loudly; 5. scurried—around

**B** 1. In what manner?—completely; 2. When?—promptly; 3. Where?—away; 4. In what manner?—genuinely; 5. When?—immediately

## Assess, p. 117

**A** 1. difficult—very; 2. began—early; 3. listed—first; 4. reviewed—carefully; 5. hard—quite; 6. slept—soundly

**B** 1. When? The crash happened suddenly.
2. Where? Lights flashed outside.
3. When? The police came instantly.
4. To what extent? It was very important that an ambulance arrived.
5. When? A man promptly received aid.
6. To what extent? His arm was badly hurt.
7. In what manner? The traffic moved slowly.
8. When? An officer soon fixed that.
9. Where? Trucks pulled the cars away.
10. To what extent? It was particularly frightening to watch.

### Grammar: Comparative and Superlative Forms

## Practice, p. 118

1. longest; 2. most; 3. best; 4. older; 5. longest; 6. clumsier; 7. closer

## Assess, p. 119

**A** 1. worse; 2. farthest; 3. safer; 4. best; 5. wealthiest; 6. sunnier; 7. earliest; 8. farther; 9. more; 10. heavier

**B** 1. The Jacksons are the friendliest people on the block.
2. Teddy seems to be the brighter of the twins.
3. She is the more popular of the two candidates.
4. Venus is the most brilliant of all the planets.
5. The largest of all snakes is the anaconda.

## Writing: Biographical Sketch

### Practice, p. 120

**A** Sample answers:

1. My Uncle Royce is not wealthy, but he is one of the richest men in the world.
2. Any two of the following: He runs errands for sick or elderly neighbors. He volunteers for the fire department, the Red Cross, and other local organizations. During the holidays, he visits hospitals and homeless shelters, spreading cheer and optimism.
3. <u>His pockets may be empty, but his heart is full.</u>

**B** Students' paragraphs should clearly state why they admire their subjects, provide at least two supporting details, and conclude by restating their main idea.

### Assess, p. 121

Student answers should reflect an understanding of how to write a biographical sketch. Students should choose a topic; clearly state the main idea in their first sentence; include the person's qualities, accomplishments, and other details that support the main idea; and end with a strong conclusion.

## Writing: Reflective Composition

### Practice, p. 122

**A** Sample answers:

1. chopping wood when he is angry
2. Any two of the following: (1) *To me, chopping that wood was nothing more than a punishment.* (2) *. . . after an hour or so of slamming my ax into thick logs, I felt lighter—if not quite "happy," then at least less stressed.* (3) *It felt good knowing that my hard work was keeping my family warm.*
3. *My dad showed me how to turn my anger into something constructive, and that's a lesson I can take with me throughout my life.*

**B** Students' paragraphs should include their reflections on the work of art and why it is meaningful to them.

### Assess, p. 123

Student answers should reflect an understanding of how to write a reflective composition. Students should choose a topic, express their thoughts and feelings about the experience, and explain why it is important to them.

## Writing: How-to Essay

### Practice, p. 124

**A** Sample answers:

1. how to make homemade applesauce
2. Ingredients: apples, sugar, cinnamon; Equipment: large covered pot, colander or strainer, food mill, large bowl
3. a food mill; the writer thought the term might be unfamiliar to readers.
4. first, then, next, after that, finally

**B** Essays should clearly explain a process. All equipment and materials should be mentioned, and unfamiliar terms should be defined. Steps should occur in chronological order, with transitional words and phrases used to make the order clear.

### Assess, p. 125

**A** Sample answers:

1. how to make cornbread
2. Ingredients: cornmeal, flour, baking soda, salt, sugar, egg, and milk; Equipment: a cast-iron skillet or a baking pan; a mixing bowl; a wire whisk or wooden mixing spoon; and a wire cooling rack
3. the cast-iron skillet; the writer thought that readers might be unfamiliar with that piece of equipment.
4. first, now, begin, then, next

**B** Essays should clearly explain a process. All equipment and materials should be mentioned, and unfamiliar terms should be defined. Steps should occur in chronological order, with transitional words and phrases used to make the order clear.

## Reading: Fact and Opinion

### Practice, p. 126

**A** Sample answers:

**1.** Fact; the score could probably be seen on a screen or scoreboard; **2.** You could replay a videotape to show what the referee did; **3.** The writer used the clue word *wrong*, which shows a judgment; **4.** The fourth sentence is a fact because her loss can be proved.

**B** 1. F; 2. O; 3. F

### Assess, p. 127

**A** Sample answers:

**1.** Someone could have seen the family sit down, or they could have heard the photographer tell them to sit quietly and smile, so it is a fact; **2.** Anyone in the room could prove that the baby screamed; **3.** Their embarrassment cannot be proved—you would have to ask the parents whether they felt embarrassed (the clue words are *awful* and *embarrassing*); **4.** It is a fact because other people could see the father walking around with the baby.

**B** 1. F; 2. O; 3. O; 4. F; 5. F; 6. O

### Reading: Analyze Proposition and Support Patterns

**Practice,** p. 128

1. Yes. The opinion is that everyone should exercise the privilege of voting.
2. There have been many elections, including the presidential election in 2000, where the winner was determined by just a few votes.
3. One of the most patriotic things you can do is to take advantage of your right to vote.

**Assess,** p. 129

1. There are many abandoned and suffering cats and the problem is made worse by too many cats being born because adults are not spayed or neutered.
2. Yes, it states the problem but not the author's solution.
3. His solution is to attempt to spay and neuter cats.
4. Yes. The Feral Cat Coalition and veterinarians
5. Yes. It seems like it make sense to stop so many cats from being born and suffering. Although I don't think it is possible to do this for all cats.

### Literary Analysis: Persuasive Techniques

**Practice,** p. 130

1. B; 2. C; 3. <u>Aren't actors supposed to act, and aren't directors supposed to direct?</u> 4. D; 5. C

**Assess,** p. 131

1. D; 2. B; 3. <u>What should a mayor do for his city—lead the people or play a lot of golf with his pals?</u> 4. C; 5. B

### Literary Analysis: Word Choice

**Practice,** p. 132

1. B; 2. D
3. **Sample answer:** Roberto was munching on a spicy meatball sub.
4. **Sample answer:** golden toast; juicy pear

**Assess,** p. 133

**A** 1. P; 2. N; 3. N; 4. P; 5. P; 6. N; 7. P; 8. N; 9. N; 10. P

**B** 1. B; 2. A

3. **Sample answer:** positive attitude—reach out and keep going; courageously; rescued; warm food and the kind generosity of a helping hand
4. **Sample answer:** negative attitude—exhausted; labor; devastating; battered building; helpless; violent storm; raged on and on

**Practice,** p. 134

1. A: to explain a process. B: to entertain
2. B
3. Passage A: To make; you mix; They cook best on; Just pour in; brown . . . gently; Passage B: the best pancakes in the world!; just the right amount; My mouth waters

**Assess,** p. 135

1. A; 2. A
3. **Sample answer:** The orchard was all she had left these days; Roy wasn't much company for anyone; She gazed out at the orchard and remembered a time when it had echoed with the laughter of rough-and-tumble boys
4. B
5. **Sample answer:** It's time to take action! It's time to say YES, we care! Let's help our children help themselves!

### Vocabulary: Word Roots *-bell-*, *-vad-*, *-pass-*, *-tract-*

**Practice,** p. 136

**A** invaded; passively; passionate; rebellion; attract; distract; evade

**B** -bell-: rebellion; -vad-: invaded, evade; -pass-: passively, passionate; -tract-: attract, distract

**Assess,** p. 137

**A** 1. A; 2. C; 3. A; 4. A; 5. B

**B** Sample answers:

1. F; Someone who is rebellious tends to resist the people in charge.
2. T; An impassive person does not show emotion.
3. T; To detract from something means to take away from it.
4. F; If you evade something, you get away from it.

### Grammar: Conjunctions

**Practice,** p. 138

1. and; 2. either/or; 3. When; 4. Both/and; 5. if; 6. but; 7. while; 8. Neither/nor; 9. nor; 10. Although

**Assess,** p. 139

**A** 1. while; 2. and; 3. so; 4. Neither/nor; 5. or; 6. whenever; 7. either/or; 8. Whether; 9. yet; 10. Both/and

**B** 1. coordinating—<u>yet</u>; 2. subordinating—<u>because</u>; 3. correlative—<u>either/or</u>; 4. coordinating—<u>but</u>;

5. subordinating—since; 6. correlative—both/and; 7. coordinating—so; 8. subordinating—because; 9. coordinating—and; 10. correlative—either/or

### Grammar: Prepositions and Prepositional Phrases

**Practice,** p. 140

**A** 1. in, of; 2. During; 3. into, without; 4. underneath, near; 5. on

**B**
1. with red hair; in her hand
2. in the very center; of the huge stage
3. for the director and the producer
4. inside the wings; to the right
5. Behind him; of the cast

**Assess,** p. 141

**A**
1. From the meeting; into the restaurant
2. throughout the manager's presentation
3. of students; in front; of the building
4. of falling rain
5. At dawn
6. from the police; under the bridge
7. through the enemy town; at great speed
8. Instead of hamburgers; for lunch
9. in front; of the chalet
10. to the travel agent; about noon.

**B** Sample answers:
1. outside; The ticket holders waited patiently near the theater.
2. under; The telephone book is beneath the table.
3. across; A housing development has been built by the river.
4. near; Let's pick the strawberries along the fence.
5. on; We were sitting beside the front porch.

### Grammar: Combining Sentences With Conjunctions

**Practice,** p. 142

1. When; 2. or; 3. before; 4. If; 5. but

**Assess,** p. 143

**A** Sample answers:
1. Because we missed the bus, we were late for school.
2. According to legend, Betsy Ross made our first flag, but there is little evidence.
3. Skin divers must follow safety precautions, or they may be injured.
4. When we stood by the Washington Monument, we felt very small.
5. Although my schedule varies, I try to exercise every day.

**B** Sample answers:

1. but; 2. When; 3. If; 4. but; 5. After; 6. nor; 7. Unless

### Spelling: Homonyms and Homophones

**Practice,** p. 144

**A** 1. bored; 2. threw; 3. accept; 4. our; 5. fowl; 6. waist

**B** 1. bored, board; 2. waist, waste; 3. through, threw; 4. board, bored; 5. our, hour; 6. except, accept

**Assess,** p. 145

**A** 1. bored; 2. our; 3. waist; 4. foul; 5. through; 6. except

**B** 1. B; 2. B; 3. A; 4. B; 5. B; 6. A

### Writing: Evaluation

**Practice,** p. 146

Sample answers:
1. Sixteen-year-olds are too young to drive.
2. Supporting points: Sixteen-year-olds have a higher crash rate than drivers of any other age. They're three times more likely to die in a car crash. These points are convincing because they show how dangerous teen drivers can be.
3. The speaker uses attention-grabbing headlines: "Teen driver killed in crash," "Teen driver causes pile-up." This technique is effective because most people have seen headlines like these; they are emotional appeals that tap into our fears.
4. Those things may be true, but there are alternatives, such as carpools and public transportation.
5. This speech is effective in that it made me think about the dangers of teen driving and the need for caution, but I still plan to get my license as soon as I can.

**Assess,** p. 147

Student answers should reflect an understanding of how to write an evaluation. Students should choose an advertisement to evaluate, clearly state the ad's position and supporting points, identify any persuasive techniques and counterarguments, and describe the ad's overall effectiveness.

### Writing: Response

**Practice,** p. 148

**A** Sample answers:
1. The writer expresses a preference for block scheduling in high school.
2. I disagree with the idea of block scheduling.

3. I like the idea of juggling many different classes at once in high school. I do it now, and it's manageable. My 17-year-old brother never had a problem with traditional scheduling. He says traditional scheduling allows room for free periods, which are really useful when you need extra time to study for a test or do homework.

**B** Students' responses should clearly state whether they agree or disagree with the idea and explain how the idea applies—or does not apply—to their own experience. They should provide at least one example that supports their explanation.

### Assess, p. 149

Student answers should reflect an understanding of how to write a response. Students should explain the author's opinion, write a statement that clearly expresses their agreement or disagreement with the idea, and explain how the idea applies—or does not apply—to their own experience, using examples to support their point.

## Writing: Editorial

### Practice, p. 150

**A** 1. D; 2. B; 3. A

**B** Editorials should begin with a clear statement of opinion, followed by strong supportive evidence (facts, statistics). Students should also predict and respond effectively to an opposing viewpoint and use persuasive language effectively to sway readers.

### Assess, p. 151

**A** 1. C; 2. A; 3. B; 4. A

**B** Editorials should begin with a clear statement of opinion, followed by strong supportive evidence (facts, statistics). Students should also predict and respond effectively to an opposing viewpoint and use persuasive language effectively to sway readers.

# Unit 4

## Reading: Context Clues

### Practice, p. 152

**A** 1. Context clue: fascinated; Meaning: interesting, fascinating

2. Context clue: natural ability; Meaning: natural ability

**B** 1. It is used to describe a person's size. Context clues: "shorty" and "small fry"

2. It is a synonym.

3. Explanation: "Won't they be surprised when they can't find their uniforms!"

### Assess, p. 153

**A** 1. D, 2. A, 3. A, 4. B

**B** 1. C; 2. experienced, skilled; 3. A

## Reading: Compare and Contrast Features of Consumer Materials

### Practice, p. 154

1. aerobics and basketball or bowling and frisbee
2. soccer or swimming; because they burn the most calories so you are getting the most exercise
3. No. I think frisbee and bowling burn the least calories because you are not moving most of the time playing them. They are not as active as some of the other activities.

### Assess, p. 155

1. equipment, ingredients, instructions, nutritional content
2. There are many more grams of carbohydrates than protein in this recipe.
3. Yes, because it lists the amount of carbohydrates in a serving
4. A person who is trying to control the intake of calories or certain nutrients would know if the recipe would be a good one for them. If all recipes had nutritional information, it would be much easier to compare how healthy they are.

## Literary Analysis: Sound Devices

### Practice, p. 156

**A** 1. C; 2. D; 3. B; 4. C; 5. A

**B** 1. B; 2. C

### Assess, p. 157

**A** 1. D; 2. B; 3. A; 4. D; 5. C; 6. A

**B** 1. B; 2. C; 3. A

## Literary Analysis: Figurative Language

### Practice, p. 158

**A** 1. simile; 2. metaphor; 3. personification

**B** 1. B; 2. A; 3. A

### Assess, p. 159

**A** Student responses will vary but should indicate the elements of each type of figurative language listed.

**B** 1. simile; 2. personification; 3. simile; 4. personification; 5. metaphor; 6. metaphor; 7. metaphor; 8. personification

## Literary Analysis: Comparing Poetry and Prose

### **Practice,** p. 160

**Sample answers:**

1. The language has a musical quality not heard in everyday life. It uses deliberate line lengths as well as sound devices such as rhythm and rhyme. It uses figurative language such as "jaws of Death" and "mouth of Hell."
2. Thundering cannons on three sides; "Storm'd at with shot and shell."
3. desperate

### **Assess,** p. 161

**Sample answers:**

**A** 1. Poetry; 2. Prose; 3. Prose; 4. Poetry; 5. Poetry

**B** Sample answers:

1. The language has a musical quality not heard in everyday life. It uses deliberate line lengths as well as sound devices such as rhythm and rhyme. It uses the ship as a metaphor for the ship of state and the captain as a metaphor for Lincoln.
2. "The port is near, the bells I hear, the people all exulting,"; "the vessel grim and daring"
3. mournful

## Vocabulary: Prefixes and Suffixes *im-, -ous, -ive*

### **Practice,** p. 162

**A** 1. immediate; 2. improvise; 3. improvement; 4. immature

**B** 1. glorious; 2. disruptive; 3. outrageous; 4. progressive

### **Assess,** p. 163

**A** Sample answers:

1. into; My grandfather was an *immigrant* from Poland.
2. not; The ship was *immobile* because there was no wind.
3. into; I *immersed* my dirty shirt in the soapy water.
4. into; Coffee is one of this country's *imports*.

**B** Sample answers:

1. virtuous; He is known to be *virtuous*.
2. responsive; She is always *responsive* to my suggestions
3. humorous; The TV show was very *humorous*.
4. instructive: My quick lesson in skating was *instructive*.
5. luxurious; Their house was *luxurious*.

## Grammar: Subject Complements

### **Practice,** p. 164

1. astronaut—PN
2. he—PP
3. proud—PA
4. career—PN
5. strange—PA
6. heroes—PN

### **Assess,** p. 165

**A** 1. PN; 2. PA; 3. PN; 4. PA; 5. PP; 6. PN; 7. PA; 8. PN

**B** 1. (have been)—useful; 2. (is)—breed; 3. (would be)—weight; 4. (must look)—beautiful; 5. (are)—they

**C**

1. knowledgeable—PA
2. she—PP
3. country—PN
4. dry—PA
5. capital—PN

## Grammar: Direct and Indirect Objects

### **Practice,** p. 166

1. direct object—courses
2. direct object—victims
3. direct object—lesson; indirect object—me
4. direct object—techniques; indirect object—students
5. direct object—rescue

### **Assess,** p. 167

**A** 1. OP; 2. OP; 3. IO; 4. OP; 5. IO

**B**

1. direct object—tickets; indirect object—us
2. direct object—us
3. direct object—part
4. direct object—orchestra
5. direct object—lakefront; indirect object—group
6. direct object—tickets; indirect object—man
7. direct object—variety

**C** 1. IO; 2. DO; 3. N; 4. IO; 5. DO

## Grammar: Revising Active and Passive Voice

### Practice, p. 168

1. passive; Aunt Lila took photographs of the mountains.
2. active
3. passive; Bill put Aunt Lila's photographs in the special frames.
4. active

### Assess, p. 169

**A** 1. was enjoyed—P
2. were detected—P
3. performed—A
4. admired—A
5. served—A
6. were offered—P
7. sold—A

**B** 1. Patrick Henry delivered a powerful speech against the Stamp Act.
2. okay
3. The orchestra conductor flashed a bright smile.
4. The Toltec Indians built large pyramids with temples on top.
5. okay

## Writing: Introduction

### Practice, p. 170

**Sample answers:**

**A** 1. [a haunting tribute to a beautiful maiden who has died.]
2. It describes the love shared by the narrator and the maiden, the illness that she suffered, and the sorrow he feels now that she is gone.
3. repetition of certain sounds, phrases and rhythms; rhyme pattern
4. a sorrowful mood

**B** Students' introductions should include an overview about the song, draw attention to the methods the composer or performer used, and describe the effect the song will probably have on the audience.

### Assess, p. 171

**Sample answers:**

**A** 1. Three examples of vivid descriptions are "the wind was a torrent of darkness," "the moon was a ghostly galleon," and "the road was a ribbon of moonlight."
2. An example of alliteration is "ghostly galleon."
3. An example of repetition is the use of the word *riding* three times in a row and then again in the next sentence.
4. Pairs of words that rhyme are *trees/seas* and *moor/door.*
5. Students might mention the rhythm, the imagery, the action, or the sense of drama in the poem as elements that a listener would most appreciate.

**B** Students should turn their answers into an introduction that they might use before a poetry reading.

## Writing: Study for a Poem

### Practice, p. 172

1. open-air market on Saturday morning
2. **Sample answer:** fruits, vegetables, flowers
3. **Sample answer:** sweet aromas of fruits and flowers, silky feel of oils, sounds of coins changing hands
4. sense of taste
5. sense of touch

### Assess, p. 173

**Sample answers:**

1. the beach
2. waves, sand, people, bathing suits, sunshine, beach umbrellas, beach towels, seagulls, boats, lifeguards, boogie boards
3. waves: sound of crashing on the shore; sand: gritty feel on feet; bathing suits: bright colors of the fabrics; sunshine: heat on my skin
4. The crashing waves are like cymbals in a band because they are so loud.The sand is like sandpaper because it is so rough.
The bathing suits are like flags of all nations because they come in so many colors.
The sunshine is like a space heater because it heats the air around me.

## Writing: Problem-and-Solution Essay

### Practice, p. 174

Students should write three more steps for the solution as well as evidence demonstrating why each step is important.

### Assess, p. 175

Students should supply four steps to demonstrate how newly arrived immigrants can shop successfully at a grocery store or mall, as well as evidence that explains why each step is important.

## Reading: Paraphrase

**Practice,** p. 176

**Sample answers: 1.** Her courage is seen by the poet as strong and lasting; **2.** I wish she had left me her courage instead of a piece of jewelry because I need it. She no longer needs courage because she has died.

**Assess,** p. 177

**A** **Sample answers: 1.** to understand the sweetness of success; **2.** most desperate; **3.** army; **4.** *Forbidden* in this case means "prevented," because if a soldier is dying, he will not hear any sounds of triumph. Those sounds will only be heard by the people who won the battle.

**B** **Sample answer:** People who never succeed appreciate its sweetness the most. None of the people in the victorious army today can really understand what victory means as well as the dying soldier who feels the pain of its loss.

## Reading: Analyze Technical Directions

**Practice,** p. 178

**1.** C; **2.** C; **3.** A

**Assess,** p. 179

**1.** A; **2.** C; **3.** C

## Literary Analysis: Lyric and Narrative Poetry

**Practice,** p. 180

**1.** "Paul Revere's Ride"; **2.** Paul Revere

**3.** an old town

**4.** **Sample answer:** An old town lies between two hills. There are houses and trees, and the normal passage of days and seasons.

**Assess,** p. 181

**A** **1.** to tell a story

**2.** **Sample answer** (any two of the following): characters, plot, setting, conflict

**3.** to express the thoughts and feelings of the speaker

**4.** The speaker "says" the poem.

**B** **1.** "The Raven"

**2.** At midnight on a dark night, a speaker is interrupted in his reading by a mysterious tapping at his door.

**3.** a cherry tree in bloom

**4.** **Sample answer:** As he or she rides through the woods on a spring morning, the speaker notices the beauty of the cherry trees, which are full of white flowers.

## Literary Analysis: Imagery

**Practice,** p. 182

Sight: wind billowing out the seat of my britches, chrysanthemums, streaked glass, flashing with sunlight, a few white clouds, elms plunging and tossing like horses, everyone pointing
Hearing: feet crackling splinters, shouting
Smell: chrysanthemums
Taste: none
Touch: wind, feet crackling splinters of glass, dried putty

**Assess,** p. 183

**A** **1.** D; **2.** C; **3.** A; **4.** B; **5.** E

**B** Sight: pasture spring, leaves, water, calf, mother; hearing: rake the leaves; smell (none); taste: (none); touch: rake the leaves, licks it with her tongue

## Literary Analysis: Comparing Types of Description

**Practice,** p. 184

**1.** an iron fence

**2.** **Sample answer:** It is made of vertical iron bars, and each bar has a sharp point on the top.

**3.** to keep out all intruders

**4.** D

**Assess,** p. 185

**A** **1.** B; **2.** B; **3.** C

**B** **1.** **Sample answer:** They have the choice of how to greet each other: with clenched fists or open hands, held out toward each other.

**2.** **Sample answer:** anger, conflict, suspicion, force

**3.** **Sample answer:** helpfulness, friendship, accommodation, tolerance

**4.** A

## Vocabulary: Prefixes and Word Roots *in-, trans-, -cede-, -vert-*

**Practice,** p. 186

**A** **1.** insufficient; **2.** exceed; **3.** transfer; **4.** divert

**B** **1.** C; **2.** C; **3.** B

**Assess,** p. 187

**A** **Sample answers:**

**1.** transplant; to move a plant; I will *transplant* the rosebush to my yard.

2. indirect; roundabout; I took an *indirect* route to school.
3. inadequate; not enough; The school gym was *inadequate* to hold all the students.
4. transaction; an exchange; I made a *transaction* at my bank.

**B** **Sample answers:**

1. I was offended by his ingratitude for all the favors I had done him.
2. The vertical stripes ran all the way down the wall from top to bottom.
3. I had to flip back to the preceding chapter to remember what had just happened.
4. The politician was forced to concede that he had lost the election.
5. I needed a translator because I did not speak the local language.

### Grammar: Prepositions and Prepositional Phrases

## Practice, p. 188

**A**

1. Snacks before dinner may spoil your appetite.
2. We agreed to the plan without any hesitation.
3. The wagon in the barn once belonged to my grandfather.
4. Paul Revere rode through the countryside on his horse.
5. We walked along the riverbank until sundown.
6. Mom found my keys in the clothes hamper.
7. The wood stove in the kitchen heats the whole house.
8. Jerry hasn't changed much since last year.
9. Carrie brought her camera with her to the museum.
10. Steam sometimes rises from warm water.

**B** **Sample answers:**

1. The news reporter stood near the candidate.
2. Lisa sat between Kristin and Jackie.
3. The squirrels chased each other around the park.
4. The cat raced up the stairs.

## Assess, p. 189

**Sample answers:**

1. We planted marigolds around the vegetable garden.
   We planted marigolds along the house.
2. The huge dog dragged his master along the path.
   The huge dog dragged his master through the woods.
3. The person standing near the kitchen seems angry.
   The person standing by the ticket office seems angry.
4. Every morning he passes by on roller blades.
   Every morning he passes by with his briefcase.
5. Katherine walked out the door.
   Katherine walked toward the exit.
6. The child played outside the pool.
   The child played in the basement.
7. The runners raced up the hill.
   The runners raced past the park.
8. No one can make that horse go over a bridge.
   No one can make that horse go along the highway.
9. An old house near the glen caught fire last night.
   An old house beside the office building caught fire last night.
10. He hid the money in a tin can.
    He hid the money under his bed.

### Grammar: Infinitive Phrases

## Practice, p. 190

1. To become a professional dancer—noun
2. to see the Grand Canyon—adjective
3. to speak to about zoning—adjective
4. to climb Mount McKinley—noun
5. to visit Cambodia next year—noun
6. to get to San Francisco—adverb
7. to take a long bike ride—adjective
8. to leave for the Earth Day Festival—adverb

## Assess, p. 191

**A**

1. To find information about Peru
2. to read more poems by Alice Walker
3. to learn
4. to leap over obstacles
5. to propose a solution
6. To master the martial art of judo
7. to ask
8. to take a scenic tour of New Hampshire

**B** **Sample answers:**

1. It took us a full day to hike to the summit of Wheeler Peak.
2. To get into a good college, you will need to have good grades.
3. Janelle always likes to try new hobbies and activities.
4. Kate's dream is to travel to Brazil.
5. We were happy to meet the new neighbors.

## Grammar: Revising to Vary Sentence Patterns

### Practice, p. 192

**Sample answers:**

1. On that early Saturday morning, the park was crowded.
2. Eager, Sara approached the soccer field.
3. Then she asked the coach to let her try out for the team.
4. She emptied her gym bag's contents, two shin guards and a pair of cleats, onto the grass.

### Assess, p. 193

**A** 1. Stonehenge; 2. an ancient monument; 3. a county in southwestern England; 4. R.J.C. Atkinson; 5. June 21

**B** Sample answers:

1. Somberly, Darren lumbered out of the room.
2. Exhausted, the puppy flopped down on the rug and immediately fell asleep.
3. In the middle of the night, we went to the back yard to watch the meteor shower.
4. Next week our team will take on the Lakeland Tigers, last year's state champs.
5. In 1985, a team of French and American scientists found the wreckage of the *Titanic*

## Spelling: Words With Prefixes and Suffixes

### Practice, p. 194

1. tasteless; 2. reference; 3. traveled; 4. immovable; 5. illegal

### Assess, p. 195

**A** 1. tasteless; 2. dizziness; 3. occurrence; 4. collapsible

**B** 1. impractical; 2. reenact; 3. immovable; 4. illegal

**C** 1. C; 2. B; 3. A; 4. D

## Writing: Lyric or Narrative Poem

### Practice, p. 196

**Sample answers:**

**A**

1. The speaker is upset to have his or her quiet evening interrupted by a noisy intruder and a blast of cold air.
2. Any two of the following: glowing embers, crash and stomp, cold air, freezing, current of cold in a warm lagoon
3. Student answers should reflect an understanding of how to write a lyric poem. Students' lines of poetry should continue to express the speaker's thoughts or feelings and include at least one vivid image.

**B**

1. Donna-Lee and her little sister are introduced.
2. The little sister wants to play with Donna-Lee, but Donna-Lee thinks she's a pest.
3. Student answers should reflect an understanding of how to write a narrative poem. Students' lines of poetry should advance the plot, introduce one or more additional characters, and include at least one detail that describes the setting.

### Assess, p. 197

Student answers should reflect an understanding of how to write a lyric or narrative poem. For a lyric poem, students should express the thoughts and feelings that a rainy day evokes for a single speaker. The poem should include vivid images that convey these thoughts and feelings and have a musical quality. For a narrative poem, students should tell a story that takes place on a rainy day. The poem should include one or more characters, details that identify the setting, and a conflict or problem that the characters face.

## Writing: Review

### Practice, p. 198

**Sample answers:**

1. The reviewer thinks that the poetry is amusing.
2. The reviewer thinks that the word choices and imagery are appropriate because they are humorous, and limericks are supposed to be humorous.
3. Students should mention in their paragraphs that the sounds and rhythms of the limerick are appropriate. Reasons might include that the rhythm is perky or bouncy; the rhymes have a nursery-rhyme quality; the rhythm and rhyme are suitably silly.

### Assess, p. 199

**Sample answers:**

1. The subject of Poem A is the forest at night.
2. An image from Poem A is shadows drifting and disappearing.
3. The image is suitable to the poem because it brings to life the picture of the forest at night.
4. The subject of Poem B is rain.
5. Repetition is an element of the sound of Poem B. The poem begins each line with the words "Let the rain . . ."
6. The sound element of repetition is appropriate to the subject because it imitates the repetition of falling raindrops.
7. Students should write a brief review of the two poems, evaluating sound and imagery in

each one, and offering an opinion of each poem. Students should demonstrate an understanding of the idea of suitability of imagery and sound in relation to the subject.

### Writing: Comparison-and-Contrast Essay

**Practice,** p. 200

1. (block)
2. The need for companionship; the ability of pets to be trained
3. **Sample answer:** A third point of comparison between cats and dogs might be the amount of exercise each needs.
4. Students should write a paragraph comparing two kinds of animals, using at least two points of comparison. The organization of the paragraph may be either block or point-by-point.

**Assess,** p. 201

1. Students should write their chosen topic on the line.
2. Students should list facts and details about the two subjects that they are comparing and contrasting.
3. Students should list three similarities or differences that they will discuss in their essay.
4. Students should select a style of organization.
5. Students should write the first paragraph of a comparison-and-contrast essay. It should show an understanding of the chosen organization and an understanding of the basic elements of a comparison-and-contrast essay.

## Unit 5

### Reading: Draw Conclusions

**Practice,** p. 202

1. C
2. Jean is probably taller.
3. Sarah cannot reach the top shelf for the cake pan; Jean can.
4. C

**Assess,** p. 203

1. Kevin has probably never visited Todd in his current home.
2. Kevin does not recognize the sound of the Pacific; "I never realized that you lived so close to the ocean."
3. C
4. Kevin is eager to learn how to surf; he wants to wade in the ocean as he talks with Todd.
5. C

### Reading: Compare and Contrast Features and Elements

**Practice,** p. 204

1. Student-Parent Athletic Participation Information
2. never participate in hazing

**Assess,** p. 205

1. Checkmarks are placed next to the items that may be recycled. X's are places next to the items that may not be recycled. In addition, the items are divded into the may and may no groups and placed under those headings.
2. Italics are used for the sentences about bins and their placement.
3. Generally plastic, metal and glass containers along with newspapers and mailed paper items may be recycled.
4. The intended audience is people who wish to recycle their trash as much as possible and correctly.

### Literary Analysis: Stage Directions (Setting and Character)

**Practice,** p. 206

1. The time is the middle of the night. The setting is a baby's nursery.
2. C

**Assess,** p. 207

1. C; 2. C; 3. B; 4. B

### Literary Analysis: Setting

**Practice,** p. 208

**A** 1. A; 2. C; 3. A

**B** 1. B; 2. C; 3. B; 4. C

**Assess,** p. 209

**A** 1. B, C; 2. A, B; 3. A, C

**B** 1. A; 2. B

**C** 1. T; 2. F; 3. F; 4. T

### Literary Analysis: Comparing Adaptations to Originals

**Practice,** p. 210

1. C; 2. B; 3. D; 4. C

**Assess,** p. 211

**A** 1. T; 2. F; 3. F; 4. T; 5. T

**B** Sample answers:

JESSE. [frowning, and pulling his hat down over his eyes] Why do we always end up doing what you want to do?

LUKE: [grinning and tugging Jesse's hat back up] Because I'm the one with all the good ideas. Now, come on, let's go, we'll have a good time.

### Vocabulary: Suffixes *-ory, -ist*

#### **Practice,** p. 212

**Sample answers:**

1. (val); worth; The jewels had a very high value.
2. (sum); to use one's own words to give a shorter version of; Please use your own words to summarize the story.
3. (val); to prove as true; You can validate your claim by submitting evidence.
4. (sum); to eat or take in; You should consume fresh fruits and vegetables every day.
5. (val); worthy, truthful, and brave; The valiant knight saved our village.

#### **Assess,** p. 213

**Sample answers:**

1. a person in poor health
2. form an opinion; take for granted
3. courage and worth
4. add; total
5. proof
6. not assuming or pretending greatness; modest

### Grammar: Participles and Participial Phrases

#### **Practice,** p. 214

**A** **Sample answers:**

1. violinist; A strolling *violinist* played in the restaurant.
2. satisfactory; The student's work on the quiz was *satisfactory.*
3. promissory; He gave me a *promissory* note when he borrowed money.
4. bicyclist; The *bicyclist* rode five miles every day.
5. illusory; The quiet appearance of the town was only *illusory.*
6. geologist; A *geologist* studies the nature of rocks.

#### **Assess,** p. 215

**A**
1. migratory
2. directory
3. mandatory
4. celebratory
5. transitory

**B**
1. piano; pianist
2. loyal; loyalist
3. humorist; humor
4. psychiatry: psychiatrist
5. scientist; science

### Grammar: Revising Sentences by Combining With Gerunds and Participles

#### **Practice,** p. 216

**Sample answers:**

1. The butterfly, performed correctly, can be a graceful swim stroke.
2. Jack enjoys learning and practicing new swim strokes.
3. Jack thanked his father for teaching him the sidestroke.
4. Struggling, the favored swimmer took third place in the 200-meter backstroke.

#### **Assess,** p. 217

**A** **Sample answers:**

1. Practicing basketball is just about all Teresa does.
2. Juan's plans for the weekend include cleaning his room and reading.
3. The team gets to their away games by riding on the bus.
4. Taking stones from the Indian ruins is illegal.
5. Playing soccer and hiking are good exercise.

**B** **Sample answers:**

1. "The Tortoise and the Hare" is a well-known fable about a race. (fable)
2. Becoming too sure of himself, the hare stops to take a nap. (hare)
3. Plodding along steadily, the tortoise eventually passes the hare. (tortoise)
4. Stunned, the hare watches his opponent cross the finish line. (hare)
5. Pleased by his victory, the tortoise goes on his way. (tortoise)

### Writing: Scene With Dialogue

#### **Practice,** p. 218

**A**
1. Harry's apartment
2. Harry and Charlie
3. The stage directions tell where each character is standing at the beginning of the scene—Harry is opening the door, and Charlie is entering the apartment.
4. Harry has been waiting for Charlie, who is late getting home. Harry is angry because Charlie's lateness may make them late for a game.

**B** Scenes should be written in correct dramatic form, with tag lines indicating each speaker. Setting should be clear, and bracketed stage directions should indicate how characters are to move and speak.

## Assess, p. 219

**A** 1. at a school bus stop, in the early morning

2. Rhonda, Greg, and Ramon
3. **Sample answer:** Rhonda tries to grab the paper away from Ramon.
4. **Sample answer:** Ramon speaks sharply to Rhonda to show some anger.
5. **Sample answer:** Rhonda, Greg, and Ramon talk as they wait at the school bus stop one morning. Suddenly, Ramon finds a crumpled piece of paper on the ground and discovers that it is a treasure map showing Greg's backyard.

**B** Scenes should feature Rhonda, Greg, and Ramon and involve the treasure map. Scenes should be written in correct dramatic form, with tag lines indicating each speaker. Setting should be clear, and bracketed stage directions should indicate how characters are to move and speak.

### Writing: Business Letter

## Practice, p. 220

**A** 1. inside address; 2. closing; 3. heading; 4. greeting

**B** Students should use either the block style (all elements aligned on the left margin) or modified block style (heading, close, and signature aligned on the right side).

**Sample answer:**

I'm writing to ask if you could please write a letter recommending me to the Student Film Study Program that will take place this summer at Carter University. The program is very selective and challenging, and I know that my work in film would really benefit from what I could learn there. I enjoyed my film class with you last year and thought that you would be able to give the program a good idea of my ability and commitment. The program's address is. . . .

## Assess, p. 221

**Sample answers:**

**A** 1. B; 2. E; 3. block style

4. to return a purchase, explain the reason for the return (the dent), and request a refund

**B** Students should use modified block style, with heading, close, and signature on the right side.

**Sample answer:**

I'm writing to tell you how much I appreciated the assistance of your employee, Jordan Phillips, when I shopped at your store last week. I was having trouble finding what I needed, but Ms. Phillips listened to me very patiently, asked some helpful questions, and looked very hard to find what I needed. I'm happy to say that she found it. You are lucky to have such a bright, responsible, motivated person working for you.

### Reading: Cause and Effect

## Practice, p. 222

1. D; 2. B; 3. C; 4. B

## Assess, p. 223

**A** 1. false; 2. false; 3. true; 4. true

**B** C

### Reading: Evaluate Unity and Coherence

## Practice, p. 224

1. news, history, shop, visitor information, contact
2. location here, garden and landscape project photos. You can tell they are links because they are underlined.
3. follow the location here link or click on the map.

## Assess, p. 225

1. C
2. A
3. B
4. A

### Literary Analysis: Dialogue

## Practice, p. 226

1. C; 2. A; 3. B; 4. D

## Assess, p. 227

1. B; 2. B; 3. C; 4. D

### Literary Analysis: Character's Motivation

## Practice, p. 228

**A** 1. C; The fact that they keep trying despite their failures shows they are determined to come up with a solution.

2. C; The external motivation is the dog showing up on his porch, which is an event beyond his control. The internal motivation is his loneliness; taking in the dog will fill up his empty house.

**B** 1. E; (three-car pileup)

2. B; (afraid to stay home alone), (rustling noise)
3. I; (adored her brother)

## Assess, p. 229

1. B; 2. C; 3. A; 4. A; 5. B

## Literary Analysis: Comparing a Primary Source With a Dramatization

### Practice, p. 230

**Sample answers:**

1. They both cover the same experience and include the actions of Kate and Secretary Carson.
2. The primary source directly states Kate's thoughts and feelings, and includes her narration concerning the actions of Secretary Carson. The dramatization turns the experience into a dialogue, which reveals all of the actions and thoughts. Secretary Carson expresses herself directly. Stage directions indicate specific gestures and methods of speaking.

### Assess, p. 231

**Sample answers:**

1. They both cover the same experience and include the actions of Pete, Hal, and Ralph.
2. Although it does not identify the journal writer by name, the primary source directly states Pete's thoughts and feelings. It is written purely from his point of view. By contrast, the dramatization turns the experience into a dialogue, which suggests his inner feelings, and gives the other characters lines to speak. Stage directions help make the actions and feelings clear.
3. Stage directions; for example, when Pete responds to Ralph's initial question, the stage directions indicate that he should speak as though trying to appear brave.
4. The dramatization is more exciting because it presents the action more immediately and shows the characters shouting.

## Grammar: Prefix *in-*; Suffix *-ory*

### Practice, p. 232

1. B; 2. B; 3. A; 4. B; 5. A

### Assess, p. 233

**A**
1. N; <u>included</u> means to let her join in. The students <u>included</u> the new girl by inviting her to play with them.
2. Y; a <u>laboratory</u> is a place where scientific research is done.
3. Y; you would take antibiotics to fight a skin <u>infection</u>, or disease.
4. N; an <u>introductory</u> passage would appear at the *beginning* of a narrative. The <u>introductory</u> passage appeared at the beginning of the long narrative.
5. N; when one <u>inhales</u>, one draws air *into* the lungs. The air rushed into my lungs as I <u>inhaled</u>.
6. Y; one lists items when an <u>inventory</u> is taken.

**B** 1. inserted; 2. dormitory; 3. intake; 4. advisory; 5. infer

## Grammar: Independent and Subordinate Clauses

### Practice, p. 234

1. SUB; 2. NC; 3. IND; 4. SUB; 5. SUB; 6. IND; 7. SUB

### Assess, p. 235

**A** 1. SUB; 2. SUB; 3. IND; 4. SUB; 5. IND

**B**
1. independent—Mammals . . . are called marsupials; subordinate—that bear extremely underdeveloped offspring
2. independent—Kangaroos are in the macropod family; subordinate—which also includes wallabies
3. independent—they do not belong to the same family of marsupials; subordinate—Although rat-kangaroos are related to kangaroos
4. independent—Kangaroos usually search for food in the late evening and early morning
5. independent—Baby kangaroos are only about one inch long; subordinate—when they are born

**C** Sample answers:
1. He spends weekends at a farm where he works as a stable boy.
2. Although he does not get paid much, he likes being around the animals.
3. He tries to learn about them because he wants to become a veterinarian.
4. He hopes to be a large animal vet, which can be a rewarding career.
5. If you love animals, consider a career helping them.

## Grammar: Revising to Combine Sentences With Subordinate Clauses

### Practice, p. 236

**Sample answers:**

1. Susan B. Anthony published a journal that demanded equal rights for women.
2. When Anthony voted in the presidential election of 1872, she was arrested and fined.
3. Although she never paid the fine, the authorities did not take further action.
4. Susan B. Anthony died before women got the right to vote.

### Assess, p. 237

**A**
1. <u>which usually consist of series of trills and chirps</u>
2. <u>when they rub their two front legs together</u>
3. <u>Because they help male and female crickets find each other</u>

4. <u>where they feed on the baby ants</u>
5. <u>Although crickets are related to grasshoppers</u>

**B** Sample answers:

1. William Penn, who was an English Quaker, founded Philadelphia in 1682.
2. Because many of the early settlers were Quakers, the city became known as the Quaker City.
3. Since it was located near trade routes, Philadelphia became an important shipping center.
4. We toured Independence Hall, where the U.S. Constitution was signed.
5. The Delaware Indians lived in this area before the Europeans arrived.

## Spelling: Plurals

### Practice, p. 238

**A** 1. half; 2. fish; 3. property; 4. patch; 5. reason; 6. tomato

**B** 1. Add *s* to the noun.
2. If a noun ends in an *o* that follows a vowel, then add *s*.
3. Add *es* to nouns that end in *s, sh, ch,* or *x.*

### Assess, p. 239

1. D; 2. D; 3. A; 4. D; 5. B; 6. C; 7. C

## Writing: Diary Entry

### Practice, p. 240

1. The writer describes going to see a production of *A Christmas Carol.*
2. The writer thought the production was excellent, the costumes were spectacular, and that Sally's mom did a good job on the costumes.
3. Students should name a recent community event in which they were involved.
4. Students should record their own thoughts or feelings about the event.

### Assess, p. 241

1. Students should choose one event from their own lives.
2. Students should record specific details in chronological order.
3. Students' diary entries should describe events in chronological order, should include their own thoughts and feelings about it, and should be written from the first-person point of view. They should also include a date for each entry.

## Writing: Letter

### Practice, p. 242

1. start allowing her to baby-sit for the neighbors
2. (Grandma agrees with me)
3. **Sample answer:** <u>Baby-sitting for just six hours a week will enable me to save enough money in three years for a good used car</u>.
4. **Sample answer:** [I know that you would be proud of me if I could buy my own car when I am sixteen.]
5. Students' letters should identify their request and why they are making it. They should also include supporting facts and ideas and offer a strong conclusion.

### Assess, p. 243

**Sample answers:**

Topic: the dangers of heavy backpacks for students

1. students, teachers, parents
2. Heavy backpacks, full of textbooks and other school supplies, can damage young people's backs.
3. Backpack straps dig into students' shoulders. Heavy packs cause posture problems and can affect growing bones. Back problems could continue into adulthood.
4. Dear Teachers:
   Many teachers think nothing of assigning homework that requires students to carry heavy textbooks home. The poor students stuff these books into their backpacks and drag them home day after day, damaging their backs in the process. One solution to the problem is for students to start using backpacks that have wheels. Instead of carrying the burden on their backs, they can just roll their books home. However, not everyone can afford to simply buy a new, expensive backpack. Maybe the answer is to keep the students' textbooks home, and keep a set of books in the classroom for classroom use.
   I know you want to watch our backs! Please be considerate when assigning homework.

## Writing: Research Report

### Practice, p. 244

**A** Sample answers:

1. A better topic for Mori's report might be the history of his hometown, since he is particularly interested in it.
2. Students should create a thesis statement, such as *Two centuries of change have occurred in Clarksville, from 1806 to 2006.*

**B** 1. Students should choose an ancient civilization such as Egypt, Rome, or China.

2. Students should select a topic that is narrow enough for a research report, such as the major Egyptian pyramids.
3. Students should create a thesis statement such as *The pyramids of ancient Egypt are amazing examples of architecture and design.*

**Assess,** p. 245

**A** Sample answers:

1. Mara's thesis is that factors such as ratings and opinions influence television news.
2. Mara might ask the anchorperson how he or she feels about opinions shaping news. She might also ask if there is a good example of an important story that was not aired in favor of a story with more popular appeal. She might ask if different networks have policies about choosing which stories will be aired.
3. The problem with Mara's research report topic is that it is already big enough without the addition of the history of broadcast news. She should leave that part out.

**B** 1. Students should select an appropriate topic.
2. Students should create a thesis statement.
3. Students should list three sources where they would be likely to find information.

# Unit 6

## Reading: Summary

**Practice,** p. 246

1. C; 2. A; 3. D

**Assess,** p. 247

**A** 1. C; 2. A; 3. B; 4. A

**B** **Sample answer:** Paleontologists believe that *Compsognathus* was the smallest dinosaur. About 2 feet long, it had a maximum weight of only 22 pounds.

## Reading: Use Text Features to Analyze Information

**Practice,** p. 248

1. negative
2. never-ending series, gullible readers, drivel,
3. "gullible readers," people who will believe anything
4. The reviewer thinks the book is a waste of time. She does not think it is helpful to people. She thinks they should spend their money on candy instead, that that will make them happier than this book.

**Assess,** p. 249

1. positive
2. entranced, engrossing, enjoyable, interesting, believable
3. negative
4. not enough, weak, least, cranked out, auto-pilot

## Literary Analysis: Mythology

**Practice,** p. 250

1. Goar
2. his courage and strength
3. the North Wind
4. why the people of Mort always pray to the North Wind before sailing out to sea
5. **Sample answer:** People must respect the power of nature.

**Assess,** p. 251

**A** 1. C; 2. B

**B** 1. Ida
2. courage and a willingness to help her people
3. Rain Cloud
4. **Sample answer:** why Goran is situated on the banks of the river KooToo; how the river KooToo came to be.
5. **Sample answer:** People must dare to do difficult things in order to help society.

## Literary Analysis: Oral Tradition—Dialect

**Practice,** p. 252

**A** 1. afraid
2. left for, started out for
3. before
4. **Sample answer:** I almost pulled my neck out of joint, trying to pull my hat off.
5. **Sample answer:** animals he was hunting for dinner, such as squirrels or rabbits

**B** **Sample answer:** One day when it was so cold that I was afraid to open my mouth because I might freeze my tongue, I took my little dog named Grizzle and set out for Salt River Bay to kill an animal for dinner. I was far from home before I recognized where I was, and because I had sweated a bit before I left the house, my hat was frozen tightly to my head, and I almost had to pull my neck out of joint in order to pull it off. When I sneezed the icicles crackled all up and down the inside of my nose, the way the icicles on a bog crackle when you walk over them during the winter. The animals I wanted to hunt were so scarce that I couldn't find one.

## Assess, p. 253

**A** 1. Sample answer: The creek is a rich source of gold.

2. Sample answer: pull out tonight/resume our travels tonight; What say you?/What do you think?

3. terribly cold; really cold

**B** Sample answer: "Well, certainly you can keep warm by jumping off the sleds and running alongside the dogs!" cried an Irishman. "And who wouldn't? The creek's as valuable as a United States mint! Truly, here's an elegant chance to really get a run for your money! And if you don't hurry, perhaps you won't get that money."

### Literary Analysis: Comparing Heroic Characters

## Practice, p. 254

1. Yes, both are historical figures. The actual day or year of each character's birth is given.
2. Geronimo: Qualities: courage, respect for tradition; Action: <u>led successful raids</u>. Johnny Appleseed: Qualities: friendliness, courage, concern for humanity; Action: <u>made friends with humans and animals alike</u>
3. Geronimo: he could hold off the dawn so his people would be safe. Johnny Appleseed: Johnny curled up beside them [hibernating bears] and slept through the night.

## Assess, p. 255

1. John Henry is probably a historical figure because the C. & O. Railroad was a real company that employed many hardworking men. Paul Bunyan is not a historical figure; his stories are wild exaggerations meant to entertain.
2. John Henry: Qualities: strong, hardworking, determined; Paul Bunyan: Qualities: strong, helpful
3. John Henry: Heroic Actions: proved he could work faster than a steam drill; Paul Bunyan: Heroic Actions: stops the rain, straightens the road
4. John Henry: Exaggerated Actions: swings his hammer so hard that it thunders and lightnings; Paul Bunyan: Exaggerated Actions: uses saplings as rattles, swims up a waterfall to turn off the rain, pulls the road straight

### Vocabulary: Word Roots and Suffixes *-sacr-, -eer, -ful*

## Practice, p. 256

**A** 1. B; 2. B; 3. A

**B** 1. regretful; 2. mountaineer; 3. musketeer; 4. deceitful

## Assess, p. 257

**A** Sample answers:

1. T A musketeer is a soldier who carries a gun.
2. T Something that is sacrosanct is extremely holy.
3. F A vengeful person is seeking revenge.
4. F Mutineers are sailors who rebel against the ship's captain.

**B** Sample answers:

1. tearful; The mother and daughter had a *tearful* parting.
2. balladeer; The singer was best known as a *balladeer.*
3. hopeful; I feel *hopeful* that I will get into the college of my choice.

### Grammar: Sentence Structure

## Practice, p. 258

1. compound; 2. simple; 3. complex; 4. compound-complex; 5. simple; 6. complex; 7. compound; 8. compound-complex

## Assess, p. 259

**A** 1. complex; 2. compound; 3. compound; 4. complex; 5. compound-complex; 6. compound

**B** Sample answers:

1. The article was interesting, but it did not have the information I needed.
2. Cats vary in size, and many have wild colorings.
3. We had been traveling for ten hours, so we were happy to reach the motel.

**C** Sample answers:

1. School closings were announced on TV and radio because the storm was approaching.
2. Do your homework first if you want to have your friends over.

### Grammar: Commas

## Practice, p. 260

1. After they built a sand castle, they had a picnic.
2. Baseball, basketball, and soccer are my favorite sports.

3. She was tired, yet she was determined to finish the race.
4. Red, blue, and silver fish flashed in the lagoon.
5. After the brief rain shower had ended, the sun began to shine.
6. Sarah, stop talking and listen to me.
7. Wind rattled the windows of the cabin, yet the campers slept soundly.
8. His words, I believe, struck home.

## Assess, p. 261

**A** 1. If you are easily frightened, don't see that movie.
2. I've called the guests, bought the food, and warned the neighbors.
3. Do you want to bring pretzels, salad, or soda to the picnic?
4. Goodness, no one could lift this rock without help.
5. The praying mantis, on the other hand, kills many harmful insects.
6. Mowing the lawn on such a hazy, hot, humid day was no fun.
7. Lost and frightened, the child began to cry.
8. Claire saw two of her friends in the grandstand, so she went to sit with them.
9. Mrs. Whitman, I am happy to say, will be back in the classroom soon.
10. If Mr. Wilson complains, we'll invite him for a snack.

**B** 1. I; The road ran around the mountain, across the river, and into the town.
2. C
3. I; Jimmy Carter, the former president, was also governor of Georgia.
4. C
5. I; Ernest Hemingway, the famous author, wrote *The Old Man and the Sea*.

### Grammar: Using Language to Maintain Interest

## Practice, p. 262

**Sample answers:**

1. Some of them wanted to own land or find work, and others wanted religious freedom or self-government.
2. Immigrants from the same country often settled together in their own neighborhoods, which were often poor and crowded.
3. As a result, prejudice against the new immigrants was not uncommon.

## Assess, p. 263

**A** 1. For example; 2. However; 3. Finally; 4. In a like manner; 5. All in all

**B** **Sample answers:**

1. Tubman escaped from slavery in Maryland, but she returned nineteen times to help other slaves escape.
2. Harriet Tubman had the support of many Americans, who provided hiding places, or stations, along the "railroad."
3. However, many other runaway slaves were not so lucky.

### Writing: Myth

## Practice, p. 264

1. Why do giraffes have long necks?
2. **Sample answer:** Long ago, during a terrible drought, a giraffe named Nika stretched and stretched to reach the leaves in the tall, tall trees.
3. a giraffe named Nika and Old Man Sun
4. **Sample answer:** Hard work pays off; less lazing about and more work will solve problems.

## Assess, p. 265

**A** 1. Students should choose a topic to write about.
2. Students should devise a creative answer to their topic question.
3. Students should create a cast of characters, using some superhuman characters.
4. Students should come up with the action that will take place in the myth.
5. Students should offer a lesson to their myth.

**B** Students should write the opening paragraph of the myth outlined in Section A.

### Writing: Critical Analysis

## Practice, p. 266

1. The writer says that Pecos Bill is a hero who uses the skills of a cowboy to defeat one of a cowboy's greatest enemies, the cyclone.
2. The writer points out that Bill has riding ability, courage, humor, and pride in his accomplishments.
3. The writer should describe events from the story in which Bill shows his riding ability, courage, humor, and pride.

## Assess, p. 267

In Steps 1–4, students should name the heroic character they want to write about, write a sentence expressing their main idea about the hero, list the hero's admirable qualities, and describe three scenes in which the hero demonstrates these qualities. In Step 5, students should write a critical analysis of the character, using the information they prepared in Steps 1–4.

### Writing: Multimedia Report

**Practice,** p. 268

1. It is too broad. Sara can't possibly cover all the animals of Africa.
2. Sara could cover only one type of animal—butterflies, for example.
3. **Sample answer:** She could include video of the life cycle of a butterfly and photographs showing various types of butterflies found in Africa. She could obtain and present an entomologist's collection of butterfly specimens.

**Assess,** p. 269

**A** 1. Kevin's topic is too broad; maybe he should concentrate on just a few athletes.
2. Kevin could ask for help at the library; he could also interview a sports editor from his local newspaper or ask the opinions of a coach or P.E. teacher at his school; he could also ask his uncle, obviously a big sports fan, for some advice.
3. Instead of doing just a slide show with music, Kevin could include posters or trading cards of his chosen athletes; he could also display and explain some of the equipment his chosen athletes would have used.

**B** Students should list a topic that is narrow, a clear focus for the main idea, two examples of media, and an explanation of how research will be done. They should also write a brief description of their plans for the multimedia report.

### Reading: Setting a Purpose for Reading

**Practice,** p. 270

1. C; 2. D; 3. A

**Assess,** p. 271

**A** 1. B; 2. C; 3. B

**B** 1. What I Want to know
2. **Sample answer:** Questions that explore what I want to know (variations should be acceptable, as long as they include the ideas of asking questions and wanting to know)
2. **Sample answer:** a purpose for reading

### Reading: Analyze Treatment, Scope, and Organization of Ideas

**Practice,** p. 272

1. C
2. A
3. A

**Assess,** p. 273

1. interviewer, art nathan
2. (laughs), (sighs)
3. It gives an idea of what the tone of voice and way he said it was.
4. Speakers are identified with all-caps, what they say is indented. Things you hear that are not words are in parentheses.

### Literary Analysis: Cultural Context

**Practice,** p. 274

1. B; 2. B; 3. C; 4. A

**Assess,** p. 275

1. A; 2. C; 3. A
4. **Sample answer:** The author used to share our cultural context but now is living in a world in which people have been flying by means of their own bodies for some time. His new world is more advanced technologically than ours, which he finds exciting. Also, in his new world, humans, regardless of their ethnic makeup, are a minority.

### Literary Analysis: Identify Author's Influences

**Practice,** p. 276

1. D; 2. B; 3. A

**Assess,** p. 277

1. C; 2. B; 3. A

### Literary Analysis: Comparing Works on a Similar Theme

**Practice,** p. 278

1. D
2. **Sample answer:** Both pieces feature sights and sounds existing in nature. Both mention birds. The poem mentions sea birds flying and the hum of their beating wings. The essay mentions a chirping bird and the sight of a white flower.
3. **Sample answer:** Both include descriptions of elements of a specific setting and a child's delight in experiencing them. The poem begins with a vivid description of those elements and then brings in the child's reaction. The essay begins with the speaker's own experiences and then contrasts the solitary experience to the shared experience.

**Assess,** p. 279

1. B
2. **Sample answer:** Both pieces are about children who are forced to work in terrible

conditions. The poem is about children working as factory workers, and the editorial is about children working in agricultural settings.

3. **Sample answer:** Both make a strong statement against child labor. The poem has a sad tone and speaks through the imagined voices of "men" criticizing the city. The editorial has an outraged tone and speaks to the readers, trying to persuade them to agree that laws must be passed to protect these children.
4. **Sample answer:** Both include descriptions of the hard labor and the dusty environments that some children must endure. Both speak of the shame; the poem uses the phrase "The worst. . . . ," and the editorial uses the phrase "terrible secret." The poem develops its theme through free verse, whereas the editorial develops it through a persuasive essay.

## Vocabulary: Word Roots *-nat-, -grat-, -hor-, -and-*

### Practice, p. 280

**A** 1. grateful; 2. heritage; 3. audience; 4. national

**B** 1. B; 2. C; 3. C

### Assess, p. 281

**A** Sample answers:

1. The worker tried to ingratiate himself with his boss by flattering her.
2. I like to go to the park to spend time in a natural setting.
3. I like to download and listen to audio files on my computer.
4. I inherited my blue eyes from my father.
5. Prenatal care is very important during pregnancy.

**B** Sample answers:

1. -aud-; a tryout for a performing group; I had an *audition* for the school play.
2. -nat-; inborn; The musician had an *innate* sense of rhythm.
3. -grat-; thankfulness; The family felt *gratitude* to the firefighters who saved their home.
4. -her-; passed down between generations; Some illnesses are *hereditary*.

## Grammar: Semicolons and Colons

### Practice, p. 282

1. Gradually the water evaporates; the salt forms crystals.
2. The basic unit consists of three rooms: a living room, bedroom, and kitchen.
3. They decided not to go shopping; instead, they went walking in the park.
4. Four states border Mexico: California, Arizona, New Mexico, and Texas.
5. Some cheeses are made from cow's milk; others are made from goat's milk.
6. Becky is fascinated by sharks; however, she has not yet met one close up.
7. Their new home is beautiful; no one would guess it was once a barn.
8. Add these things to your list: soap, bread, eggs, and milk; then, come back as soon as you can.

### Assess, p. 283

**A**

1. We expect to win easily; nevertheless, we are still practicing very hard.
2. Running through the park, Gail tripped; she scraped her knee badly.
3. The man did not show up for his appointment that morning; instead, he left town.
4. Steve sent the hamburger back; it was too rare.
5. Kerrie had a cast on her leg; nevertheless, she was the first one on the dance floor.
6. This was the heaviest snowfall in years; it broke all records.
7. I love tennis; in fact, I play four times a week.
8. If I am not awake by five o'clock, call me; otherwise, I will be late for work.

**B**

1. This semester we are studying several civilizations: Egyptian, Greek, and Roman.
2. My list for camp includes the following items of clothing: shirts, shorts, sneakers, socks, sweatshirts, and swimming suits.
3. We saw many types of dogs at the show: collies, setters, poodles, beagles, and boxers.
4. Four team sports are popular in U.S. schools: basketball, baseball, football, and soccer.
5. Campers should bring the following items: sheets, blankets, and towels.
6. Nick chose three poets to study: Dickinson, Frost, and Sandburg.
7. In this wallet are my life's savings: six dollar bills, eight quarters, and two nickels.
8. Their birthdays were all in the summer: June 23, July 11, and August 9.

## Grammar: Capitalization

### Practice, p. 284

1. Wow! These fireworks are spectacular!
2. Whenever I see Andrea, she is with Rachael.
3. The city of Cleveland lies on the shore of Lake Erie.

4. My brother will enter the University of Wisconsin in September.
5. George Washington fought on the side of the British in the French and Indian War.

## Assess, p. 285

**A** 1. as soon as i met janet scott, i knew we would be friends.
2. it was emma lazarus who wrote, "give me your tired, your poor."
3. the yellow sea separates south korea from china.
4. the matterhorn is one of the mountains in the alps.
5. my brother jason is going to a class reunion at the university of chicago.
6. she asked, "have you ever appeared on late-night TV?"
7. hoover dam is in nevada, southeast of the las vegas.
8. the rose bowl parade is televised every new year's day.
9. how could the owner have said, "my dog is friendly?"
10. my whole family went to visit aunt cecilia.

**B**

| | | |
|---|---|---|
| 1. | A. Korean War | B. Korean soldier |
| 2. | A. Roman Empire | B. Roman architecture |
| 3. | A. Italian Renaissance | B. Italian pastries |
| 4. | A. Kentucky Derby | B. Kentucky people |
| 5. | A. French Revolution | B. French dressing |

### Grammar: Revising Run-on Sentences and Sentence Fragments

## Practice, p. 286

1. fragment; 2. complete sentence; 3. run-on; 4. complete sentence; 5. fragment; 6. complete sentence; 7. run-on

## Assess, p. 287

**A** **Sample answers:**
1. We expected the senator to arrive tonight. She has just returned from Africa.
2. Here is the package you ordered. It was delivered this morning.
3. Karen writes music, and she is a fine pianist.
4. The storm flooded major highways; motorists were warned to stay at home.
5. A trip to the state park seemed like a good idea. Everyone agreed to go next Sunday.

**B** **Sample answers:**
1. I was fast asleep when the delivery man rang the bell.
2. The glider landed on top of the hill.
3. A policeman standing on the corner was giving information to the lost tourists.
4. So much has changed since my last visit to Los Angeles.
5. Please keep this secret between you and me.

### Spelling: Vowel Sounds in Unstressed Syllables

## Practice, p. 288

**A** 1. buoyant; 2. epilogue; 3. benefit; 4. hesitate; 5. anonymous

**B** The jurors were desparate to get to the end of the trial. They were so bored by the prosecutor's remarks that they hoped that the judge would edjourn the trial so they could leave. Nevertheless, they did their duty by listening to every syllible of the presentation. They even hoped that the defense lawyer would try to plea-bargan to cut the trial short. It was a pleasunt surprise when the prosecutor finally ended his remarks.

1. desperate; 2. adjourn; 3. syllable; 4. bargain; 5. pleasant

## Assess, p. 289

**A** 1. C; 2. A; 3. D; 4. D

**B** 1. B; 2. C; 3. D; 4. B; 5. D

### Writing: Research Proposal

## Practice, p. 290

1. B; 2. D
3. **Sample answer:** A book on European history would contain information about life in the 1300s and the conditions that may have led to the Black Plague. The encyclopedia and an Internet search would turn up entries and articles containing factual information about both the disease and the time period.
4. **Sample answer:** My research report will discuss the Black Plague that threatened Europe in the fourteenth century. In my report, I will answer the following questions: What were the symptoms of the disease? How quickly did the disease spread? What effects did the disease have on society? The sources I use to answer these questions will include a book on European history, an encyclopedia, and an Internet search. The book on European history will provide a good overview of life in the 1300s and how people were affected by the disease. The other two sources will provide specific factual information about the disease, such as symptoms, how quickly it spread, and the number of people affected.

**Assess,** p. 291

Student answers should reflect an understanding of research proposals. Students should choose a research topic, present three questions about the topic, identify specific sources they would use to find answers to their questions, and explain why each source would be useful.

### Writing: Speech

**Practice,** p. 292

**A** 1. Students should circle the first paragraph.
2. Students should underline the repeated phrase "ask the."
3. **Sample answer:** Vivid language includes the following phrases: bereaved family, solemn service; labor of love; struck the nation with dismay; bowed heads in grief.
4. **Sample answer:** A good place to pause for effect would be after the first sentence.

**B** Students should write the introduction to a speech in tribute to their personal hero.

**Assess,** p. 293

**A** 1. Students should describe the friend's accomplishment.
2. Students should describe the audience.
3. Students should state the main point of the speech.
4. Students should tell how they would support the main point.
5. Students should say what phrase they would repeat for effect.
6. Students should tell where they might pause for effect.
7. Students should write three phrases with vivid language.

**B** Students should write the beginning of a speech, indicating where they might pause for effect.

### Writing: Cause-and-Effect Essay

**Practice,** p. 294

**A** 1. A; 2. B; 3. C

**B** Type of organization: Single Cause / Many Effects

Essays should discuss the possible effects of not using sunscreen and should employ the organization of devoting a paragraph to each effect.

**Assess,** p. 295

**A** 1. B; 2. B

**B** 1. Students should state the cause of the topic they have selected
2–4. Students should list three effects of that cause.